To Work and to Weep

The Ethnographic Locations

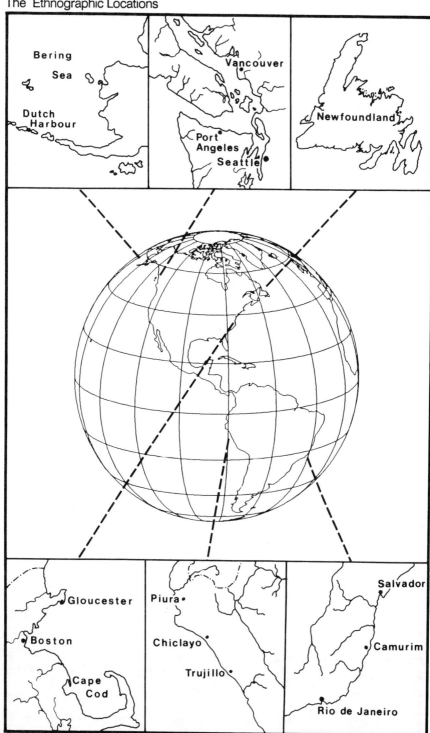

Cartography by Arnold Balisch.

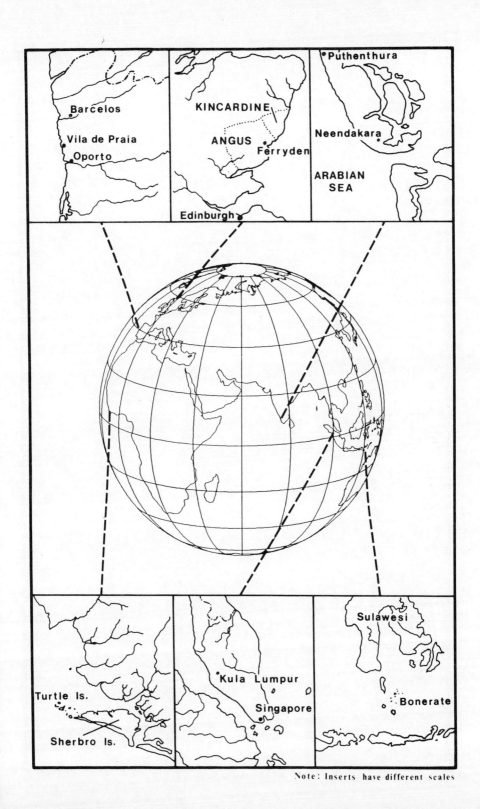

Barcelos

Vila de Praia

Oporto

KINCARDINE

ANGUS

Ferryden

Edinburgh

Puthenthura

Neendakara

ARABIAN
SEA

Turtle Is.

Sherbro Is.

Kula Lumpur

Singapore

Sulawesi

Bonerate

Note: Inserts have different scales

To Work and to Weep

Women in Fishing Economies

Jane Nadel-Klein and Dona Lee Davis

Social and Economic Papers No. 18
Institute of Social and Economic Research
Memorial University of Newfoundland

Canadian Cataloguing in Publication Data
To work and to weep
(Social and economic papers ; no. 18)
Bibliography: p.
ISBN 0-919666-60-4
1. Women Employment. 2. Women Social
conditions. 3. Fishing villages Social
conditions. I. Nadel-Klein, Jane, 1947-.
II. Davis, Dona Lee, 1948-. III. Memorial
University of Newfoundland. Institute of
Social and Economic Research. IV. Series.
HD6073.F65T6 1988 305.436392 C88-098627-1

Contents

Preface

This book examines the nature and significance of women's roles in communities in which fishing is a primary mode of subsistence. Fishing is commonly viewed as men's work, but evidence from a variety of fishing communities indicates that women's participation is vital. We explore the implications of women's work for gender and community identity, and for social relations both within and between communities.

The book had its origins in a symposium organized by Jane Nadel for the 1983 meetings of the American Anthropological Association in Chicago. Our call for additional papers generated more interest than we had expected. While some of the contributors had originally set out to do research on women in fishing communities, many others had collected data on women's activities but had not yet had the opportunity to write about them in a focused way. A common reaction was, "This is a good idea. I have a lot of stuff on women but I've never gotten around to using it." We hope that this volume will help to fill the gap in our awareness of the diversity of women's roles in general, and enhance our understanding of maritime adaptations, another subject which has only recently begun to draw much serious attention.

While the book focuses upon women in fishing communities, we have chosen to make its scope as wide as possible. Thus we use a broad definition of fishing, not limiting the literature review which follows in Chapter Two to sea fishing, but including the riverine, lake, swamp, and coastal fisheries. Nor have we confined our attention to only one or a few particular aspects of women's lives, but rather have sought to examine as broadly as possible the kinds of questions that have been asked, and answered, about women in

fishing economies: about their work, their social structural positions, their values, and their places in the symbolic order.

The contributions span cultural and geographical settings from
Malaysia to Massachusets, and reach from subsistence to industrial fishing. They present a compelling diversity in the sexual
division of labor, and in the extent to which gender ideology appears
to be a dominating factor in organizing the relationship between
family, community, and occupation. The authors share a concern
for history and political economy, for recognizing the complexity of
social change and the importance of cultural flexibility. Thus the
book is not only about sex roles, but about the social construction
of gender, and its relationship to ecology in the broadest sense.

We have divided our introductory material into two chapters.
The first delineates the book's theoretical orientation and rationale,
and explains the relationship of the separate chapters to our main
ethnographic and theoretical concerns. The second is a review of
the literature available on women in fishing. We have done this for
several reasons: first, in order to assess the state of the art and to
clarify the significance of this volume's contribution; second, to
provide what we hope will be a useful guide to those interested in
fishing more deeply in these waters.

The editors would like to acknowledge the help of a number of
people. First we would like to thank our contributors, the editorial
staff at ISER, and anonymous reviewers for the great patience they
have shown while we have struggled to put the volume together.
Benjamin Orlove kindly served as discussant for the original panel.
Jane Nadel-Klein thanks Bradley S. Klein for his ruthless and invaluable criticism. She also thanks Daniel Bradburd, Krystyna
Starker, and Eve Stoddard for their editorial comments. Finally, for
her love and her very mature understanding of her mother's work,
a special thanks to Cory Ellen Nadel. Dona Davis would like to acknowledge the University of South Dakota Research Institute for its
help with travel funds and the invaluable help of Ruth Weigert. She
would also like to thank Richard Whitten.

J. N-K. and D.D.   September 1988

Notes on Contributors

Charlene J. Allison received her Ph.D. in Social/Cultural Anthropology from the University of Washington in 1980. She is currently working as a Research Scientist with Seattle's Fred Hutchinson Cancer Research Center.

Harald Beyer Broch is curator and Associate Professor of Anthropology in the Ethnographic Museum at the University of Oslo.

Margaret Elwyn Clark is a doctoral candidate at Syracuse University. She is writing her dissertation on the Gloucester Fishermen's Wives Association, based on data collected in Gloucester, Massachusetts in 1982-84.

Sally Cole received her doctorate from the University of Toronto. Based on fieldwork conducted in Northern Portugal in 1984-85, her thesis examines the transformation of women's work in a rural fishery.

Dona Lee Davis is an Associate Professor of Anthropology and Sociology in the Department of Social Behaviour at the University of South Dakota at Vermillion. She is author of *Blood and Nerves: An Ethnographic Focus on Menopause* (ISER).

Mary Schweitzer de Grys is an Associate Professor of Anthropology at Winthrop College in Rock Hill, South Carolina.

Leela Gulati is an economist working at the Center for Development Studies in Kerala, India.

Thomas S. Krabacher has taught at California State University, Sacramento, and received his doctorate in geography from the University of California, Davis.

Jane Nadel-Klein is an Associate Professor of Anthropology at Trinity College, Hartford, Connecticut. She spent two years as a Fellow in the Marine Policy and Ocean Management at Woods Hole Oceanographic Institution.

Barbara S. Nowak received her doctorate in Anthropology from the State University of New York at Buffalo. She has done fieldwork in West Malaysia and her research intersts include problems in development and gender relations. She is now teaching at Grinnell College in Iowa.

Antonius C.G.M. Robben teaches in the Anthropology Department of the University of Michigan at Ann Arbor. His work on fishing has been previously published in *Anthropological Quarterly, Ethnology,* and *Cultural Survival Quarterly*

M. Estellie Smith is Professor of Anthropology at the State University of New York, Oswego, and has just finished her second term as Senior Fellow in the Marine Policy and Ocean Management Program at Woods Hole Oceanographic Institution.

Introduction: Gender in the Maritime Arena

Jane Nadel-Klein and Dona Lee Davis

Images of fishing tend to be male: men stand with hook and line in cold water; men brave the perils of the sea, while women are bad luck on boats. It is safe to say, in fact, that Western tradition has stereotyped fishing as an exclusively male occupation. Unfortunately, this perspective robs us of the ability to think about women in fishing communities, to ask what women do and to contemplate the possibility that "fishing" as an economic enterprise might require— and even value— women's labor.

Studies of women in society challenge a long androcentric tradition. The point of feminist ethnography is to provoke some radical rethinking of long-accepted anthropological "truths," and to open up new areas of investigation. Feminist ethnography reminds us to look at women as significant actors in the social system, and at gender as a conceptual device employed by people everywhere— but not in the same way. This reminder is particularly salient when we look at the social dynamics of fishing communities where female roles— both in the social relations of production and in the reproduction of culture— have been largely overlooked or ignored. Moreover, the study of gender in society can benefit from a focus upon fishing peoples, whose wide ranger of adaptive problems can raise some interesting questions regarding the relation of practice (Bourdieu 1977) to the formation and consequence of gender ideology.

To look at women as dynamic and creative actors in the challenging and stressful environments which are so often a part of the fishing way of life is one way of countering anthropology's explicit and implicit androcentric bias in describing social systems as male artifacts. This volume highlights the nexus of subsistence and ideology in fishing economies in order to examine some complex systemic relationships between work, gender, power, and prestige. We look at the social fields in which gender asymmetry may be either elaborated or muted, hoping to shed some light upon how these fields and concepts may change. The volume thus addresses several broad issues for the theoretical study of women in society and for the application of feminist theory to problems in economic development.

We begin with two underlying premises. The first is that the study of women as social beings cannot be separated either from other spheres of social inquiry or from the study of men, as Rosaldo reminds us (1980:396). The chapters which follow emphasize the importance of male-female relationships both in terms of material and psychological factors. The contributors all address aspects of conjugal relationships and place these relationships within a framework of larger social issues. This approach, which stresses the dynamic interplay of gender roles with gender identity, is one which also could be profitably employed by those whose focus is on male activities in society. In order to avoid the tendency to regard women as "residual," it is not enough to produce a body of literature classified as "women's" studies. If women are truly to be seen as creative social agents, then we must develop an anthropology which automatically encompasses gender, in the same way that we automatically encompass subsistence. The second premise is that women's status is neither a unitary construct in theoretical terms, nor is it necessarily internally consistent in any particular cultural setting. As Atkinson points out, "it is too facile...to presume that women's influence in one context cancels out their degradation in another" (1982:248).

Several topics are central to any discussion of women in fishing economies and communities (which may be partially or wholly dependent upon fishing): the specific nature of women's work in fishing economies; gender, status, and the sexual division of labor in fishing economies; socialization, gender ideology, and the expressive dimension of status; and the implications of all of these for social change and development.

Four key, although not mutually exclusive, themes underlie all the following chapters, most explicitly in the literature review chapter which follows this introduction. While these themes overlap to some extent, we find it useful to distinguish them. One of these themes is the focus on women in the technological, subsistence, and social structural realms of fishing economies. Taken as a whole, the volume presents a broadly ecological look at the nature of women's work in different fisheries and at women's subsistence contributions in different cultures, economies, and political arenas, including hunting and gathering, peasant, and modern industrial societies. In their portrayals of women's subsistence and work roles in fishing societies, the authors explicate such social structural factors as division of labor, kinship organization, community, ethnicity, and social class. The chapters by Broch and Nowak illustrate two non-Western, relatively "low-energy" fishing economies; the chapters by Cole, David, de Grys, Gulati, Krabacher, Nadel-Klein, and Robben illustrate problems attendant upon the transformation from marginal to more complex and central markets for fishing; Allison, Clark, Cole, and Davis examine women's roles in highly capitalized contemporary Western fisheries.

The second key theme concerns the problem of women's status and the evaluation or ranking of women's activities in both public and domestic domains. Here we turn our attention to some of the cultural and social factors in fishing economies which relate to prestige rankings and gender ideology. The chapters by Allison, Broch, Clark, Cole, Davis, de Grys, Nadel-Klein, Nowak, and Robben illustrate both intra- as well as inter-cultural variation in female roles and status. Age, kin affiliation, distribution and marketing processes, and individual skills all affect the assignment of roles and status for women within the same culture or society.

Thirdly, women are viewed as individuals, as dynamic and creative actors in both the expressive as well as the material realms of fishing economies. The mental environments and psychological aspects of women's lives in fishing economies are explored by Allison, Clark, Cole, Davis, de Grys, and Robben. Special attention is paid to distinguishing ideal culture from actual behavior, precisely because accounts of women's lives so often reveal sentiments of personal conflict, of discontent, anger, and frustration. The issues of self-esteem and social honor become important dimensions of gender ideology; local prestige systems play powerful roles shaping social action.

Fourthly, we stress the practical or applied importance of these issues for problems of social change and development. Planning for economic change without acknowledging the input of roughly half of the population is not only ineffective and wasteful of human resources, but often damaging of both happiness and productivity. The contributions of Allison, Clark, Cole, Gulati, and Krabacher are particularly relevant here.

FISHING ECONOMIES AND FISHING COMMUNITIES

The terms "fishing economy" and "fishing community" require definition. A "fishing economy" may entail the activities of an entire
society or of an occupational subgroup. Fishing peoples are often
found in rural settings where whole communities weave their lives
around a single adaptive strategy, or they may be found as occupational enclaves within pluralistic and even urban settings.

People may fish full-time or part-time, for subsistence, for the
market, or a combination of these alternatives. Increasingly, fishing
peoples are caught up within the capitalist world-system which
reduces—though does not necessarily eliminate—their ability to
make choices about such things as where, when, and how to fish,
as well as how to dispose of the catch. Smith's concluding chapter
takes up this theme. Thus, while a fishing economy may be discussed as a relatively restricted range of activities and transactions,
such as the household or village-level economy, the social and cultural systems of contemporary fishing peoples must nonetheless be
viewed as being at least partially determined, constrained, or, for
that matter, enabled, by a set of activities and exchanges which link
household and community to the state and to aspects of the international political economy. We believe that it would be misleading
to refer simply to "fishing societies" since fishing peoples often exist
as specialized occupational groups within larger heterogeneous
societies, and because the term "society" itself implies the existence
of some kind of internal political autonomy and separation from
others, which is seldom warranted. We would not go as far as
Thompson does in assuming *a priori* that fishing communities are
necessarily isolated or distinct enough to form "clear, coherent
cases" with which to test the relative influence of social variables
(1985:4). While fishing peoples sometimes do appear to be *relatively* isolated or marked off from other groups, it is also true that some
movement of individuals in and out of such communities does take
place. Furthermore, relatively few groups of people are *wholly* dependent upon fishing, in the sense that there is no other source of
subsistence.

There is great variation in the importance which fishing holds
for peoples who fish, both from the standpoint of self-ascribed identity, and from the standpoint of food consumption. Friedl (1975)
notes that among foragers, for example, fishing is a dominant food
resource for 33 percent of the societies studied. Many other productive activities contribute to community or household welfare,
including agriculture, wage labor, trade, and even the public assistance programs provided in some modern nation-states. However,

we may speak of a fishing economy when fishing constitutes a resource significant enough that its elimination would mean a sharp drop in the standard of living, or a serious change in a community's way of life and its sense of identity.

As several writers have noted, fishing as a mode of subsistence has received relatively little attention compared to other human adaptations (Leap 1977; Smith 1977a). In their eagerness to establish a societal type, however, maritime researchers have tended to focus on the commonality of fishing societies. Andersen and Wadel (1972a), Smith (1977b), and Acheson (1981), have all pointed out that fishing appears to be a distinctive way of life and set of adaptations that warrant cross-cultural analysis. Specifically, people in fishing communities have special sets of technological and social problems: their prey tend to be not only elusive, but invisible, so that substantial uncertainty accompanies every fishing event. Capture techniques must often be highly specialized, requiring special skills and equipment, as well as considerable social cooperation. At the same time, many fishing peoples depend upon a wide variety of species, so that fishers must be flexible and innovative in their approach to subsistence. For many fishers, danger and risk are constant companions. The catch is highly perishable and special skills, risks, and hardships are often necessary in order to market it at all. In a recent article, Raymond Firth notes the special territorial and property definition problems which mobile marine resources pose for economic and political relationships (1984:1145-1170). Furthermore, fishers are very often separated socially from neighbors who pursue other occupations; their adaptive strategies may also lead to distinctive social arrangements, particularly in complex, stratified societies where fishers are very often at or near the bottom of the local status hierarchy.

The maritime literature as it relates to women has also focused on a few common themes, of which the most predominant is the issue of male absence. Among those fishing groups where men are absent for long periods, women are held to play a proportionately greater role in managing both the household and the local community. Smith (1977b:4) points out that many maritime communities are characterized by "a greater dependency on women to control land-based food production; greater role differentiation among males/females because of the above; and a greater economic independence for women."

At this point, however, we feel we must introduce a caveat. Similarity can be overemphasized. While acknowledging substantial validity in Acheson's statement that "fishing poses similar

problems the world over" (1981:275), we would caution readers that
there has also been a widespread tendency to overstress the homogeneity of fishing peoples with respect to gender, to assume that
women's roles in fisheries the world over have been the same.
Thompson, for instance, asserts that "the character of women's work
in fishing communities has again and again taken parallel forms in
fishing societies" (1985:3). We believe this to be a misleading claim.
In this volume alone we can see women as commercial fishers, fish
plant laborers and proletarian processors, subsistence or artisanal
fishers, processors and marketers, political agents, financial managers, dependent housewives, and complementary work partners.
The data suggest that to understand fishing communities and
economies, the adaptive challenges of fishing must be placed within
the specific contexts of history, political economy, and gender ideology. The interplay of subsistence, mode of production, and prestige
systems generates many permutations. One of the tasks of this
volume is to analyze and explain these permutations.

One factor in fishing economy variability lies in fishing people's
range of contemporary and historical connections to other social
groups and networks. All of the chapters present fishing peoples as
both separate from and part of a wider social network, and their
uses of gender emphasize this ambiguity differently in each case.
Newfoundland is characterized by considerable variety in outport
culture, and Davis carefully explains that Grey Rock Harbour must
not be seen as a template for other communities with different histories and ecological relationships. Robben explicitly notes that
machismo in Camurim is articulated differently from practices in
other Bahia communities, whether they depend upon fishing or
agriculture. Broch presents Miang Tuu as a rather complex case of
the adaptability of occupational norms in the context of ethnic diversity within a small community, where women of Bajau descent are
expected to perform certain fishing tasks which non-Bajau women
are not. Cole explains that until quite recently, the women of Vila
da Praia, in Portugal, stood in contrast to rural women with respect
to their dominance in household management. Moreover, Vila da
Praia was known as the only north coast fishery in which women
went to sea. Nadel-Klein also notes that fishwives in Scotland acquired a public image of being physically strong and socially
aggressive, which helped to set them apart from others. The
fishermen's wives of Gloucester clearly deviate both from Sicilian-
American norms and from wider community norms in their practice
of occupational political activism. Gulati indicates that women of
the Araya Hindu and Christian fishing communities of Kerala have

responded differently to birth control and educational opportunities offered through the Indo-Norwegian Fisheries Development Project. Krabacher's women of the Sherbro coast in Sierra Leone appear to have weathered the impact of capitalization more successfully than their counterparts in agriculture. Nowak's Btsisi' women and men maintain complementary work roles within a highly diversified and plural economy, with plantation wage labor available as an alternative occasional occupation.

WOMEN'S WORK IN FISHING ECONOMIES: TO WORK OR TO WEEP?

Popular images of women in fishing communities often convey a sense of female passivity: in the words of Charles Kingsley's poem, that "men must work, and women must weep...and the harbour bar keeps moaning." This volume addresses a number of such misconceptions about women's work, illustrating that women in fishing economies have a number of highly specialized roles to play in production and in domestic management, as well as in linking fishing communities to the world outside.

While none would deny the dangers and anxieties of life in a fishing community, the work/weep dichotomy suggests that women's main task lies in waiting and worrying, rather than in doing anything more important (e.g., directly productive). This image of women introduces two popular and misleading conceptualizations of life in fishing communities which this volume sets out to correct. First is the idea that women's roles are divorced from direct participation in the fishery. Second is the idea that the so-called "passive," expressive, and household roles of women in fishing economies are themselves of little import and of even less theoretical significance. Both of these misconceptions stem directly from an androcentric and capitalist (wage-oriented) bias in the definition of what constitutes "work."

Work in our own culture is all too often assumed to be only that activity which extracts resources (whether directly or indirectly, as in market exchange) from the physical and social environment. Activities concerning the "unpaid" allocation, preparation, and distribution of these resources, as well as those concerning the care of human beings themselves, are not seen as other forms of work, but as something else which is often simply dismissed or ignored. (See Wadel on the "Folk Work Concept" in Wallman 1979.) This can be illustrated by the common American habit of distinguishing between "housewives" and "working women," as if the former have lives of total leisure. As Wallman (1979) points out, the social meaning of work varies from culture to culture, and within culture as well. We must thus be aware of the frequent Western bias of valuing work according to the gender of the performer. As certain occupations (teachers, secretaries) have become identified as female, their prestige has tended to decline. Ultimately, some forms of "female" work, like motherhood, cease to be regarded as work at all.

Anthropologists describing fishing communities have not been immune from these conceptual oversights and tend to commit two errors: they ignore the enormous diversity of techniques and tasks which fishing peoples employ, and they overlook the amount of fish extracting which women actually do. Murdock and Provost (1973), for example, cite fishing as a predominantly male occupation. As the contributions to this volume will show, that assumption both distorts and devalues the work of women in fishing communities. Most studies of fishing communities devote considerable attention to such issues as the organization of fishing crews, or the social relations of production between fishermen and their creditors, without looking very closely at women's roles in both the productive and expressive spheres of fishing life. A closer look reveals that what women do in these communities is, in point of fact, both diverse and essential to the maintenance of family and society. We have already learned that women in foraging societies make vital subsistence contributions (Dahlberg 1981) and considerable attention is being paid to women's roles in agriculture (Boserup 1970; Burton and White 1984; Linares 1985). Without wishing to pose the existence of an abstraction called "woman the fisher," we must insist that the subsistence strategies and division of labor among fishing peoples are more complex than a sketch of work done by adult males alone can tell us. It is time to turn our attention to the variety of contributions that women make to life in fishing communities and to the ways in which women see themselves and their work. In doing so, we believe that we can contribute both to the development of gender theory and to the understanding of maritime peoples.

As the chapters in this volume clearly demonstrate, whether or not men are the only ones actually capturing fish, women's livelihoods and senses of self are also inextricably bound up with the fishery. As economies are transformed, so are women's roles. Women may be explicitly conscious of this, particularly as members of occupational communities embedded within larger, heterogeneous societies. The Gloucester Fishermen's Wives Association, described by Clark, acts politically to defend the North Atlantic fishing grounds of Georges Bank against the threat of offshore oil and gas development. The fishermen's wives of Gloucester feel themselves to be part of a fishing community, and are threatened not only with loss of income, but with loss of identity as well. The fishwives and fish processors of Scotland described by Nadel-Klein saw themselves (and were seen by others) clearly as active members, creators, and re-creators of specialized and socially encapsulated fishing villages. The older women of Cole's Portuguese village deplore what they see as their daughters' loss of pride and independence, as a result of their withdrawal from the fishery.

In fact, it is likely that most contemporary fishing groups provide an excellent setting in which to study the impact of class and of capitalist transformations upon gender ideology. That such transformations need not, however, always be seen negatively is shown in Davis' chapter on the women of Grey Rock Harbour, whose recruitment into proletarian fish plant labor does not appear to disrupt social norms or to make the women feel devalued. In a different context, the Pacific Northwest women described by Allison are attempting to take advantage of the mobility and opportunities afforded by commercial fishing there. While most use prior ties to fisher*men* to facilitate their entry into work at sea, many are emotionally and cognitively tied to the fishery itself and endure considerable hardship to remain there despite the presence of alternative occupations. Krabacher's description of successful women fish traders in Sierra Leone also indicates an active and entrepreneurial response to change (although he notes this may be temporary). And, as Gulati describes, at least some women in the Kerala fishery have reaped benefits from the development efforts of the Indo-Norwegian Project.

WORK, PRESTIGE, AND GENDER STATUS

This section indicates the ways in which the chapters address the formation, use, and symbolic expression of gender ideology, emphasizing status issues as related to the sexual division of labor. Much recent literature on women has focused upon the universal existence of a sexual division of labor, variable in task content, but nearly always assigning greater prestige to men's work. Far from reaching any definite conclusions about the ultimate, or species-wide causes of such asymmetry, however, most researchers have found themselves awash in a sea of problematic definitions and complex and intertwining variables which require extensive historical and sociological analysis to sort out. Many forays seem to end in at least some degree of retreat when confronted with apparent ethnographic exceptions or accusations of ethnocentric patterning. Arguments over such posited universal male-female dichotomies as culture-nature (Ortner 1974), or public-private (Rosaldo 1974) have been provocative and stimulating, but hardly definitive (Rosaldo 1980; Ortner and Whitehead 1981). Most writers explicitly disavow biological-determinist models, but are not prepared to assume that biological functions and our evolutionary history play no role at all.

One issue for this volume then is that of the circumstances under which gender becomes or remains a salient social category or basis for action. Nadel-Klein argues that for the fisherfolk of eastern Scotland, gender was historically of major significance in the organization of the fishing economy. Women's contributions to subsistence were high, but their status was ambiguous. Women could not enter boats, but could dig bait, bait lines, process and market fish. They were regarded as strong and essential, but for the same reasons, also as dangerous and possibly polluting.

Davis' Newfoundlanders of Grey Rock Harbour also separate land and sea domains according to sex. Women who work in fish plants do not violate cultural norms of propriety; they are still seen as complementing, supportive "grass widows" who maintain the arena of domestic emotional support for their seafaring men. However, women who take an active role in fishery finances and crew recruitment are seen as "shore skippers" who cross the boundary of acceptability and generate considerable hostility from both men and women in the community.

Cole tells us that women in Vila da Praia participated in all aspects of the fishery; some women regularly went to sea, most often as crew for fathers or brothers. However, husbands did not want their wives aboard, and actively discouraged their presence, though they did not (apparently) mind as much if their wives crewed for other boats.

Clark reveals that the (mostly Sicilian) fishermen's wives of Gloucester, Massachusetts are perceived as inhabiting a separate, land-based world, and do not go out to sea. They are not, however, relegated to a purely domestic realm. Along with their political activism and promotional endeavors, they are responsible for running the financial side of the family business, keeping the books and taking care of land-based, fishery-related business, such as negotiating with fish dealers and arranging for boat repairs. Their public activities generate considerable ambivalence among both the older, more "traditional" women, and among some of the men who believe that they overstep the bounds of proper behavior.

Allison writes about the non-native American female fishermen of the Pacific Northwest, who find opportunities to act as crew members, cooks, deckhands, and even boat skippers. Their numbers are still relatively few, and all the women interviewed indicated that they had encountered problems because of their sex. They insist on being called "fishermen," but freely acknowledge that both sexuality and motherhood make this choice of livelihood a difficult, and for many, only a temporary situation. While considerably more open to women than most fishing regions, the Pacific Northwest remains very much a man's world.

When we turn to South America, we find the sharp division of labor much more conspicuously mixed with an ethos of male dominance and a devaluation of women. De Grys notes that the *machismo* complex which the Catholic Spanish conquest brought to many indigenous communities, has complicated what would appear to be a fairly straightforward division of labor and authority: with deep sea artisanal fishing and extended male absence, the women of San Jose, Peru, become responsible not only for housekeeping and childrearing tasks, but also for marketing the catch and managing family finances. Along with this, they develop a sense of personal authority and competence, and are not normally shy or reticent about speaking their minds. *Machismo*, however, demands female deference to male authority, along with an assumption of male superiority, a belief which women do not share. However, anxious to conform to the culturally dominant mores of neighboring agricultural peoples, the women of San Jose switch modes of demeanor according to whether their men are present in the village or not. They acquiesce in following the *machismo* code, but both women and men know that this is only a temporary situation. Robben's description of the strength of men's insistence on male superiority in Camurim presents an even more extreme case. There men feel that women should confine themselves to domestic roles. This becomes most problematic for those women married to men who fail to live up to their cultural expectations of being the household "provider."

One difficulty in explaining gender status variation in fishing communities may stem from the uncritical application of Western-biased (and hence stratification-biased) models of what a social system based upon fishing must look like. Schlegel notes that "classless societies at the 'middle range' of complexity— horticultural, herding, or fishing societies— can go in either direction" (1977:5) with respect to gender inequality. Maranda's data on the Lau "sea people" of Malaita seem to indicate that the absence of class does not necessarily indicate the absence of sex-antagonism for fishing peoples (Maranda 1974). There the widespread Melanesian pattern of inter-sex hostility seems just as strong as elsewhere.

However, it is striking that the two societies discussed in this volume which fall largely outside the capitalist cash nexus— Nowak's Hma' Btsisi' of Malaysia, and Broch's Miang Tuu of Indonesia— both display a much greater degree of gender equality than the other fishing groups presented here.

Both Nowak and Broch stress the flexibility of the sexual division of labor, and the ease with which men and women take over each others' tasks when needed. In both Miang Tuu and Hma' Btsisi' society, neither men nor women regard the performance of cross-sex tasks as threatening their gender identity. The division of labor exists, but does not rule. There is a minimal emphasis upon gender as a source of prestige assignment. Nowak explains that for the Hma' Btsisi', gender-role determination in fishing is relatively unimportant, with males and females performing tasks when and as needed. The Btsisi' ethic of conjugal cooperation and egalitarianism overrides notions of appropriate gender work.

Broch also sees a generous degree of overlap in fishing task performance among the horticultural and fishing Miang Tuu of Bonerate Island who display a very high status for women and an institutionalized degree of matrifocality. A clearly influential factor is the regular absence of men on overseas trading expeditions. Miang Tuu women are socialized to expect conjugal respect and cooperation, and are also ritually important within the village.

One crucial problem is how we determine appropriate measures for ambiguous concepts such as status and hierarchy. Davis, who has raised the issue elsewhere (1983a), points to the fact that women may play many different roles within a single society, and that these are interpreted in different ways. Several scholars have reminded us that both gender and status are abstractions which should not be reified but placed in the context of culture and of individual experience. Sanday (1974) points out the difficulty of treating status as a monolithic construct, noting that women's status appears different depending on what is being measured: power, authority, or deferential treatment.

Men and women often differ in their evaluations of their own and of the opposite sex. "Culture" itself breaks down as an explanatory unit when we realize that gender functions to isolate interest, and that men and women may constitute different interest groups even in small-scale, fairly egalitarian societies. This may come about in a variety of ways. Broch tells us, for example, that while Bonerate women are not devalued, and have subsistence and central ritual roles which are complementary with those of men, gender remains an important factor in socialization. Because they are not under severe economic stratification pressure, they do not display the antagonism Robben describes in Camurim, where class and gender expectations co-exist in uneasy tension.

One analytical theme upon which there has been considerable debate is the relationship of gender asymmetry to other forms of social stratification. Both Old and New World North Atlantic fishing communities, for example, often display a fairly clear-cut division of labor, with women's work restricted to shore-side tasks only. A number of studies of Newfoundland history and political economy indicate a correlation of gender asymmetry with low socioeconomic status. Indeed, Faris (1972) concludes from these cases that fishing societies in general tend to display a rigid sexual division of labor, as well as varying degrees of sexual antagonism. This perspective reflects the impact of dependency and colonial hierarchy upon marginal peoples, but clearly does not address those fishing societies for whom stratification is not (yet) a problem.

The significance of stratification, in fact, becomes very interesting for fishing peoples, as they are often noted for maintaining a high degree of internal egalitarianism even when embedded within stratified societies. (See, for example, K.F. Norr 1978.) Fishing communities are often of very low status when compared to other occupational groups within such societies. In this volume, Nadel-Klein discusses the stigmatized identity and commitment to internal class-equality of Scottish fisherfolk, and elsewhere has explored their conflicted sense of needing to adhere both to intra-community and extra-community values (1984). This complexity highlights the difficulty of evaluating the relationship between intra-community gender values and the mode of production in which they are enmeshed.

GENDER IDEOLOGY AND THE EXPRESSIVE DIMENSION OF STATUS

Several of the chapters examine the construction and expression of gender ideology. While they view ideology as rooted in the interplay of ecology and structure (vide Ortner and Whitehead 1981), they also recognize its dynamic power in shaping the position and self-image of women in fishing communities (cf. Firth 1984 and Thompson 1985). Gender ideology becomes a conspicuous and problematic factor in the world of deep sea fishing, where men are away for prolonged periods of time. If, as Ortner and Whitehead (1981:9) say, there is a "general tendency to define women in terms of their relations with men (the 'world of heterosexual relations') which contrasts with the way men are defined in terms of their occupation of certain exclusively male roles or statuses (the 'world of men')," then we might expect to find those communities where deep sea fishermen go on extended voyages to manifest particularly deep gender divisions and hostilities. And indeed, there is some evidence to bear this out. In this collection, Robben notes that offshore motor-boat fishermen who cannot fulfill the normative provider role because of poverty and debt, have very antagonistic and fearful relationships with their wives. The gulf between the sexes grows also because long voyages enable men to avoid facing their families directly.

That women's behavior may defy accepted gender ideology when males are absent from home for long periods of time is the subject of Mary de Grys' study. De Grys provides a detailed account of how the male/female gender ideologies of the *machismo/marianismo* complex affect women's lives in fishing communities on the northern coast of Peru. Although on the surface (or in the ideal realm of culture), the women of San Jose display the ethos of *marianismo* (the virtue of being long-suffering and responsible by deferring to patriarchal authority), young wives will side-step their husbands' or mothers-in-law's demands by using gifts of money secretly to buy contraceptive pills. De Grys thus shows that formal gender ideology does not always enable us to predict actual female behavior.

Clark also describes a situation where women take initiative despite a prevailingly patriarchal ethos. Sicilian-American Gloucester fishermen's wives refuse to conform to traditional Sicilian gender ideologies and have constructed their own individualized self-image in order to underwrite their actions in the public, political sphere.

Davis deals with the sociocultural dynamics which lie behind locally constructed female gender ideologies in a Newfoundland fishing village. She considers deviant (shore skipper) as well as acceptable (grass widow) gender ideologies and analyzes the complex strategies which women employ to maintain the proper or publicly valued gender image. Allison chronicles the lives of women who are exceptions to the rules and explains why gender ideologies on the West Coast are more conducive to women fishing than are the gender ideologies which underlie the division of labor and fishing traditions of the United States East Coast.

Gender ideologies entail more than just the simple sex-linking of mental habits. They are also related to prestige structures or evaluations of "social honor" and "social order" (Ortner and Whitehead 1981:13). Cole illustrates a case where women perceive men as prone to vices and burdens on the finances of a household. Men's responses to their wives' control of cash ranged from violence (which might be reciprocated) to tears. Davis, Clark, and Nadel-Klein show how romanticized, occupationally gender-specific ideologies of fishermen's wives can command deference and respect, generate high self-esteem and prestige, and underwrite or legitimize social action. Davis and Nadel-Klein also show how the romanticization of the fisherwife role helps to integrate male and female spheres in the moral order of the community.

The relation between women and the supernatural order also provides a way to investigate women's status. Nowak shows how marriage rituals integrate men's and women's work in Btsisi' society. Broch tells us that Miang Tuu women have important public trance roles and can communicate with the supernatural. Nadel-Klein spells out the relationship between religion and stress in the symbolic domain, where Ferryden women were seen as powerful, dangerous, necessary, and polluting. Clark demonstrates the integral roles that Catholicism plays in Sicilian fisherwives' cultural and personal interpretations of life by examining religious motifs which link women to the fishing, such as the Madonna and child symbolism seen in two bones of a lobster's head.

Finally, several of our studies address the emotional factor. Clark's women "speak from the heart" to manipulate the emotions of their political audience. Robben's study deals in great detail with the affective quality of the husband-wife relationship— a relationship founded upon mutual mistrust. Davis addresses the primacy of the expressive order over the instrumental roles of women in her analysis of the saliency of worry as the primary duty of a fisherman's wife.

CONCLUSION: SOCIAL CHANGE AND DEVELOPMENT

Fishing peoples are more often than not economically and politically marginal to the polities they inhabit and thus are seldom tied in effectively to sources of power and patronage; more often than not they seem to be at the mercy of middlemen and entrepreneurs. Indeed, the continuation of their livelihood may even depend upon isolation. If their beaches or their waters become desirable for other purposes, the fishers must often give way. For example, Parkin (1979) reports that the Muslim fishermen of coastal Kenya must now compete for beach land with capitalist speculators building hotels. Similarly, whether through pollution or simply through restricted access, offshore oil development poses a threat to fishing grounds in a number of places, particularly Malaysia, Indonesia, and New England (Nadel 1983; 1985).

It is essential to inquire about the consequences of such marginality for the sexual division of labor and for women's status in the context of externally imposed economic and technological change. There is an unquestionable need to document the impact of such changes upon women's lives in fishing economies, but without an understanding of women's economic centrality, it is unlikely that many researchers will undertake such projects. As Gulati points out, both here and in her longer analysis of the Indo-Norwegian Fisheries Development Project in Kerala (1984), women's roles in fishing are most often seen as purely ancillary and fishery development planners simply omit taking women into account. (An exception to this can be found in the recognition of women's roles indicated by the ILO's 1984 manual for West Africa on improving village technology for women's activities, which includes a section on fish processing).

Technological, social, and economic changes in the fisheries have ramifications for gender identity. Allison reports that while the women who fish off the Pacific Northwest coast feel that they are breaking with tradition, some fishermen's daughters are beginning to enter the fishery. The new generation thus has role models not available to women before. Should the trend continue, this change in the division of labor could affect the content of gender for these women and their families. Women of Grey Rock Harbour, Newfoundland, on the other hand, maintain historically cherished values as fishermen's wives while they take advantage of new wage labor opportunities to supplement the small family income, harmonizing technological innovation or "modernization" with their understanding of the past. Cole tells us that capitalization has reduced women's participation and independence in Vila da Praia. Krabacher explains why the fisherwomen of Sierra Leone have actually improved their economic status vis-à-vis men as a consequence of "modernization." Gulati notes that, despite their exclusion from developers' plans, the women of Kerala fishing villages have found new sources of wage work, and although the conditions of such work are often very poor, such women are less dependent upon males and less restricted in their activities.

Thus, it is here that we both illustrate and make our plea for the importance of setting the historical context for any study of gender. For without a knowledge of the past, we can hardly presume to assess the future. Moreover, historical research reminds us forcibly of the malleability of human institutions. De Grys notes, for example, the foreign origin of *machismo* ideology in South America, while both she and Robben point out the contradiction which *machismo* imposes for fisher people. Nadel-Klein's chapter is entirely ethnohistorical, describing women in contexts which have disappeared, although women still remain central in the fisherfolk's oral reconstruction of the past. Davis explains the activities which Grey Rock Harbour men see as appropriate for women, as well as those which women choose to enter, regardless of male opinion. Women in Grey Rock Harbour weigh against losses, and sometimes enter nonconformist roles. Putting Allison's paper on women in nontraditional, offshore roles into historical perspective, we can see the seeds of change for the future in individual women's actions.

Fishing economies in many places are imperiled by "modernization" and development. Groups such as the offshore oil industry may press the rhetoric of "national interest" into their own service, persuading powerful allies that economic "progress" lies in backing their desires. Parts or all of fishing communities are often left stranded in the rush to exploit new resources. Such transformations threaten equally to eradicate work-based identity for women as well as men. (See, for example, Mina Caulfield on "Taxes, Tourists, and Turtlemen: Island Dependency and the Tax-Haven Business" (1978), in which she spells out some of the consequences of a changing subsistence base for women's roles in Grand Cayman.) In this volume, we see the problem highlighted in Margaret Clark's chapter, which shows how the women of Gloucester have mobilized to defend their community's livelihood because their own identities are threatened.

The absence of the recognition of women's importance in fishing communities—which are often poor and faced with shrinking resources— suggests that the idea of progress through technological change is informed not only by Western, class-based assumptions, but by gender-bias, as well. Not only may women's activities be affected by new management schemes designed to promote some larger "efficiency," but their very sense of self, as well.

Terra Cognita?   **2**
A Review of the Literature

Dona Lee Davis and Jane Nadel-Klein

INTRODUCTION

Maritime anthropology and women's studies have thus far been the most likely subfields of anthropology to look at women in fishing economies; however both perspectives have seldom been combined to study any specific society. Until recently, most studies of communities either partially or largely dependent upon fishing focused on such issues as the organization of fishing crews or the social relations of production between fishermen and their creditors. Women's roles in both the productive and the expressive spheres of fishing life were generally simply ignored. Yet there is evidence in the literature that the subsistence strategies and division of labor among fishing peoples are more complex than a sketch of the work performed by adult males alone can tell us.

Since numerous myths of female passivity or insignificance appear to characterize much of the literature on fishing communities, though perhaps only by default, we feel that the subject of women in fishing communities deserves special attention, particularly since the newly burgeoning women's studies literature contains relatively little on women in the kinds of geographically and socially marginal areas which fishing peoples often inhabit.

This chapter presents a review of the literature which addresses women's contributions to life in fishing communities, as well as the ways in which women see themselves and their work. Although we found a surprising amount of information available on these issues, we also found that it tends to be scattered, diverse, and piecemeal, in many cases lacking either a clear theoretical focus or ethnographic coherence. Here we hope to provide the specialist and the nonspecialist with insight into how the subsequent chapters both complement and amplify work already done.

When we look at the literature on fishing peoples, two general features of the sexual division of labor stand out. First, the division of labor is highly variable across cultures, rather than uniform. Second, although the tasks allocated by gender cannot be predicted with much certainty, women actively participate in various aspects of the fishery almost everywhere. In some places, both men and women fish; in others, only men fish. In some places, women weave nets; in others, that is a man's job. Scholars debate the rigidity of this division of labor. Faris (1972), for example, claims that fishing societies tend to display a fixed sexual division of labor. Murdock and Provost (1973) classify fishing as a predominantly male occupation. Löfgren (1979), however, points out that in many maritime communities the boundary lines between male and female work can be fuzzy. There are also many cases in which descriptions of men and women at work in fishing societies show a distinct degree of overlap. In any case, the data show that women, whether they catch fish or not, play important roles in the subsistence production system. The conclusion to be drawn about predicting the sexual division of labor in fishing economies would, at this stage, seem to be, "it depends," and the problem of identifying the significant variables remains.

Our survey reveals that women play a number of vital roles in the technological, economic, and social processes by which fish become sources of protein and human income. We find that women may themselves be "fishermen," fishprocessors, fish vendors, or political activists defending their communities in the public arena. Indeed, not infrequently it is their economic contribution that underwrites or provides the risk fund necessary to sustain fishing activities. Women are essential to the fishing economy in innumerable ways, including, but hardly restricted to the formation of fishing families.

A corollary of the assumptions that, first, where fish are a resource, only men catch them, and second, that women's tasks are purely domestic, is the idea that the roles played by women in fishing societies are largely passive and have limited impact on sociocultural facets of the fishing adaptation. Yet the work of a number of scholars demonstrates that women act as well as react to events in the economic sphere, and that they should be portrayed as socially dynamic elements of fishing societies. Moreover, an exclusive emphasis on the material division of labor overlooks other important roles which women play in the symbolic order. For example, Davis (1983c) describes the expressive role of women in Newfoundland, showing the positive social function of the female institution of public and private worrying. Symbolically, women's worry keeps their husbands' boats afloat. Jorion (1976) discusses the instrumental role that female networks play in the evaluation of who is to be considered a good fisherman in Brittany. And Porter (1983) describes the active role a young woman plays in her husband's choice of whether or not to become a fisherman. It should therefore be clear that in order to understand the structure and dynamics of the fishing adaptation, as well as a fishing community's relationship to the world around it, the place of women cannot be relegated to a vague, subsidiary realm.

Yet only a limited number of researchers in women's studies have begun to take an interest in women in fishing economies, and to question the androcentric bias of some earlier work. These scholars examine the complexity and diversity, as well as the similarities of women's lives in maritime settings. Some studies combining the methods and theories of women's and maritime studies are emerging and the literature is beginning to grow in both depth and diversity. At this point, we should state that although our own review refers to work in several disciplines, the analysis and evaluation of the sources are solidly rooted in the perspectives and methods of anthropology. We agree with Greenwood and Stini (1977:vii) that the human condition is a "complex amalgam of environmental conditions, social structures, and symbolically based cultural meanings which have interacted through human evolution and history." With this in mind, we have surveyed the available literature and divided the review into six parts, organized by the subject matter and primary orientation of each work: (1) previous cross-cultural literature reviews, (2) methods of study, (3) women in primary and secondary production, (4) social structure and the occupational community, (5) affect and symbol, and (6) general conclusions about the status of women in fishing economies.

PREVIOUS REVIEWS

In our search through the literature, we found seven review articles which address the topic of women in fishing economies from a cross-cultural and theoretical perspective. The earliest is that by Andersen and Wadel (1972). In their review of comparative problems in fishing adaptations, they were first to note the paucity of materials on women in fishing economies. Although their key objective is "to bring light to new information and ideas about fishermen and fishing" (1972:141), they criticize assumptions about the sexual division of labor in maritime sociocultural adaptations which rest on simplistic, implicit or explicit notions of a "natural" or "universal" male: sea:/female:land dichotomy, and maintain that culture rather than biology shapes women's roles in fishing societies. They call for a greater interest in women as active participants in fishing, as well as for the incorporation of female land-based activities into maritime themes.

Arguing that maritime studies can constitute a legitimate subfield of anthropological research, Smith (1977a) states that maritime communities must be viewed as including multiple and differentiated land as well as sea production strategies. Male absence at sea fishing results in greater role differentiation between males and females, and this in turn leads to a greater dependence on women to control land-based food production. Therefore, female economic independence and control in family and community affairs characterizes maritime adaptations much more frequently than other socio-ecological arrangements.

In a similar vein, Acheson reminds us that maritime adaptations are among the most "extreme achieved by man" (1981:277). Maritime peoples share the problems of life in uncertain and risky environments. Acheson's review of maritime anthropology includes a section on "Women and Family Life" which contains eleven references to women's roles, reiterating the theme that "men fish while women mind the household" (1981:297), and focusing primarily on the problems of male absence, particularly in industrialized fishing.

Taken together, the works of Andersen and Wadel (1972), Smith (1977a), and Acheson (1981) display several common concerns. They recognize the many contributions women make both directly and indirectly to the fishery. This becomes obvious when we remember that the "fishery" itself entails far more than the capture of fish, not the least of which is the procurement of the necessary "tools." Before capture, various preparations must be made, while after capture, the fish must be processed or distributed and sold. In many cases, women must also tend the family farms or work for wages in order to help sustain men's ability to continue as fishermen. These authors also are concerned with the ways in which fishing as an adaptation affects the nature of male and female and family relations in maritime communities. Their reviews show a predominantly materialist focus which brings attention to the division of labor and the resulting features of social structure which make maritime societies a distinct type of environmental and social adaptation.

Finally, they reflect the fact that most of the case studies available to them were based on deep sea, high risk, commercial fisheries where the separation of male and female spheres of activity tends to be a dominant theme, and where fish capture itself generally appears to exclude women.

The more recent reviews of Pollnac (1976, 1984b, 1986), Thompson (1985) and Porter (1984) are also centrally concerned with the division of labor in fishing economies. Their theoretical concerns show different emphases, however. Pollnac's approach to his data may be described as ecological and evolutionary. Using the Standard Cross Cultural Sample of Murdock and White (1969), Pollnac (1976) identifies the sociocultural consequences of the division of labor by sex in the light of fishing as a subsistence activity. By cross-tabulating the degree of emphasis on fishing in a particular society with the division of labor in other productive activities (such as land-bound hunting and gathering and animal and plant domestication), Pollnac establishes fishing dominant, fishing co-dominant, and fishing important/unimportant typologies. His data show that women's participation in the fisheries of subsistence-based "traditional" societies is significant, although females are more likely to participate in co-dominant (39%) fishing societies than they are in dominant fishing societies (26%). In both types of society, males tend to dominate the deep water marine fishery, while women collect shellfish and conduct shore and reef fishing. According to Pollnac's analysis of the data, fish dominant and co-dominant patterns associate statistically with the following sociocultural features: (1) root, tuber, and fruit rather than grain cultivation or animal domestication; (2) semi-nomadic settlement patterns; (3) lack of a supreme deity; (4) absence of patrilineal kin forms; and (5) relative absence of social stratification. In a later, related article, Pollnac (1984b) again uses the Standard Cross Cultural Sample to show that as the subsistence emphasis shifts more towards fishing, land-based activities are increasingly performed predominantly or exclusively by women. Pollnac points out that this is more true for marginal than for technologically developed, capital-intensive societies. Pollnac (1986) also suggests that these increased responsibilities may be associated with more prestige, independence, and self-reliance for women in fishing communities, especially if their contributions are already valued by their society. Although he does address the issue of how social change and development policies can affect the position of women, Pollnac chooses not to grapple with the issues of cause and effect, and does not attempt to explain the sociocultural dynamics underlying the interrelationships within

male/female labor patterning, overall subsistence strategies, levels
of technological and structural complexity and religious ideologies.
To a limited extent, Pollnac's work follows the ecological and evolutionary paradigms used by Lenski (1966), Martin and Voorhies
(1975), Friedl (1975), and, more recently, O'Kelly and Carney (1986),
who view human evolution as having occurred through several
major ecological adjustments, each entailing significant differences
in the sexual division of labor and the overall structuring of society.

In Thompson's (1985) recent review of the maritime literature
on women in fishing, he devises a model for understanding the position of women in fishing communities across cultures, both past
and present. He confronts the limitations of those feminist studies
which persist in viewing transhistorical female subordination or
patriarchy as the primary concept for analysis. According to
Thompson, because of their crucial roles in fishing economies (e.g.,
direct production, rearing the next generation, household responsibility in male absence) women in some fishing societies tend to
show a degree of power and independence which is unusual in other
societies. He seeks to identify the roots of power by examining the
complex interactions among economy, property, space, work, family, religion, region, and personality, and the vital roles such
interactions can play in changing the balance of domestic and community power between the sexes. Using information from diverse
geographical sources, Thompson argues that ascendancy (e.g., independence and power) of women is the result of the conjunction of
two dimensions of the sexual division of labor in fishing societies:
the spatial and the economic. Male absence from home can accord
women with a kind of territorial autonomy in the domestic sphere,
while active roles in domestic production or financial decision
making give them vital economic responsibility. Yet these two
dimensions must be mediated by a social recognition of this independence and power. According to Thompson, when one considers
the juxtaposition of power between the sexes, one can see women's
power undermined to the extent that their menfolk are exploited by
merchants or employers. Such exploitation hardens men and drives
them to compensatory self-indulgence and assertiveness when they
return home. Yet Thompson's model goes beyond a sole reliance on
economic determinism. Thompson recognizes that cultural factors
(such as family, ethnic or regional traditions, or the maintenance of
separate gender-based cultural traditions) can override economic
factors, since even in highly adverse circumstances, women may
retain their balance of power with men. A problem with Thompson's
theory is that although he spells out in detail the socio-dynamics of

economic factors in the gender power balance, he fails to subject ideological factors to similar analysis, preferring to see them as "givens," rooted in a culture's history and traditions. Although he claims to have developed a cross-cultural model for understanding the position of women in fishing communities, most of Thompson's examples are drawn from Europe. This European bias, along with a heavy emphasis on commercial fisheries may give unwarranted salience to the male absence theme.

In a paper focusing on "gender and the sea," or the division of labor in marginal maritime societies, Porter (1985) criticizes anthropologists in general for their tendency to lump all kinds of fishing (e.g., high technology and simple technology fishing strategies, urban and rural fishing communities) into a single analytic category. Instead, Porter suggests that more limited, intensive studies of maritime societies as regional and marginal may have particular value for examining some of the theoretical questions which feminists have addressed. Porter formulates a case for re-examining the political economy of peripheral regions in advanced capitalist societies in the context of feminism by revising the notion of patriarchy. Unlike Thompson (1985), Porter, after a brief review of the literature, is not willing to dismiss the usefulness of the patriarchy concept. Instead, she questions the simple equation of patriarchy with oppression, by stating that although men may hold culturally legitimated power, there are factors which mediate or mitigate male power, such as: (1) countervailing strategies and multiple and diverse loci of power, (2) a ceaseless process of negotiation between males and female, and (3) the separation of male and female spheres. Porter calls for a refinement of the concept of patriarchy by specifying its different forms and by assessing (through fieldwork) female resistance to and co-opting of patriarchies. Porter states that more research should directly focus on both production and reproduction as analytic categories, since family and household are important productive units in marginal economies. Porter's purposes are ambitious. She sees a potential to reveal or identify any Levi-Straussian "deep structures between gender and the sea" or to unravel the systemic relationships by which women have universally become the prey of men (Rubin 1975). By focusing on marginality and refining the concept of patriarchy, she agrees with Thompson (1985) that the interrelationship between ideology and economy denotes a vital area of gender negotiation, and one which the Marxists have tended to overlook. A problem with Porter's analysis is that although she cites sources with contrary definitions of patriarchy, she never directly defines what she means by the term, specifically as related to marginal maritime societies.

Methods

The literature which relates to women in fishing economies represents a very diverse range of methods and analytic perspectives. The most frequent method employed is the time-honored anthropological field method of participant-observation. Participant-observations which tell us something about women vary from the community study (e.g., Firestone 1967; Rosemary Firth 1966; Muir 1976), to the occupational community study (e.g., Andersen and Andersen 1964; Horobin 1972; Lummis 1977 and 1985), the comparative or multi-community study (Raymond Firth 1984; Hammel and Hasse 1962; Klausen 1968), and the extensive study of one element or group within a particular community (Acheson and Lello 1980; Forman 1970). Life histories or extended case studies of single individuals (e.g., Gulati 1984; Wadel 1973) have also been used to supplement more general types of community analysis. Participant-observation studies have been conducted in many different areas, although there is a relative scarcity of literature on cultures from Africa, the Caribbean, and the Middle East. All levels of sociocultural development and diverse subsistence patterns, including hunter-gatherers (e.g., Estioko-Griffin and Griffin 1981), horticulturalists (e.g., Firth 1967), agriculturalists and peasants (e.g., Firth 1946) and modern industrial societies (e.g., Tunstall 1962; Saugestad 1980; Gronbach and Gerrard 1987) have been examined by anthropologists. Fieldwork has also been conducted at sea aboard boats (e.g., Nimmo 1972; Ward 1965; Zulaika 1981).

A problem common to many of the participant-observation studies stems from their male bias or emphasis on male activities to the virtual exclusion of female activities. The large majority of studies have been conducted by men, but even in the rare cases where a female ethnographer conducted the research, men tended to remain the focus (e.g., Ward 1965). It was extremely frustrating to read such genderless descriptions as "'the people' went out to fish every morning," or "'the shaman' blessed the catch."

Questionnaires and interviews have also been used to supplement other methods (e.g., Akerele 1979; Davis 1983a; Dixon et al. 1984) or as the sole method of data collection (e.g., Connelly and MacDonald 1983, 1985; Lamson 1983). The quantitative analysis of questionnaire data figures prominently in the studies of industrial (e.g., Andersen and Andersen 1964; Danowski 1980; Poggie and

Gersuny 1974) and artisanal fisheries (e.g., Akerele 1979; Gladwin 1975; Quinn 1978).

Limited use has been made of the Human Relations Area Files or of clinical studies. Pollnac (1976, 1984, 1986) has used the HRAF, as have Murdock and Provost (1973). Tiller's (1958) clinical and experimental study is unique. Tiller used doll play observations and clinical interviews of parents and children to assess the effect of prolonged periods of father absence on male and female gender identity and comportment among children in fishing and sailor families.

Although studies such as those by Antler (1982) and Porter (1983) for Newfoundland, and Löfgren (1972) for Sweden are based entirely on historical materials, most ethnographies are accompanied by chapters or sections on history (e.g., Faris 1972). Oral folklore has been used to supplement historical data (e.g., Thompson 1985 and Taylor 1983) and has also served as the sole basis of information (Murray 1979). Archeological data dealing directly with women are rare. One exception is found in the volume edited by Gunda (1984), where Kreuzer indicates a symbolic association of women with fish in discussing the evidence for female fish-goddesses in Fourth Dynasty Egypt. There the goddess Hatmehit was called "First of the Fish"; in lower Egypt, the goddess Neith was associated with the large Latus fish.

WOMEN IN THE FISHERY: PRIMARY AND SECONDARY PRODUCTION

Generally speaking, women take part in the fishery as members of fishing families or fishing communities where the sexual division of labor essential to the survival of the fishery includes domestic or household tasks. Women as independent entrepreneurial fishers appear relatively rarely, the Pacific Northwest providing a notable contemporary exception (see Allison's chapter, this volume). Women's roles in fishery production may be complex and overlapping, but for the convenience of discussion, we will divide them into rough categories of primary and secondary production. Primary production refers to tasks related to the actual capture or harvest of fish or other marine products in both subsistence and commercial settings. Secondary production refers to other roles in preparing fish gear or in the processing, marketing, and distribution of fish. The latter category includes women employed in fish plant wage work as well as women who process and sell fish either as independent or domestic agents. We also distinguish here between subsistence and commercial fishing, as the enormous differences in modes and relations of production have equally enormous consequences for women's participation and status.

Subsistence and Artisanal Fishing

Fishing has been and continues to be a major source of protein in many foraging and farming subsistence economies in various parts of the world. A number of ethnographic accounts show that women may have active roles in subsistence or non-commercial fishing. Dahlberg (1981) points out in the introduction to her book, *Woman the Gatherer*, that women's subsistence contribution can be crucial for a group's well-being and survival. In many subsistence oriented societies, however, gathering and hunting may be difficult to categorize by sex, despite that fact that we emphasize "man, the hunter," and "woman, the gatherer." For example, while Lee (1968) classifies shell collecting as gathering, Meehan (1977) speaks of shellfish "hunters" and with this usage, of course, women may be hunters. Further, in many cases, there does not appear to be a necessarily fixed division of labor in fishing. Grumet (1980:56) tells us, for example, that for the Coastal Algonkian of the seventeenth and eighteenth centuries, "fishing...was a cooperative venture. Both sexes produced the weirs and nets that collected a portion of the enormous anadromous fish runs every spring. Men and women further speared, netted, and hooked fish from the shore and from canoes."

Generally, among the hunting and gathering Phillipine Agta, women "participate in all the subsistence activities that men do," although a few Agta groups do reserve some tasks for men (Estioko-Griffin and Griffin 1981). Women use many different fishing techniques, including spearing fish underwater, and teenage girls are considered especially capable fishers. Women from childhood to old age fish with men in the lowland rivers, unless incapacitated by pregnancy, lactation, or extreme age. When fishing individually, women may be major contributors to the daily catch. Old women and children also gather shellfish, shrimp, and amphibians in coastal reefs and fresh water rivers. With the adoption of nets from the lowlands, however, women's participation in fishing appears to drop off in accordance with lowland patterns of labor (Estioko-Griffin and Griffin 1981). This provides a rather intriguing comparison with the impact of agricultural modernization in Africa, where women are actually pushed out of traditional roles with the adoption of new technology and changing market relations (Boserup 1970). However, development policies do not always divorce women from fishing. Among the Nata Tyna of northern Botswana, the introduction of hooks and fishing lines, along with diminishing access to land, have increased the involvement of women and children in river fishing (Ebert et al. 1987).

Women in many places play very important roles in inshore and riverine fishing, particularly in shellfishing. Among the Miskito women in Eastern Nicaragua, who live in a mixed subsistence and market economy, sea fishing for turtles, manatee and shrimp is considered men's work. Women collect crabs and oysters and occasionally fish with line in the rivers (Nietschmann 1973). Tiwi women also collect crabs, cockles and oysters in mangrove swamps (Goodale 1971). Among the Ifaluk, women help to set lines and nets for inshore fishing (Burrows and Spiro 1970). They also tighten the nets once the fish have entered them. Sahlins (1962) notes similar complexities of fishing strategies among the Moala women of the Fiji Islands. Here women collect prawns, crabs, and shellfish, and dive for fish. They also fish with baited lines from boats, poison fish in tidal pools, and practice communal netting in groups of twenty to thirty women and girls. Pomponio (1983) says that Siassi Island women dive for clams and fish with hook and line. In the Korean village of Sok'po, Brandt (1971) reports that women's shellfishing activities can contribute significant amounts of protein and cash income to the household. Ruth Landes (1938) has pointed out that for the Ojibwa of western Ontario fishing is about equally important for men and women.

Commercial and Industrialized Fishing

The commercial fisheries are generally regarded as male domains to an even greater extent than the subsistence and artisanal fisheries. This is in some respects true, but since, as Andersen and Wadel (1972) point out, there is no biological reason why women cannot fish, we must ask why this is so. In fact, we find there are many exceptions. Examples of women fishing commercially are not difficult to come by in the ethnographic literature, although they seldom comprise the focus of analysis.

Hart and Davis (1982a-d) interviewed women involved in deep sea and river fishing on the North Carolina coast. Most of the women they surveyed fish mainly to help male kin who are short-handed for a specific trip or a particular time of year. Once on board, they perform the tasks traditionally assigned to women on shore (e.g., cooking). However, Hart and Davis found one woman for whom fishing is a full-time operation. She operates her own crab boat, does some drop netting, regularly crews on trawlers and scallop boats, and also works as a mate on recreational fishing charter boats. She maintains that " I am a fisherman and mean *fisherman* [emphasis ours]. I'm not a fish person or a fisherette or any of those strange words. The word says what I do, I fish. The word has been around a long time and it deserves respect" (Hart and Davis 1982b:1).

There are other examples. Perhaps the classic case of women who fish is found in Hornell's (1950) brief account of the skilled oyster divers of Japan. Where pearl diving is a family enterprise, wives or daughters dive while the husbands or fathers row. Women abalone divers in Japan have also been noted by Maraini (1962), Kalland (1983), and Plath (1986). Norbeck (1954) says that in the Japanese community of Takashima, women and girls regularly help with fishing if the household is short of male labor. They also dig clams and assist their husbands with net fishing. And among the protected fjords of the Pacific Alaskan fisheries, nuclear families composed of men, women, and children fish while living aboard small boats, gillnetting, trolling, and purse seining for salmon from spring to fall (Miller 1977). Miller also makes a passing reference to all-women crews but fails to give details. Nimmo (1972) tells us that among the Sulu "sea gypsies" of the Phillipines, women assist their husbands in fishing, although their primary responsibility lies in "boat as household" tasks. Even among people who perceive fishing to be a solely male activity, exceptions can be found. The boat people of Hong Kong spend their lives fishing on boats crewed by nuclear family members, and a fisherman's helpmate is often his wife. Ward (1965) indicates that while it is very rare, women have been known to captain fishing boats. The women of Notre Dame Bay, Newfoundland, are reported to have taken to fishing when their husbands were away working on longliners. In their husbands' absence, these Newfoundland women, caught, dried, and sold squid, which the Japanese bought for its aphrodisiac qualities (Porter 1983). Szala (1977) reports that southwest coast Newfoundland women often fished for subsistence when their husbands were absent. According to Porter (1983, 1985), there are Newfoundland women who join their husbands in commercial fishing; there are also a couple of dozen women around the island who fish in their own right. Christiansen-Ruffman (1982) reports that women on Newfoundland's northern peninsula have grouped together to protest rules on unemployment insurance which deny benefits to wives who fished with their husbands. The Newfoundland women's fishing activity has its historical antecedents:

> In the Labrador 'floater' cod fishery, which was operated from the late eighteenth to the mid-twentieth centuries from the Newfoundland outports on a seasonal basis, fishermen...took up girls

and young women with them, both as fishworkers and as cooks, who would work aboard the boats as well as in the huts. These Newfoundland outport women were often already notably handy with a gun from going out to hunt for the winter food; so in the cod season some would take their chance for a little 'jiggering' for fish for themselves (Thompson et al. 1983:174).

Thompson (Thompson et al. 1983:78) also claims that women not only fished from boats in southern Brittany and in north-west Spain, but also had inheritance rights to boats, while women in parts of coastal Wales, Sardinia, Northern Ireland, and Eire have been reported working as crew or even as skippers. In the Baltic fishery, women sometimes took active part, unmarried women working as crew members in strenuous fishing operations such as deep sea drift netting (Löfgren 1979).

Unfortunately, such tantalizing incidents of women's participation are often relegated to "remarks in passing" (e.g., Löfgren 1979; Thompson et al. 1983). Women seem to be viewed as interesting only in their nonfishing roles, with little attempt to see the cultural context or theoretical import of such roles. Given the extent to which women participate either on board or on shore in fishing activities around the world, it is tempting to speculate that the prevailing perception of fishing as an exclusively male occupation reflects the western bias of conceiving of fishing as an aggressive capture enterprise, or in other words, as hunting. Since the next assumption is that males are to hunting as females are to gathering, fishing is perceived *a priori* as a male endeavor. As we shall see, the crucial nature of women's work in preparing gear, and processing and marketing the catch means that in many places, the fishery's survival depends upon women's work. It is even appropriate in some cases to see women as having the greater role, at least in terms of the number of tasks.

PROCESSING THE CATCH

Women in fishing economies are perhaps most widely known for their involvement in fish processing and marketing. Women in almost every fishing community play some role in processing, gutting, sun-drying, smoking, pickling, canning, or freezing fish so that it can be preserved either for sale or use. Fish perish so quickly that something must be done as soon as possible after they are removed from the water. That women often have sole or major responsibility for this task comes as no surprise, particularly in those cases where it is the men who labor to bring the catch to shore. It is also interesting to note that women play major roles in processing fish in subsistence, small-scale market, and capitalist economies. In fact, it is here, along with the closely related set of tasks concerned with selling fish, that women's roles are particularly conspicuous and take on very great importance for the survival of fishing as a way of making a living. In many, if not most cases, women's efforts in processing represent labor dedicated to the service of the household as family firm. Whether the cash or goods realized from the sale of fish represents women's contribution to the household income, or whether women keep part of their profits for personal use, women's work enables the fishermen to keep fishing. As Gerrard (1987) succinctly states, women constitute the "ground crew" of the Norwegian fishery. Women automatically become fisherwomen by entering into a permanent alliance with a fisherman. For every man recruited into the fishery, one must assume a woman ought to be recruited. Without women's investment in time and energy, the fishing enterprise would quickly cease. However, it is here also that women become particularly vulnerable to social change. Modernization and development programs designed to improve the technological capacity of local fisheries or the management of scarce resources may have a serious reorganizing effect upon the division of labor and the cultural significance of work. We have relatively little information about the impact of such changes on women's lives in fishing communities; further work focusing specifically upon such problems would be very useful.

Descriptions of fish processing tasks and techniques are sporadically available in the ethnographic literature. Among the Malay, both men and women process fish, smoking it for sale for high profits (Raymond Firth 1967). Fanti women smoke fish in order to increase profits, as well as to preserve the highly perishable catch. Both men and women in Peru clean and dry fish (Hammel and Hasse 1962). Japanese fishwives process dried squid, which has a very high commercial reputation throughout Japan (Chang 1971). Taiwanese women of K'un Shen shuck oysters and tend fish ponds for the upper classes of the village (Diamond 1969). Around the turn of the century, Scottish fisherwomen employed by commercial fishcurers traveled from their home villages to herring ports around Britain to gut and pack herring. In Newfoundland until the 1950s, women were an integral part of the family based household production of lightly salted, sun-dried cod. This skilled labor required group effort and considerable time expenditure (Antler 1977, 1982).

Sometimes, like the herring curing women of Scotland, Newfoundland women would migrate to Labrador to help with the summer fishing. According to Antler (1982), women did not get paid for their labor, but their fish processing efforts approximated from 30 to 40 percent of the family's earning power. Antler's historical overview surveys the roles of women in the Newfoundland fishery from the early colonial, servant-planter fishery to the family salt fishery, through to the modern frozen-fish industry. She views land tenure, marriage and residence rules, and kinship categories as responding to the requirements of the traditional salt-drying fishery. Although a Newfoundland woman still salts fish for home consumption, the sole surviving commercial, family-based salt processing industry ceased to exist in Newfoundland in the mid-1970s (Andrews n.d.). In Peace Harbor, Maine, women used to can lobster before live sale predominated. Today, some women pick crabmeat to sell to supermarkets and restaurants (Kunhikannan 1980). Women in the Soviet Union and Norway have moved from factory to sea as boats have expanded to include processing facilities (Löfgren 1972).

Fish Plant Labor: Studies in Atlantic Canada and Norway

Several studies of women in fish plant labor have contributed significantly to our knowledge of one aspect of changing modes of production within the modern capitalist world-system (Wallerstein 1974). Studies of women as wage laborers in fish plants incorporate a variety of themes. These include: (1) explanations of how women perform the multiple roles of fish plant laborer, mother, and housekeeper, allocating and organizing their time and priorities (Muir 1976); (2) evaluations of the status of women within the fish processing industry (Lamson 1983; Nyseth 1987); and (3) the availability of female labor as a factor in the semi-proletarianization of the poor inshore fisherman (Connelly and MacDonald 1983, 1985; Thompson et al. 1983).

McCay (1983) discusses women fish plant laborers on Fogo Island, Newfoundland, not only in terms of their need for wages, but also of their need for the unemployment stamps for which their work qualifies them. She analyzes the multiple strategies women use to maximize their financial contribution to household income, addressing the issue of who gets priority to work at the fish plant. According to local judgement, fishermen's wives should be hired first, since if it were not for their husbands, there would be no work for anyone.

Margaret Muir's (1975, 1976) studies of women's networks in French and English speaking lobster fishing villages in Isles-de-la-Madelaine, Quebec, show how fishermen's wives who work in the fish plant exploit traditional female labor networks to run their homes while they are working. They maintain domestic authority by "apprenticing" younger women; a married woman's status and reputation rest on her ability as a housekeeper. Regular employment of women outside the home is valued, but not expected.

According to Nyseth (1987), although women are numerically dominant in the Norwegian fish processing industry, the existing division of labor favors men. While men work with machines or at the quay where fish are landed, women work at the conveyor belt cutting, slicing and packaging the fish. Women earn less than men and their work is more monotonous. Moreover, women's jobs are more prone to seasonal fluctuations. Dissatisfied with careers as fish plant laborers, young Norwegian women are migrating out of the fishing districts to seek better employment opportunities.

Lamson (1983) reports on women fish plant laborers in their communities in Newfoundland and Nova Scotia. She administered a questionnaire to fifty-five women to elicit information about their general working environment. Her data sharply contradict local myths about women as fish plant laborers: that women work only for luxuries, that women won't travel more than a few miles to a job, that they are lazy, irresponsible workers likely to steal or sabotage the product.

Connelly and MacDonald (1983, 1985) demonstrate how people in fishing communities respond to changing conditions, not just as individual workers but as members of households; this in turn affects the workload and well-being of women. Women in Atlantic Canadian fishing communities have always constituted a cheap, available labor reserve, consistently responding to every wage labor opportunity open to them. Connelly and MacDonald conclude that women's domestic role continues to constitute a pool of reserve labor and to underwrite the costs of the reproduction of labor. Examining changes within the fishing industry as related to a particular Nova Scotia community,they interviewed fish plant managers and employers concerning changes in the sex distribution of jobs within the plant, working conditions, and sources of labor. In the traditionally prosperous fishing community of Big Harbour, women are most likely to work in the fish plant under the following conditions: (1) when their husband's income is low, (2) in winter, when the husband is home to tend the children, (3) for extra household goods (e.g., a refrigerator), and (4) as a middle-age replacement activity for childrearing. Underdevelopment is perpetuated and wages are kept low by the fact that when Big Harbour women can afford not to work for poor pay in bad conditions, employers can always recruit female labor from a less prosperous nearby lumbering community. Thus development for the whole regional economy is undermined.

Another account of proletarianization in the female fish processing labor force is found across the Atlantic in the historical accounts of women as transhumant herring gutters in Scotland in the late nineteenth and early twentieth centuries (Buchan 1977; Gray 1978; Thompson et al. 1983; Nadel-Klein this volume). Scottish women from dozens of small fishing communities were contracted to gut, salt, grade, and pack herring at major fish processing centers. The work was hard, the living and working conditions poor, and the pay low. However, the herring packers interest Thompson because they were one of the labor groups most likely to go on strike. Thompson attributes this to the sense of community and solidarity built up by the fact that these women were isolated from their own homes and lived together, but it should also be noted that Scottish fisherfolk have a long tradition of political and religious radicalism.

DISTRIBUTION, MARKETING, AND FINANCING

In addition to their work in fish processing, women often work as fish merchants, marketing and distributing fish. This has been documented and described in a number of areas, including (but not restricted to) India (Gulati 1981, 1984; Klausen 1968), Brazil (Forman 1970), Malaysia (Rosemary Firth 1966), Peru (Hammel and Hasse 1962), Ghana (Christensen 1977; Gladwin 1975; Pollnac 1984a; Quinn 1978), Liberia (Akerele 1979), and Scotland (D. Fraser 1983; Gray 1978). In this volume, both Nadel-Klein and de Grys discuss women's roles in processing at length. We will briefly elaborate on a few of these examples.

In a comparison of Hindu and Christian fishing villages and their responses to an Indo-Norwegian technical development project in Kerala, Klausen (1968) found that fishermen in the Christian community give part of their catch to their wives who, in turn, sell it to merchants. Although the fishermen sell most of their catch to non-spouse middlemen, women keep the money from their allotted share to invest in gold and other goods for themselves. Because it is considered very vulgar, only very poor women act as fish merchants on a much larger scale. These women carry fish in baskets on their heads and run inland as fast as possible to sell the fish before it starts to spoil. As wives, they have greater access to newly landed fish than the merchants and middlemen from non-fishing families.

In some groups, fish dealing is seen as a purely female domain. For example, in Fraser's study of the Malay fishing villages of South Thailand, we find that women are solely responsible for the fish once they are landed. Although fishing is largely seasonal here, women play an important role in the product's distribution and marketing. Men's responsibility in the fishery ends when wives or mothers of the crew unload the fish. Women distribute the catch, each collecting the shares due her. Putting some aside for family use, the women travel by bus to the market where they sell fish to Chinese fish dealers. If individual catches are small, women may combine them for sale or sell directly to the market consumers to get a higher price. Malay women also turn to netting crab themselves for retail sale (Fraser 1966).

Some of the marketing behavior studies are rather severely limited for our purposes in that they do not focus on gender issues; some mention women simply in passing, or only in relation to men. An exception is Gulati's (1981, 1984) detailed life histories of women fish vendors and processors. Most studies relegate women to chapters on household and family. The work of Rosemary Firth (1966) and Raymond Firth (1967) on the Malay fishermen of Kelanton have also been more thorough in their coverage of women, and point out the complexity that may accompany women's indirect participation in the fishery. One of the most notable features of Kelanton peasant life is the extent of women's freedom, especially in matters such as the control of family finances. At least 25 percent of adult women have some definable occupation which yields a regular income. If casual or intermittent work such as selling or gutting fish is taken into consideration, the percentage rises to 50. Women fish dealers operate commercially on the same terms as men, and mother and daughter often join together as dealers. A woman may use her natal kin as buyers if she has married outside her own village. Among these peasants, fish dealing is a fairly specialized trade which fluctuates with the success of the fishermen. A type of equality between males and females is indicated by the fact that women advise their husbands on matters of investment, such as decisions to buy or sell boats, although we are not told whether or not such advice is followed (Rosemary Firth 1966).

Both Christensen and Gladwin have written extensively on the Fanti fishing people of Ghana, where a complex system of marketing is accompanied by equally complex processing and financing. Without women's contribution, the rural fishery could not exist in its present form. Christensen (1977) demonstrates how technological change has resulted in the movement of market women into positions as entrepreneurs who finance expensive boats and gear. Fanti women were not traditionally involved in this way, but had simply sold the fish either fresh or oven-smoked. When the costs of equipment increased to a point where fishermen could no longer finance their resources through kinsmen, fishermen began to run to the market women for loans. Some women lend the crew money for operating or for living expenses when fish are scarce, and, in return, have the right to purchase future catches at favorable prices. They get high interest rates as well as a share of the catch for the equipment financed.

The Gladwins discuss Fanti women fish-sellers in terms of marketing strategies. Hugh and Christina Gladwin (1971) present a formalistic model of market decision-making and Christina Gladwin (1975) models market strategies to demonstrate the rational factors that inform sellers' judgements. In this matrilineal society, husbands do not view their wives as necessarily dependent on a spouse's income; a fisherman prefers to sell his fish to his sister rather than to his wife.

Christensen (1977), Akerele (1979), and Pollnac (1984b) warn against seeing marketers necessarily as examples of high status among women; in Ghana, for example, women have tried to fill a void created by changing economic and technical demands. Akerele (1979) contrasts artisanal fishing among the Fanti with industrial fishing in Liberia. One fish company operates in Liberia, sending out trawlers and returning fish to refrigerated packing plants. "Fish-mammies" purchase fish from these plants and sell them through groups of submammies or market women. While some women have become entrepreneurs of note, most merely eke out a living. Quinn (1978) also says that women fish sellers in West Africa often fail and that their marketing efforts can be a mask for increasing under-development and poverty.

As noted, women occasionally play a role financing fishing operations. Malay women help their husbands finance vessels; Fanti women in Ghana have become part owners of motor and fishing canoes. Pollnac (1984a) describes female money lenders of Tombo, who assume financial control over fishermen. Some 14 percent of boat owners in the herring and bonga fishery of Tombo are widowed women over fifty years of age.

WOMEN IN THE FISHING COMMUNITY

Women and the fishery are most often studied in terms of women's participation as members of fishing communities. However, the prototype of the small, isolated, and traditional community dom-inated by the family fishery with its characteristically rigid division of labor by sex may be, in part, an artifact of the predominance of North Atlantic (mainly British and Canadian) studies in the fishing community literature. The importance of the household in its support and processing functions for the fishery, as well as being a primary unit of subsistence production, is recognized as a basic adaptation to local fishing ecology and marketing demands.

An important criticism of the study of women in fishing communities is, as Porter (1983:4) so aptly puts it, that women are too often discussed as "O's" or as the by-products of patrilineal groupings. Porter refers specifically to studies of fishing in the North Atlantic which present fishing as an agnatic enterprise. "O's" symbolize women on the kinship charts which illustrate the workings of crew recruitment, virilocal residence, and equipment inheritance rules (Britan 1979; Byron 1975; Cohen 1982b; Firestone 1967; Fox 1978; Gaffney 1972; Jorion 1982; Knipe 1979; Löfgren 1972; Nemec 1972; and Stiles 1979). Much of the North Atlantic kin crew recruitment literature deals with how modernization and change have broken down the traditional agnatic organization of crews along with the institutions of the extended family. Kinship is seen as the basis of economic cooperation and social structure, but women in these studies are apparently of little importance except as links in kin chains. Some, however, see the patrilocal extended family as more ideal than real (Chiaramonte 1970; Gaffney 1972; Knipe 1984; and Stiles 1979). For example, Davis (1983b) has questioned the structural saliency of crew recruitment and the patrilocal extended family pattern in Newfoundland. According to Davis, the emphasis on this ideal obscures the actual variation of family forms which may occur in the Newfoundland outport, particularly along the southwest coast, where the inshore ecology has never supported the kinds of trap-sharing agnatic fishing enterprises that are found on the east and northeast coasts.

The Family Fishery and the Sexual Division of Labor

The nature of the sexual division of labor in maritime communities is quite diverse, varying with such factors as technology, mode of production, and market strategies. Scholars disagree about the general significance of the division of labor, depending, we suspect, upon the cases considered. Faris (1972) maintains that fishing societies characteristically show a rigid sexual division of labor, while Löfgren (1979) states that in many maritime communities, it is impossible to uphold such a rigid division. Nowak, Broch, and to some extent, Cole, in this volume, present cases upholding Löfgren's viewpoint. Andersen and Wadel (1972) concede that there are exceptions, but generally uphold Faris, as does Acheson (1981). Ellis (1983) contrasts two Chesapeake Bay shellfishing communities along this axis. In one, the division of labor by sex was sharply upheld, with women largely confined to domestic tasks. In the other, generally less prosperous community, "women have been doing a variety of shore and water work as long as locals remember" (1983:16).

Very little research has been done on family fisheries within industrial, multi-occupational complex economic settings. Hart and Davis (1982a, b, c) interviewed four North Carolina women who described themselves as co-partners with their husbands in independent family fishing businesses. They handled the paperwork, drove trucks, weighed fish, and ran the family store. Although their activities were primarily onshore, they occasionally fish, net crab, and dredge oysters.

More is known about family fisheries in less industrialized settings. The importance of women in household production has been well documented for the traditional fisheries of Atlantic Canada and the British Isles. In Newfoundland, for example, the saying that "a woman is more than 50 percent" reflects the recognized importance of women's contribution to the subsistence effort (Murray 1979). The significance of women's household contributions to the community and to family fishing is well described in a number of places, including Queen and Haberstein (1974), Weatherburn (1977), Philbrook (1966), Porter (1983), Murray (1979) and Davis (1983a, 1986b). The impact of repeated and prolonged male absence upon women's work loads is a common theme in the literature of Quebec (Muir 1975; Doran 1974), the Shetlands (Thompson et al. 1983), Denmark (Andersen and Andersen 1964), Sweden (Löfgren 1979), Norway (Saugestad 1980), and the Dutch oystermen of Long Island (Taylor 1983). Women must raise food, care for livestock, make clothes, preserve food, care for children, run the household, make and sell crafts for extra cash, and care for the aged. Young girls often work for wages in the fishery or in nearby factories to bring money home to the family. They constitute a mobile and underpaid labor force.

Thus the importance of women in traditional economies cannot be over-estimated. However, talk of women in fishing economies must be accompanied by more analysis of how modern fisheries, industrialization and modernization, and improved standard of living have all affected women's roles in contemporary fishing communities.

THE IMPACT OF CHANGE AND DEVELOPMENT

Although there are several studies which refer to the effects of so-cial change on women in fishing economies from a historical perspective (Löfgren 1979; Antler 1982; Cole this volume; Nadel-Klein this volume; Porter 1983), this section focuses on the industrialization of fisheries and their incorporation into the capitalist world market through "planned" development programs in a more contemporary perspective. Gulati, in this volume, insists that government development policies should take women's roles into account, as does Pollnac (1984a). He also points out, however, that such policies may displace women from established roles. In Liberia and Ghana, for example, as the profitability of fisheries rises, men tend to become more involved in marketing.

This section on change and women's roles points to some cru-cial problems for further investigation and analysis. It is clear that fishing communities still tend to be characterized by relative pover-ty and low status, despite a number of community development programs. Modernization and development in general have come in for serious criticism by some North Atlantic ethnographers. The rise of the highly capitalized, centrally-owned industrial fishery with its huge offshore trawlers has been blamed for the decline of family fisheries and the undermining of economic viability and quality of life in many North Atlantic fishing communities (Gray 1978; Grobech and Gerrard 1987). This is particularly well-documented in Newfoundland through a series of case studies of local responses to post-Confederation provincial attempts to develop the fishery and modernize the island (Iverson and Matthews 1968; Brox 1972; Wadel 1973; Firestone 1967; Philbrook 1966). However, few of these studies directly concern women. Some exceptions are Antler (1982), Davis (1983a, b), and Porter (1984), whose research was strongly influenced by Faris's study of Cat Harbour (1972).

Faris and other researchers have seen development as operat-ing to women's detriment in the Newfoundland outports. Faris (1978) is particularly concerned with the effects of modernization on kin organization and the place of women in the social fabric of the community. According to him, capitalism, development, and de-pendence on wage labor have adversely affected the quality of life. As Antler and Faris (1979) see it, government sponsored fishery development programs and resettlement have undermined tradi-tional agnatic crew formation and have had a socially negative impact on local organizational structures, such as marital and postmarital residence patterns. Since young men no longer fish, there is no longer the same pressing need to establish households as productive units incorporating wives and children; thus, fewer women marry locally. This leads to conjugal instability, alcoholism, drug abuse, alienation, and suicide. Increased consumerism also leads to an increase the accident rate from automobiles and appliances. Women who work at the frozen fish plant must often use part of their earnings to hire household help. In addition, baby bonuses and welfare payments undermine women's roles in salt fish production and thus compete with the fishery.

Antler (1977, 1980, 1982) echoes Faris's macrostructural views and agrees that women have become both proletarianized and alienated. Sealy (1975), in assessing the impact of development programs in a Canadian maritime community, concludes that people fail to recognize women's exploitation because they are deluded by the idealization of the fishery; and that frozen fish processing has widened the gap between male and female incomes as well as limiting female opportunities for employment. McCay (1983) contends that while the introduction of fish plant labor on Fogo Island, Newfoundland, has led to new opportunities for women to get wage work and the unemployment stamps for which wage work qualifies them, it has also led to disputes over whether fishermen's wives should have priority in getting fish plant jobs.

The view that women's status declines with modernization in fishing is not, however, shared by all Newfoundland ethnographers. Davis (1983b) takes issue with both Faris and Antler by stating that they have overly romanticized the past position of women in outport society. Her informants claim that they are much better off now that they no longer have to work like slaves in the salt fishery. While Wadel (1966) recognizes the exploitation of female labor in fish plants, he also cites the continued importance of women in the home, equality between husbands and wives, and separate esteem systems for men and women as having survived Newfoundland's transformation into a welfare state. Porter (1983) says that change and community development have had little effect on male labor, but that the female processing sector of the outport fishery has been radically affected. Younger women now take advantage of their education and of their ability to drive, to go to St. John's, where they acquire new values and life styles. After some time away from home, they resist reabsorption into traditional family roles as well as into commercial fishing enterprises.

WOMEN AND THE FISHERY: FAMILY, SOCIAL STRUCTURE, AND OCCUPATIONAL COMMUNITY

Fishing groups enmeshed in complex stratified societies may be usefully regarded as occupational communities (Lipset 1956; Blauner 1960; Lummis 1977; Davis 1986b; Nadel 1984, 1986). They tend to live in distinct areas, such as fisher-towns and villages, to have a high rate of endogamy and to share a strong sense of occupational identity. Like other work groups whose occupation separates them from others both at work and at home, fisher people are often considered to be "a group apart" (Horobin 1972:343). The peculiar nature of their occupation tends to isolate them from their neighbors and concomitantly to reinforce their ties to one another. Geographically, there may or may not be much physical distance between them and non-fishing communities, but the social gulf is often considerable, and is frequently marked by such devices as a distinct orientation of houses. Fishing peoples are often stigmatized as inferior by outsiders (Nadel 1984; Smith 1977a; Wright 1981; Ward 1965). We may ask a number of questions about the lives of people in segregated—geographically or socially—occupational communities. How do members see themselves vis-à-vis the larger society, and how does that larger society view them? What relationships cut across the boundaries of such communities, and how much and what kinds of individual mobility across these boundaries is there? How are social categories such as age, gender, and rank affected? By paying some attention to women's roles and perceptions, we hope to shed some interesting light on these and other questions. For example, while fishermen's lives are focused on the sea, women may have many ties to land-based activities, particularly if they process and market fish. Women may even be the major links between the occupational community of fishers and others (as Nadel-Klein argues in this volume). Davis's (1986b) critique of the androcentric bias of occupational community typologies demonstrates that an exclusive focus on the organization and ethos of men's work underrates the active and important roles which women also play in the establishment of family and community-wide occupational identity.

Many studies of occupational fishing communities have been done in the North Atlantic maritime area. Some tell us more about women than others. The studies reviewed in the remainder of this chapter fall into two essential types: (1) those which deal with husband-wife and family relationships within the occupational community (Tunstall 1962; Dixon et al. 1984; Horobin 1972; Lummis 1977, 1985; Orbach 1977; Poggie and Gersuny 1974; Tiller

1958; Okraku 1975); and (2) those that primarily focus on women as representatives of the fishing community to the outside world (Danowski 1980; Acheson and Lello 1980; Smith 1978).

To begin with those studies dealing with women as members of family and community, Tunstall (1962) portrays the women of Hull as married to "men apart." Deep sea trawler fishing keeps men from home for more than ten days at a time. As Tunstall sees it, this way of life tends to attract men who feel uncomfortable with women. After a short time at home, the fishermen feel a pressure to return to sea. They see little of their families, spending most of their limited shore time with other men or with prostitutes in bars. Divorce rates are high. Women become very attached to their sons, who in turn grow up to see women essentially either as their obedient servants or as exploitative sex partners. Horobin (1972) adds that Hull fishing families tend towards matrilocality, which he attributes to the pattern of male absence.

By contrast, Lummis (1985) reports that while the ecology of East Anglian fishing produced a much weaker involvement of women in fishing-related activities, their control over family finances, and their involvement in wage work and domestic labor indicated a "sense of partnership in work" (1985:134) between husbands and wives. Lummis notes the contrast between the East Anglian and Hull patterns of labor and attitudes, and concludes that:

> In the East Anglian trawling there was not the separation at the psychological level that Tunstall postulates between work and home...the smacksman's life may have been male only, hard and dangerous but there is no evidence to support the view that it devalued wife, children or home (1985:136).

Orbach's (1977) study of Portuguese tuna seinermen also stresses the separation of the fisherman from his family. However, San Diego tuna fishermen differ from the fishermen of Hull in that they see themselves as relatively well paid. This affects their self-esteem and their relationships with the community and the family onshore. However, a fisherman at home feels that he lacks control, and this sense of helplessness drives him back out to sea. His wife agrees that "it is nice to have him home, but it is good to have him gone again" (1977:278). Orbach, like Tunstall, shows how a husband's alienation from his wife and family and his overriding loyalty to his crew mates can undermine male-female relationships.

Tiller's (1958) occupational study discussing the effect that prolonged father absence has on the psychological development of sailors' versus non-sailors' children reiterates the common theme of stress when the father is home and the simultaneous disappointment and relief upon his departure. Tiller finds that sailors' wives use their sons as emotional substitutes for absent husbands, and that sons react to maternal overprotection by becoming anxious about their identities. They express this anxiety through super-macho behavior.

On the other hand, being married to deep sea fishermen may also bring women some rewards. Poggie and Gersuny (1974) found that women may experience a degree of gratification when their husbands are happy with their work. They examine psychological factors in a Rhode Island fishing community and suggest that "fishermen's wives are as different from their 'landbound' counterparts as are the fishermen themselves" (1974:88). Poggie and Gersuny compare interview data with mill workers, fishermen and their wives within the same community and find that fishermen's wives, unlike mill workers' wives, do not generally want their husbands to find different work, despite the danger and long hours associated with fishing. Women like the money their husbands bring home, but also appreciate and share their husbands' commitment to fishing as a way of life. We should note, however, that this support is apparently not manifest in all east coast United States fisheries. In a similar study conducted among fishermen's wives on Harkers Island, North Carolina, Dixon et al. (1984) found little support for the husbands' choice of occupation.

Danowski (1980), who participated in the Poggie and Gersuny study, explores the psychodynamics of cognitive dissonance theory to explain why women ignore the danger of their husbands' occupation. She finds that women are capable of considerable adaptability when faced with a source of chronic anxiety. Interviewing fifty fishermen's wives, she finds that women must adjust to unpredictable and irregular schedules, and must learn not to worry. They must cope with the disruption that their husbands' return from sea invariably brings. However, they also play active roles in the fishing enterprise: keeping accounts, cooking for the crew, and relaying messages. However, despite this degree of involvement, women's lives are not wholly determined by their husbands' occupation. Many also have a wide range of activities apart from the fishery and friends from non-fishing families. Danowski reminds us that "there is no one way to be a fisherman's wife" (1980:2).

Okraku (1975) conducted a study of the effects of fishery-related occupations on reproductive patterns in a Nova Scotian fishing village. Comparing the fertility patterns of wives of inshore fishermen, offshore fishermen, and fish plant workers, Okraku concludes that either fishing attracts men with low family orientation, or that fishing makes them that way. Conclusions are based on data which show that birth rates are highest for wives of fish plant workers and lowest for offshore fishermen's wives. Although they complained of wanting more children, offshore fishermen's wives were more likely than the other two groups to terminate their reproductive careers earlier and to choose the permanency of sterilization.

Acheson and Lello (1980) discuss fishermen's wives who are becoming a political force by forming effective pressure groups to influence fishery-related legislation, a topic which Margo Clark takes up in this volume. Wives are learning to represent the fishermen's vested interests before government hearings. Smith (1978, 1982:83-85) also shows how this "occupational marriage" works. Gloucester fishermen's wives are active in regional politics and fishery management council planning. Women usually conduct their business in the forum of the local community, through petitions and delegations to congressional representatives, through letter writing and use of the mass media, and, most importantly, through the preparations of materials which fishermen's associations can use in their attempts to get backing from various sources of influence. She sees this as due to the increased role of government following the extension of territorial limits, and of increasing paperwork which has brought family women into bookkeeping, payroll, and secretarial roles for their husbands. Even when keeping a low profile (which, more and more, they cannot and will not), these women are a force to be reckoned with.

However, studies of the Norwegian trade unions show that the nature and effectiveness of women's political action organizations may be tempered by a variety of complex factors. Gerrard and Haavind (1987) describe how women in Norway have become progressively more involved in local fisheries trade unions. Although women may gain important union positions at the local level, where they are a numerical majority, women have a more limited influence at the district and national levels. Gerrard and Haavind conclude that Norwegian women have limited possibilities of influencing their own working conditions through organized political activities. This is especially marked when the interests of women conflict with those of men.

WOMEN AND THE FISHERY: AFFECTIVE AND SYMBOLIC REALMS

Another theme in the study of women in fishing economies, which occurs either singly or along with other themes, is the importance of women in the symbolic and emotional realms. Although a few studies stress the notion of female pollution and elaborate on the theme of the separation of male and female spheres, most studies in this category emphasize the integration of male and female domains and their common purpose in fishing communities.

In Newfoundland fishing communities, Szala (1977, 1978) and Sider (1976) provide insightful analyses of female fishery-related phenomena. Szala's (1977) study of meaning and metaphor in a Newfoundland fishing community highlights the importance of women in the symbolic realm, and the importance of the family in rural fishing community life. Her study goes beyond subsistence roles and social structure to the very heart of life in an outport fishing community. She discusses the concept of family as a source of metaphors for the conceptualization of a Newfoundland fishing village and its interpersonal relationships. Key symbols, such as naming systems, kin terminology, and concepts of belonging, as well as emblems like tatoos and rings demonstrate the recurrent theme of family in village life. Women, children, and men are seen not as things apart, but in terms of their total involvement in the entire community. In a subsequent article on "Clean Women and Quiet Men," Szala (1978) shows how traditional patterns of courtship and marriage, including notions of the ideal spouse, have survived culture change.

Sider's (1976) analysis of mumming in a Newfoundland outport also addresses the community's ethos by reflecting the egalitarianism of family and community life. Mumming and cross-dressing by outport men and women provide an escape valve for tensions built up by the patrilocal extended family system and its accompanying complex of reciprocal relations. The fact that women are given license to drink with men in this context symbolizes women's participation in the production of cured fish and in subsistence activities.

Lessa (1966) suggests symbolic elements of women's relationship with the fishery in Micronesia. Among the Ulithi, who practice subsistence fishing and horticulture, women are an important part of the creation myth. A certain spirit, grateful to women for giving him/her a yellow wraparound skirt, reveals to a woman the secret of fishing. She teaches her husband and two sons how to fish. All commercial fishing magicians (who perform two-month fishing rites every year) must leave her offerings.

Lest we imagine that gender-related maritime magic is neglected in our technological age, Silvia Rodgers (1984:1) notes that in Great Britain, "the relationship between women and ships and mariners" persists today. Ships are personified as female, and complex beliefs and rituals attend their namings and launchings. Two images predominate: the all-powerful mother who nurtures and protects and the enchantress of whose intentions a man can never be certain.

Women often appear to be negative, rather than positive symbols, and in many fishing cultures, women are popularly regarded as bringers of bad luck. Raymond Firth (1984) notes that both the Tikopia and the Kelantan Malays "have tended to associate men positively with ritual performances concerned to promote success in fishing, and women negatively with ritual observances of avoidance of major items of fishing equipment" (1984:1149). However, he also indicates that for the Tikopia, the female principle is regarded as very powerful, particularly in bonito fishing. Firth claims that the ambiguity evident in this belief system stems from the more abstract principle that "food is support, sex is danger, though each gives its own satisfactions" (1984:1159). For the Malay Kelantan, the "female principle of power" also affects the fishing, usually maliciously (1984:1167).

Peter Anson (1932), the Scottish folklorist, illustrates the rituals which proliferate in fishing communities and which express both gender relationships and anxieties about the sea. Examples he offers include the belief that "after a fisherman had been married a bad storm would take place" (1932:40). Judith Cook (1984) reports that among the pilchard fisherfolk of Cornwall, "women were not supposed to go on the piers and it was considered to be poor luck if a woman walked over a net which was about to be put on a boat. This signified that the net would surely be lost" (1984:89).

Thomas Gladwin (1970) says that on Pulawat Atoll, women are seen as anathema to the forces of the ocean, and when on board ship, are confined as polluters. Mullen (1978) says that the fishermen of the Texas Gulf area strongly resist the entry of women in the fishery, and feel very uneasy when a fisherman brings his wife on board. Faris claims that in Cat Harbour, women who marry into the community are seen as strangers and thus as potential sources of evil, even witches. They have the power to "jinx" boats. He says that in this strikingly male-dominated society, feminine gender is associated with weakness and unreliability, while maleness is associated with strength and vigor. Faris places this system of gender symbolism in a historical and material context, pointing out that women are and have been economically essential to the survival of the fishery, but that an outport woman is regarded as "an item of her husband's capital, just as a cod trap or an engine" (Faris 1972:75). In his discussion of fishing magic among Martiniquans, Price (1966) notes the existence of menstrual taboos relating to fishing: a menstruating woman must not step over a fisherman's canoe, nets, or lines, for example. Some suggest that such taboos indicate hostility to women. Wilson (1973) states that for Caribbean males, fishing is pleasurable because it gets men away from women.

Affect and Mental Ecology

Analysis of realms of meaning can also be extended beyond myth and symbol to focus on elements of the affective or emotional aspects of women's lives in fishing societies. By "affect" we refer to what Zulaika (1981) has termed "mental ecology," Faris (1972) "the moral order," Wright (1981) and Messenger (1969) "ethos," Davis (1982, 1983c, 1984) "affect," Poggie and Gersuny (1974) and Danowski (1980) "the psychology of fishing," and Jorion (1976) "status ideology."

Zulaika's (1981) study of Spanish trawlermen provides an insightful view into the crucial role that women play in men's mental ecology. Zulaika describes the interrelationship of natural and mental ecology in terms of: (1) how trawlermen conceptually order their environment, (2) how economic needs lead to institutional deprivation, and (3) how distance shapes emotional needs. Although Zulaika also describes the now familiar process by which men alternatively are emotionally driven home and then driven back to sea, he more thoroughly develops the idea of an "affective reciprocity" that exists between fishermen husbands and wives (1981:37). To show fishing as a cultural system, Zulaika notes that it is necessary to uncover modes of thought developed by fishermen in the course of pursuing their occupation. Specifically, because he is torn between home and sea, the fisherman has "no place where his mind and body are one" (1981:42). The fishermen love and idealize their wives and children, cherishing their memories and their photographs during the long months at sea. At the same time, fishermen are hoist by the petard of the double standard. For them, marital infidelity merely satisfies marital needs, but for their wives to be unfaithful would represent betrayal. In fact, fishermen worry that their wives are being "mentally unfaithful" (1981:43). All these factors together shape the ethos of the fisherman. How the wives themselves view the situation is, by the nature of Zulaika's shipboard study, unavailable to us.

Not all studies find women in a peripheral or disadvantaged position. Davis (1983a, c), Green (1976), Donnelly (1974), and Cheryl Brown (1980) have all noted the ethos of stoicism, of enduring hard times, and the importance for women of character traits such as strength, stamina, courage, and acceptance. Donnelly (1974) says in her review of the popular romantic image of the Newfoundland outport women that the same environment that threatens to destroy also gives a peculiar form of strength. Davis (1983c) relates this highly valued affective quality to the fishery and to husband-wife relationships, showing how women share in the glory and the drama of the fishery. Women's duty to worry about their husbands makes them folk heroines in their own culture and strengthens the intimate dimensions of the relationship between spouses. Given the danger of fishing, women become the affective core of the community.

Jorion (1976) reiterates this view in his analysis of strategies for prestige in a South Brittany fishing village, where, although women and children are excluded from competing for the status of "good fisherman," the village women use their gossip networks to constitute the jury that decides where each individual fisherman will stand. A good fisherman risks danger willingly and works hard; a good woman endures misfortune.

CONCLUSION: SOME IMPLICATIONS FOR UNDERSTANDING WOMEN'S STATUS

This review has been fairly extensive, but far from complete. The authors have found that while there are relatively few entire studies devoted to women in fishing communities, there is a good deal of scattered information included (sometimes buried) in studies with a different focus. There is a great need for further cross-cultural and intensive area and community studies. Area reviews and annotated bibliographies such as Grobech and Gerrard's (1987) English translation and summaries of social science materials available for the study of women in the Norwegian fisheries are most useful. Similar efforts should be undertaken for other culture or national areas. We apologize for the inevitable omissions, but hope that this survey helps to highlight the areas of research which have as yet been largely unexplored. We conclude this review chapter with some thoughts on the implications of the material presented for the problem of women's status.

Studies which focus on evolution, ecology, and the division of labor seem to suggest that the degree to which women produce valuable goods and exercise some control over the distribution of these goods influences the degree to which their status approaches (but never exceeds) that of men (Pollnac 1976; Firth 1984). In simple, subsistence fishing societies with a fairly fluid division of labor, women's status most often appears to be close to that of men. However, any attempt to fit fishing societies into standard evolutionary-ecological "levels" generates problems.

At present, the only systematic attempts to establish an ecological-evolutionary typology of fishing societies are those of Lenski (1966) and Pollnac (1976). In Lenski's model, fishing is seen as marked by accumulation and stratification unequaled among hunting and gathering societies. Pollnac (1976) distinguishes between simple fishing production and more complex forms of fishing, in addition to supplementary forms of production. Clearly, more attention must be directed to the technology and ecology of fishing, to the relations of fishing to other subsidiary subsistence patterns, and to the social relations of production governing both fishing and other activities, before general rules about the construction of female status can be developed.

The question of status becomes extremely complicated when one turns from women in simple, subsistence fisheries to those in more complex societies. Such features of social organization as descent and inheritance systems may mediate the status of women in family and community (e.g., see Broch, this volume). The presence or absence of female sodalities, public roles for women, and women's control of significant cultural events can also influence status (Sanday 1974; Sack, 1975). Davis (1983a) has shown how a society may distinguish between individual and collective female power in social interaction (the former being acceptable, the latter negatively sanctioned). The organization of women's work is also important. Is it homebound or public? Public labor is said to enhance women's status (Rosaldo 1974; Sanday 1974; Sacks 1975). Further structural factors such as class, region, relationship to overarching polities, the capitalist world market, and the relative degree of development or underdevelopment may affect female status in a multitude of ways. The studies of Davis (1983a), Friedl (1967), Susan Rogers (1978), Goldschmidt (1966) and Gerrard and Haavind (1986) have shown that while women may lack access to power in regional or national terms, they may have high status in the local setting. Yet, as Akerele (1979) has demonstrated, the "high" status of the West African fishmammy is the by-product of exploitation in the world-system which has forced some women into marginal and risky occupations.

The "position" of women certainly varies with the methods and objectives of each study. Whereas Marxist works tend to stress conflict between men and women, (Faris 1972) or between the local and the wider society (Porter 1983), other approaches are apt to see complementarity between male and female roles (Raymond Firth 1984). For example, Muir (1976), McCay (1983), and Davis (1983a) see positive aspects to women's work in fish plants; Antler and Faris

(1979), Connelly and MacDonald (1983) and Nyseth (1987) do not. Porter (1984) sees such work as a reification of the sexual division of labor. One important structural dimension to remember is that women's roles may also vary among social groups within a single society. Women of one clan, class, region, age group, or occupation may enjoy greater or lesser prestige than that of other women.

Ideology and symbol systems also mediate women's status. The value placed on female labor in male and female spheres is important. Female deities, women dealing directly with the supernatural in powerful roles, or the simple ability of women to pollute or contaminate are important ideological aspects of power (Sanday 1981). As Maranda (1974) points out in his analysis of the Lau "sea people," despite an egalitarian division of labor, there is a widespread pattern of intersexual hostility which permeates the fabric of Melanesian life. Also important in the ideological realm are such psychological factors as women's perceptions of self (Davis 1983a, c; Danowski 1980). Do they believe that they have autonomy and independence? Are male and female gender evaluation systems the same or different? Sanday (1974, 1981) and others (e.g., Ortner and Whitehead 1981) have pointed to the importance of ideology and belief systems in assessing overall female status. Our review has shown that deferential romanticization of the female role may be especially significant for women in fishing economies (e.g., Zulaika 1981; Thompson 1985), yet this dimension is presently underanalyzed.

Given the heterogeneity of fishing adaptations, we will leave it to others to develop measurable status variables. There are not yet sufficient data to reach a consensus about "rules" such as the universal exchange of women (e.g., Rubin 1975). What our review does show is that women's status in fishing is not *simply* or *directly* related to women's work. Women's contributions to fishing economies do not automatically guarantee them high status. We can say that women's status in fishing economies is an amalgam of environmental, structural, and ideological factors. As yet, the plethora of material, cultural, and social variables render generalizations premature and unwise. Thus we will content ourselves at this point to ask, not *why* women's status is problematic, but *how*, or in what ways does it vary? More cross-cultural studies viewing women and men in a holistic context may help us to begin sorting the exceptions from the rules. For now, we must begin with the beginning, with ethnographic data.

The Cooperative Nature of Women's and Men's Roles in Btsisi' Marine Extracting Activities

3

Barbara S. Nowak

INTRODUCTION[1]

This chapter presents a brief description of gender relations and the division of labor among the Hma' Btsisi', a Southern Aslian speaking group of roughly 1300 people who live on the Selangor coast of West Malaysia.[2] In contrast to general comparative observations which appear to assign fishing principally to men, this chapter describes how Btsisi' ideational, economic, and social organizational factors contribute to the integration rather than the segregation of men's and women's roles in marine resource exploitation.

Diversity and flexibility characterize Btsisi' socioeconomic organization, and women regularly participate in a wide variety of marine extracting activities.

The Btsisi' have access to resources in a variety of subsistence zones. Exploiting estuarine forests and tidal rivers, the littoral and the sea, hinterland forest, and (since the turn of the century) oil palm plantation wage work, Btsisi' have for a long time had a variety of choices to make when deciding which activities to perform. Rather than depending on one or two primary productive activities, the Btsisi' have developed a broad repertoire of economic skills. Foreshore topography, seasonal and tidal cycles, village location, Malaysian government policies, the development cycle of the family, and individual initiative are all factors which influence Btsisi' exploitation of marine resources and other economic activities. The following description focuses on Btsisi' use of marine resources, and how socioeconomic and ideological factors act to allow for "cross-over," integrating men's and women's work.

The majority of ethnographic studies on women and development conclude that cross-culturally, women's status in subsistence economies is consistently lowered with the intrusion of capitalism (Beneria 1982; Boserup 1970; Etienne and Leacock 1980). Women find themselves either locked into the household, economically dependent upon individual men (Buenaventura-Posso and Brown 1980), or performing a double day doing wage labor along with their household duties (Beneria and Sen 1981). Boserup (1970) and Rogers (1980) discuss how development agencies impose their male bias by employing men over women in activities that were traditionally female. The Btsisi' present a striking exception to the general trend.[3]

Today, the Btsisi' depend on a cash economy. Their repertoire of tasks is still very broad, including cash cropping and wage labor, as well as commercial and subsistence fishing, crabbing and shellfish gathering.[4] The planned economic development administered by the Malaysian Government centers solely on men. For example, men receive subsidies in the form of fishing nets, small outboard motors, cash crop saplings, and cash loans to purchase large diesel powered boats. However, despite the bias of government development programs towards men, women have not been locked out of the economy nor into the household. The Btsisi' socioeconomic organization and the ideology of cooperation seem to buffer the negative effects on women which are commonly associated with "modernization" and development.

THE IDEOLOGICAL RELATIONSHIP BETWEEN HUSBAND AND WIFE

In order to understand Btsisi marine exploitation, we must examine the basic unit of economic production, the conjugal pair, or *odo'*. Btsisi' believe that marital relations should be based on cooperation and equality between husband and wife. The system for naming and identifying individual couples beautifully illustrates Btsisi' notions of marital cooperation and egalitarianism. When nearing the end of a primary wedding ceremony, the Btsisi' shaman presiding over the ceremony bestows a married name on the couple (*galah odo'*). Thereafter, the bride and groom address and refer to each other by their *odo'* name, and the community also begins referring and addressing them individually and as a couple by this name. The *odo'* name has no relation to the couple's birth names. The couple's identity thus changes from that of two separate individuals to an inde-

pendent, culturally distinguishable social unit, in which the individuals work together for mutual benefit.

The Btsisi' define women's area within and around the village,
swidden, and mangrove. The Btsisi' and the neighboring Senoi-
Semai (Dentan 1979:68) and Senoi-Temiar have a similar long:short
gender metaphor which expresses this spatial relationship. Roseman (1984:431) quotes a Senoi-Temiar man who explains the
metaphor:

> We call the longer (bamboo tube stamper) "father," because a man
> is brave and travels long distances; he goes out at night, wherever,
> to hunt game, without a second thought. Women, they go short
> distances, within the community, to the swidden fields or to cut
> banana stalks. So the "mother," we make it short.

Btsisi' express the notion of male:long and female:short in a
variety of contexts. For example, a blowpipe contains two inner
tubes of different lengths. The longer tube they call *lmpl*, or "hus-
band/man" and the shorter tube is *kdow*, or "wife/woman." This
dichotomy also appears with the musical instruments called bamboo tube stampers. Two stampers of varied lengths form a sonic set
which a single woman musician plays during a song and dance
cycle. The longer stamper with the lower pitch is the male, and the
shorter, higher-pitched stamper is the female. At least two pairs of
stampers must be played, and again, the longer set is the male, and
the shorter set is the female. If there is a third set, it is called *knan*,
or "child" (Skeat 1896:382).

The items mentioned above symbolically express not only Btsisi'
ideas regarding men's and women's spheres, but also ideas concerning husband-wife and male-female relations and the primacy of the
conjugal pair. For example, if a blowpipe is to work, the "husband"
and "wife" inner tubes must be fused to form one continuous tubing.
The "husband" and "wife" tubes operating jointly allow the blowpipe
to work. Musically, a "husband" and "wife" stamper are both necessary to form a complete sonic set; and a complete set must include
a "husband" and "wife" set of stampers. Btsisi' also extend the pair-
ing idea into the spiritual world where all spirits have a spouse.

The ideal division of labor between husband and wife is based
on a complementarity of tasks. At a young newlyweds' wedding, their
elders both formally and informally instruct the couple about their
proper roles and duties. The couple hears that the bride's primary
duties center around the household and children; it is her job to
cook, clean, wash clothes, collect firewood and water and to care for
her children. The groom's major responsibility is to provide economically for his wife and children. A husband must hand over his cash

earnings to his wife, who manages the household finances. Newly-weds are also instructed in the importance of helping each other with their respective responsibilities. At one wedding ceremony, a man told the new couple: "If you [the groom] finish your work and your wife is busy with the children, you cook the meal. If you [the bride] are done with your tasks, ease your husband's work load and help him." This exemplifies the fluidity and lack of proscription in Btsisi' division of labor.

The pliancy of Btsisi' social organization makes it easier for people to shift from one activity to another and from one subsistence zone to another. Although a culturally prescribed sexual division of labor assigns complementary tasks to men and women, in practice, Btsisi' view these distinctions as optative. In fact, there are few if any sexually *proscribed* economic tasks. Btsisi' sexual division of labor is flexible. A person may easily perform tasks assigned to the opposite sex and "cross-over" is a very common occurrence.

SUBSISTENCE AND COMMERCIAL MARINE RESOURCE EXPLOITATION AND THE ORGANIZATION OF WORK

Crossing over the delineated role assignments is thus not only culturally permissable, but highly valued, particularly when the role cross-over is done in the performance of cooperative household activities. Fishing and other marine-related activities must be seen in this light. While some fishing strategies are performed more by men or more by women, no Btsisi' fishing strategies ideologically or actually prohibit women from participating. Women perform some fishing techniques only when partnered with their husbands, however. This is also true for men; there are marine related tasks men perform, but typically only when partnered with their wives. A married pair with children forms the most efficient collecting group for strand resources, and Btsisi' generally prefer to keep economic activity a household affair, although sometimes women prefer to work in female groups.

Hook and line fishing is an example of a task women perform more regularly than men. Women enjoy the relaxed social atmosphere of line fishing in the nearby rivers and plantain irrigation ditches. On afternoons when the tide is high and when there is nothing to eat, a woman angles for an hour or two in the company of female relatives or her husband. Men rarely go angling, either on their own or with male friends, but they often accompany their wives, especially when their wives want to angle at a distant location.

Women also share each other's company in small groups on the littoral, when searching for clams, cockles, and turtle eggs, and when gathering mud clams, mud lobsters, mussels and snails in the mangrove forests. Strand and mangrove gathering activities, like angling, are tasks women perform side by side, synchronistically. By traveling in small groups, women not only have company, but they also feel secure from wild animals and non-Aslian men.

Btsisi' collect razor clams, cockles, and snails for their commercial value, as well as for subsistence. The easiest time to go snailing is on the rising tide, as the snails make themselves visible by climbing up the mangrove trees to escape the water. People continue snailing until the water level rises high enough to inhibit easy movement through the mangrove forests and until it is difficult to see dangers such as approaching crocodiles.[5] Razor clamming requires a little more skill than snailing. Btsisi' use a three-foot metal wire with a sharp barbed hook at one end to catch the clam. They search for the razor clam's breathing hole along the beach as the tide recedes. Since a variety of sand-dwelling animals leave holes, people searching for razor clams must recognize its distinctive breathing holes. When a woman finds a razor clam's breathing hole, she stamps on the ground to enlarge the hole, then jabs the barbed hook wire down into the hole. She must do this quickly and accurately with a straight downward motion, making sure the hook catches both the animal and its shell. If she is slow or inaccurate, the clam may escape. On a good day, a skilled person may collect three or four hundred razor clams. In order to protect the resource, Btsisi' go clamming only intermittently.

Crabbing is of primary economic importance. Both men and women use the same techniques. At high tide, when the crabs feed in water away from their holes, the Btsisi' use floated crab lift-nets. Both men and women make and use the lift nets, which are square nets eight- to ten-meshes wide. Split bamboo laths crossed over the top are attached to the diagonally opposite corner, with shells acting as weights. In the middle, a thin wire hangs down to hold the bait (usually a "hard" meat fish like manta ray). A ten- to twelve-foot line with a floater attached also hangs from the center. A crabber throws as many as twenty to thirty traps at one time, retrieving them after about a half hour. If necessary, the crabber replaces the bait and throws the nets out again. When two people work together, one takes responsibility for the boat and the other for the nets. When a man and woman work together, they take turns maneuvering the boat and caring for the nets. At low tide, when the crabs are back in their holes, both men and women use crab hooks. A crab hook is made of a heavy gauge wire approximately six-feet long, attached to a wooden handle at one end. The working end curves up toward the handle in a "U" shape. The crabber jams the hook in and out of the hole. In defense, the crab grabs on to the hook, at which point the crabber pulls the hook out, grabs the animal and ties up its claws (see Burdon 1954:7, 1959:21-22).

While waiting to pull in lift-nets, crabbers either angle or gill net. Although women do not gill net alone or in partnership with other women, they do actively participate as work mates with their husbands. The woman most typically takes responsibility for steering the boat while her husband tends the net, but the roles may be reversed, with the man steering and the woman tending the net. Because the catch is small, it is inconvenient to share it with members of other households. Thus, men prefer to partner with their wives, particularly when searching for mangrove fauna.

Gill net fishing in the mangrove at night is a favorite activity for many couples. People consider night fishing enjoyable and economically productive, since it does not interfere with daytime activities. A high tide in the late afternoon and early morning allows a couple to go fishing after the day's work and return before the next day's work begins. Staying out at night alone is scary and supernaturally dangerous; men are glad to have their wives along. When a couple goes night fishing, they take their very young children along with them, leaving the older ones behind with relatives.

Deep sea gill net fishing contrasts with other techniques in being more clearly dominated by men, although only a few of them participate in it. The expense of equipment, including diesel-powered boats, fuel, and commercially bought nylon nets puts deep sea fishing beyond most men's economic means. Very few men own diesel-powered boats and only a few men who own boats go out daily. The cost of diesel fuel and the unpredictability of returning daily with a large, profitable catch prohibits most boats owners from depending solely on income from deep sea gill net fishing. Women go along with their husbands only when the fishing expedition lasts more than a day. When couples do schedule long trips, the whole household goes along and lives on the boat. The boat returns to shore every couple of days to sell the catch and replenish the ice supply. In these household expeditions, the woman plays a major role in the fishing activities, helping to steer the boat and tending to the net and fish.

Seine net fishing is the most profitable and popular littoral activity Btsisi' perform. It is most lucrative just before and just after the full moon, when prawns feed close to shore. Seine nets cannot be pulled at high or spring tides, when there is no dry spot on the beach onto which to haul the nets. The best time to pull a net is before the tide begins to rise, until just before high tide. Seining is also an activity which Btsisi' describe as men's work. But, as is the case with gill net fishing, women frequently participate. In fact, almost as many women as men pull seine nets. Pulling a seine net requires at least two people. The most common work team is, again, husband and wife. Husband and wife together discuss and decide where to pull the net. When a woman pulls a net, she takes the anchor position just below the shoreline, while her husband pulls the net out and around back to shore. When the net is on the strand, both partners gather the catch and prepare the net to pull in again. If a woman is unable to partner with her husband, the man teams up with another man, usually a relative such as a father or son who is in a similar position. Women do not pull seine nets unless they are in the company of men.

On a good day, if the beach is not crowded with fellow Btsisi' and Indian plantation workers who are also pulling seine nets, a team can pull its net three or four times. On returning home, either the fishing team or their relatives divide the catch into two piles: one for subsistence and one for sale. The smaller, non-marketable "bone" fish are kept, and the rest sold. If two men from different households have paired up to work together, each man or his wife takes what fish they need; after the fish are sold by either partner, the cash is split evenly. The man who owns the net rarely gets a larger cut. Women and sometimes men salt and dry fish in excess of the family's immediate consumption needs.

Several older, traditional fishing methods are now falling into disuse. Barricade fishing, for example, a method which involves blocking egress from the mangrove waters by lowering and raising nets, requires round-the-clock work. Women rarely participated in barricading on the strand. Other barricade techniques, some involving the use of now-illegal fish stupeficants are being abandoned because of decline in fish stocks, pollution, and government taxation policies. Since these fishing techniques were, in Btsisi' theory if not in practice, the provenience of men, the methods available to men are less diverse than they were before other peoples began their more destructive exploitation of the environment. Women's fishing is relatively unaffected, except by the depletion of resources.

COMMERCIAL AGRICULTURE AND ENVIRONMENTAL CHANGE

Before the introduction of commercial agriculture, the Btsisi' made extensive use of the forest environment. According to early observers, the Btsisi' relied more on horticulture than hunting (Bellamy 1895:229). They were dry rice swidden cultivators. For varying periods of time, although never permanently, the Btsisi' would move into the forests, building temporary shelters either in the middle of their fruit orchards or at the edge of their cleared swiddens. Men took responsibility for clearing and burning the land; women planted and weeded. Together they harvested and pounded the rice, and women were responsible for roasting and winnowing the grains. Skeat and Blagden (1906, 1:231) mention that the rice crop was the envy of local Malays to whom the Btsisi' sold and bartered their surplus. Seasonal fruits, collected by women (Bellamy 1895:230; Skeat and Blagden 1906, 1:360-361) were an important component of Btsisi' diet, in addition to being an important commercial item. The Btsisi' grew banana, coconuts, maize, sweet potatoes, tapioca, and yams. The income from the sale of rice, durian, and other fruits provided the Btsisi' with cash to buy market products including salt, matches, cigarettes, iron tools, and cloth. Besides rice and fruit, Btsisi' traded rattan, resins, and monkeys with Malays and Chinese (cf. Dunn 1975; K.M. Endicott 1984).

The forest also provided Btsisi' with wild plants and animals. Women gathered wild plants and tubers, and men hunted with blow-pipes, spring and fall traps, game fences, and bird-lime. Btsisi' consider hunting men's work, but there is no restriction against women's hunting (cf. Dentan 1965; K. L. Endicott 1979). An English woman (anon. 1896) living in Malaya at the turn of the century mentions that on a trip she made to a Btsisi' household she saw women and children returning with men from hunting monkeys.

Wage labor activities have been part of Btsisi' life as early as the beginning of the twentieth century. With wage work came deforestation. In 1905, a British planter received two large land grants from the Sultan of Selangor to open a rubber plantation on Carey Island (Nowak 1983, 1984a, 1984b). Initially, plantation managers hired 75 Btsisi' men to clear forest land for rubber and coffee growing. They also employed women to work in the plantation coffee nursery and to weed. By 1980, the plantation owned over half of Carey Island (Nowak 1983, 1984a, 1984b)— some 49,000 acres of land— now mostly planted with oil palm.

The plantation had a serious impact on the Btsisi'. The plantation evicted them from their settlements. When the plantation opened, the managers, under pressure from the land grant conditions, began planting in areas inhabited by the Btsisi', since their land was already cleared (Karim 1977:45). The Btsisi' lost many of their fruit trees as well as their houses to the plantation. Also, rapid destruction of the forests reduced the animal population. The increasing scarcity of the Ipoh tree (*Antiaris toxicaria*), a tree which grows only in primary forest, and from whose sap the Btsisi' made dart poison, diminished the economic importance of hunting (Evans 1913:2).

Before World War II the Btsisi' could still continue traditional subsistence activities in the mangrove and on the beaches. They were also still able to plant dry rice and other crops and to fish and collect mangrove animals. When anyone wearied of working for the estate they would return to the swamps and forests and resume living as semi-nomadic foragers and horticulturalists.

In the 1950s the estate had cleared enough forests on Carey Island to begin hindering rice production. Loss of forest land impeded the Btsisi' semi-nomadic existence and they became dependent upon store bought rice and commercially manufactured items which they paid for with their wages and the income from cash crops, crabs, and fish.

A more sedentary existence followed the loss of forest lands. By the early 1950s, the government began establishing aboriginal reserves on Carey Island. The reserves are small isolated islands of land surrounded by oil palm and mangrove. On Carey Island today, there are five reserves ranging from under 100 to almost 400 acres of land and there are four coastal mainland reserves.

Despite the plantation's inroads on Btsisi' land and the introduction of wages, plantation work has not intrinsically altered Btsisi' household work patterns. Plantation labor provides the Btsisi' with another alternative activity which they have fit into traditional socioeconomic organizational patterns allowing men and women to work jointly. The plantation managers employ Btsisi' as oil palm harvesters. Oil palm harvesting is back-breaking work which requires at least two laborers; the most common partnership is a husband and wife. The husband takes responsibility for cutting the oil palm and branches, while the woman piles the bunches up for the man to collect and transport to the road. She also individually picks up and bags all the loose fruits which fall from the bunch.

Today, a cash income is essential for a household's survival. Btsisi' are no longer able to subsist solely on products they produce, but must also purchase many food stuffs, including rice. People obtain the necessary cash not only by selling fruit, fish, and other marine fauna, but also from logging activities, thatch manufacture, and oil palm harvest work. However, the great diversity of subsistence zones the Btsisi' exploit give them considerable freedom to vary their activities with changing opportunities. Within the group on any given day, different activities are performed. In order to exploit available resources efficiently, people adjust their activities to daily and monthly tidal fluctuations and seasonal rhythms.

Btsisi' distinguish between working for themselves and working for others. Crabbing and fishing, for example, are not "work." Instead, people say they are "going to the sea" or "looking for crabs." However, someone going to harvest oil palm is going to "work." Btsisi' prefer working for themselves, but some people discover they are not as economically secure, and decide to harvest oil palm. Working for the plantation insures a monthly income which can be much more than a family could making working for themselves. Oil palm harvesting is a fairly inflexible activity which is incompatible with other activities. After a year or two, most households tire of the hard, constant work on the plantation, take a formal leave of absence, and turn to fishing or crabbing, activities most people prefer. A conjugal couple reaches the decision to change occupations jointly, as any decision affecting the household requires mutual consent.

The cooperative and complementary nature of men's and women's work described for marine related activities is also found in these other work environments. Women are more likely to pursue particular activities such as making thatch, gathering wild plants and animals, and cultivating small vegetable gardens; men's responsibilities include hunting, wood carving, and logging. Other activities, such as fruit cultivation and oil palm harvesting for the plantation are not sex-typed. Although there is a prescribed complementary sexual division of labor for forest and village activities, men and women work cooperatively, often crossing over the prescribed division of labor and sharing duties. For example, the prescribed sexual division of labor for dry rice swiddening assigns the clearing and burning of the land to men and the planting and weeding to women, while both sexes together harvest the crop. Deforestation has made dry rice growing less attractive, but the few households who continue to grow dry rice find it easier to work cooperatively within the household unit, so that women also clear and burn the fields, and men plant, weed, and husk rice.

Deforestation has resulted not only in the decreased importance of rice swiddens but also in the decreased emphasis on traditional hunting and gathering activities. Cash crops, especially seasonal fruits, provide an important component of the Btsisi' diet, as well as providing households with additional income. Women and men both own and cultivate cash crops, including durian, rambutan, mango, coconut, banana, coffee, and oil palm. Btsisi' consider an individual who plants or inherits a crop the sole owner, but most typically the owner's family help in caring for and harvesting the crop. When strangers come into the village to purchase fruit, women take over the bargaining and cash collection. However, men are responsible for transactions outside the village, such as selling fruit in neighboring non-Aslian communities and to storekeepers.

LOCAL VILLAGE ECOLOGY AND ECONOMIC PURSUITS: MANGROVE AND INLAND DWELLERS

People decide to switch their primary occupation for a variety of reasons, including boredom, the desire for more money, seasonal and tidal cycles, changes in household membership, and change of residence, although change of residence often follows upon such a decision. On the broadest level, Carey Islanders distinguish between "mangrove people" and "inland people." People living in the mangrove rely almost exclusively on gill net fishing and crabbing for a living. Mangrove dwellers either live full time on their boats, or they reside in small settlements of two to ten households scattered along the mud banks of the mangrove rivers. At any given time, about ten households reside full time on boats.

Boats give families mobility to wander in and out of small tributaries. Reasons mangrove people give for living on boats include dodging creditors, having profitable work, and enjoying life in the mangrove away from people. Small oar-powered boats of approximately twelve to fifteen feet can provide a home for about four conjugal couples, but more commonly a nuclear family will occupy a diesel-powered boat.

Families living on diesel boats move with all their possessions, including portable cassette radio players and televisions. On the bow of the boat the family members build a frame for a plastic sheet for shade during the day and cover and protection at night and during the rain. Women cook on small wood burning stoves. Fresh water is no more problematic on water than on land. In both places six gallon containers hold a household's drinking water. The boats come to shore often so two or three containers of water is enough for one trip. Boat dwellers use salt water for bathing and washing clothes.

Subsistence and commercial crabbing, fishing, and snail collecting are the primary occupations of mangrove dwellers. Men, women, and children by the age of eight or nine all participate in one or more of these activities daily. Gill nets, barrier- and hook-and-line fishing are the favored methods. However, many people prefer crabbing to fishing. Fish are perishable, requiring fisherfolk to return to port

every other day to sell their catch and purchase ice. Crabs and molluscs can be kept live, making returning to port less urgent.

Among boat dwellers, there is, in fact, no distinction between
the workplace and the home. A family's physical separation and
cooperative organization of labor means that a wife and husband,
along with their children, are continually at work and at play
together. Each boat-dwelling family travels on its own, working
independently. As a consequence of the boat-dwelling family's physical isolation, a couple and their children depend heavily on each
other. Living full time on boats creates an environment conducive
to continuous cooperation and sharing between husbands and
wives. At one time or another, a husband and wife must perform
each other's prescribed tasks. If, for example, a woman is caring for
her infant, her husband takes on the cooking chores. On boats, men
and women pay close attention to their children to ensure that they
do not fall overboard.

Mangrove villages on the mud banks of forest reserves are far
from fertile, dry land. Anyone wanting to cultivate the land must
reside, at least part time, at an "inland" village. Some people divide
their time between mangrove and cash cropping, spending a few
weeks in an inland village caring for their plants and trees and
returning to the swamps when their work on the land is complete.
Others lead a more sedentary life, dividing their time between
horticulture and fishing activities, or harvesting oil palm on the
plantation.

Not only do inland villagers' activities differ from mangrove
villagers', but the predominant occupations of the inland villages
also vary. As people move from village to village, they adjust their
activities to the varying environmental conditions. Because of the
great distance by land and river from the sea, people at Dg. Bum-
bun depend less on the sea and fishing, and more on cash crops
than other inlanders. They do fish with hook and line for subsistence, and occasionally men, women, and teenage boys wander into
the adjacent mangroves in search of crabs. Unlike the mangrove
dwellers, however, they do not crab for commercial purposes, and
use only crab hooks, rather than the more profitable and efficient
lift nets.

Mainland Btsisi' have a harder time following traditional economic occupations than Carey Islanders (see Ayampillay 1976).
When commercial agricultural plantation workers cleared the
forests and drained the mangroves to plant coffee and rubber, main-
landers turned to cash cropping and wage labor. On Carey Island,
where the soil is too saline to be very productive, cash crops for most

people only provide extra income. The logging of mangrove wood for charcoal by the Chinese and Indonesians, destructive crabbing by local Indian plantation laborers, and the general over-exploitation of mangrove animals is beginning to affect mangrove resources. But the mangroves still provide Carey Islanders with fish, molluscs, and crabs, and wood for housing, boat building, and firewood. Now plantation managers on Carey Island are beginning to drain the mangrove and plant oil palm. Draining the mangrove disturbs the Btsisi', who are aware of their relatives' situation on the mainland, where the swamps are already dried up; where housing can no longer be built from mangrove wood and thatch but requires buying wood planks and zinc roofing; where firewood consists of coffee branches, which burn quickly and unevenly; and where shellfish are now scarce.

OCCUPATION AND THE HOUSEHOLD DEVELOPMENTAL CYCLE

Thus far, the chapter has described some of the many activities available to Btsisi', focusing on the complementarity of gender-prescribed tasks and the continuation of cooperation between women and men at work, despite the impact of plantation agriculture. Now the focus shifts to the family's developmental cycle in order to elucidate women's central role as economic contributor.

In over half of all primary marriages, the bride's and groom's grandparents or parents arrange the marriage. A girl should marry into her mother's family, preferably her mother's older sibling's son; ideally a boy should marry a relative of his father's, preferably his father's younger sister's daughter.

Ambilocality characterizes a young married couple's first year or two of marriage. Alternating residence between the bride's and groom's natal homes results in a reciprocal brideservice and groomservice; and, as Dentan (n.d.) suggests, this symmetry is "not payments but proofs of equality in status" (Collier and Rosaldo 1981:279). According to customary law (*adat*), a couple eventually settles down neolocally, building their house near the bride's family. While they reside with parents, the couple maintains economic autonomy, cooking and eating independently with separate food supplies. However, their parents continue to correct them, either individually or together, if they do not perform their roles properly. Primary marriages often end in divorce; in part this is attributable to the couple's lack of choice in the arrangements. Divorce is relatively simple and can be initiated either by a wife and/or husband. The birth of children, however, does seem to stabilize a marriage and the birth of a couple's first child is typically the time when young couples move out on their own. Polygyny is acceptable but in most cases the first wife opts to terminate her marriage after a year or two.

Btsisi' believe that fetuses and infants are susceptible to spirit attack and "soul-loss." The forest and sea are places an expectant mother or infant should not regularly frequent. A pregnant woman can go to the forests or sea no more than once or twice. If a married pair are working jointly at the time an infant is born, the productive unit they form temporarily dissolves. Some Btsisi' women today bottle-feed their babies instead of nursing. They say that bottle-feeding frees them to leave the vicinity of the home to work with their husbands, at least sporadically. If a woman has no one with whom to leave her infant, she remains at home to look after it. In her spare time, she may fish for the evening meal with hook and line, or make thatch to sell to Chinese middlemen. If she or her husband has an unmarried sister who is not helping out in her natal household or who can be spared, the sister will move in and take over the childcare, becoming part of the household, eating, sleeping, and working within and for it.

Since a man depends on his wife's labor, he must find a different economic activity for a time. If the couple has been working on the plantation, he will usually take a leave of absence, since a man cannot harvest enough oil palm alone. Working independently at fishing, crabbing, making thatch, doing contract work, or collecting mangrove wood for charcoal factories are his alternatives, and he can vary his tasks daily according to tides, weather, and inclination. Sometimes he may find another man in a similar position with whom to form a temporary work team. However, Btsisi' prefer not to form work teams with people outside their own households. Working with someone from another household entails the division of produce and profits between the two households. Earnings are so small that sharing the money leaves each with too small a share. As soon as a woman can either leave her child with someone, or take it along with her, she reenters the work force, teaming up again with her husband. Together they make the decision to return to their former task, or take on something different.

Children begin helping with small household tasks at a young age. Their parents send them on errands and give them small roles in taking care of their younger siblings. Boys, as well as girls, care for younger siblings and continue to do so up to the age of thirteen or older. Parents often take children along with them into the mangroves or to the beach, and by the age of four, children begin to perform simple gathering tasks such as collecting snails. By eight to ten years of age, children begin following their parents to the sea and help to gather the fish from the drag net, or to search for littoral fauna. By the age of fourteen, children can participate in most activities and they are major contributors to the household economy.

A household with a teenager is in an enviable position. The members of such a household try to optimize the use of their (at least) three-person labor force. After finishing Standard School at around the age of twelve, children will either join their parents' work team or will pair up with one parent (usually the mother). The other parent is then free to work on a complementary activity. For example, a woman and her teenage child usually work for the plantation. The mother does the heavier labor, cutting down the oil palm fruit, and the child gathers them from the ground. If they need help, the husband joins in intermittently. In such a case, the man does not take over his wife's task of cutting (which is usually defined as man's work), but helps the child in gathering fruit.

Households must attempt to strike a balance between the relative advantages of subsistence and wage labor. Subsistence production reduces a household's daily cash outflow. A household working for the oil palm plantation can earn more cash on a regular monthly basis than a household dependent upon fishing. However, plantation laborers must then buy fish along with other necessary items such as rice and spices. When there are three workers in a household, the unpartnered parent can perform an activity which complements the work of the other two. Consequently, a man usually fishes when his wife and child work for the plantation.

Dissolution of a household, either as a result of divorce or of death, does not put women in any more marginal a position than it does men. Women, as well as men, own and inherit land. Customary law is for all siblings to share equally in their parents' fruit trees and today, in land.[7] Every person has rights to any property she or he helped to clear and plant. If a woman helped her ex-spouse clear and plant a field, she has rights to share in the produce. Men and women both find it easier to have a partner and most widowed and divorced people remarry as soon as possible. Only the very old or ill do not remarry. Single women and men who remain unmarried try to remain as self-sufficient as possible. Even the very old try to live on their own. They may attach themselves to a child's household, but if possible, they maintain their own food supplies and cook for themselves.

WOMEN'S STATUS AND POLITICAL CHANGE

In response to my question— "If you could be reborn tomorrow and could choose whether to return as a woman or man, which would you pick?"— no one said they wanted to return as a woman. Women responding to my question explained their answer in terms of their biological role: menstruation, gestation, and childbirth. Interestingly, women did not include their role as nurturer. The Btsisi' have great regard for a mother's nurturing role. Those who are disrespectful and uncaring for their mothers can expect God to punish them when they die and try to enter *Pulaw Buah* (lit., Fruit Island), the Btsisi' "Garden of Eden" where all the fruit and other choice foods are there for the picking.

Men and women also explained their desire to return as a man because of men's greater freedom to travel (Nowak 1984a; cf. Dentan n.d.). Men's hunting and fishing activities take them to the sea and deeper into the forests than women's activities. The Btsisi' consider the forest and sea to be dangerous areas because of wild animals, spirits, and rapists. Women entering the forests typically travel short distances and in groups large and noisy enough to scare off wild animals (K. L. Endicott 1979:35; Roseman 1984). The more malevolent Btsisi' spirits desiring to injure humans reside in the forests and at sea (Karim 1980).

Women's fear of rape is probably relatively recent. This may be the result of the increasing numbers of Tamil, Chinese, Malay, and Indonesians living in close proximity. The Btsisi', like most *Orang Asli*, distrust outsiders. *Orang Asli* distrust stems in part from their victimization in slave raiding expeditions (see K.M. Endicott 1983:237). Btsisi' women encumbered with children would be more vulnerable than men, who could defend themselves with blowpipes. Many *Orang Asli* teach their children to fear outsiders (Dentan 1978; K.M. Endicott, 1983:237).

The extent to which women's roles have changed with respect to political activity is somewhat ambiguous. Btsisi' leadership is village-based. Each village is a localized kin group and has a Council of Elders (Karim 1981:24). The Council of Elders include both ascribed and achieved positions. Btsisi' women no longer hold any official position on the council. Older Btsisi', however, do remember when there were women *Batin* (the symbolic leaders of the village/kin group). A *Batin* acts more as a figure-head than as an administrator or judge since villagers reach decisions by consensus. A *Batin* inherits the position. A woman *Batin* inherits her office on the death of her mother or mother's sister while a man inherits his office from his father or father's brother. When a person holding an inherited position on the Council of Elders dies without an heir, the position is left vacant within the village. The last woman *Batin*, according to older Btsisi' who remember her, died without an heir. The lower ranking ascribed positions on the council are open to all villagers by "election." In principle, Btsisi' women can fill the lower ranking positions on the council by studying customary law and learning to speak persuasively with clarity, wit, and force (Dentan 1979:68). However, it is claimed that Btsisi' women, like most Senoi women, do not desire formal leadership roles (Dentan 1979; Benjamin 1968:42). But women married to men on the Council of Elders do have important, though informal, leadership roles in the community, and Btsisi' do in fact mention that these women know how to speak, and do so if they feel strongly about the issue under discussion. The position of *penghulu'* is a relatively recent introduction into *Orang Asli* political life (Benjamin 1968). A *penghulu'* receives his authority externally from the Malaysian government. His purpose is to act as mediator with the outside world. As such, the *penghulu'* is unquestionably always a man, conforming to outsiders' notions of gender roles (Benjamin 1968; Dentan n.d.).

The Malaysian government's stated goal for Orang Asli is to "upgrade the socio-economic well-being of [the] Orang Asli community and to accelerate their integration into the mainstream of society" (Malaysia 1981:392). "Mainstreaming" includes Orang Asli acceptance of Islam and their blending into rural Malay life. The majority of the Orang Asli, however, are unwilling to assimilate (see Dentan 1979; K.M. Endicott 1979a; K. L. Endicott 1984; Nowak 1985). The more nomadic groups living in the deep jungle are resisting the government's attempts to force them to settle down and take up agriculture, and they, as well as the already settled Orang Asli, are resisting conversion to Islam, the national religion. Conversion to Islam means changing dietary habits, abandoning traditional religious beliefs, and for women, an acceptance of a subordinate position vis-à-vis men, a notion inherent in Islam, and to a lesser degree in traditional Malay society (see Manderson 1979; Strange 1980).

For example, the Malaysian Government's Department of Aboriginal Affairs (Jabatan Hal Ehwal Orang Asli JOA), is the principle government office involved with the Orang Asli. The JOA's primary responsibility is to raise the Orang Asli standard of living and to facilitate the mainstreaming of the Orang Asli into Malaysian society. The JOA programs focus on three major areas: education, medicine and economic development (see Malaysia 1981). The JOA is attempting to provide all Orang Asli children with schooling. Both boys and girls attend school, but girls do not continue on to secondary school as frequently as boys. Secondary schools are not located in the villages, requiring children to live away from home in dormitories. Some girls' parents persuade them to remain home and take care of the daily running of the household. But this educational differential is small and up to the present has not affected relations between men and women.

Malays believe that a woman's first and most important responsibility is to her husband and children. Following through with this idea, the JOA, for a short time, provided adult education "home science" classes to a group of Btsisi' women. A Malay woman taught Btsisi' women domestic arts, including cooking and sewing. The teachers attempted to teach Btsisi' women that household and childcare are their major responsibility while men's primary duty is to provide financially for their families. Btsisi' women quietly rejected the Malay ideal of women's segregation and the classes ended.

Btsisi' appreciate the medical help the government gives. The JOA runs a hospital and smaller medical facilities providing the Orang Asli with free treatment. Most Btsisi' women use the hospital facilities at least once to give birth. Hospital delivery exempts a woman and her husband from an expensive traditional cleansing ritual. Couples who cannot afford the bathing ritual decide on hospital delivery. The medical clinics also provide women with free birth control pills. Women do not begin using birth control until they have three or four children. Women like the idea of being able to plan their families, giving them the freedom of deciding whether they would prefer to work or stay home.

Government development programs sponsored by the JOA focus almost solely on men, whom Malays consider the appropriate target group for economic progress. The JOA administers agriculture and fishing programs providing Btsisi' men with young cash crop seedlings, boats, motors and fishing nets. By providing the economic programs only to men and by teaching women "domestic science," the JOA is segregating women and locking them out of modern-day Btsisi' economic life.

CONCLUSIONS: THE COMPARATIVE CONTEXT OF WOMEN AND FISHING

Most studies of fisherfolk describe a sharply defined sexual division of labor with men preeminent in fishing itself (Smith 1977:8). Women's exclusion from deep sea fishing is sometimes so complete that they may not even touch the equipment or boats. In contrast with men's central role, women's participation is often seen as peripheral to the actual fishing, centering instead around marketing (Christensen 1977; Forman 1970; Kuchikura 1977; K. Norr 1978) and processing activities (Faris 1977), or their part in the organization of work groups and crew recruitment (Breton 1977; Nimmo 1972). This has also been emphasized in studies of fishing among Malays. In Raymond Firth's work on the Malay fishermen, he stressed women's participation in the "secondary processes" (1946:3) of the fishery and Rosemary Firth (1966) and Fraser (1960) both support his observation.

Explanations for women's exclusion from deep sea fishing tend to center around the uncertainty and unpredictability of the task. Fishing requires frequent and lengthy absences which conflict with women's household and childcare tasks (Norr and Norr 1978; Thompson 1983). For example, Samal Philippine fisherfolk say that a woman with young infants or many children to care for should remain ashore because she cannot give the children the nourishment and warmth required on a boat (Randall 1977:208). Among the "Sea Nomads" of Southeast Asia, nuclear families reside on boats, forming the primary fishing unit (Sather 1975, 1976; White 1922). However, Nimmo (1972:17-27) mentions that women's fishing activities on a boat may be limited by childcare.

There is a different pattern in the sexual division of labor among fisherfolk whose focus is on a littoral or mangrove environment. Ethnographic descriptions of fishing in such environments describe women as playing a central role in fishing. For example, Ciprianni notes for the Andamanese that "[women's] ...contribution to the everyday diet is by no means negligible, and during the season of very low tides, their daily haul is tremendous" (1966:166). But Ciprianni is also quick to maintain that "the real fishing, however, is done by the men" (1966:117) who use harpoons while women net-fish.

Although women play a more significant and central role in fishing among shallow water fishing peoples, Ciprianni's example highlights the fact that women's fishing activities and technology differ from men's. Bascom (1965:82) also describes a similar sexual division of labor on Ponape, in which both men and women fish and cultivate the land, without cooperating in their work on water or on land. Women fish only at low tide using their hands, hand nets, and poisons, whereas men always fish in the morning whatever the tide, using spears or seines. Even when a husband and wife work together performing parallel tasks, each person "owns" his or her individual produce. Raymond Firth (1984:1150, 1152) also brings up this point in his description of fishing on Tikopia, emphasizing the complementary division of roles.

The Btsisi' sexual division of labor is unique even among littoral fishing peoples because of their "mechanistic" (Bacdayan 1977) level of cooperation in economic pursuits. To efficiently exploit a broad spectrum of resources, Btsisi', as is characteristic among all Orang Asli, have a flexible organization of labor (e.g., Benjamin 1973:viii; K.L. Endicott 1979:87-93; K.M. Endicott 1979b:8). The ideal sexual division of labor rests on the complementarity of women's and men's roles. Customary law assigns household and childcare tasks to women and subsistence activities to men. However, while the Btsisi' sex-type activities, no tasks are totally restricted to one sex or the other. Rather, cross-over in task performance is the rule. By not restrictively sex-typing activities, the Btsisi' are able to optimize all situations.

The egalitarian nature of Btsisi' economic life parallels the egalitarian relations of the *odo'*, the basic socio-economic unit in Btsisi' society. The lack of a rigid sexual division of labor and the need to have a partner for the successful completion of work reinforces the interdependence and cooperation between husband and wife. For a woman to participate in economic activities her husband must take an active role in caring for the children and household. If a man does not "help" his wife out with her responsibilities she doesn't have the time to partner with him and "help" him. The pattern of men and women cooperating in work is most pronounced among the boat-dwellers, where the division between work and home is blurred.

The Btsisi' have been remarkably successful in resisting the imposition of alien work patterns but the pressures continue. In Islam and in traditional Malay society, women and men are not equal and are to some degree segregated. The Malay idea that women's primary roles are wives and mothers has implications for how the Malaysian Government approaches Orang Asli women and men. The government imposes Malay expectations of sex roles onto Orang Asli society, and development programs are directed almost solely towards Btsisi' men (Nowak 1984b). For example, since Malays assign fishing (except for angling) to men (Fraser 1960; Raymond Firth 1966, 1984; Rosemary Firth 1966), Government programs distribute boats, motors, and nets only to Btsisi' men. Btsisi', although assigning drag net fishing to men, do not emulate Malays, but instead integrate the technique into their repertoire of activities in the traditionally flexible pattern of cooperative work within the conjugal household.

The type of wage work the Btsisi' perform also makes it possible for a couple to continue to work together. Oil palm harvesting requires the cooperative labor of a couple. If, for example, instead of working for commercial agricultural plantations, Btsisi' worked in factories, a different organization of labor might develop to deal with that particular circumstance. The introduction of a new technology may be sex-typed, and men may be the focus of Malaysian development programs, but the type of work the Btsisi' perform and their traditional notions of the organization of labor and gender relations have helped to dilute the unequal effect direct and indirect modernization programs have on women.

Notes

1. My research was carried out from May 1980 through October 1981 and in April and October 1982. I would like to thank Dr. Baharon Azhar Raffie'i, Director-General of Jabatan Hal Ehwal Orang Asli for his assistance, and Dr. Robert K. Dentan for his encouragement, insightful comments and suggestions. I would also like to thank Dona Davis, Karen and Kirk Endicott, Elizabeth Kennedy, Peter Laird, and Jane Nadel for their suggestions.

2. Hereafter I will use the term Btsisi'. *Hma'*, an Austroasiatic word glosses as "people." Btsisi' are people who speak Btsisi' (or *Besisi'*, *Siseq*). The origin of this word is unclear. Btsisi' may originate from the Austronesian *sisi*, "edge," which describes the people's location vis-à-vis Temuan-Belanda, who the Btsisi' say named their language (Benjamin 1986).

3. For other documented exceptions see McElroy (1979) and Weiner (1980).

4. Murdock (1967:154-155) classifies shellfish exploitation as "fishing." Participants of the symposium on "Man the Hunter," "...recommended that shellfishing should be classed under gathering, not fishing" (Lee 1968:41). Lee, however, does not explain why the panelists redefined subsistence strategies. Suttles (1968:61-62) agrees with the symposium panelists' new classification. He says: "...shellfish gathering has more in common with the gathering of plant foods than with fishing. Both plants and shellfish are immobile and were collected (on the Northwest coast) mainly by women using digging sticks and baskets. They differ only in food value..." The classification of shellfish exploitation as gathering seems based, in part, on a traditional male anthropological bias of woman the gatherer. Although some varieties of shellfish are immobile, not all are. Razor clams and crabs do move and both can escape capture. The Btsisi' do use baskets in shellfish "collecting" but they also use them fishing.

5. I did not see any crocodiles although the Btsisi' say they are still living in the mangrove.

6. The Btsisi' have a Hawaiian cousin terminology. Ego's age in relation to her cousin's is based on the relative age of the linking kin, in this case ego and alter's parents.

7. Traditionally, the Btsisi' do not have a western concept of land as alienable or exclusive property. But as land becomes scarce it takes on the character of private property. Technically, all reservation land is communal and administered by the Council of Elders. The council gives land to anyone asking for some and they also exclude outsiders from ownership. Although the Btsisi' do not individually "own" land, and technically cannot buy or sell reserve land, a person controlling the land has the base to plant cash crops. Presently, women as well as men "own" land, but the Malaysian Government's Department of Aborigines (Jabatan Hal Ehwal Orang Asli or JOA), is beginning to title every land lot. They automatically put the male household head's name down. The JOA does this even in the cases where the Btsisi' recognize not the man as landowner, but the woman household head. What effect this JOA action may have on Btsisi' women's economic position vis-à-vis land ownership is not yet apparent. So far, the JOA rule of male ownership has had little effect (Nowak 1984b).

Between Field and Sea: The Role of Miang Tuu Women in Village Economy and Society

4

Harald Beyer Broch

This chapter focuses on Miang Tuu women, residents of one of Bonerate's coastal villages.[1] Bonerate, a small coral island fringed by extensive reefs, is approximately seventy square kilometers in area. It is one of the lesser islands in the Sea of Flores, situated south of Sulawesi and northeast of Bali in Indonesia. In spite of poor soils, the islanders are dependent on slash-and-burn agriculture (corn followed by cassava are staple crops) as well as fishing. Fishing is carried out around the reefs, and in lagoon-like areas. Bonerate islanders do not carry out offshore or deep sea fishing although the waters are rich in fish. Marine animals gathered along the shore are important in the composition of the daily diet.

The purpose of this chapter is threefold: (1) to analyze the role of Miang Tuu women in the economy, (2) to show how their central position in community life is reflected and strengthened through ritual responsibilities, and (3) to trace important traditions of socialization which are significant to the development of Miang Tuu female gender roles. The first section of this chapter is primarily descriptive and emphasizes the dominant pattern of gender role distribution. While fishing is often regarded as a strongly gender-differentiated activity, Miang Tuu provides an exception which is instructive. Although men are responsible for most of what the villagers call fishing, women also contribute their labor to such tasks. Given certain household settings, and other particular social contexts, individual women may apply fishing techniques which in most instances are usually carried out by men. (Both men and women, however, normally carry out activities which we would classify as fishing, although they themselves regard them differently.)

The sharpness of distinctions drawn between culturally recognized feminine and masculine roles varies widely between different cultures. On the one hand we find societies like our own, Western industrial society, where:

> Gender distinctions are commonly rationalized by beliefs about the central importance of women's role in childrearing and the imputed operation of maternal 'instinct.' There is also the assumption that all men are 'naturally' incapable of nurturing children and to compensate are 'naturally' stronger than all women, who are deemed incapable of heavy work (Rogers 1980:14).

Or in broader, more general, terms:

> Cooking the food, cleaning the house, purchasing the food, and other household activities are usually duties of women. That women may be confined to these roles or basically responsible for them is a result of different socialization for males and females. Males are also socialized to believe that housework is a sole legitimate sphere for women and given the *male-dominated power structure*, their sexist views usually result in actions that perpetuate the oppressed position of women (Lindsay 1980:304).

In Miang Tuu, however, the division of most labor, authority and village power is flexible. It has previously been stressed that where women withdraw periodically from their family, men have to participate and do housework and childcare even when this is ideally considered women's work (Mead 1975: 165-170). That the opposite is also true, that women are not restricted to housework where their fathers and husbands are absent, should not be surprising. This has been shown by Tanner (1974), and the present chapter is an additional example of this.

The second section of the chapter deals with Miang Tuu women in ritual life. It is argued that female ritual experts are acknowledged because their skills are seen as positive and of crucial importance to all villagers. Where men and women possess similar means to provide ritual security, women are often superior to men. This applies to ritual communication with *Iblis* (a deity) through possession trance in order to gain existentially important information.[2]

The final section of the chapter is devoted to how the socialization of Miang Tuu girls prepares them for adult status. It is my conviction that socialization patterns are crucial to our understanding of sex role and identity formation. In the present context, the institutionalized custom of periodic male absence seems important. Relatively little anthropological research focuses on the consequences of father and husband absence. In this chapter, some attention is directed to this phenomenon and how it may influence psychosocial aspects of Bonerate culture. This section also describes and offers a tentative analysis of a girl's puberty ritual. The ritual contains important messages about ideal female conduct, about what is regarded as central to femininity, and stresses some important aspects of Bonerate culture such as gender complementarity and the sharing of responsibility.

The village of Miang Tuu, in which my field investigations were carried out, is situated approximately five kilometers from Baranka-/Bonerate, the administrative and market center of the island. The village is placed approximately one hundred meters from the shore. The houses are built on poles and made of locally obtained materials like bamboo and rough wood. Mats of coconut palm leaves are used for thatching. At the end of my stay in Miang Tuu, there were forty-six houses occupied by forty-three households and 196 people. The village fields are situated between the village perimeter and an approximate walking distance of twenty minutes. The people have not experienced any land shortage, although Miang Tuu has been growing rapidly during the last thirty-five years. The local population are experiencing the effects of this growth in the form of gradually diminishing seashore fauna.

MIANG TUU WOMEN AND THEIR ROLE IN THE VILLAGE ECONOMY

There are three sectors of the Miang Tuu economy, two mostly subsistence and one market oriented. One is swidden horticulture, another is fishing and the gathering of other marine animals, and the third is the sailing of merchant *perahus* in the copra/spices trade between the Moluccas and Java.[3] To pinpoint one sector as more important than the others is difficult and could shift, depending upon one's analytical viewpoint.

For two reasons, I shall not examine the *perahu* trade activities in this chapter. Firstly, because women are not directly involved in this activity; secondly, because the major effect of this trade is not economic, in terms of the wages earned by the sailors. Only shipowners and captains make a profit, and only one household in Miang Tuu is involved at this level. Rather, the most important effect of this trade is that a large number of young village men are absent from four to eight months a year. Their time away coincides with the months of the annual food shortage in the village. Thus their absence is economically important, if not necessary, in order for the

Miang Tuu environment to provide enough food for the population at its present size without external inputs.

Although both Miang Tuu men and women regard themselves primarily as agriculturalists, their Bonerate neighbors regard them as primarily dependent upon and directed towards the sea. Indeed, Miang Tuu fishing and agriculture are actually integrated to such an extent that it would be meaningless to separate the two economic activities from each other.[4] This notion has important consequences for our understanding of the society. The interdependency of Miang Tuu fishing and agriculture is also reflected in how the villagers assess their happiness. When fish are scarce or absent, the people complain about how the quality of their lives has been reduced.

FISHING AND GATHERING OF OTHER MARINE ANIMALS

Fishing in Miang Tuu is generally a male occupation, but there are important exceptions to this pattern. We must first notice how the islanders themselves define fishing. Both agriculture and fishing are regarded as heavy work, while gathering is not. The only gathering activity not carried out by women is diving for rockborer bivalves. The villagers give two reasons why women never collect rockborers: they believe the activity is too strenuous for women and that women should neither swim nor dive.

While most Miang Tuu women do not fish on the open sea, they often urge their men to go fishing. Fish are highly desirable, but they are periodically scarce in Miang Tuu. The local fishing techniques are unsuitable during bad weather. In spite of a continuous demand for fish and recurring periods of fish scarcity, fish are rarely preserved for storage. This is not due to an ignorance of technique. The residents know how to prepare sun-dried fish and like the flavor. The explanation appears to lie in the small size of catches. Catches are usually poor, and when they are exceptionally good, the fish are distributed throughout the village and are eaten immediately. During my stay in Miang Tuu, only two net owners caught enough fish on two or three occasions to carry them to the market. On these occasions, the households had special needs for cash. The calculated risk of these fishing efforts was high, and the nets were severely damaged. (See Broch, in press a.)

In Miang Tuu, two sizes of weirs or fish traps, both identical in shape, are used. Large weirs are placed outside the reef at depths from three to twenty meters. Only men use these weirs. Inside the reef, both men and women place small weirs. Both sizes of weir are damaged by rough weather. They are regarded as most effective after the monsoon ends in March, and the season lasts about thirty to forty days. Small weirs can be used for a longer period than the large ones.

During the peak season of fishing with large weirs, small groups of people from the inland villages come to buy fish from the two best fishers in Miang Tuu. Payment was often delayed and paid by the customer's participation at the harvest. In the two "richest" households, both husbands had quit sailing and were more engaged in fishing than other male villagers. Thus, both of them could convert fish into agricultural labor. In this way, they gained even more time for fishing.

When a big catch is landed, women and children usually help to bring the load home. Once all the fish are home, the fisher helps his wife and other adult or adolescent female household members clean the catch. If some fish are to be sold or bartered, this is the job of women. They evaluate the quality of the different fish according to both taste and price. Special delicacies, such as rock lobsters or cuttlefish, are usually put aside to be prepared as snacks to eat while preparing regular meals. (As sailors, men become skilled cooks and may also prepare special fish-dishes at home to ensure that they get their share of rare delicacies such as crabs and mantis shrimps.)

As already mentioned, according to local ideology, Bonerate women do not fish. The reality is different (see Table 1). What holds true is that most women do not fish alone. When some women still do, it is usually in a setting where they are the lone providers. This may be due to the fact that their husbands are dead or gone on an extensive voyage. Women, however, never fish when this involves diving, and rarely fish from canoes. Both boys and girls are excellent swimmers, but girls stop swimming shortly after they have passed the initiation ceremony. Miang Tuu women most commonly fish by wading waist-deep into the lagoon, using a bamboo rod equipped with a nylon line and a tiny hook. This is also the most common technique used by boys and men. Some women also own small fish weirs which they place in shallow water in the lagoon. The weirs are visited when the tide is out, and it is possible to walk without getting wet above the knees.

The picture of women's roles in fishing in Miang Tuu is complicated by the fact that some Miang Tuu women are of Bajau origin, an ethnic group heavily dependent on the exploitation of fish and other marine animals. Bajau women not only fish, but are indeed skilled at it (for ethnographic accounts of the Bajau, see Nimmo 1972; Sather 1975). Although Bajau women married into Miang Tuu households have "accepted" the islanders' notion that fishing is not fit work for women, they use their skills in times of need. Bajaus are highly respected on Bonerate (Broch 1981a) and admired for their marine skills.

TABLE 1: Role Distribution in Fishing and Connected Activities

Activity	General Participation		Occasional Participation	
	women	men	women	men
Net Fishing		x	x	
Hook-and-line Fishing				
a) with rod	x	x		
b) from canoe	x			
Diving		x		
Small Weirs	x	x		
Poison	x	x		
Tidal Zone Collecting	x	x		
Cleaning Fish	x	x		
Drying Fish	x	x		
Cooking Fish	x			x
Selling Fish	x			

All Miang Tuu men and women are supposed to contribute to their household's subsistence activities. Alone, a woman gains respect and is not stigmatized if she manages her household, even if she cannot live up to such ideal norms as the belief that women should not fish. In this context, different standards of evaluation are applied to judge female conduct in the village. This flexibility indicates that information on ethnic and cultural variation in behavior is well-distributed among the villagers. In some instances, questions of household viability or of Bajau status may overrule Bonerate role ideals. Culturally irregular or even idiosyncratic behavior which is observed in the village is sometimes referred to in an ethnic context. When a woman is fishing, people say she might have Bajau roots. On Bonerate, double ethnic identity is culturally accepted and is transferred with force from both mother and father (see Broch 1981b). Other social positions complicate gender role play. "Rich" and "poor" have different options in Miang Tuu. Thus, women belonging to the two "richest" households are not likely to go fishing, whereas less fortunate women may easily find themselves in a situation where fishing becomes necessary to provide adequate food for their dependents.

Under certain circumstances, it is regarded as beneficial to all households that women participate in the final stages of fishing operations. When a wife or daughter joins forces with the men, there will be fewer people outside the domestic economic unity with whom to share the catch. But there are limits to the distribution of tasks.

When fishing takes on the character of "gathering," female participation is high. This happens, for instance, when tiny inlets or parts of the lagoon have been barred by gillnets. When the fisher waits for ebb-tide, he may summon his wife and perhaps other household members. When almost no water is left, fish hide in small ponds. Equipped with *parangs* men and women hunt the trapped fish.[5] In this activity, many women are great experts. They know where the fish are likely to hide and are quick to deliver their blows at the fish. Also, when poison is used in the lagoon, women participate in the gathering of half-dead fish. Most gathering activities are carried out by males and females of all ages. Foods gathered include bivalves, gastropods, cephalopods, sea urchins, marine sandworms, mantis shrimps, and other sand-dwelling crustaceans. None of these is sold. If such foods are bartered, it is only on the principle of delayed exchange in kind. When the tide is out, all household members may either go into the shallow lagoon or search along the exposed reef. During periods of rough weather, or when there have been few or no fish for a long time, gathering reaches a peak. During the agricultural harvest, there is little time left for fishing. Then, husbands and wives often put their children to sleep before they light up a petromax lantern and walk out to gather on low tide. The night catch of small fish and octopus is often good.

MIANG TUU AGRICULTURE

Miang Tuu villagers work long hours each day, spending most of their time spent in the fields. During the peak agricultural periods, over ten hours of work are normal. Agriculture is given priority in the minds of the villagers, and they assign it a higher status than fishing.

Let us examine the agricultural workload of Miang Tuu women. During the last decade, we have been presented with information that emphasizes the large amounts of leisure time available to hunters and gatherers (Sahlins 1972) and horticulturalists. The following quotations may serve as illustrations of general conclusions reached about the distribution of work and the general work load in technologically simple societies: "in every sparsely populated region where shifting cultivation is used, men do little farm work, the women doing most" (Boserup 1970:35). And, according to Friedl:

"The human energy expended by horticulturalists in obtaining subsistence is probably not appreciably greater than that among
foragers. An average, over the year, of some three hours work daily
per person is a reasonable estimate" (Friedl 1975:48). However,
neither of these quotations represents the economic setting of Miang
Tuu. Men older than thirty-five to forty years are usually not active
sailors any more. With the younger men at home from the sea between voyages, they work along with their women in shifting
cultivation. Most activities, such as the harvesting of cassava, corn
and fruit, weeding, and also the burning and clearing of new fields,
are done jointly by men and women. Sowing is the only agricultural
task in which the roles of men and women are strictly separated.
Women carry the seeds and are responsible for their storage. The
men enter the swidden field first and use digging sticks to make
holes in the soil for corn seed. Then the women drop one seed into
each hole, firming the soil with their hands to protect the seeds.

Much new land is cleared by cooperative workgroups (*gotong
royong*) whose gender composition may be mixed or homogeneous
(either male or female). However, when all-male workgroups are
clearing new land, Miang Tuu women also contribute to the task.
Women activate kinship relations such as sisters, husbands, brothers, and brothers-in-law to invite potential male participants.
Workgroups are commonly rewarded by a large meal, which is
prepared by groups of women recruited from the close female relatives of the organizers, assisted by other young village women. While
food preparation in this context is a solely female enterprise, the fish
used in some dishes is caught by a male household member, and
boys or men gather most of the wood needed for cooking. Thus, even
when male work groups are recruited, the female contribution in organizing and in compensating the workers is essential.

Goyong rotong can also be organized along principles of delayed
exchange in work. This makes it possible for single Miang Tuu
women to manage all stages of swidden horticulture. Although the
fields of a widow or woman left alone while her husband is at sea
will be small, she can get help in growing at least a substantial portion of the staples needed to keep her household viable.

Agricultural products among Miang Tuu are considered prestige
goods, and it is interesting to note that, contrary to Friedl's observation that among horticulturalists, women raise staples and men
raise prestige crops, among Miang Tuu, men's agricultural efforts
are directed particularly towards such staples as corn and cassava
(Friedl 1975:55). Any prestige crops are raised by the women. Such
crops (bananas, green peas, black beans, papaw, and gourds) are

sold at the island market. Women keep the money they receive, but they seldom sell more than is necessary to purchase immediate necessities.

We can only speculate about the reasons for this unusual agricultural division of labor. It may relate to the fact that young men's time at sea conflicts with the demands of agricultural work, particularly at harvest time. In any case, Miang Tuu women are the household treasurers. They manage the finances, keeping track of loans and debts of food and labor, including what might be left from a captain's or *perahu* owner's profit (in the case of the two most affluent households), or the cash received from the sale of fish (Broch 1983:151). Given the institutionalized household development pattern, where newly wedded men and young fathers leave their homes for the sea, it seems only practical that women should have this role. It is important to notice that this arrangement stays unaltered in later years, when the husband gradually settles for longer periods in the village.

THE RITUAL STATUS OF MIANG TUU WOMEN

Bonerate islanders regard themselves as Muslims, but they do not follow Koranic prescriptions strictly. The local religion is syncretic: many traditional customs, such as the belief in supernatural beings, are integrated into their belief system. Offerings are regularly arranged at small altars to provide good fortune or as thanksgiving. Ritual precautions are taken at the time of birth and in severe cases of illness to protect the life and well-being of endangered individuals. Islam also has an impact on daily village life. Food taboos are kept, Ramadan is recognized, Koranic readings are held at thanksgiving and at public events, such as the first haircutting ceremony of boys, and at puberty rituals.

There are few ritual experts in Miang Tuu. Minor rituals such as blowing the "guardian" back into a patient's chest or head, or lighting a protective fire below the house, can be done by most women and men. Some women possess ritual knowledge which makes them renowned and sought-after midwives. Some midwives are also regarded as being especially skilled as curers. When possible, the midwife is always summoned if a person she once received gets seriously ill later in life.

When it comes to communication with supernaturals, women seem in most instances superior to men. Two different situations appear to have generated much ritual activity in Miang Tuu in the past. First, information has been sought to find answers to how disasters, such as droughts or longlasting storms, should be handled.

Second, information has been and is still sought on the whereabouts of an overdue *perahu*. Only Bonerate women may obtain the ultimate truth in such existentialistic issues; through a possession-trance ritual they are able to communicate directly with *Iblis*. The ritual is led by two women dressed as male *perahu* captains. A medium dances, assisted by two young girls, until she enters a state of trance. At that moment, she cries out for embers. Live embers are brought forth and the medium smothers them with her bare feet. The fact that she is not burned is regarded as the proof of her authentic role as a medium, and thus that communication with *Iblis* is established. Actually, it is not the medium who demands the embers, but *Iblis*, who has now taken possession of the medium's body. No man could ever serve as a medium. A man would burn his feet seriously because men are never possessed by *Iblis* in this context. After possession, the medium experiences a state of amnesia. However, the ritual leaders are able to interpret the messages from *Iblis*. It is important in this context that Bonerate possession-trance is self-induced and is regarded as a benign source of power and guidance for the community at large. It is culturally accepted that all women are able to enter possession trance. This surely adds an aspect of mysticism to the general status and power of Bonerate women today (see Broch in press b).

In a somewhat wider context, I find the ritual status of Bonerate and Miang Tuu women in accord with the general gender role distribution of Bonerate culture. Given a small and relatively isolated society with a high level of relatively prolonged male absence, women have to take control to meet existentialistic needs. These needs are not only economic and ecological, but also of a religious character. What makes Miang Tuu interestingly different from many western cultures with a high degree of male absence, is the development of a matrifocal society.[6] Just as Miang Tuu women cannot afford to sit idle or to regard many forms of work as male occupations, the same holds true of the men. They must be largely self-sufficient in most activities, and also work on board the *perahu*. The matrifocal ideology of Miang Tuu society stresses a relatively egalitarian role composition between men and women, the economic and social independence of women, a cultural emphasis on the mother-child tie, and an emotional focus on the mother role (Broch 1983:144-159). Thus, men or boys are not stigmatized or ridiculed when they help their wives or mothers, or when they show dependence on these most significant women in their lives. This is not the behavior of some few, atypical men or boys, but a culturally sanctioned and anticipated life style. This dependence is also ritually elaborated.

THE SOCIALIZATION OF MIANG TUU GIRLS TO ADULT STATUS OR MOTHERHOOD

Two features of Miang Tuu family structure and household composition can be singled out as crucial to our understanding of Miang
Tuu socialization: periodic father absence and matrifocality.
Residence is not uxorilocal, but mothers are the focus of emotional, economic, productive, and reproductive attention.

During their first years of life, children of both sexes receive quite
similar treatment. As children grow, boys and girls are delegated
the same tasks, such as fetching water, gathering bivalves and sea
urchins, or tending younger siblings or other tiny village children.
Instead of being assigned by sex, tasks are related to the current
household composition and the social status of parents. Thus more
work is delegated to children from "poor" households or where the
father is absent, than to children from more affluent households.

It is widely assumed that mothers cross-culturally identify differently with their sons than with their daughters. Since a mother
was once a girl herself, and the identification with her mother and
mothering is strong, we might expect that a woman's identification
with a girl child might be stronger than her identification with a boy
child. This would then lead a mother to treat infants of different
sexes in different ways.

As a girl grows up, her gender identification is primarily achieved
through her mother. In Miang Tuu, the mother-daughter dyad is
strong and lasting. It is culturally a positively laden relationship
which is the focus of much village attention. The quality of this dyad
inculcates the girl with a strong sense of gender role identity.
Feminine identification is based on the gradual learning of a way of
being familiar with household management exemplified by the person with whom the girl has been most involved (Chodorow
1974:43-66).

A son's case is different. In Bonerate, he is to a large degree
brought up by women, but he sees himself as different from them.
He identifies with his father and with other close adult male villagers. These men are, however, relatively more remote and, for
extended periods of time, inaccessible to the boy. As a result, the
boy's sex role identity becomes a "positional" identification with
aspects of his father's not-so-clearly defined male role. His sister is
prone to identify with the more total female role of her mother. Thus
a boy is likely to define his masculinity in a negative way, in contrast to the sex of his omnipotent mother. If, as Ember (1973:437)
says, "parents' anticipation of task performance in adulthood may
affect social behavior acquisition in much the same way as differen-

ces in task assignment to children," this also, to some degree, legitimates the systematic delegation of household chores by mothers to their children of both sexes in Miang Tuu. Because the context of the task situation seems more critical than the task itself, it becomes somewhat misleading in the Bonerate context to mark out most household work as female activity or to regard wood-cutting or heavy agricultural labor as typical men's work. To be a single mother is as normal for a woman as to be a member of an all male *perahu* crew is for a young man. The single mother has to carry out much heavy work; the sailors have to prepare food and keep the vessel clean and tidy. If it is true that boys who do a great deal of "feminine" (according to our western culture) work in the home are more "feminine " in their social behavior than boys who are not delegated such chores (Ember 1973:432-433), then Miang Tuu boys may be well prepared for a sailor's life. But it is just as important to recognize that the absence of fathers may provide daughters with both emotional and physical strength, and qualities required from them in motherhood and as primary or single providers.

The socialization will always have to be accommodated to the economic and productive role of the caretakers. It is argued that the busy mother will be bossy and that she has little time to be permissive and indulgent. The busy mother expects and demands help from her children (Brown 1963). This, of course, only holds true as long as the mother is the only major caretaker. In Miang Tuu, mothers are generally busy, but they have the necessary help available to tend their children while they are occupied with other things. This situation probably makes Bonerate mothers somewhat more permissive and indulgent than they would be if they had to look after their children continuously by themselves, along with their work. The mother-child dyads in Bonerate social structure are also based on the idea of the ever-nurturant and indulgent mother figure. However, as Chodorow points out:

> A daughter's identification with her mother in this kind of setting is with a strong woman with clear control over important spheres of life, whose sense of self-esteem can reflect this. Acceptance of her gender identity involves positive valuation of herself, and not admission of inferiority (1974:64).

An initiation ritual is staged for Miang Tuu girls before they are approximately twelve years old. The ritual, which lasts for two days, is led by a female expert who is usually also a midwife. The home of the novice is decorated with coconut flowers before the guests are invited to an evening meal. The reception room is cleared, except for a large bed which is supplied with lots of white sheets and pillows.

The girl sits cross-legged, dressed in a bright *sarong* and a blouse. She wears shining bracelets on her upper arms and golden coins are hung around her neck. At her side in the bed, five colored eggs are placed on a small tray. The ritual expert is seated on a chair close to the novice, and a boy in his teens sits on the floor at the end of the bed. This adolescent boy prepares a mush called *batiranga*, probably from henna leaves. The ritual experts paints the girl's fingernails with the *batiranga*, which has a bright, dark red color when it dries. Little else happens except that all the guests, both women and men, are served some food.

The next morning, all the villagers are served a meal: rice, fish, and cucumbers. Late in the afternoon, the girl is accompanied by her mother and the ritual expert across the village where the initiation of "circumcision" takes place. This "circumcision" is a symbolic act. It consists of a light scratch with a bamboo knife at the inside of the upper thigh. No blood, no wound, no pain, and no health risk are involved. It is important to the villagers to stress this, because male circumcision is regarded as painful and as a health risk for the novice.

Inside the house again, the girl's body is covered all over with a mixture of rice and corn flour which is blended with pleasant smelling herbs. Her eyebrows are painted golden with corn flour. She is then dressed in a costume brought by the ritual expert. Her hair is covered in a transparent shawl.

After approximately three hours, the novice appears in the doorway, and everyone present whistles and cheers. She walks slowly down the wooden ladder, alone. At the bottom of the ladder two young men wait to carry her home. When they lift the girl, the ritual expert appears and throws rice down over her. An adolescent boy shades her head from the sun as she is quickly carried home. Before entering her house, more rice is thrown upon her. Then another public meal is served. Before the guests start to eat, the oldest man in Miang Tuu reads from the Koran in Arabic to bless the food. While all the guests eat, the girl sits in the bed, from which the sheets have been removed. She is alone with the eggs at her side. The guests seem to ignore her, and she herself is shy, or *malu*; she looks down and is not served food until the last guest has left the house.

During the period following her initiation, the girl behaves as she did before. She will play with the other village children, boys and girls, initiated and uninitiated alike.

I shall not contribute here to the debate over the explanation for such initiation rituals (Brown 1975:42), but suggest that "female circumcision" in Bonerate is not a ritual which transforms children

into adults. Here, initiation inaugurates the children into a culturally accepted notion of a period of gradual development which leads
towards adult life and status. During the ritual Miang Tuu girls are
taught aspects of ideal Bonerate conduct which they need to know
as they mature both physically and mentally. The ritual does,
however, also serve other goals. It is, for instance, important to acknowledge that the initiates themselves serve as symbols to all
Miang Tuu villagers by their display of idealized social norms.

During female initiation, much ritual activity is directed to en-
suring future fertility. According to what both male and female
informants say, the worst disaster a woman can experience is to be
barren. If a marriage remains childless, the woman is always
blamed; but if no more children are conceived after a first child is
born, the father is stuck with the blame as a token of lacking virility
(see Broch 1983:154-155).

Through all stages of the female "circumcision" ritual, symbols
of fertility are explicitly present. The container-shaped coconut
flowers attached to the wall, the eggs in the bed, the white sheets
(although these may symbolize bride-wealth and marriage), and the
throwing of rice should all be familiar symbols of fertility. Further,
it may be no coincidence that a renowned midwife is the preferred
ritual leader to carry out the proper "circumcision" act.

Miang Tuu female initiation rituals support the findings of
Judith Brown. First, female initiation rites occur in societies in
which the young girl does not leave the domestic unit of her parents
after marriage. Second, those female initiation rites which subject
the initiate to extreme pain are observed in societies where conditions during infancy and childhood result in a conflict of sex identity.
Third, female initiation rites are found in societies in which women
make a notable contribution to subsistence activities (Brown
1963:849-851).

Throughout childhood, girls hang around their mothers and are
provided with models which explicitly present them with an unam-
biguous sex role pattern. From an early age girls experience
confidence in their own sex. Women are respected for their reproductive ability, for their productive skills in food production and
processing, for ritual know how, and for their role as family
treasurers. Thus, a Miang Tuu girl experiences few identity
problems regarding her sex role and circumcision rituals further
reinforce her sense of feminine identity.

During the ritual, the novice herself appears as a symbol of
femininity. She does not symbolize female identity as experienced
in an everyday village context; rather she symbolizes an idealized

component of the role repertoire stressing *malu* behavior. To be *malu* is an especially important component of female conduct which embraces a wide spectrum of affect. To be *malu* is to be shy, to feel embarrassed, and it also carries connotations of losing face or feeling guilt (see also Lundström-Burghoorn 1981). Sitting on the bed, the initiate is trained in screening. The room is teeming with stimuli, but they have to be ignored for the sake of her *malu* presentation of self. As Erikson (1978:228) says, "From a sense of self-control without loss of self-esteem comes a lasting sense of good will and pride." In the modern village setting, to be *malu* is also attached to Islam. In everyday life, these rules are not followed strictly, but the ceremonies serve as reminders; when strangers arrive in Miang Tuu, women and girls are *malu.*

Cooperation between the sexes is another theme which is repeated in different ways during the "circumcision" ritual. It is an adolescent boy who mixes the *batiranga*; men and women cheer the novice when she is "circumcised"; young men carry her back to her mother's house; and it is an adolescent boy who shades her from the sun. The young men strengthen the female self by serving the young girl. In addition, the young girl symbolizes an aspect of community stability to the men. It is to their women, the houses of wives and mothers, that men return after a voyage.

When girls enter puberty they are already mature women in miniature. They have acquired the prerequisite skills to carry out their female roles and are busily engaged in all kinds of work in close company with their mothers and sisters. When they experience menstruation, they wash before dawn and after sunset, but that is the normal practice of all women and men on most days. Girls often stay in bed a day or two because of menstrual pains, but they are not secluded. A menstruating woman is not regarded as contaminating and may, if she herself feels fit, help in the preparation of food for all household members.

CONCLUDING REMARKS

The Miang Tuu economy is characterized by its composite nature. The level of work specialization is low. All households are involved, in at least one stage of their developmental cycle, in all three economic sectors (horticulture, fishing and gathering, and *perahu* sailing). The economy is primarily subsistence-oriented and there are no specialists, such as full-time ritual experts, smiths, or boat builders, who work for wages and not in primary production. With the exception of participation in the *perahu* sailing, Miang Tuu women actively participate at most significant levels in the village economy. The most important consequence of the involvement in the *perahu* trade is the substantial reduction of the pressure on scarce food resources.

Miang Tuu culture conforms neither to most generalized accounts of societies based on swidden agriculture, nor to the ideology commonly expected of fishing communities. The most striking cultural trait is the rather authoritative, respected, and in several ways, self-sufficient position of Miang Tuu women. It is all too tempting to view not only the economic, but also the ritual self-sufficiency of Miang Tuu women as a consequence of a high level of seasonal absence of young men.

I will not attempt to explain the development of the social position of Miang Tuu women. But some determinants can be suggested without being too speculative. Miang Tuu gender ideology is an elaboration of a theme described for many Southeast Asian cultures. Throughout this region women and especially mothers are held in high esteem. Mattulada, for example, says of the Bugis (one of Bonerate's close neighbors):

> The brother has strong feelings towards his sister, that is he feels called upon to protect her in any situation. This is based upon the notion that the sister is the living representation of his mother, the highest symbol of honour within the family connected *siri* (dignity) (1982:17).

On Bonerate, a man's social position and honor are dependent on his mother and later his wife. But a woman, Miang Tuu villagers say, never loses or reduces her social identity or position by marrying a man below her own status. Within limits, a hard-working groom may, with the help of his wife and her family, raise his own position.

The position of Miang Tuu women is probably also influenced by an ethnic integration of Bajaus, and the culturally accepted idea of double ethnic identity, which is transferred in equal shares from both parents. It should also be mentioned that the local rules of inheritance prescribe equal shares to all children regardless of their sex. The one exception to this rule is that the youngest daughter inherits the house from her mother.

Ideology provides motivation for both men and women to share their products and pool their resources, relating the mode of production to spirits, nature, and sex. When we consider sex roles in Miang Tuu, these should also be related to the marginal character of both agriculture and fishing. The villagers rightly view their situation as one which requires long hours of daily work in order to make a living.

The Miang Tuu economy and the villagers' ecological adaptation grant neither men nor women the possibility of sitting idle.

In Table 1, it was shown that women participate in many different fishing activities. They are particularly occupied in various time-consuming activities such as gathering semi-dead fish after the water has been poisoned, and collecting small fish and crustaceans during low tide. These occupations are not properly regarded as fishing activities by the villagers. But from a nutritional point of view, collecting is also recognized as important by Bonerate people. Women are the household treasurers and have the responsibility for the sale of all fish. Also, in fishing and connected activities, cooperation between the sexes is strong and the related sex roles are generally not rigidly elaborated.

When young men and fathers leave the island to spend at least half-a-year at sea, this influences both male and female sex identification. Because boys must help their mothers and because girls as much as boys are only familiar with some aspects of the father's role, this influences the way girls identify with their own sex, and how they experience and elaborate in their minds the image of an adult male role.

Miang Tuu culture stresses complementarity and equality between the sexes. These elements are also expressed during the initiation of girls. On the personal level, this ritual is an important event in the young girls's life. It is the only event in which all girls experience being the center of attention of the entire village. Dressed like a Malay princess, a girl receives presents, admiration and recognition. Initiation is a good day to remember, adolescent girls told me in Miang Tuu. It is an event to celebrate an emerging female status (future mother) and an event to cement pride in female status generally.

Notes

1. This article is based on data gathered from a one year (1978) period of anthropological fieldwork in Bonerate, Indonesia. The study was sponsored by LIPI and the Hasanuddin University (Udang Pandang). Financial support was granted by Institutt for Sammenlignende Kulturforskning, Oslo (Norway) and the Scandinavian Institute of Asian Studies, Copenhagen (Denmark).
2. *Iblis* is the deity to whom Miang Tuu villagers prepare offerings at small altars. Some people referred to *Seta* as a synonym for *Iblis*. *Seta* is a term commonly used to denote spirits and ghosts in much of Indonesia. In my view, the villagers' preference for the Arabic derived term, *Iblis*, reflects a strong desire to appear Islamized and thus to blur

connections to a traditional religion of spirit worship (see Broch in press b).

3. Bonerate *perahu* are sailing ships made for merchant voyages on the open sea. Some modern *perahu* are equipped with small engines, but most were in 1978 solely dependent upon sails.

4. We can only speculate about why Miang Tuu villagers regard themselves primarily as agriculturalists. People living in inland villages on Bonerate claim that Miang Tuu is indeed a fishing community. The reasons may be of historical origin. Contemporary Bonerate Islanders claim to have immigrated five or six generations ago from agricultural areas on Butong. Also, in the present Indonesian context, agriculture seems to rank somewhat above fishing as an occupation.

5. Long-bladed bush knives used by both women and men.

6. In many Western societies and other male dominant groups, father and male absence leads to what has been termed "momism." See Tanner (1974:132) on the important contrasts between "momism" and matrifocality.

Does Absence Make the Heart Grow Fonder or only the Influence Stronger? Women in a Peruvian Fishing Village   5

Mary Schweitzer de Grys

INTRODUCTION

On the most concrete level, this chapter is about women in a Peruvian fishing village. On an intermediate level, it is about how the fishermen's subsistence strategies encourage women's personal independence and social influence, while the prevailing regional ideology discourages it. On the most theoretical level, it is about what strange bedfellows ideology and economy can make. From village women to mega-concepts is a large step and some might argue an unwarranted or a foolish one. Yet Geertz (1973:23) reminds us that "social actions are comments on more than themselves...Small facts speak to large issues, winks to epistemology, or sheep raids to revolution, because they are made to." By the same token, village women's activities speak to the relationship between ideology and economy. What is interesting in this instance is that the particular ideology, rooted in *machismo*, seems totally incompatible with the particular economy, deep sea fishing, which takes men out of the family and village social arenas for long periods of time. This instance offers us the opportunity to look at the relationship of ideology and economy through the "bodied stuff" of Peruvian villagers.

Let us begin with a comment on the theoretical level. Ideology and economy are often imagined as two very different poles. One is seen as primary in terms of influencing or even determining the other; one is the shaper and the other is the shaped. From this perspective there are two basic positions: one in which ideology determines economy, the other in which economy determines ideology. Although there are many variations and nuances of differences within these two positions, there is enough common ground that it makes sense to talk about two basic positions. Proponents of the various primacy-of-ideology positions hold the common opinion that belief systems or networks of ideas are powerful in negotiating and establishing social and economic realities. An example is when *machismo* is seen as negotiating the social reality of perception and behavior. Stevens (1973), Ortner (1974), and Nunez del Prado Bejar (1975a, 1975b) take this position. A description and brief history of the *machismo* complex is given later in this chapter, but I have not taken the primacy-of-ideology position.

The primacy-of-economy positions are represented in the whole range of stances of cultural materialism and Marxism. The collection of essays on Latin American women, *Women In Latin America: an Anthology from Latin American Perspectives* (Leacock (ed.) 1977) is squarely within the Marxist tradition. The essays clearly show the characteristics of class conflict and its role rather than that of ideology, in determining the mode of production. The economic base of fishing is described in the first part of this chapter, and is seen as a very important factor, but I have not taken the primacy-of-economy position.

Neither set of basic theoretical positions seems helpful in understanding this concrete ethnographic situation. We are driven to a new examination of the relationship between economy and ideology when we take a closer look at the "small fact" of a fishing village in Peru. Specifically, the "small fact" is that the demands of the Peruvian fishermen's subsistence strategies conflict with the maintenance of the prevailing regional ideology. Paul Thompson (Thompson et. al. 1983:6) came to the same conclusion when he did research among fishermen in Scotland: "We need new theories: interpretations firmly rooted in the variety of fishing experience. And there is a logic in each local story on which we can build." This chapter is an attempt to unfold the logic of one local story, and to interpret it in a way that might point to new theory.

This brings us to the intermediate level. The fishermen in this local story are involved in a particular subsistence strategy, artisanal deep sea fishing.[1] The characteristics of the strategy itself, as well as the matter of women's participation, are important to note. Women's participation in artisanal deep sea fishing differs significantly from their participation in shellfish gathering and river fishing. It is common for women to do all of the tasks of the fishing even from beginning to end in shellfish gathering (cf. Goodale

1971:152; Gonzalez 1969:46) or in river fishing as among people living along the Xingu and other Amazon tributaries. In artisanal deep sea fishing, women are excluded from the fishing expeditions, although they may do the work of processing or selling fish which is essential to the particular economic arrangement.

As artisanal deep sea fishing always involves a time investment of several days or longer, and it is men's work, it necessitates the physical separation of fishermen and their female counterparts— wives, daughters, mothers, and sisters—for a period of time.[2] The subsistence strategy, however, simply necessitates the separation, and does not dictate how the separation will be treated or what meaning it will have. In societies where males are seen as dominant, and that dominance is maintained at least in part by their presence, their regular and sustained absence becomes problematic. Conditions arising out of this particular subsistence strategy do not permit a social patterning which is consistent with the historical, social ideology of male dominance. This is precisely the case in our local story.

Finally, we come to the most concrete level. How do the women in this local story reconcile the inherent contradiction between the conditions of the subsistence strategy and the demands of the ideology of male dominance? The starting point is the role that women play in the fishing economy. How do they process and market fish? These ethnographic questions are the point of departure for understanding the deeper questions of how men control the actions of women when they (men) are absent. When men's absence is significant and repeated, how can daily life be carried on if the ideology maintains that men should direct those activities? How do women respond to structural subordination when the superordinates are away fishing? These are the questions and problems which face the people of a fishing village on the northern coast of Peru. The remainder of this chapter will explore these questions in the following sequence: first, a description of the economy with particular reference to women's work; second, a discussion of women in their roles as mothers and mothers-in-law; third, a brief review of the *machismo* complex; and finally, women's strategies for coping with the apparent contradiction between the demands of their lives and the prescriptions of their culture.

WOMEN'S WORK IN THE LOCAL ECONOMY

The people of San Jose, a fishing village on the northern coast of Peru, have a centuries-long tradition of artisanal deep sea fishing.[3] Their pre-Columbian ancestors also lived by the sea, both as fishermen and as traders. New World colonization forced them out of trading, but as a subjugated people they still fished. While colonization brought the "loss" of trading, it also brought the "gain" of values and a worldview which gradually developed into the *machismo* ethic which spread throughout the continent. From the *machismo* complex, the social structure was shaped so that men held primary positions in all key institutions. Men were structurally dominant; women subordinate.

The village of San Jose lies in a desert, about six degrees south latitude of the equator, but enjoys the cool ocean breezes of the Humboldt Current, swept up the South American coast from Antarctica. A peculiar combination of factors, including ocean currents and breezes, as well as land features, makes this desert one of the driest in the world. The sandy land strip along the coast is saturated with salt. There is no possibility of agriculture in this area without an elaborate irrigation system and leaching the land of salt.

About 70 percent of the adult male population fish and another 20 percent build fishing boats for the fishermen of San Jose and neighboring fishing villages.

The men are away from the village for four to eight days at a time, with two days or so spent in the village between expeditions. During the winter months, the cool Humboldt Current takes the plankton on which fish feed farther from shore, so expeditions must go farther out to find fish, sometimes as far as the islands of Isla de Lobos and Isla de Afuera, some one hundred miles from the village. During the summer months, expeditions may set out in the direction of the islands, but usually encounter sufficient fish along the way to fill their boats and return to the village.

Each fisherman has two nets and the crew string their nets together to form a curtain, a seine. The seine net is suspended between floats along its top edge and weights along its bottom edge. The seine net is checked periodically, and when it is full it is hauled into the boat. Each fisherman tends to his own nets, marking each fish with his own mark as he takes it out of the net. When the crew returns from the expedition, men may help one another unload the catch, but each fisherman's catch is piled separately on the beach. Each fisherman pays the captain and the "boat" (i.e., the owner) a share of the fish.

The women, that is, a crew member's wife, mother or sister, take over the responsibility for the fish as they are piled on the beach. At all times there is need to be wary lest any fish be stolen from the piles. Middlemen from the city of Chiclayo come to buy in the village. They truck the fresh fish back to the city to sell to restaurant owners and fish retailers. The fishermen's women bargain with the middlemen in an assertive, sometimes aggressive way, arguing strongly for the price they want. As the fish are sold the women pocket the money. Meanwhile the fishermen unload their nets, beach the launch and wash it down. This work takes the crew two or three hours after the fish have been unloaded.

Through this division of labor all income from the sale of fish goes into women's hands; they literally hold the purse strings. Sometimes women tell their fishermen how much they have received from the sale, and sometimes they do not. They seem more likely to divulge the amount when it is low or barely adequate, complaining that fish are scarce or that the price of fish is so low these days. They are much more reluctant to reveal higher amounts. Whether or not they reveal the amount they retain control of the money.

Women desire to sell all fish fresh because it is easier to sell fish immediately than to have to process it. Fresh fish sale means the women will be finished with their responsibilities for a particular catch within a matter of a few hours. Sometimes the supply of fish outstrips the demand. There may be so much fresh fish available to the buyers that the less desirable varieties of fish are unwanted, and even the more desirable varieties bring a very low price. Therefore, it is frequently not economically feasible to sell all fish fresh.

Fish not immediately sold have to be processed. Salting and drying are the two major ways to process fish. A third method utilizes both salting and drying. After the buyers have left, the fish are eviscerated and washed on the beach. In the salting process, the fish are rubbed thoroughly with coarse salt, both inside and outside the fish cavity, and are then packed in burlap bags ready for the market. In the drying process, the cleaned fish are stretched on cross-sticks and hung on wooden racks in the open. The particular climatic conditions of the area favor a slow, reliable drying. After several days, the fish are packed in burlap bags and are ready for the market. When fish need to be kept for a long time, they are first salted, then dried. Fish thus processed will be edible for months. Whatever the method, women have to work at processing for the rest of the day, or even for a second day after the expedition returns.

The marketing of processed fish is also women's work. These fish are taken to the city by truck and unloaded at a prearranged place in the central market. The San Jose women rent market stalls for the morning or for the day. Early buyers are usually householders, purchasing only for a family. As the day wears on, wholesale buyers come upon the scene. These are middlemen who will take the fish into the sierra, or who may even "hawk" it in the city streets.

The later the hour, the harder the bargain driven by the middlemen and the more vulnerable the sellers. No woman wants to pay to have her fish trucked back to the village at night, and then trucked back to the city a day or so later. Although there are several different kinds of opportunities for selling, women consistently do the marketing.

In summary, San Jose women stay in the village while men are on fishing trips. When the expedition returns, women take charge of the fish as they are unloaded on the beach. Women sell fish fresh in the village or process it for sale in the city, and they keep all money received from the sale of fish.

WOMEN AS MOTHERS AND MOTHERS-IN-LAW

The most important kinship positions a woman has are as mother and mother-in-law. Of the two, it is the latter which makes a significant difference. It has been assumed in the past that all women will become mothers, hopefully the mother of sons. The one or two unmarried women in the village are in ambiguous positions. These women live with married kin. Married women without biological children will raise a child for a sister. The expression which such a woman frequently uses is, "My sister gave me a child...she took away my shame." In the normal routine, children accompany their mothers everywhere, to the beach, the market, the church, and the *municipalidad* (court house). Women whose offspring are past the age of childhood often "borrow" a relative's or neighbor's child to accompany them. Motherhood, obviously displayed by the accompaniment of children, deserves respect. The respect derived from the status of motherhood endures as the offspring become adults.

When an adult son marries, the dynamics of the mother-son relationship alters and the woman's status changes. The mother-son bond is not weakened, but is complicated by the additional element of the son's wife. The relationship that was basically dyadic becomes triadic; the son's new wife is also expected to respect his mother, and the mother's sphere of influence is broadened to include the son's wife. Even though the mother-son relationship may have been an easy one, the inclusion of the daughter-in-law produces tension. The difficulties of the triadic arrangement are reinforced by the residence pattern.

A couple usually lives with the groom's family for several years after marriage. The young couple works for the groom's parents to repay them for the wedding expenses. Weddings tend to be elaborate and may easily cost the equivalent of six months income of the average fisherman. The groom's parents and their *compadres* (sponsors) bear the brunt of this expenditure. The fruits of the labor of the young couple belong to the groom's parents as long as they reside in their house.

The young groom continues to relate to his mother socially and economically as he did before marriage. When he returns from a fishing trip, it is his mother who takes charge of his fish, not his wife. The mother sells as much of the fish fresh as she can. The unsold fish must be processed. The interesting fact is that it is the new bride who bears the brunt of the fish processing, rather than the groom's mother. When market time comes, the new bride is likely to be at home washing clothes or cooking, rather than selling fish. If she does accompany her mother-in-law, it is the latter who makes all of the sales and holds the purse strings. So the mother continues to garner the income. The new bride is used as supplemental labor without receiving remuneration.

While living in the mother-in-law's house, the daughter-in-law is subordinate to the mother-in-law. It is the mother-in-law's duty, her prerogative, to "teach" the new bride the ways of the family into which she has married. The mother-in-law assigns the bride the most exhausting and lowly tasks. She gives her few privileges and frequently demeans her. For example, when the bride is sent to the market, her absence is timed. On return her purchases are scrutinized, and the change returned to the mother-in-law is carefully counted. If her performance does not meet the standard in any of these areas, she may be severely reprimanded or even beaten by the mother-in-law. Years later, women recount these early years of marriage with bitterness and resentment toward their mothers-in-law. Middle-aged women will say with deep emotion, "*Me enseno!*" ("She taught me!")

Young women probably have always chafed under the control of their mothers-in-law and tried to outwit them, but the focus of the concerns changes with the times. Mothers-in-law are very pronatalist in their orientation, as women in general have been until recently. However, young women want fewer children than the older parental generation. Contraceptive medication and devices were slowly making their way into the village in the early '80s. The concerns of younger women and their successful wit are illustrated in the following incident which occurred in June of 1982. A young woman still living with her mother-in-law was sent shopping one day. She carried her first-born, a six-month-old, into the general store, and good-humoredly asked her friend the store-keeper for chocolates. Both laughed heartily and the clerk reached for a package containing a one-month supply of contraceptive pills. From time to time, the mother-in-law would treat her daughter-in-law to money for chocolates, and the daughter-in-law would treat herself to contraceptives. "Wouldn't my mother-in-law be furious?" she whispered. Concerns may vary, but cunning ways persist.

After several years of marriage, when the wedding has been paid off, and the bride has learned the ways of her new family, the couple may set up their own household. By this time they usually have a few small children. Thus they begin their residential independence without finances and with many obligations. Nevertheless, the transition is welcomed by both, but especially by the woman. While the mother-in-law may ease her dominance as the years of marriage increase, she will remain a persuasive figure for life.

THE MACHISMO COMPLEX

Besides the conditions set by the fishing economy and the kinship patterns surrounding mothers and mothers-in-law, it is important to look at the ideology of *machismo* which purportedly permeates San Jose society. Only the briefest of descriptions is possible here, but it should be noted that *machismo* has a history that is long and important on the continent.

The origins of *machismo* are difficult to untangle. Gissi (1980:30-45) sees it rooted in sexual division of labor in general and in *patria potestad* of the early Romans in particular. The nature of these origins is economic and legal. Stevens cites "ancient roots in Old World cultures" (1973b:91) as antecedent to the New World phenomena, but she also sees *machismo* as primarily an image or value. A. J. R. Russell-Wood (1978:60-100) asserts that the antifeminist stance of colonial Brazil differed little from the mother country of Brazil. "Male-oriented, male-dominated, patriarchal societies, both ascribed a marginal role to the female, isolating her from the mainstream of developments in the colony" (1978:68). There is evidence of *machismo* in colonial Mexico (Couturier 1978:129-149) and sixteenth century Peru (Burkett 1978:101-128). Regardless of the ambiguity of the beginnings, *machismo* permeates the history of Latin America.

The practice of *machismo* varies according to geographical area and type of community. Chaney (1979:32-33) argues that *machismo* also varies according to social class. *Machismo* may describe an image or worldview, social relations between the sexes, legal and juridical realities, or personality characteristics. Stevens, who sees *machismo* as a mindset of the cult of virility, describes its characteristics as "exaggerated aggressiveness and intransigence in male -to-male interpersonal relationships and arrogance and sexual aggression in male-to-female relationships" (1973:90). Foster (1967) says that *machismo* entails the exercise of authority and dominance. "They (Tzintzuntzenos) find it difficult to believe that a husband and wife can share domestic responsibility and decision-making, without the husband being deprived of his *machismo*, his masculinity" (1967:130-131).

Whatever the variations, the general description of *machismo* is male superiority. Men need to be, and to portray, the supermale: obvious strength to the point of rigidity and brute power, authority over women to the absolute, sexuality to the point of prowess, and the proliferation of offspring. Men are physically strong and morally weak. Their moral weakness is often seen as being analogous to a child's—they just cannot control themselves. They lack self-control especially in regard to sex relations, drinking, and physical violence.

The complement to *machismo* is *marianismo* or *hembrismo*. Women, men's opposites, need to portray the ability to endure suffering in silence, to be humble in demeanor, and responsible and maternal in caring for children and men. They are to be patient and nurturant in all situations. An incident which I witnessed in San Jose exemplifies the *marianismo* characteristic beautifully. A middle-aged man, somewhat inebriated, returned home one evening just after visiting his lover. His wife met him in very soothing tones, "*Ay, ay, ay, hijito, quieres cafe?*" ("Ay, ay, ay, my little son, do you want some coffee?") Her response to his behavior was maternally supportive and not condemning. She exhibited *marianismo* behavior in the face of his *machismo* behavior.

San Jose men take a typically *macho* attitude toward their work as fishermen. In social conversation they are fond of elaborating tales about the dangers of the sea. They state that only men are brave enough and strong enough to face those dangers. They flex their arm muscles and say with a smile, "*Fuerte*" ("Strong.") In addition to being brave and strong about the dangers of the sea, men also say that they "know" the sea. They know the currents, know how to read the stars for directions, know the winds. Women, on the other hand, are said not to understand these phenomena because they do not have men's intelligence. There is much evidence of the presence of *machismo* in San Jose.

In accordance with the *marianismo* principle, San Jose women engage in a broad range of activities in the home. Women are adept at caring for children because they are nurturant and emotionally sensitive, as well as spiritually strong. Many *Sanjosefinas* are like the "good woman" who is monogamous and practices sexual self-denial (Jaquette 1973:23,26). Women thus come to signify the integrity, strength and stability of family and society. San Jose women strongly portray these aspects of the *marianismo* image.

There is a high degree of correlation between the traditional image of *machismo* and *marianismo* and the public behaviors of men and women when fishermen are in the village between expeditions. Women stay in their houses more than at other times. They defer to men in public and sometimes in private. Ostensibly, they have little influence over men's behavior. When men are on fishing expeditions, the correlation between image and behavior slips. Women may continue to be nurturant but they become more public figures. They are seen more often on the street and in other public places. Women seem to make the best of these opportunities.

STRATEGIES EMPLOYED BY WOMEN

The problem of the conflict between the dominance of the *machismo* complex and the limitations of its exercise and expression in this artisanal deep sea fishing community is very long-standing. San Jose is in a region, nation and continent with centuries of male-domination experience, and shares that social history. An equally important historical factor for the village is the long tradition of living by the sea. Both historical strains are strong, and apparently incompatible.

In the present situation, San Jose is structurally and institutionally similar to nearby agricultural communities where the *machismo* complex is not inhibited by the subsistence strategy. In both, men's power is evident in all of the patterned social relationships, and the economic, political, and religious organization. For example, men hold all of the political offices and the religious offices within the villages. Men make the decisions regarding the public expenditures of money. Women in both communities are in structural positions which are disadvantageous. While women in both communities employ strategies for limiting the power of men, some strategies are available to fishermen's women that are not available to agricultural women. The advantageous strategies of San Jose women are made possible by the conditions of the fishing economy.

The particular technology used and the subsistence strategy adopted by Sanjosefinos provide a source of influence for women. Men are away on fishing expeditions for four to eight days at a time. This translates into an absence of 60 to 75 percent of the time during a fisherman's active labor years. When fishermen are absent, women, children, and old men are left in charge of the village. *Machismo* demands that men make decisions, take care of public and legal affairs and determine the behavior of women and children, but under these circumstances, these demands obviously cannot be met.

Daily life in the village must continue whether men are present or not. Children study, work and play, get sick and get well, and even die while their fathers are fishing. Women buy and prepare food, market fish, run the households and the village while men are fishing. Only a very few activities are postponed or deliberately planned so that the fishermen of the family may attend. Among these exceptions are baptisms, marriages, and the greater fiestas of the village. Postponed with much less regularity is the burial of a child or the registration of the vital statistics of birth and death. During the active years of a fisherman's life, he spends much more time at sea than he does on land. Some of his land time he spends drinking with crew men with whom he has just spent five or six days on sea, thus extending his absence in a certain respect.

Men and women both acknowledge women's ability to run the household and the village, at least tacitly. Women are not timid in the *municipalidad* or with public officials, or with outsiders who come to the village for special purposes, such as paramedical personnel, school teachers or itinerant salesmen. Women seem to make decisions with as much boldness and deliberation as men, and the decisions they make seem to withstand the test of time as well as those of men. San Jose women do not follow the *marianismo* pattern in the foregoing instances, either in their stance vis-à-vis persons of higher status or in situations requiring decisions. San Jose men seem to accept this state of affairs with little difficulty. Men joke among themselves that all that women do while they are at sea is to pray until they return. Nonetheless, they realize that daily life flows on, even when they are not there. This realization is evident when they do return and notice what changes have occurred in their absence. Their usual response is silent acceptance. Occasionally, they may grumble a complaint or, even less often, a word of affirmation. A husband would never seriously complain or be angry unless his wife acted whimsically. Since the behavior of young women is subject to the ever-present purview of older women, especially their mothers-in-law, aberrant behavior is virtually non-existent. Women's competence in guiding village and household affairs is a source of influence for them.

As noted earlier, women hold the purse strings. Women not only sell fish, they also retain effective control over all expenditures, even those of the men. When fishermen are in the village between expeditions they fill their days with repairing the nets and drinking with their friends. The money which they need for this socializing is given by the women. It is expected that a woman will always give some money to her man even if the budget is very tight, but she may not give as much as he wants. Men may fuss or grumble but it is the women who determine how much will be given. It appears that many women are as adept at bargaining and negotiating with their fishermen about drinking money as they are with middlemen over the price of fish. Disagreements are never aired in public but the privacy of the controversy does not tranquilize the waters of dissent.

Women have leverage in this situation because they have the responsibility for feeding children and buying necessities while men are away. They are in a better position than men to allocate resources on a daily basis. It would not be practical for a man to try to take charge of expenditures (even his own personal ones) for one or two days, and then hand over the charge to someone else for four or five days.

The pragmatics of the situation arising from men's absence makes women structurally important, but the facade of the *machismo* complex keeps women structurally subordinant. Given the circumstances of the subsistence strategy, the question of the stability of the male-dominant structure arises. How do men maintain dominance if women are so important structurally and so influential? The continuity and stability of the system lies in the mother-in-law, the focal position of the mother of a married son.

At first blush, it may appear that the mother-in-law is betraying fidelity to her own sex. After all, why would a mother-in-law lord it over a daughter-in-law when they are both women who are dominated by others? One might argue that it is simply a matter that the mother-in-law feels like it is finally time for her to dictate rather than be dictated to. The mother-in-law in her younger days was tyrannized by others, and now it is her turn to tyrannize. Such an answer is too simplistic. The larger social and historical context must be considered.

It will be remembered that San Jose is immersed in an historical and contemporary social context of male domination, commonly and loosely referred to as the *machismo* complex. The social structure of San Jose is similar to the neighboring agricultural villages. In order to perpetuate this structure of male dominance, *someone* has to act as men's surrogates in the exercise of power. In this instance it is young married men's mothers. Even though the mother-in-law is female, she acts as a surrogate for the male, her son. Thus the pattern of male dominance is reinforced, and San Jose continues to resemble its neighbors in its institutions.

CONCLUSION

The local story is about women who live in a fishing village on the northern coast of Peru, and how they and their fishermen participate in a subsistence strategy of artisanal deep sea fishing. This strategy necessitates the absence of men from the village for significant periods of time. The absence of men is problematic because the prevailing regional ideology of *machismo* is maintained at least in part by the presence of men. Thus arises the basic conflict between the requirements of the economy and those of ideology.

An examination of the way the *Sanjosefinos* act would not support either the primacy-of-economy position or the primacy -of-ideology position, at least not consistently. The economic arrangement of artisanal deep sea fishing remains intact in spite of the regional history of *machismo*. The ideological arrangement also seems to remain intact if one observes the activities of women when the fishermen are in the village. However, if one observes the activities of women when their fishermen are absent, the ideology of *machismo* and its consequent behaviors seem to be muted. Women make decisions wisely and execute them competently, both in everyday affairs and in times of crises. They are assertive in their relations with others. Their speech gives no clues that they feel inferior to men either socially or intellectually.

What are the San Jose women (and men) really doing in this situation? Are the women blindly switching from one set of behaviors to the other, the change triggered automatically merely by the presence of men? Are the men so naive that they do not realize the competence of women in their absence, and that their (women's) behavior changes rather dramatically at that time? How much self-awareness is there on the part of both men and women?

The clue to understanding this oscillation of behavior lies in the assertion that both women and men are fully aware of their own and others' abilities and activities. Women are assessing the situation wisely and choosing from a whole repertoire of skills they have carefully and knowingly cultivated. They have acquired a very sophisticated and extended knowledge in the areas of interpersonal relations, interactional spheres within the village, and the intricacies of household finances. They can perform the multiple and demanding tasks required for survival in a peasant village which offers few comforts of contemporary civilization, and even fewer luxuries.

I maintain that San Jose women know the *machismo* complex very well, and that at times they choose to act within its parameters and at other times, they choose to act in opposition to it. By acting within its parameters when their fishermen are in the village, they comfortably conform to the prevalent ideology. They appear to be like their agriculturally based sisters and in no way odd or peculiar. Their men still maintain the aura of male dignity and do not lose face before their agriculturally based brothers. To put it simply, conformity to the norm brings the general approval of others and the comfort that one is not odd. In this phase, both men and women choose to act in a way that supports the primacy-of-ideology theory.

The other phase occurs when men are fishing. Then women choose to act in a way that contributes more to the survival of themselves and their families than the traditional *machismo* complex would permit. Not only do they make such a choice intellectually and deliberately, but they have acquired the skills to execute that choice. In this phase, if women are humble in demeanor, it is simply a mask for the real influence they exercise. Women appear subordinate and remain structurally subordinate but have wide-ranging and effective control over much of their own lives and those of their families. The artisanal deep sea fishing creates the conditions which allow a significant break with the consequences of the *machismo* tradition. This is the phase which supports the primacy-of-economy position.

Men's absence limits the effectiveness of their power in all areas of life, including the economic. Purse strings are held by women, and women regulate the flow of money. In men's absence, they also strongly influence the flow of life. In our society, there is a saying, "Absence makes the heart grow fonder." San Jose women might alter that saying, and assert boldly and truthfully, "Absence makes our influence stronger."

Notes

1. Shellfish gathering and river fishing are generally classified with the activities of hunting and gathering as a basic subsistence strategy. When traditional societies do deep sea fishing, their activity is more difficult to classify. The methods, though variable, do not employ complex technology and are not highly mechanized. Because their success depends to a great extent upon the fishermen's skill or "artistry" rather than technological sophistication, they are often called "artisanal." This designation does not solve the problem of classification, but it does emphasize simple rather than complex technology, and personal skill rather than mechanization.

2. For an interesting discussion on the extended time periods involved in commercial deep sea fishing, see David R. M. White's essay "Environment, Technology, and Time-use Patterns in the Gulf Coast Shrimp Fishery" (Smith 1977a:195-214). Other economic activities

which demand the absence of men may also affect women's responsibilities and the society as a whole. Sanday (1981:121) notes the prolonged absence of men "engaged in hunting, warfare, trading or migrant labor." Sanday then gives an interesting ethnographic example of the Abipon of South America.

3. Fieldwork was conducted during three periods: May 1970 - August 1971, May - July 1974 and May - July 1982. The methodology was basic participant-observation which was deliberately reflective (de Grys 1983:14-19).

Conflicting Gender Conceptions in a Pluriform Fishing Economy: A Hermeneutic Perspective on Conjugal Relationships in Brazil

6

Antonius C.G.M. Robben

This chapter examines the influence of different modes of fishing on the social and economic position of women and on the relationship between husbands and wives.[1] Men and women of Camurim, a town in the state of Bahia, Brazil, have opposite gender ideologies, with each sex claiming to be superior to the other, but they share similar notions about the normative standards of the conjugal relationship. Women should remain at home to take care of the household, and men should go out to sea to sustain the nuclear family. Men work to reproduce the material basis of the domestic world, while women use their services to give substance to the life at home. The social and economic arrangements at work and at home, however, are not unattached or independently constituted. The productive effort a man chooses to attain the seemingly straightforward economic objective of feeding, clothing, and housing his family tends to modify the nature of the domestic world. Women who marry receive the promise of adequate material support, but the extent to which fishermen realize their good intentions depends greatly upon their mode of fishing. Different technical and organizational requirements used to exploit distinct ecological zones influence the translation of ideological conceptions of gender into normative priorities, and the translation of norms into everyday actions. Ideologies, norms, and actions are not logically interrelated but have numerous ambiguities that lead to conflicting interpretations among actors. The focus of this chapter is on these interpretational tensions and how they affect the conjugal relationship and the status of women in Camurim.

The approach to the ethnographic material is interpretive, and the analysis is sociological.

In the groundbreaking book, *Sexual Meanings*, editors Ortner and Whitehead (1981:2-6) distinguish between a culturalist analysis that elucidates the inner logic and structural relations among gender symbols, and a sociological analysis that reveals the relationship between the social order and cultural perceptions of gender. The sociological analysis is, in my opinion, more congenial to the study of gender-related issues in maritime societies, because it shows best the influence of the production mode on the interplay of ideologies, norms, and actions. Most fishing economies are characterized by a stark sexual division of labor that makes it impossible to understand the place of women independently of the type of economic activities performed by men to sustain the conjugal relationship. If the economy does not offer men the possibility to fulfill their conjugal obligations, or when these responsibilities are given less importance because of new interests engendered by the economic activities, severe repercussions will follow for the domestic relationships and the female household members. The status of a woman in the pluriform fishing economy of Camurim depends on the occupation of her husband, on his position in the ensuing relationship between domestic and public spheres of activity, and on the few economic roles accessible to women. A dominant male ideology that confines women to the private world of the home keeps them from developing public identities independent of the social statuses of their husbands. Women are categorized as "the wife of ..." because men are the principal social referents.

The relational status of women and their enclosure in the domestic hearth are common in many societies (Ortner and Whitehead 1981; Rosaldo 1974), but these characteristics are very intense in Camurim. Fishermen, unlike peasant farmers, exclude women from all primary production activities because of their alleged physical inability, while the male-dominated Latin culture of Brazil— "the place of women and old men is in the house"— further enhances the division of domestic and public domains. Although this state of affairs impedes the self-realization of women, it does not necessarily lead to tensions in domestic relationships as long as men can satisfy the needs of the household and women are content with the role of housewife. The mutual satisfaction of normative role expectations makes both sexes accept status definitions that are grounded in a male ideology. Boat owners and canoe fishermen in Camurim reasonably succeed in living up to their wives' expectations, but many boat fishermen periodically fail to maintain their households adequately. A boat fisherman who cannot secure the economic foundation of the household loses his respect at home and feels that he has failed as a husband, a father, and a man. He feels estranged from his wife and isolates himself from the family. The domestic marginalization leads to a public marginal life in bars and on street corners. Unable to attain public esteem because of his economic and domestic failures, he eschews these existentially painful realities and sojourns in an interstitial world of fleeting relationships without lasting commitments or responsibilities.

In such a situation, the discrepancy between what a woman expects and what she receives will inevitably lead to marital conflicts. The financial weight of the household falls on the female head who has to enter a fishing economy that, because of its male bias, does not provide a secure occupational niche for women. She has to enter an unfamiliar public domain and accept employment under conditions set by men. If a woman cannot obtain well-paid work, nor rely on help from her children, then she must try to develop relationships with wealthy townsmen and resort to social strategies that capitalize on this network. The repercussions on the conjugal relationship are far-reaching and make her place in the community significantly different from that of other women.

The discussion of the place of women in Camurim is restricted to wives of men in three social categories: canoe fishermen, boat fishermen, and boat owners. The lives of these women clearly portray the constraints of their relational status and the decisive influence of the types of domestic and public realities that are created. The place of the male heads of households in the two fishing modes predisposes men and women alike toward particular statuses in the two domains which, in turn, affect their conjugal relationship. The data will be approached from a hermeneutic perspective that explicitly demonstrates the different interpretations of the conjugal relationship among and between men and women. By drawing an analogy between text and action, this approach tries to understand and explain how actors interpret symbols, ideologies, and social actions, and through these interpretations reproduce the social world and endow their existence with meaning (Ricoeur 1981:36-38, 197-221). Underlying this perspective is the epistemological assumption that people arrive at an understanding of meaning through a hermeneutic circle of perpetual reflections on the meaning constituting relationships between the general and the particular, between the totality of existence and its constituent parts (Bauman 1978:28). "It concerns the circular relation between the whole and its parts: the anticipated meaning of a whole is understood through the parts, but it is in light of the whole that the parts take on their illuminating function" (Gadamer 1979:146). Thus, a discussion of conjugal relationships must not be confined to the narrow social realm of the household in which husband and wife interact, but must encompass all relevant aspects of the social and cultural context that impinge on their relationship. What is considered relevant or not is indicated by their interpretational conflicts. By focusing on issues which differ across social categories, and about which men and women are in conflict, the crucial interpretational junctures of the parts within the whole of meaning are unfolded. The hermeneutic circle of understanding is entered at interpretive pressure points that expose the conflicts between different ideologies, normative expectations, and actual actions, and show the disagreements about the translation of one level of meaning into another.

After a brief description of the fishing economy and the economic status of women, I will proceed with a discussion of conflicting gender ideologies and conjugal expectations. Finally, I will provide an extensive analysis of the social and economic differences among the three categories of women, showing how their positions are largely the result of their relational statuses, but that they still find ways to exert some power in the household and force men to seek compromises among conflicting interests.

THE PLURIFORM FISHING ECONOMY

Camurim is a town of almost 6,000 inhabitants in a county whose main income comes from cocoa plantations, cattle ranches, lumber exploitation, sawmills, small ceramic industries, brickyards, and fishing. Fishing offers potentially the highest personal income of all economic activities. Most men who start out as fishermen will never switch to wage employment ashore, despite years of toil and hardship at sea that yield just a bare existence.

The pluriform fishing industry consists of two main fishing modes: sail-driven canoes that exploit marine resources in the shallow coastal waters and motorboats that face the high seas. Boats fish with four- to six-men crews at distant coral reefs and at the edge of the continental shelf. Small boats can stay at sea for up to three days. These multi-purpose boats use gill nets, handlines, and trawl nets. Large, eleven-meter vessels fish exclusively with handlines for a period of seven to ten days. Dugout canoes are manned by one or two fishermen who make daily trips with handlines and gill nets.

The relationship between canoe owners and their crews is harmonious and cooperative. Both work hard to remain independent producers, even though one owns the canoe and the other only contributes a number of fishing nets. The term independence implies the self-determination to decide when, where, and how to fish, and not to be subject to the demands and commands of captains or boat owners. Canoes are financially within reach of most canoe fishermen. Those who have a conflict with a canoe owner can always find ways to buy a used dugout and pay for it in installments. Although canoe owners earn more money than crew members, there are no significant differences in their conjugal relationships, hence I will treat them in this article as an undifferentiated group.

The relationship between boat owners and fishermen is antagonistic and conflict-ridden because of opposed interests. Capital owners want to maximize profits while fishermen want higher revenues. The owner is disgruntled when the men return with a small catch, charging that they were lazy. The fishermen counter that the owner is greedy and inconsiderate. These tensions become stronger when fishermen owe money to the owner after an unsuccessful fishing trip. Owners and fishermen share equally in all running costs i.e., fuel, oil, ice, bait, hooks, lines, anchors, and food. The running costs are deducted from the total value of the catch and the remaining amount is divided in two equal parts: one for the owner and the other for the fishermen. When the running costs exceed the value of the catch then all or some fishermen, depending on the size of the individual catches, will be in debt. Those who caught more will be able to compensate their part of the running costs, while others will not. However, a fisherman does not always receive the net value of his catch because often the owner advanced him or his wife money before embarking. The advance (*vale*) is intended to cover household expenses during the fisherman's absence. The longer the trip, the higher the advance. It is obvious that after several small catches many fishermen will have an accumulated debt of running costs and *vales* that will be difficult to pay off.

The social and psychological effects of a continued state of indebtedness are very serious and partly explain why boat fishermen and their wives are estranged. These fishermen tend to shy away from home because they cannot confront their spouses' claim that they fail to fulfill their obligations as husbands and fathers. They will drift towards colleagues who can empathize with their situation. This flight from the domestic world may result in heavy drinking. Fishermen will spend much money on rum and will not even leave the *vale* at home before they go off on another fishing trip. The household is left without money and the woman will be obliged to earn some money or ask the boat owner for another advance. This situation will increase the fisherman's marginalization from the domestic life, and the estrangement from his wife. Of course, not all boat fishermen are in this position, but many who fish on large vessels are, because liners spend more time at sea than small boats. Since the running costs for long trips are higher, the possible debts are also higher. Furthermore, fishermen are away from home for long periods and more easily develop some callousness towards their domestic problems. Even the small number of boat fishermen who have reasonably good yields often have tense conjugal relationships because of their urge to display their wealth publicly and to divert earnings away from the household into activities that bring social esteem. Their relationships with their wives resemble those of boat owners and will therefore not be discussed here. This chapter presents only the data on poor boat fishermen in order to enhance the contrasts with canoe fishermen and to show the consequences of a trend toward scale enlargement that will eventually affect all fishermen.

The variation in income among boat fishermen is far greater than among canoe fishermen. Some boat fishermen do extremely well while others earn less than half of the average income of canoe fishermen. However, the living standard of boat and canoe fishermen with similar incomes is not identical because of the high public spending of boat fishermen. Concern for public prestige corrodes the economic foundation of the household and leaves their families worse off than those of many canoe fishermen. Low-income boat fishermen, who would fare better in shallow coastal waters, are prevented from switching to canoes by the social problems of a peer group change and especially by the difficulties of paying off debts to boat owners and accumulating enough money to buy canoes and nets. As long as these men cannot disentangle themselves from the debt relationships, it will be difficult for their wives to improve their social status, because the economic opportunities for women to raise their living standards are almost nonexistent.

THE ECONOMIC STATUS OF WOMEN

In many fishing communities in northeast Brazil, women have always been directly involved in the fishing economy (Forman 1970; Oliveira 1966; Robben 1982). Women have been known to collect mollusks and crustaceans, and to cook, dry, salt, and barbecue fish. With the exception of some women who clean fish, and a few, very poor women who help to pull a tattered beach seine ashore, none of the almost 3000 females in Camurim is involved in the production

or processing of marine resources. Women do not work as mid-
dlepersons selling fish on the market; instead, boys hawk the
catches of canoe fishermen in the street, and the produce of boats
is bought by wholesale dealers from Rio de Janeiro and Vitoria.

The wives of canoe fishermen have very few opportunities to earn
money. Men want them to be at home to have a warm meal ready
when they return from the sea. Furthermore, they believe that
women who work are more likely to develop adulterous affairs, especially when they are employed by townspeople. Still, a number of
married women hold steady jobs as charwomen and cooks in the
hospital, the city hall, and the schools of Camurim. Women also
work in the houses of tourists during summer. They are paid better
wages than women who work in public jobs, and often receive gifts
of clothes and food. They have no insurance benefits, although loyalty to the employers is rewarded with clientelistic relationships that
may ensure assistance in case of illness or old age.

Camurim does not have an artisanal tradition of embroidery,
lacework, or straw plaiting as is common in other fishing communities along the northeastern coast. Tourism in these places has
made handicraft industries flourish and has reduced the financial
dependence of women on men. Tourism is a fairly recent phenomenon related to the development of cocoa plantations in the
hinterland of Camurim during the 1970s. Women are not yet aware
of many of the possibilities to earn money from tourists, but occasionally, some couples do rent small bars on the beach. The
husbands supply fish and the wives sell beer and prepare seafood
dishes. During this period, they rent their own houses to tourists.
A few women sell Afro-Brazilian delicacies on the beach, but in
general the female involvement in the tourist industry is small compared to other fishing villages in the state of Bahia (Kottak 1983).

The most important display of female entrepreneurship is the
production of popsicles (*geladinha*). Almost every household that
has a refrigerator sells popsicles. Women spend at least one day a
week preparing thousands of small plastic bags filled with artificial-
ly flavored ice. They invest in a few cool boxes and have children sell
the popsicles in the street and on the beach. The wives of canoe
fishermen do not work because of pressing financial needs, but to
have some extra money for themselves. The strict separation of the
budgets of men and women is a remarkable aspect of the fishing
economy of Camurim. The explanation must be sought in the formal role expectations of the husband-wife relationship. Men attend
to the material needs of the household and women supply the services. Only under the worst of circumstances will a woman spend

her earnings on food items that are supposed to be bought by men. During weeks with very low catches, some men purchase bread on credit and others borrow money from their wives, who have more than enough money to cover these expenses. Women spend their earnings principally on kitchenware and clothes for themselves and the children. They argue that if they were to take over some male household responsibilities, then this would discourage men from confronting the sea under less than ideal circumstances.

Many wives of boat fishermen are less fortunate. They have to work to be able to satisfy basic needs, because the men leave them very little housekeeping money due to high liquor expenses, small earnings and sizable debts to boat owners. These women have even fewer possibilities of making money than the wives of canoe fishermen because they live at the riverside, a part of town that has not attracted any tourists. Tourists prefer a relatively isolated area near the beach which is situated closest to the houses of canoe fishermen. Hence, wives of boat fishermen have no chance to work for tourists. Poor women, of course, do not have refrigerators at home to make popsicles, although they do encourage their children to sell these to be able to buy some food. A number of women have public jobs as cooks and cleaners. Their incomes exceed those of many boat fishermen and are further enhanced by child support, retirement benefits and a health insurance. Street-cleaning, and the making of charcoal and bricks are the only three other means of full-time support for uneducated women in Camurim. None of these occupations is considered by fishermen's wives. Only the poorest women take these jobs. They are the most exploited of all Camurimenses, a socially marginal group that survives on a starvation budget. The pay and the status of the work are so low that wives of boat fishermen prefer an irregular income from sewing clothes, cleaning fish, peeling shrimp and, above all, washing clothes. There is a large demand for laundresses. Women have to go to the river with heavy loads of clothes on their heads and spend hours in the hot sun till all is clean and dry. Everybody who can afford the expense, even wives of boat and canoe fishermen, has the laundry done by washerwomen.

Families of low-income boat fishermen lead a precarious existence. Like all people who live off the sea, they are not assured of stable incomes, but unlike canoe fishing households, this uncertainty is enhanced by an unfavorable remuneration system, debt relationships, alcoholism, adulterous affairs, and estrangement between husband and wife. The load of the household's welfare weighs disproportionately on women who have hardly any possibilities to

earn money. Still, these women play a far more crucial role in the
survival of the family than men are willing to admit (Figueiredo
1983). When poor funds cannot meet the barest demands of the
household, then women have to resort to degrading social strategies
that will be discussed later.

Boat owners take good care of their households and hire servants to relieve their wives of most domestic tasks. These women do
not have the financial need to take low-paying menial jobs. Still,
several women work as teachers at primary and secondary schools.
They enhance the social status of their husbands through professional contacts with local authorities. While boat owners would
certainly forbid their wives to take jobs that would involve too many
contacts with men, they approve of a prestige-giving educational
position, which they regard as a variation on the role of women as
educators at home.

GENDER IDEOLOGIES AND NORMATIVE EXPECTATIONS AMONG SPOUSES

Men believe that women are physically, socially and mentally inferior, are capricious, irrational, ambiguous, only serve for the
kitchen and for having children, and engage in adulterous affairs
whenever the opportunity arises (Freyre 1961; Willems 1953). These
characteristics arise from and are accompanied by an ideology of
male superiority or *machismo* that manifests itself in arrogance, intransigence, sexual aggressiveness, boasting, self-importance,
independence, and callousness toward women (Stevens 1973a).
Women cannot be trusted and therefore should be confined to the
house so that they are under strict male supervision. The most suc-
cinct statement of this attitude toward women was written in 1650
by the Portuguese author D. Francisco Manuel de Melo in his *Guide
for Married Men*:

> A young lion can be tamed; a little bird can become fond of the bars
> of the cage in which it lives imprisoned; the former being fierce and
> the latter being free by nature. Education is a second birth, and if
> it differs in something from the first, it is only in that the second
> is more forceful (Melo n.d.:26).

A woman should be married when she is young and pure, because men are convinced that only a virgin can be effectively
dominated and "trained" (*treinado*) by the husband. Virginity is
regarded as a sort of anticipatory loyalty that gives a future husband the privilege to educate a woman according to his desires.
However, the combination of loyalty and opportunity gives rise to
the ambiguous nature of women. Men are convinced that "woman

is opportunity" (mulher e'oportunidade), which means that any woman can be seduced if the opportunity is there. Women agree that they can be tempted, but counter that men actively search for the right opportunity.

Female conceptions about men show that women note a discrepancy between male behavior inside and outside the home. Women say that men are not loyal, that they easily forget their conjugal obligations, search for opportunities to seduce other women, or otherwise exploit their position of power and authority to make improper propositions. Although they cannot openly express their opinions, women regard themselves as superior to men in character and in moral and spiritual strength. This cult of female superiority or marianismo exists in other parts of Latin America (Stevens 1973b). Women have to confront many unknown situations alone, while men support each other in difficult times. Machismo makes men boast about their hardships at sea and belittle the daily worries of women who, in their eyes, just have to keep the household functioning. Women believe that men are cowards deep down inside. They mention six situations of much anguish in their lives which show that women are more courageous than men: (1) the wedding night, (2) pregnancy, (3) childbirth, (4) post-delivery defenselessness against spirits, (5) raising children, and (6) personal suffering. Men usually have pre-marital sexual experiences, while women do not know what to expect, not even knowing if their husbands are going to be overdemanding or abusive. Everything associated with pregnancies is only felt by women, who have to endure pains which would be unbearable to men. Upon delivery, the mother is left with an "open body" (corpo aberto), as opposed to the father's "closed body" (corpo fechado), that is a natural causeway for evil spirits to enter and harm her. She has to raise the children and bear the responsibility for their well-being when the husband is absent. Finally, when the burden becomes too heavy, she has to suffer at home alone and in silence in order not to harm her husband's reputation. Men, on the other hand, take out their frustrations on their wives, get drunk, solicit help from friends, or simply go to sea to escape any problems ashore. The emotional isolation of women becomes especially intense when the husband offers no consolation during important periods of their lives. One woman told me how a few days before she gave birth to a fourth child, her husband had left with his mistress for another town. She cried during the entire delivery and was devastated when the next day her husband walked in as if nothing had happened. In a festive mood, he demanded that she prepare snacks so that he could celebrate the birth with a couple of drinking companions. Such painful experiences add to the importance of motherhood for women. They cannot conceive of womanhood without having children. With young children women can create feelings of intimacy they lack with other women, and they project onto children the love that remains unreciprocated by men.

The predominance of the male ideology is expressed in the complementary roles of men and women. Once the sexual division of economic and domestic tasks is taken for granted, men and women share clearly defined role expectations without relenting their own gender conceptions. The husband expects his wife to bear children, prepare food, wash clothes, clean the house, look after the children, and respond promptly to his sexual desires. All household work devolves on his wife and daughters. Both men and women do not regard domestic services as labor; only men work because they earn the money that sustains the nuclear family. The wife expects her husband to provide a shelter, to show sexual interest in her, and to pay for all household expenses such as food, rent, utility bills, school fees, and medical costs. The obligations of husband and wife are considered complementary, but imbalanced. Marriage is seen as a transactional arrangement which a couple hopes will create an intimate, independent domestic world that is emotionally and existentially fulfilling for a nuclear family that shares mutual affection, warmth, understanding, and trust.

Since men feel that they contribute more to the household than women do, they try to settle for cohabitation arrangements that can be easily dissolved if they are unhappy with the reciprocated domestic services. Men say that they want "to leave the door open" (*deixar a porta aberta*). This metaphoric expression associates the husband-wife relationship with the house and suggests that the door marks the social and spatial threshold between the intimate domestic unit, with its mutual obligations, and an open-ended, public domain where men can engage in extramarital affairs and choose other, more suitable partners. To leave the door open implies that they can break the transactional arrangement and reappear as uncommitted men. Some married men go even so far as to say that once they leave the house they are bachelors, conceptually speaking, who can do whatever they desire without being held accountable for their public acts by their wives.

Women, of course, can never take such an ambivalent attitude towards men. Men try to resort to common-law unions (*amasiado*), but most women refuse to accept the low social and moral status of concubinage. Furthermore, since women are suspicious of losing their virginity without any formal commitment, they will resist cohabitation. Hence, men try to get married either by church or by law, but not both. Before divorce was legally recognized in Brazil, men preferred religious to civil marriages so that in case of a separation their wives could not claim alimony and a share of the property. The local Roman Catholic priest, however, has recently begun to demand that civil weddings must precede all religious ceremonies. This condition has made church weddings less attractive and has reduced the power of men to dominate women with the threat of abandonment. Civil marriages enhance the women's negotiating power whenever conflicts arise. Quarrels among common-laws result most often in the woman going with her children to her parents' house; among couples married in civil ceremonies, the husband leaves the home.

Husband-wife relationships are assessed in terms of their degree of obligation (*obrigacao*) and consideration (*consideracao*). Obligation refers to the acting out of duties that pertain to the status of a spouse and indicates the partner's rights and expectations. If a person cannot fulfill the obligations mentioned above, as is the case with boat fishermen, then he or she undermines the role relationship. The degree to which spouses feel satisfied with each other's role performances varies with their social status. A woman will avoid marrying a man who cannot provide her with a living standard comparable to that of her parents, and her expectations will rise with the upward social mobility of her husband.

The relation between obligation and status applies, of course, especially to men. Household services can only be improved so far, but luxury and wealth are without limits. The fulfillment of obligations beyond what is formally expected is a sign of the consideration between husband and wife. Consideration expresses a person's emotional involvement in the conjugal relationship. Love (*amor*) is not a synonym for consideration. Camurimenses certainly acknowledge the importance of love in any intimate relationship, but they feel that romantic love confessed during courtship must be acted out in marriage. What counts is how one acts, not what one proclaims. Most people live on the edge of subsistence, where material contributions to survival weigh more than good intentions. Consideration encapsulates but also transcends obligation in that duties are felt as voluntary actions that sprout from the emotional attachment to a partner. A person who has consideration tries to anticipate the other's needs instead of just reacting obligatorily upon his or her expectations. Consideration replaces obligation as the principal motive of action when the bond between spouses is strong. For example, a woman may wash her husband's clothes out of consideration, not because she thinks it is her duty. Her husband may buy her a stove or extra clothing, and she may make him a hat or a shirt. These tokens of affection and generosity, imbued with true feelings of care for the other's emotional well-being, heighten mutual consideration, while their absence makes the husband-wife relationship seem very transactional and calculated. In the latter situation, the wife will still wash clothes but now out of a sense of duty. In general, a couple will remain together as long as both spouses perform their role obligations satisfactorily.

Obligation and consideration describe the long-term standing of the conjugal relationship. The term *media* is a short-term indicator, a sort of emotional barometer of the present harmony between husband and wife. The *media* will be low after a woman discovers her husband's visit to a brothel. She will be angry and demand some show of repentance before her *media* will rise. She does not lose her consideration because the incident is too small to affect her long-standing emotional bond with her husband. If, however, he continues to spend his time with prostitutes, then the prolonged low *media* will reduce her consideration until there is only obligation left. The *media* does not subside, it remains the emotional evaluator of everyday interaction that indicates the highs and lows of the conjugal relationship. A consistently high _media might even give rise to renewed consideration and improve the conjugal relationship.

POWER AND STATUS OF WOMEN

The actual interaction between wives and husbands depends on how they interpret formally agreed upon role expectations, how everyday experiences influence these interpretations, and how their enactment is intersubjectively negotiated. Due to the exclusion of women from most fishing activities and the separation of workplace and household, there exists much mutual incomprehension about the daily problems of the opposite sex. In Brazil, this division of male and female spheres of activity, so typical of fishing economies, is intensified by the strong opposition between domestic and public domains in Latin cultures. Men do not allow their wives to enter places such as bars and brothels where eventful experiences at sea are recounted, and women avoid talking about their personal feelings and frustrations in the presence of men. Because of the unfamiliarity with each other's activities, men and women do not understand the contextual circumstances that might impede a proper enactment of role obligations. Hence, explanations for failure are often sought in personal defects or personality disorders, and only seldom in social and structural circumstances. A person is regarded as lazy or weak, rather than tired or undernourished, and a drunk is shameless (*sem-vergonha*), immoral and rotten (*safado*), instead, of exploited and in despair. Women hardly comprehend the peer pressure among men to publicly spend their earnings for reasons of honor, prestige, and power. Men, in turn, do not understand the humiliation women feel when they have to buy milk on credit or ask a boat owner for a loan. The degree to which this lack of empathy can be moderated depends on the opportunities for interaction at home, because women cannot enter male domains, but men do observe female activities around the house. The lopsided sexual division of space makes the house the most important meeting place for spouses and thus enhances the opportunity of women to influence the husband-wife relationship. The man may be the head of the household and the family (*o patrao e o pai da familia*), but the woman is the lady of the house (*a dona de casa*). Her carefulness with food and clothing prevents unnecessary waste of income, raises the standard of living, and maximizes the satisfaction of household needs with limited means. She can embitter the domestic life if her demands are not met. The man may supply the material means, but the woman presides over their consumption in the home (Freyre 1961:32-38; Woortmann 1982:121-126). Another source of female power is the male belief in her inbred ambiguity. Her alleged propensity for infidelity and hence her ability to undermine the moral standing of the house and her husband's reputation give a woman considerable power (Brandes 1981:227-228). At home, a woman may make her husband realize that his material support is deficient and if this awareness does not foster some understanding for her problems, then she cannot be blamed for committing adultery. Domestic conflicts in Camurim, therefore, tend to be less frequent when nuclear families spend more time together.

The wives of canoe fishermen share many domestic experiences with their husbands. They watch the men mending nets, overhear some of the conversations, ask them to help with household chores, and notice their influence on the education of the children. At times women feel burdened by the male presence and relish the hours when they are among themselves. They turn on the radio, open doors and windows, sweep the floor, place some chairs outside, and make the sidewalk an extension of their house: a communal, female space to chat, sew clothes, clean beans, and hum to their babies. As soon as the fishermen return, the women move to the backyard to prepare dinner. The men take a quick shower to wash off the salt of the sea and sit down to eat. Depending on the hour, a woman and her children may share the meal. After a brief rest, the fishermen again take command of the street, mending their nets till sundown and discussing the day's events.

Although men will always proclaim that they are in charge, arguing that they bring in the money so that they have the right to decide about its use, women have considerable power because of the day-to-day contact. Casual but well-aimed remarks about the poor state of the house, the neighbor's new furniture, or the lack of food and clothes incite men to try to meet such demands. Women make their husbands aware of the dire needs at home. A poor household confronts a fisherman with his failure to do what is expected of him: to sustain the members of the nuclear family and their social position in the community to the best of his ability. A well-fed, well-clothed family in a brick house with a bathroom, a refrigerator, a gas stove, a radio, and a television is an ideal attained only by few but strived after by many.

Canoe fishermen rank each other according to the height of their living standard. Those who are shown respect are not just fishermen who catch much fish but those who wisely invest in fishing gear and durable consumer goods. The social prestige of women among this group of canoe fishing households reflects the informal hierarchy among fishermen. Comments about other women who show off a new blender or tablecloth are intended to convey that their social position and consequently that of their husband is declining in relation to others. Such social pressure tends to channel earnings into the household. Honor and prestige among canoe fishermen are translated into a display of domestic wealth instead of the conspicuous consumption in bars that in part determines the social status of boat owners and fishermen. Canoe fishermen are, of course, far from being total abstainers but they only go on a binge on special occasions. They are honestly concerned about the welfare of their families because of the emotional proximity. They say that they dislike boat fishing because it takes them away from their families. They want to be near to help when financial or health problems arise, knowing that women will have greater difficulties than men in dealing with such emergencies. As a result, women are socially restricted to their immediate surroundings and only leave occasionally to make a purchase or to go to the market or to church on Sundays.

The married woman is almost entirely dedicated to servicing an all-absorbing household that leaves hardly any time or possibility for pursuing other activities outside the home. Although she does not sustain the domestic reality materially, she plays an important part in its constitution through a process of continuous negotiation with her ever-present husband. She realizes that the alternatives to her subservient position are worse, as the plight of wives of boat fishermen will show below. Hence, conjugal quarrels are not about the basic conditions of the husband-wife relationship and the maintenance of its transactional content, but about the household's prestige and ranking in the community. Tensions are not about the household's existence but about its appearance to others and the living standard of its members.

The wives of boat fishermen complain about their men's insensitivity to the suffering they have to undergo to keep the household functioning. Most women do not steadily receive housekeeping money. Sometimes boat fishermen are ashore for weeks due to bad weather, repairs, or religious festivities but boat owners will only reluctantly advance money, knowing that an increasing debt will take a long time to be paid off. At other times, fishermen might spend the advances on liquor, and leave the penniless household to scramble for itself.

Boat fishermen acknowledge that they like to be far from the domestic preoccupations of their wives. When they leave the harbor, everything is behind them, and they prefer to concentrate on the catch to come. They learn to consciously eliminate troubling thoughts about home in order to maximize their mental effort on fishing. Once I witnessed a dramatic scene in one of the bars of Camurim where fishermen were paid their meager shares of a ten-day fishing trip with lots of bad weather and few fish. One unfortunate young man received the balance of US$0.03, not even enough to buy a beer. Furthermore, the owner reminded him that he still had an outstanding debt of US$10 from advances given for previous trips. The demoralized fisherman lamented that he had hardly been able to sleep, worrying about his pregnant wife. The boat owner replied that all men go through such a phase during their first year of marriage but that aboard ship one had to think only about fish, fish, and more fish. "Don't worry about your woman being in need of money, she will struggle her way out" (*ela se vira*). This allusion to illicit sexual behavior to obtain money was immediately followed by the explicit statement: "If your woman turns you into a cuckold, then you put horns on her head." Such crushing statements are made often. They make the neglect of the home seem somehow less grave and instill fishermen with a sense of suspicion toward women. Men, of course, dismiss all hurt that women feel about their going to brothels as inappropriate sentimentality.

The relationships between many boat fishermen and their wives are founded upon a mistrust that harms the conjugal bond in the core of its existence. The suspicion is always there, even though the incidence of female infidelity seems to be relatively rare. With reason, women feel resentful when their husbands arrive ashore and without even stopping by at home squander the small earnings on prostitutes and drinking-sprees with equally poor colleagues. Men drift to brothels when their neglect of conjugal obligations makes it more difficult to demand sexual satisfaction at home. Once a prostitute is paid, all obligations are fulfilled and the relationship can be cut without further compromises. Some women encourage their men to go fishing so that the burden of shame and, at times, the physical abuse by a drunken husband will be temporarily relieved. But once alone, they are cornered in a destitute situation with few solutions. Motherhood becomes therefore very important for their emotional as well as economic well-being. Once they become adults, children can secure their mother's livelihood in case of divorce or old age.

In an earlier section, I discussed the economic activities of women; here I will concentrate on the social strategies of survival. The most common means open to a woman to obtain food for herself and her children is to buy on credit. Storekeepers do not demand interest on such loans, despite the high price inflation in Brazil, but their merchandise is higher priced than products in the two local supermarkets which sell only for cash. A household's credit rating depends, of course, on how promptly debts are being settled, a condition which can be difficult to meet. A woman may also ask her blood relatives for a loan, but these people are often not much better off.

Another, more humiliating possibility is to ask a boat owner for money. Unlike owners of small boats who accompany their crews on short trips, the owners of large vessels are often at home to attend business or simply to ostentatiously hang out in bars or spend the day playing cards with friends. A woman has to muster a lot of courage to ask for a favor in an intimidating environment of boisterous, half-drunk men. She knows that she can count on her husband's employer in case of serious illness but a plea for money to buy food will less likely be granted. Amidst laughter, she is told that her husband is a lazy bum who accumulates large debts and finds his way to a bar better than to a boat or to his home. The woman is torn between care for the welfare of her children and the possible wrath of her husband and the boat owner. If she accepts money, she enhances her husband's debt and might also forfeit her chance to get help in the future.

A variation on this strategy is the regular transfer of advances (*vales*) between boat owners and women, bypassing the fisherman. This arrangement exposes a pattern that seems inherent in the credit advance system and contributes to the estrangement between husband and wife. Because of this credit system, the boat fisherman, as opposed to the independent canoe fisherman, never really worries about the material provisioning of his nuclear family because he can always rely on credit from his employer, regardless of his labor. As long as a fisherman is a member of the crew he will receive an advance based on his average catch. Hence, in an odd way, his household is sustained by the boat owner; the credit system transfers the responsibility for the household from the fisherman to the boat owner. The home has ceased to be an independent stronghold of the nuclear family and becomes incorporated into an economic organization and its relations of production. The household becomes contingent on the quality of the relationship between employer and employee. As a result, many boat fishermen feel that the periodical credit advance should be enough as housekeeping money, while the net proceeds are entirely at their disposal. When the fisherman is heavily in debt, as many crew members of large vessels are, then his family lives by the grace of the boat owner's continued support. In this case, the wife feels that her husband is socially and materially marginal to the construction of the domestic reality. He is seldom at home to act out the role relationships that make him a father and a husband, and he fails, furthermore, to realize the obligations that are attached to these roles. This failure is even more serious because of the formal notion of the unbalanced complementarity between wife and husband. The man is supposed to provide for the lion's share of the household, but somehow he does not succeed. His behavior is in contrast with the ideal image Latin men try to convey to others of themselves as independent men who know how to take care of their families, and defies the popular saying "Mother is blood, and father is sustenance" (*Mae e' sangue e pai e' sustento*). The mother lives up to the expectations of the consanguineal relationship with her children, but the father has relinquished his obligation. This discrepancy between male ideology and the actual behavior of men prompts some women to say that their house is a "woman's house" (*casa de mulheres*), indicating that they, rather than their husbands, are the heads of the household. The men are marginal to its maintenance and social reproduction.

The third, and most extreme solution is to receive money from storekeepers, boat owners, or other well-off men in exchange for sexual favors. Women call this "to pay with bastards" (*pagar com a raca*). In other words, the woman is forced to run the risk of bearing illegitimate children who are the result of the economic failure of her husband. The boat fishermen is now marginal to the nuclear family as its reproducer as well as its producer or genitor. The woman becomes the head of household and the center of the construction of the domestic reality, while the husband retreats increasingly from that world and the social interaction it engenders. This process of estrangement between husband and wife often includes phenomena such as verbal and physical abuse of women by men, heavy drinking by men and sometimes by women, severe emotional depression for both partners, male guilt feelings interspersed with promises to become responsible again, anger toward and financial neglect of the household, conflicts with boat owners, frequent crew switching (often to boats of inferior quality), increasing indebtedness, and adulterous affairs of men and women. Many boat fishing households have experienced at least several of these manifestations of conjugal tension. Their accumulation might first lead to a temporary separation and eventually, if no improvement sets in, to divorce. Despite the frequency of marital conflict, the divorce rate seems relatively low, although high in relation to the more stable marriages among households of canoe fishermen. Men's prolonged absence is certainly a factor, but more important are the difficulties divorced women face in finding new, reliable partners, and the social stigma— divorce is condemned by church, the community, and the parents. Much has to occur for a couple to separate permanently and divide their small possessions. The feeble arrangement will not be broken as long as there is at least a small transactional flow of benefits.

The dozen or so boat and canoe fishermen who are in the privileged position of being able to switch back and forth between fishing modes are an interesting control group. They show that conjugal conflicts cannot be attributed primarily to the characters or personalities of the fishermen or their wives, but that these are consequences of structural and social differences between canoe and boat fishing. Wives of canoe fishermen understand that seasonal variations in shallow-water marine resources motivate some men to temporarily fish on boats, but they abhor its social consequences. They believe that peer pressure persuades the men to spend their small earnings in bars. The home ceases to be the central focus of their attention, but becomes a service station for dirty laundry, food, and a bed. Once a woman renders these services, the man joins his boat fishing colleagues at the harbor. Domestic tensions are of course imminent.

When a boat is under repair or an unsolvable personal conflict with the crew or the boat owner has arisen, a boat fisherman might borrow a canoe to fish temporarily in shallow waters. The ensuing changes in behavior are clearly noticed by the women. They urge the men to proceed with canoe fishing. One woman even bought an old canoe for her husband "in order to save him from liquor," but the fisherman made a few boat trips and fell back into his old drinking habit. Some men actually succeed in switching to canoe fishing permanently. None of the canoe fishermen wanted to give up canoe fishing for more than a few weeks, while several boat fishermen expressed the desire for shallow water fishing but they were unable to accumulate enough money to make the investment in canoes and gill nets.

The third social category of women in the Camurim fishing economy consists of the wives of boat owners. Their life style and social status differ significantly from those of the other two categories. Both for the women and their husbands, the domestic life of the nuclear family ranks second to their public lives. The conjugal relationships reflect the diverging social interests of the partners. Boat owners and their wives are not close, nor estranged, but distant and aloof. Boat owners spend little time at home. Those who do not go fishing can invariably be found near the river observing the movements in the harbor. Often they do not return home for lunch but go to a small eating place in the company of fish dealers. At night, they run virtually a circuit of taverns and late-night bars with occasional visits to prostitutes. While canoe fishermen realize themselves and gain social prestige in the domestic reality, the boat owners find the meaning of their existence in the creation of a public reality with conspicuous leisure and consumption in the presence of influential political friends, wealthy acquaintances, and mistresses. Those boat owners who can maintain a high living standard and a network of middle class friends without fishing themselves are attributed the highest prestige by all persons involved in the fishing economy.

The wives of boat owners are not pleased with the extramarital affairs, nor with their spouses' limited domestic life, but they do not complain as long as they can continue to live in a comfortable way and rub shoulders with women of high social status, befriended through their husbands' connections. They have an active public life of social calls to the homes of the wives of ranchers, cocoa planters, physicians, civil servants, and bank employees.

The formal obligations of husband and wife are met more than satisfactorily but without much emotional commitment or consideration. Women fulfill few domestic obligations themselves; they have servants to wash, cook, clean, and keep an eye on the children. Household chores do not fall unevenly on the shoulders of the women, as is the case among boat fishermen, nor do boat owners assist with domestic tasks as canoe fishermen do, but boat owners remark that they free their wives from their share of the conjugal obligations by paying for servants. Because of the small transactional basis of their relationship, boat owners and their wives are not strongly emotionally involved with each other, but rather pursue public acclaim to satisfy the human need of pertaining to significant social groups that give meaning to their lives.

The diverse conjugal experiences of women in Camurim modify their gender conceptions. *Marianismo* as a common ideological denominator for women differentiates into three partially distinct attitudes. The wives of boat owners have emulated certain aspects of male ideology. They are uninterested in the household, try to attain a high public status, and have a life style that is far removed from the image of the woman as a madonna-like figure who silently bears her subjugation to men and suffers her anguished fate in solitude. These women are self-confident and delight in the privileges wrested from their husbands' oversensitive male egos. The congruent interests of canoe fishermen and their wives, their complementary roles, and their desire for compromise make women feel satisfied with their position as homemakers. *Machismo* is attenuated in the intimacy of the domestic domain and makes women accept the sexual division of economy and society. They know of the suffering of other women and hence embrace the beliefs of female moral superiority but they have few everyday experiences that relate to this ideology. The wives of poor boat fishermen, however, do not receive proper support at home, and are confronted with an unmitigated aggressive version of *machismo*. Unlike the other women, who do not challenge the social consequences of male ideology as long as their demands are met, the women of poor households debunk male claims to inherent superiority as self-inflated justifications of their dominance in society. Instead of receiving help, the wife of a poor fisherman who searches for the means of livelihood is almost perceived as propositioning in public. She is taken advantage of by men who deny women a structural position in the economy. Her experience of the complete suspension of normative conjugal obligations reveals a fundamental sexual inequality which she accepts with resignation and which subsequently strengthens the belief in her own moral superiority.

CONCLUSION

Gender ideologies are not as dualistic as the sexes they depict because the interpretations of their meanings and the translation into other conceptions of male-female interaction are multiple. The capacity of sexual meanings to unite and segregate men and women is reflected in the interpretational conflicts surrounding the definition of the conjugal relationships in Camurim. A hermeneutic approach exposes these different interpretations because it does not focus on one level of meaning but attempts to understand the circular interplay of several levels of meaning that intersect within the conjugal relationship. This emphasis on interpretation does not preclude the importance of a structural approach. The position of women can be understood simultaneously through their interpretations and through the social, structural, and economic circumstances that are beyond the horizon of everyday experience. Women cannot determine the direction of their future because of a cultural heritage that confines women to the house, defines them as social extensions of men, and therefore offers few possibilities for female social mobility. These sociocultural parameters carry even more weight when men monopolize the economic activities that must produce the material foundation of the social and cultural realities that give meaning to the existence of both men and women. The spatial and social separation of the sexes in fishing economies enhances the contrast between a female-centered domestic domain and a male-centered public domain. Lack of direct experience of the other's problems make incursions into the domain of the opposite sex difficult. However, even if the sex discrimination were to vanish and women were to succeed in occupying positions in the fishing economy now monopolized by men, they would still encounter the same impediments to social mobility felt by men. Camurim's economy is part of a larger economic system whose structure does not give fishermen or their wives the opportunities to rise above the level of bare subsistence. The choice of how to earn such a living depends to a certain degree on the fishermen themselves, but is obscured by an incomprehension of the social consequences of different fishing modes, as well as a lack of insight into the overall economic structure of a highly stratified society. That choice, however, is crucial because it directs them into patterns of interaction that affect the conjugal relationship.

As the data have demonstrated, canoe fishermen are independent producers in the sense that they make all major economic
decisions. They have no influence on the prices of consumption or
of capital goods, and therefore will not be able to significantly raise
their incomes without major changes in the national economy, but
they are directly responsible for their families and businesses.
Somehow, this control makes the lower-class status and the structural inequality of the society more bearable and gives them a feeling
of pride in the little they have: their canoe, their small house, and
especially their wife and children. Many boat fishermen lack even
these positive feelings amidst the all-encompassing structural af-
front on the human dignity of an entire class. They not only earn
little and are often in debt, but they also suffer under the power of
capital owners who, in turn, are also entangled in an economic system that imposes the prices for the products they offer for sale. In
order to secure labor for their ventures, boat owners cultivate
relationships of dependency that extend into the households of
fishermen, and usurp their control over its reproduction. The prolonged absence from a home full of senseless hardships, the loss of
confidence in themselves as men, the mistrust in their fellow-men,
the disillusion about their own lives, and the lack of faith in a better future for their children, reduce men's affinity for the nuclear
family, and estrange men and women. The wives of boat fishermen
become involved in this situation almost by accident, but they are
the ones who bear the ultimate consequences. They are even more
victimized by social inequality than their husbands because parental responsibility for the children falls on them. These women have
to accept low and subjected statuses, or exploit themselves sexually to be able to survive. The wives of canoe fishermen and boat
owners are also subject to male authority but they at least are in a
continued dialogue with men inside the privacy of the home and
thus have some power to influence the actions of their husbands.
As long as they are able to preserve their husbands' inclination
toward the domestic reality, then their position offers hope for positive changes that together with an increased awareness and
self-realization will enhance their influence on society.

Notes

1. The research in Brazil, from August 1982 to October 1983, was made
   possible by a grant from the National Science Foundation.

   This article could not have been written without the help of my spouse
   Claudia Bernardi. She collected and verified many of the data presented
   here. As a male researcher, I found it easier to obtain information on

the wives of canoe fishermen, because I would visit the men and women in their homes. Boat owners and fishermen could usually be found in the harbor, in bars, or in brothels. They were seldom at home and this made it difficult to establish rapport with their wives. Claudia's assistance was therefore indispensable. The responsibility for the rendition of the data, however, is entirely mine.

Sexual Division of Labor, Risk, and Economic Success along the Sherbro Coast of Sierra Leone

7

Thomas S. Krabacher

In recent years researchers have become concerned with the declining economic status of women in many African societies. Beginning in the 1970s a growing number of field studies have drawn attention to the ways in which colonialism and post-independence development policies have tended to weaken the economic power and independence of both rural and urban women in subsaharan Africa (Boserup 1970; Wipper 1972; Bay 1982; Bandarage 1984). In many traditional African subsistence societies, female labor was important not only in childbearing and childrearing, but also in agricultural production, food processing, marketing, and various handicraft industries. In many West African societies, this involvement permitted women to participate equally with men in the domestic economy, and also afforded them a certain degree of economic independence. Throughout large parts of subsaharan Africa, this pattern has changed dramatically in recent years as a consequence of colonial policies and post-independence development efforts. Rather than improved conditions for women, the results have frequently been the opposite: increased workloads, falling production, restriction of economic roles, and declining economic security (Wipper 1972; Oppeng, Okali and Houghton 1975; Rogers 1980; Bay 1982). Even more serious, however, has been the steady erosion of the African woman's traditional independence as a consequence of modernization efforts. In many agrarian societies, change from kin-centered, domestically-oriented production systems to cash-oriented commodity production has frequently resulted in the elimination of shared economic responsibility between spouses, leaving control of productive resources such as land, tools, and labor, mainly in the hands of men (Wipper 1972; Oppeng, Okali and Houghton 1975; Rogers 1980; Bay 1982).

In contrast to women in agrarian societies, women from African fishing communities have shown considerable success in adapting to social and economic change. They have been able to maintain productivity, continue to play important roles in processing and marketing, and, in some cases, have moved directly into fishing itself (Christensen 1977). This applies to many women in the fishing communities along the Sherbro Coast of Sierra Leone. Fishing in Sierra Leone, more than in any other West African country, remains a rural activity centered around small-scale, village-based fisheries. These fisheries are currently experiencing significant social and economic change as a result of expanding markets and the introduction of new fishing technologies over the past three decades. These changes have affected not only the fishermen directly involved in production, but also the economic status of many of the women involved in processing and marketing the catch.

This chapter examines the impact of these changes on the economic status of women along the Sherbro Coast.[1] It also attempts to explain why, in contrast to the cases of women elsewhere in rural Africa, these changes have generally been positive for women in local fishing communities. It argues that female success in the Sherbro Coast fishing economy can be attributed to two factors: first, the local household women's ability to maintain independent control over the essentially "domestic" task of fish processing in face of the increased commercialization of the local fisheries; and second, the changing nature of economic risk along the Sherbro Coast.

THE SHERBRO COAST

Sierra Leone's Sherbro Coast is a 120 kilometer stretch of low-lying coastal plain extending from the base of the Freetown Peninsula in the north to Sherbro Island and the Turtle Islands in the south. The region lies at the northern edge of West Africa's forest zone where 460 centimeters of rain ordinarily fall during the April to October wet season. The coastline is a mosaic of estuaries, riverine creeks, mangrove swamps, beach ridges, sand bars, and small islands, all of which combine to create a series of diverse shallow water environments easily exploited by traditional fishing techniques.

Culturally and historically, the Sherbro Coast is part of a broader geographical region, West Africa's upper Guinea coast. Linguistic diversity is high along most of the upper Guinea coast and mutually unintelligible language groups often exist in close proximity. However, language differences tend to mask a broader cultural uniformity which exists throughout most of the region. Multilingualism, similar environmental and economic conditions, fluidity in traditional political alliances, and the influential role played by interethnic sodalities such as the male (*poro*) and female (*bundu* or *sande*) secret societies have tended to promote a common cultural heritage among most peoples of the upper Guinea coast. In recent centuries there has been a steady blurring of cultural differences, until the distinctions between groups are now primarily linguistic (Murdock 1959:261).

Members of three ethnolinguistic groups— the Sherbro, Temne, and Mende— predominate on the Sherbro Coast today. The Sherbro, from whom the region derives its name, are the oldest known inhabitants of the coast and the only group present there today with no tradition of past migration into the region. In the past, the Sherbro were one of the most prominent groups along Africa's upper Guinea coast, controlling a considerably larger section of the coastline than they do at present. In recent centuries, however, Sherbro territory has been steadily reduced due to pressure from surrounding groups; their present distribution is confined primarily to the present-day Sherbro Coast and the immediately adjacent hinterland. Traditional Sherbro life is closely linked to their littoral environment, and the Sherbro in the past have had the reputation of being "the fishermen" of Sierra Leone.

By contrast, the Temne and Mende are recent arrivals on the coast. The Temne and Mende are the two largest ethnic groups in Sierra Leone, and both have been expanding gradually into what traditionally has been Sherbro territory. Although in the past the Sherbro traditionally have been considered the most prominent fishing people in Sierra Leone, in recent years it has been the Temne who have been the quickest to adopt the more capital intensive, commercially-oriented fishing techniques that have started to appear along the coast.

The significance of these ethnic differences tends to vary along the Sherbro Coast. Ethnicity seems to be of greatest significance today in the political arena, where it frequently has a major impact on events at both local and national levels. Its role is considerably less important, however, in shaping day-to-day life on the local village level. Although every individual can claim affiliation with a specific ethnic group, numerous features of local society such as interethnic marriage, fostering of children across ethnic lines, and the pan-ethnic nature of major institutions such as the male and female secret societies,[2] have tended to blur the importance of ethnicity in daily life. In fishing communities along the Sherbro Coast, almost all villages and many households are multiethnic in nature, and as a result, social and economic interaction across ethnic lines is generally high.

Population density on the Sherbro Coast averages 34 people per square kilometer, a value that is low for Sierra Leone as a whole and for much of West Africa in general. Settlement is ordinarily in villages of 500 or fewer. Only on the Shenge Peninsula do villages approach 1000 in size. Communities are frequently isolated either by mangrove swamps or by their location on offshore islands, and are often accessible only by water. Only in a few locations do laterite roads connect coastal villages to the more heavily populated interior. Bonthe, located on the eastern end of Sherbro Island, is the only town of significant size along the coast, but due to its isolation, it plays only a limited role in the economic life of the region. Most external economic ties are with regional market centers located in the interior or with the capital city of Freetown, to the north. Depending on one's location on the coast, a one or two day journey is usually necessary to reach these urban centers.

The economy of the region is a combination of fishing and bush-fallow cultivation. Rice is the principal food crop and cassava is an important co-staple. In almost all coastal communities, fishing is the dominant activity. The household compound is the basic unit of production for both agrarian and maritime activity. A household ordinarily consists of residents related to the household head by cognatic descent or marriage, as well as non-kin who may be clients or wards of the household head (MacCormack 1982). Household members may often come from more than one ethnic group, and this is frequently the case along the Sherbro Coast, where intermarriage between Sherbro, Temne, and Mende is common. Such ethnic differences within the household, however, are generally of little importance in shaping daily household life. The household head is ordinarily the eldest member of the core descent group, and in Sherbro country it is not unusual for this individual to be a woman. A survey of selected fishing villages in 1980-81 showed that 16 percent of all households were headed by women. Local production remains geared toward meeting domestic needs, although a significant proportion of the household output now is directed into the cash economy.

The case of women's work along the Sherbro Coast reflects a pattern common to much of West Africa as a whole, where women traditionally not only maintain control of most basic household tasks but frequently have access to lucrative outside economic opportunities, such as handicrafts or trading, as well. Along the Sherbro Coast today, both men and women participate in a wide spectrum of economic activities, and both sexes derive status and profit from their participation. At the same time, economic tasks are routinely assigned to one sex or the other. The heavy work of clearing fields for planting is a male activity, while pounding rice is a female one. Even on those occasions where both men and women are engaged in the same activity (for example, planting fields), labor is organized into male and female teams so that sexes do not directly compete with each other for; ideally, male and female tasks should be complementary, not competitive. Both males and females among the Sherbro and other ethnic groups agree that such divisions of labor are just and appropriate.

Women play an important role in the village economies of the Sherbro Coast, and most men readily and explicitly acknowledge that importance. Women generally have responsibility for those tasks which are culturally defined as "nurturing" (MacCormack 1978). Nurturing tasks include not only childbearing and childrearing, but also a wide variety of activities related to household management, such as gardening, gathering, aspects of agriculture, and food processing and cooking. Food processing includes the preparation of selected items (such as palm oil and preserved fish) for market exchange. In addition to these "nurturing" activities, many women are also prominent in local marketing and trade.

THE FISHERIES

Since at least the time of first European contact in the mid-fifteenth century, village-based marine fishing has been a specialized and intensive activity for most communities along the Sherbro Coast, contributing to local diets and providing an important commodity for market exchange. As in the case of local agriculture, a generally defined sexual division of labor exists in fishing communities: men are responsible for fishing while women control the processing and marketing of the catch. There are exceptions to this general pattern, for both women and children occasionally fish the nearby creeks and tidal pools. This is usually done with an improvised hook-and-line or by using a sweep net (known locally as the *woman's net*), a small net attached to a wicker frame which can be swept along in the water while wading through the shallows. Women and children may also collect shellfish exposed at low tide, or help haul in a beach seine. These efforts are irregular, production is usually low, and most of the catch is ordinarily consumed within the household. Because of this, and because such activities are shore-bound, the local people usually view them as a form of gathering, rather than fishing. Deep water fishing, where the bulk of production occurs, is purely men's work.

Traditional marine fishing centered around the small dug-out canoe and employed a wide variety of hook-and-line and netting techniques such as bottom lines, telegraph lines, cast nets, drift nets, set nets, and the beach seine.[3] The dug-out canoe ordinarily held one to three fishermen (frequently kin, although with no fixed pattern of kin-based crew-selection), and each type of gear was suited to a particular species and aquatic environment. Fishermen sought a variety of pelagic and demersal species, particularly the bonga (*Ethmalosa fimbriata*) a pelagic fish abundant in the shallow off-shore waters.

This pattern of fishing, employing small canoes and diversified techniques, is widely practiced along the Sherbro Coast today. Returns are frequently low but so is the capital investment required. Much of the catch is either consumed locally or traded with nearby communities for items such as rice, salt, or fresh drinking water. Occasional surpluses result from the canoe fisheries and these are usually dried and then carried inland for marketing.

Since the mid-1950s, several important structural changes have occurred in the village fisheries along the Sherbro Coast. The most important of these was the arrival of migrant Mfantse fishermen from Ghana who introduced major technological changes such as nylon nets, outboard engines, and large plank canoes up to 15 meters feet in length (now referred to locally as Ghana boats) capable of carrying a crew of 12 or more. An equally important introduction was use of the *Ali* net or ring net, a large nylon net design which, when fully deployed, runs from 200 to 600 meters or more in length, and hangs between 15 and 20 meters deep. Supported by cork floats on the top and lead weights on the bottom, it allows rapid encirclement of large shoals of fish which are then driven to gill themselves in the strands of the net. Following the expulsion of the Ghanaians by the Sierra Leone government in 1968, this technology was taken over by local Temne fishermen. Adoption of the new technologies greatly increased the size of the average catch, and made possible the regular production of surpluses for market exchange. However, while these changes have increased the potential returns to the fisherman, they have also greatly increased the size of the necessary capital investments.

A second major change has been the increased integration of the local village-based economies of the Sherbro Coast into the broader national economic system. Population increases throughout Sierra Leone have led to an increased demand for fish from inland markets. This demand was further stimulated by the initiation of large-scale diamond mining activity in the southeastern region of the country between 1956 and 1961, creating a major market in mining areas for fish to feed mine workers. As a result, the once intermittent market trade in dried fish has expanded into a major economic activity for a significant portion of the coastal population.

The result is a dual fishery along the Sherbro Coast. The traditional fishery is based around the dug-out canoe, employs small crews, seeks a diversity of species, and requires relatively little capital investment. Much of the catch is used for local subsistence; fishing households often practice small-scale farming as well, with time and labor divided between the two activities. The newer, market-oriented Ghana boat fishery involves larger boats and crews and, while returns may be greater, also involves heavy capital investment. It is not unusual for building and outfitting a Ghana boat to cost 200 times what it costs to carve and equip a traditional dug-out canoe. This commercial fishery has placed an ever-increasing emphasis on catching a single species, the bonga, because it appears in large shoals, is easily caught by Ghana boats using the *Ali* net, and is highly desirable in the marketplace. More and more of the catch is now by-passing the local economy in favor of distant markets. With its emphasis on catching a single pelagic species for commercial sale and not local consumption, it is the aquatic equivalent of cash-cropping.

These technological and economic changes have produced important social changes, as well. First, the dual fisheries tend to break down along ethnic lines. The newer fishing technology first introduced from Ghana has been adopted almost exclusively by Temne immigrants, who now own and operate the majority of the Ghana boats found along the Sherbro Coast. Temne dominance of the Ghana boat fishery has occurred for a number of reasons. Since the time of their first arrival in large numbers in the 1920s, the Temne have been present on the Sherbro Coast primarily as fishermen, and, as a group, have been closely attuned to changes occurring within the local fisheries. Furthermore, as recent arrivals along the coast, the Temne were in the position of outsiders, without the necessary kin-based rights to local agricultural land; thus they have had little opportunity in the past to leave fishing and to establish themselves in agrarian sectors of the economy. Finally, the Temne are viewed as the most economically aggressive people of Sierra Leone, and as such, they have been quick to take advantage of the expanded economic opportunities offered by the rise of the Ghana boat fishery. The Temne, with their rapid adoption of the newer fishing technologies, are now the *modern* "master fishermen" of Sierra Leone. The Sherbro, historically the predominant fishermen in the region, are now seen as a people reluctant to give up their traditional techniques.

Another important change has been an increase in the size of household compounds. In the late 1970s the average size of residential compounds in the Sherbro region as a whole was ten to eleven people (MacCormack 1978, 1982). However, field surveys in 1981-82 showed that for households engaged in the more capital intensive, commercially-oriented fishing, sizes tended to be considerably greater. Compounds of 25 or more are not uncommon, and some occasionally have 50 or more members. In these cases, the household head is also usually the boatowner, and the compound consists of not only his family and wards, but also of his crew members and their families as well. In such households, all men fish and almost all women are engaged in fish processing and trading. The boatowner acts as patron; he not only pays his crew members with a share of the catch,[4] but also provides them and their families with food and other household needs. As a patron, the boatowner is responsible for settling any disputes in which a household member may become involved, and, if the individual has no other source of income, for settling any personal debts they may incur, as well.

FISH PROCESSING AND MARKETING

Men fish and women process and market the catch. This division of labor is common not only along the Sherbro Coast but in other West African fishing societies as well (Christensen 1977; Gladwin and Gladwin 1971), and reflects the dominant role played by women in the processing and marketing of foodstuffs throughout subsaharan Africa.[5]

Women ordinarily meet returning fishermen at the beach in the late afternoon or early evening, whereupon the catch from each boat is counted out and apportioned to the women waiting to receive it. The catch is ordinarily handed over for processing to a woman from the fisherman's own household. In smaller households, this is ordinarily a wife or some kinswoman of the fisherman or boatowner, although in larger residential compounds a fisherman's catch may be processed by a female household member to whom he is not directly related. Occasionally, however, buying and selling relationships will exist between fishermen and women from different households. Fish are priced according to their size and species. Although prices may be adjusted seasonally (and occasionally on a daily or weekly basis), such adjustments are minor and a uniform price is offered to all fishermen along a given beach.[6] Business arrangements between buyers and sellers tend to be long term; this provides the fisherman with a regular buyer for his catch, and the women with a dependable supply of fish.

All fish except for those immediately used in cooking are quickly processed. The bonga, which comprises the bulk of most catches nowadays, is an oily fish, and, unless it is preserved, will begin to spoil only four or five hours after it is caught. Fish are occasionally processed by salting or sun-drying, but smoke-drying is the most common form of preservation. Smoking fish is quick (it can be done overnight), relatively inexpensive, and can be done in large quantities; ordinarily only one or two women are required to process the catch of a large Ghana boat. The preserving is done in a tightly enclosed smoking hut (*banda*) where the fish are spread upon wire racks over a low, smokey fire. During processing, larger fish must be cut and gutted, some species descaled, and the size of the fire must be regulated to assure preservation yet prevent burning. Children frequently assist with these tasks, and it is as children that most women originally acquire their knowledge of processing techniques. Smoked fish to be sold at market remain stored in the *banda* until just before market time to reduce the chance of spoiling. With occasional resmoking, fish can be kept for a month or more without significant loss of quality.

Village women may personally transport dried fish to market, but the more common practice is to sell the fish to traders who visit the coastal villages on a regular basis.[7] There is no clear sexual division of labor in the fish trade, as both men and women regularly travel to the coast to buy fish for resale at inland market centers. Traders schedule their visits according to the village's accessibility and the volume of fish it is regularly capable of supplying. Communities at the tip of the Shenge Peninsula, such as Katta and Plantain Island for example, are both easily accessible by road and produce large quantities of fish. As a result, traders visit these villages by lorry to buy fish on a regular twice-a-week schedule. On the other hand, smaller, more isolated communities are visited less frequently. Fish buyers travel by boat to villages in the mangrove regions north or south of the Shenge area only once every ten days or two weeks, and to villages on outer Sherbro Island and in the Turtle Islands only about once a month.

Business is conducted between village women and fish traders on an individual basis, and once business arrangements are established, the fish processor will generally continue to sell to the same trader on subsequent visits. As in the case of business relationships between the fishermen and the women who process their catch, such long-term arrangements provide stability for both fish processor and fish trader: one is guaranteed a regular buyer for her fish, and the other a regular supply.

Village fishing increasingly involves money, and women are central to most cash transactions. In the past, when catches were small and marketable surpluses limited, a fisherman would hand the catch directly over to a wife or other kinswoman for processing without payment. In such cases, the household would then maintain a single set of accounts. However, with the increasing commercialization of today's fisheries, more and more exchanges of fish, even those between spouses or kin, are now treated as cash exchanges. Accounts are usually settled at the time the fish change hands. Women pay cash to fishermen on the beach for the fresh catch and are in turn paid cash for their smoke-dried fish by traders visiting the village. In such cases spouses engaged in production and in processing and marketing keep separate accounts and are not financially accountable to one another.

Fish processing is an attractive economic activity for most women since it requires no large initial investment of capital to get started and offers the opportunity for quick cash returns. The single largest capital investment is the smoking *banda* common to most fishing households. Because these are usually made from local materials in a wattle-and-daub and thatched-roof design, they are relatively inexpensive to construct and maintain. The only important operating expense other than the cost of the fresh fish itself, is the cost of fuel for the smoking process, which must be purchased from professional woodcutters if women or members of their household are unable to collect it themselves. In the communities of Katta and Plantain Island during 1981-82, women received a price for smoked fish that averaged 20 percent above what they paid for the fresh catch. After expenses involved with the smoking process (mainly firewood costs) were deducted, this left an average profit of 12 percent.

It is important to note that not all women have access to a regular supply of fish. Ordinarily, it is the wife of a fisherman or boatowner who has control over her husband's catch. If the household is polygynous, the senior wife has first claim to the fish, although if the day's catch was large, a portion may be allotted to the junior wives as well. However, because it only takes a few women to process even a really large catch, many women from larger households never have a chance to become involved in the fish business on a regular basis. It is common in such cases for the control of household fish processing to rest in the hands of only one or two elder women.

Household women not involved in the fish business have a number of economic options, the most common of which is to take up some form of petty trading.[8] Cooperation among wives rather than competition is the general rule in coastal households, and senior wives will frequently provide the financial backing necessary for a younger wife to get started in the trading business (MacCormack 1982). A second alternative is for a junior woman to secure her own source of fish outside the household and enter the fish processing business herself. Women newly entering the business generally offer no serious competition to women already well-established as processors and traders because the inland market demand for fish well exceeds the production levels of most coastal villages. Thus, younger women are not competing with older established women for a share of a limited market. The most common way for a junior woman to establish her own steady supply of fresh fish is by arranging to buy the catch shares belonging to unmarried crew members of a local Ghana boat. Although specific cases were notoriously difficult to pin down, one frequently heard stories during fieldwork of women who established sexual liaisons with local fishermen primarily on the basis of the amount of fish such relationships could provide them.

The most successful fish processors, and in economic terms the most successful women in the coastal communities in general, are those who can secure a steady supply of fish. For such women, fish processing can prove very lucrative. Large, commercially-oriented fishing households may easily process and sell several hundred leones worth of fish each week.[9] In line with the practice of maintaining separate accounts, all profits accrued through processing and marketing remain in the hands of household women. Frequently such women are financially well off by local standards, may occasionally head their own households, and, by investing in other activities such as shopkeeping or trading, tend to exert a strong economic influence in their own communities.

RISK AND CAPITAL ACCUMULATION

Throughout most of subsaharan Africa, the shift of rural economies towards more highly capitalized commodity-oriented production has seriously undermined the economic status of African women. In general, it is the men who have been the beneficiaries of government development programs, new technologies, and the increased privatization of productive resources, while women are seen as occupying an increasingly marginal position in the changing economy. The economic position of many African women today is considerably worse than it was for their counterparts only one or two generations earlier.

The fishing societies of Sierra Leone's Sherbro Coast have also experienced considerable technological and economic change, yet they offer an interesting counter-example to this pattern. Here, women continue to play an indispensible role in the local maritime-based economy as processors and sellers of fish. The increasingly commercialized nature of the local economy, rather than having a detrimental effect on the economic position of local women, has actually provided them with an opportunity for even greater involvement in the market economy through expansion of their roles as food processors and petty traders. Hendrix (1983) notes that in many West African fishing communities, women play a far larger role in the capitalist sector of the economy than do men. In fact, given present-day patterns of investment and risk in the Sherbro Coast fisheries, one can argue that, as individuals, women fish processors occupy a more stable position than individual men in the local economy, and have better chances than men for economic advancement and capital accumulation.

Fishing is a risky business everywhere, and along the Sherbro Coast the risks to fishermen are primarily financial. In the traditional dug-out canoe fishery, economic risk is relatively low; the capital investment in equipment is small, and because fishing is often not a full-time occupation, the fisherman can easily switch to some other activity such as agriculture during times when fishing is poor. However, with increasing commercialization and the adoption of new technologies, the financial risks assumed by fishermen have greatly increased. Initial capital investments are very high (see Table 1) and a boatowner usually must go into debt in order to enter the business. Daily operating and maintenance costs are also high, since fuel expenses for the Ghana boat's outboard engine alone will run between 35 and 50 leones on an average fishing day. In addition to direct fishing-related costs, the boatowner, in his role as patron, must also meet the daily expenses of the household residential compound, which include such items as food, clothing, medical and educational fees, and occasionally any debts or legal fees accrued by household members. Ideally, these greater expenses are offset by the higher returns to be made as a Ghana boat fisherman. On a reasonably good day a single boat can easily land 100 to 200 leones worth of fish, and occasional catches valued at 800 or 1000 leones do occur. Nonetheless, the boatowner also runs the risk that a prolonged string of bad fishing days, or a major accident resulting in loss of engine, boat, or gear, will put him out of business permanently.

TABLE 1: Outfitting Costs[1] (1981)

ITEM	COST	ITEM	COST
Canoe (carving)	Le 10	Boat Construction	Le 1300
Gear (hook and line)[2]	Le 8	Gear (net, accessories)	Le 3000
Other (paddles, sails)	Le 15	Engine (25 hp)	Le 2500
		Other (anchor, paddles, etc.)	Le 140
Total	Le 33		Le 5940

1. All values are given in leones.
2. Will be somewhat higher when nets are employed as gear.

Source: Fieldnotes, 1981-1982.

The central issue in the success or failure of a fisherman along the Sherbro Coast today is his ability to reproduce his means of production. For a Ghana boat owner this depends on whether he is able to pay off the debts he incurred with the initial purchase of his boat, engine, and gear before it becomes time to replace these items. If the initial debts have not been repaid, the fisherman will have had no chance to accumulate any savings towards their replacement, and because he was unable to pay off his first set of debts, he will be viewed as a poor risk for any future loans. However, should the boatowner manage to pay off these initial debts, he can begin building up savings for the eventual replacement of his present equipment and perhaps even for investment in additional boats and gear. Of critical importance in the repayment of these initial debts is the length of time a boatowner can maintain his original equipment in operating condition—the longer the time before replacement, the more time available in which to pay off the loan. Along the Sherbro Coast this period is often not very long, usually the working life of an outboard engine. The engines in use on most Ghana boats tend to be lightweight sport engines of 25 horsepower or less which are poorly suited for the heavy day-to-day use they receive in fishing. Such engines frequently begin to break down after about two years, and, for many fishermen, replacement after such a short period is extremely difficult if not impossible.

Events in the world economy also have begun to have an important effect on coastal economic life as fishermen increasingly have come to depend on the use of imported goods. Many items essential to the newer Ghana boat fishery, such as nylon cord for nets, nails used in boat construction, outboard engines, and gasoline are now all imported. During the late 1970s and early 1980s local prices for most of these items rose dramatically as a result of inflation, rising world petroleum prices, and the declining value of the leone against most major currencies. The result has been a further increase in the financial burden placed on local fishermen as higher prices on imported goods have increased the costs of both new and replacement equipment, and higher petroleum costs have added to his daily operating expenses. Equally unfortunate for the fisherman, fish prices have tended to remain stable over most of this period, and there has been no corresponding rise in the price received for their catch to compensate for the increased costs of production. As a result, relatively few new boatowners have entered the Ghana boat fishery in recent years, while, over the same period, a number of fishermen have been forced to leave the business, due either to debts or to the loss of equipment they were unable to replace.

In contrast, women who process and sell fish are subject to little of the economic risk facing most boatowners. Fish processing does not require use of capital intensive equipment and, unlike the case of fishermen, no large initial investment or indebtedness is necessary. The *banda* and smoking racks used for processing are relatively inexpensive and are manufactured locally; unlike a fisherman's boat, engine, or nets, if damaged or worn out these items are easily repaired or replaced. The most common form of *banda* maintenance usually consists of little more than applying a new layer of clay to the walls or rethatching a section of roof. This work is frequently performed using readily available household labor. The only commercially manufactured item used in *banda* construction is the wire mesh found in most smoking racks; such mesh, however, is inexpensive and will last indefinitely. In consequence, the task of reproducing the means of production, which can be a serious problem for many fishermen, is not particularly difficult for the women who process fish, since their initial investment, and the cost of eventually replacing that investment, is so much less.

Additionally, fish processors do not have to contend with the high daily operating costs experienced by fishermen. The amount a woman spends on fuel to smoke a given quantity of fish is ordinarily considerably less than the cost of the gasoline required to land the same catch. Furthermore, unless a women herself heads a large household compound, her daily domestic expenses will be well below those of a boatowner who is also a household head. What is most important, however, is that, unlike a fisherman, a fish processor is not required to risk her money on a daily basis against the possibility of receiving little or nothing in return. It is not unusual for a boat consuming 40 leones worth of gasoline in the search for fish during the day to return to the beach with a catch worth considerably less than this; a boatowner must, as a matter of course, be able to absorb such losses. For the fish processor, on the other hand, there is no such risk. If there are no fish to be had at the beach at the end of a day, she still has no expenses to worry about: for that day the door of the *banda* is simply kept closed, and the fires for smoking left unlit.

Consequently, one can argue that women who process and sell fish have an economic advantage over fishermen in the same community. While both may benefit from the larger catches that occur through use of more capital-intensive fishing techniques, women processors, by maintaining separate accounts, can take advantage of the larger catches without assuming any of the attendant risks of production. As a result, those women who are successful at fish processing and selling over the years often have been able to accumulate considerable wealth. In villages along the Sherbro Coast many women in the fishing business are quite well off as measured against any local standard of financial success, and wield an economic influence over local affairs comparable to that of the wealthiest males.

Division of Labor and Economic Success

The economic success of African fishing women is striking when compared to the deteriorating position of women in many African rural economies. The evidence from a wide variety of case studies indicates that, with increasing incorporation of traditional economies into broader market-oriented economic systems, the resulting sexual division of labor is one generally detrimental to the economic status of women; in such cases, female labor tends to be undervalued and underpaid, and women are progressively excluded from participating in the more productive sectors of the economy (Sacks 1979; Leacock and Etienne 1980; Bandarage 1984). A clear division of labor by gender exists along the Sherbro Coast, based primarily upon traditional sex roles found in the local economy. Nonetheless, while this division of labor is largely exclusionary (women are never involved in the highly productive deep water fisheries, and men hardly ever process their catch), it does not undermine the economic status of local women; rather, it may be argued, it forms an important basis for their economic success.

Traditional female roles along the Sherbro Coast centered around the management of the household compound and gave women control over many of those activities Rosaldo (1974) assigns to the "domestic domain" and which MacCormack (1978) has identified as "nurturing." Important among these activities are the cooking and marketing of household surpluses. MacCormack (1982) has observed that in the Sherbro region, "cooking" is a broad concept that includes not only the preparation of meals but also a wide variety of food processing activities, including the processing of fish. Petty trading, which is also a well-established tradition among West African women in general, ordinarily involved the marketing of a wide range of locally-produced items such as fruits, handicrafts and fish. In the traditional dugout canoe fisheries, production was limited and fish handling was just one part of a broader round of subsistence-related household tasks. However, with the advent of new fishing technologies and increased commercialization, fish processing and fish marketing occupy a much more prominent role in the local household economy and have become increasingly lucrative for the local women involved. Because women have been able to retain control over these expanded processing and marketing activities as part of the traditional division of labor, they have also been able to retain control over the increased profits that result.

Commercialization of West Africa's village fisheries has offered opportunities not only for those male boatowners able to expand production by investing in new fishing technologies, but also for women who have control over processing and marketing the larger catch that results. Christensen (1977) notes how women fish traders in the highly commercialized Mfantse fishing communities near Cape Coast, Ghana have become an important economic force in the local economy by serving as an important source of loans to fishermen and by investing as absentee owners in boats and gear. A similar pattern is emerging along Sierra Leone's Sherbro Coast: although the fisheries there are not yet as commercialized as those in Ghana, women who work in fish processing and selling are beginning to emerge as a powerful sector of the local economic community. Women are frequently a source of the small loans occasionally needed by fishermen to cover gasoline costs or repairs on equipment, and in some cases they have begun to invest in boats and gear themselves.

Women have thus benefited from the traditional division of labor which excludes them from actually participating in fishing, the primary productive activity. In African agrarian societies it has been the woman's loss of control over the means of production through the growing privatization of land, technology, and labor that has been one of the most frequent causes of her declining economic status. In African maritime communities, on the other hand, it is this lack of direct involvement in actual production which has shielded women from many of the financial risks and uncertainties associated with fishing. Economic risk has emerged as a major theme in a number of studies of maritime communities. In fishing communities worldwide, entrepreneurs frequently prefer investing in the commercial aspects of fishing such as processing, transportation and marketing rather than in production itself, since in such land-oriented activities, risks tend to be less and the returns safer and more reliable (Breton 1977; Acheson 1981; McCay 1981). This pattern is borne out along the Sherbro Coast: lower risk and more reliable returns are found in the processing and marketing sectors of the fishing economy. The case of the Sherbro Coast is unusual, however, in that control of these shore-based activities is dictated not so much by outside entrepreneurial investment as by the traditional division of labor in coastal West African society.

CONCLUSIONS

Compared with women in other parts of rural Africa, women in the fishing communities of the Sherbro Coast have been able to establish and maintain a high degree of financial success and independence, a situation, this chapter argues, due in large part to the sexual division of labor in West African society. Nonetheless, it is necessary to note that a number of other factors are present which also contribute to their success, and which may not necessarily apply in the case of other West African fishing societies. Quinn (1978) notes, for example, that there is a significant failure rate among women fish sellers involved in the more highly commercialized, long distance fish trade in southern Ghana. While Quinn suggests that this may be due in part to the fact that not all fish sellers are equally efficient, she also observes that Ghanaian traders operate in a more uncertain economic environment: prices paid by Ghanaian traders for fish have risen in recent years, credit with which to purchase fish from fishermen is no longer as readily available, and market conditions are often unreliable. These problems are not yet faced by the women along the Sherbro Coast, since fish prices have generally remained stable, demand from inland market centers for fish remains high, and perhaps most importantly, the costs and uncertainties of the long distance fish trade are borne by travelling fish buyers, and not by the village women themselves.

One can argue, therefore, that some of the conditions that have made fish processing and trading so profitable for Sherbro Coast women may be only temporary. Should market conditions change, or should the price of fish paid by women at the beach begin to rise, this profitability may be undercut. In the past women along the Sherbro Coast possessed relatively high social status compared to women in many other parts of the developing world; given their success in the local maritime economy, they currently occupy an influential economic position as well. The question remains whether women in local fishing communities can translate their current economic strength into the kinds of political influence which might let them exercise some degree of control over any future economic trends which might otherwise undercut their current favorable economic status.

Notes

1. This paper is based on fieldwork conducted along the southern coast of Sierra Leone between October 1980 and March 1982. Primary study sites were the communities of Shenge, Katta, and Plantain Island, although periodic reconnaissance surveys were made along the length of what is referred to here as the Sherbro Coast. Research was sponsored by a Fulbright-Hayes Grant for Overseas Study.
2. The male *poro* secret society and the female *sande* or *bundu* secret society are major institutions in most societies along the upper Guinea coast. Membership is virtually universal since almost all children are initiated into their ranks around the age of puberty. Such societies serve to perpetuate cultural values, instruct youths in the responsibilities of adulthood, and adjudicate certain classes of disputes. These societies, particularly the *poro*, were a major political force in pre-colonial times and are still influential today. Important to the discussion here is the fact that as society membership and authority cross ethnic lines, the societies serve as an important influence in settling differences and promoting cooperation and cultural uniformity among local ethnic groups along the Sherbro Coast.
3. A brief description of gear types may be useful here. Bottom lines and telegraph lines are both hook-and-line techniques used for catching larger and more valuable fish such as snapper and barracuda; the bottom line, used to catch demersal species, is a weighted line which allows a baited hook to play along the sea floor; the telegraph line rides on the surface, buoyed by floats while a series of short, weighted lines

hang down from it. Cast nets are weighted handheld nets thrown by one man from either on shore or from a canoe to capture a small shoal of fish. Set nets and drift nets are both gill nets which capture fish by entangling them in the net mesh; set nets are staked out in fence-like fashion across shallow stretches of water, while drift nets, supported at the top by floats and hanging vertically, are allowed to drift freely in deeper water (frequently overnight) to be recovered later. Beach seines in use along the Sherbro Coast are similar to those found worldwide.

4. Crew payment along the Sherbro Coast takes the form of free use of the owner's boat, engine (including free fuel), and gear one day every week (at the time of the fieldwork this was usually a Wednesday). The value of all catches made that day belong to the boat's crew to divide among themselves.

5. Female labor is critical to local food economies throughout subsaharan Africa. A United Nations study has estimated that African women supply 70 percent of the labor in food production, 100 percent in food processing, 50 percent in food storage, 50 percent in animal husbandry, and 60 percent in marketing (UNECA/FAO 1975).

6. Fish prices throughout the fieldwork period remained extremely stable, showing very little fluctuation. Because of this, there was little opportunity to observe the operation of pricing mechanisms along the Sherbro Coast. When fishermen and fish processors were questioned about how and when price changes were determined, no clear answer was received.

7. Fish buyers belong to no single ethnic group, but rather reflect the ethnic composition of the inland market areas from which they originate. Since most inland markets served by the Sherbro Coast fisheries are in Mendeland (southern and eastern Sierra Leone), the majority of the buyers in the study tended to be Mende. This, however, merely reflects the geography of local trading patterns rather than a formal control of the fish trade by a particular ethnic group.

8. Common items sold by petty traders along the Sherbro Coast include locally produced foodstuffs such as rice, cassava, fruit, and the occasional hot prepared food. Also traded are commercial food items such as canned tomato paste, bouillon cubes, soft drinks, and sweets, as well as soap, kerosene, cloth, and other frequently used household items.

9. The basic monetary unit of Sierra Leone is the leone. Originally the value of the leone was fixed at one-half the value of the British pound, and the two-leone note is still frequently referred to as a "pound." In recent years the value of the leone has been freed from that of the pound, and its worth has varied considerably. The leone fluctuated between US$0.98 and US$0.84 during the time of fieldwork; the higher exchange rate is probably more reliable for the figures in this paper.

Women's Changing Roles in the Kerala Fishery

8

Leela Gulati

This chapter examines the unanticipated consequences of the Indo-Norwegian Fisheries Project on the lives of women in Kerala fishing villages.[1] In 1953, a project to modernize traditional, unmechanized fishing technologies was begun in a block of three traditional fishing villages in the State of Kerala, India. Mechanized boats and improved gear were introduced to modernize fishing, and freezing was introduced to improve fish preservation. While the project's primary concern was to increase productivity in fishing and fish preservation, planners also envisaged providing better health services and sanitation in and around the three villages. This study documents how the resulting changes in the technology of fishing and fish preservation in these communities have affected two generations of women in fishing households.

The project, as it was conceived and designed, was mainly geared towards men in the community. Since women did not go out fishing, it was assumed that changes in the technology of fishing were of no direct concern to them. The project's basic assumption was that if men of the fishing households could be helped to improve their economic position, their womenfolk would automatically stand to gain. This assumption was defended on the grounds that women in these households did little or nothing that was economically productive. This assumption, to say the least, is quite arguable. Even though women from Kerala fishing households were never directly engaged in what may be narrowly defined as fishing—that is, fish capture—they always participated in a number of related activities (not all of which were necessarily paid), which supplemented the average household's income-earning capacity. Unfortunately, there is hardly a census or survey which has adequately captured the full extent of work participation by women from the fishing households. This is as true today as it was a generation ago. Our autobiographical case studies and limited use of survey materials hardly begin to fill the male/female information gap. Still, on the basis of whatever macro-level information we could collect,[2] it appears that women's work participation has in fact increased considerably in all three study villages since the inception of the project.

In planning for change in fishing technology, questions such as the following have seldom been raised: How do women adjust to major technological changes in the work of their menfolk? What measures should be taken to draw women into the new situations created by technological changes? Indeed, women themselves sometimes have such a low estimation of their work and its return that they may be the least concerned about their involvement (or the lack of it) in work, present or prospective. Yet when circumstances change in such a way as to deprive women of what little work they are able to do, some households can be adversely affected. Actually, the decline in census figures of women's work participation in India since the turn of the century clearly shows that technological advance has tended to take work *away* from women. In spite of clear evidence, very little attention is paid to this aspect in most schemes and projects envisaging the introduction of new technology. Is it any wonder that a project meant principally to modernize fishing and fish preservation showed little concern for the impact on women's work in the households directly affected?

DEVELOPMENTS IN THE FISHERY

Kerala is one of the leading maritime states in India. It has a long coastline of 590 kilometres and a network of rivers, lakes and water areas which make it ideal for fishing. The waters of Kerala also are by far the richest in the country because of the intermixing of the nutrient-laden waters from the 41 west-flowing rivers with the seawater all along the coast. In fact, Kerala has a fishable area as large as that of the land surface of the state. The coastline is dotted with many protected bays, estuaries and natural harbours which provide excellent facilities for the launching and landing of fishing craft. As a result, the coastline supports 249 fishing villages, amounting to almost one village for every 2 1/4 kilometres.

The fishing population of Kerala as a whole is about 770,000, forming 159,000 households. Of these, 114,000 are marine (deep sea) fishing households and 45,000 are inland fishing households; there are about 160,000 active fishermen. Additionally, the fishery provides employment to another 350,000 persons.

Fishing occupies an important place in the economy of Kerala. It is an important source of food and protein, a major avenue of employment, and in recent years, it has become a major export industry. Kerala's population is essentially a fish-eating population; the level of fish consumption in Kerala is four times the national average. Until very recently, fish was a relatively cheap source of protein. In the early part of the 1970s, fish consumption stood at 15 kilograms per capita per annum. This figure has been declining, but the fact remains that in even the humblest of households there is at least one meal with fish every day. Eggs, milk, or meat rarely enter the diet.

The people engaged in fisheries come under three distinct categories: (1) those employed in the actual catching of fish, (2) those engaged in processing, and (3) those who engage in both activities. Most often, references to fishermen indicate those in the first category. With the high population pressure and high unemployment in the state, fisheries are a great source of economic diversification. Traditionally there existed some marginal export of dried fish and prawn powder from Kerala to the southeast Asian countries. However, the major preoccupation was to meet the domestic consumption requirements for fish for the population of Kerala and the border districts of the neighbouring state. In recent years, however, prawn export has become a major national economic activity and Kerala's share in it has become very significant, being close to 50 percent of the total. The total quantity of prawns exported went up 12 times between 1963 and 1977 and the value rose 40 times. Today, marine products rank as the third largest commodity export of the country, with prawns accounting for over 90 percent of the value of such exports.

THE INDO-NORWEGIAN PROJECT

The Indo-Norwegian Project was one of the earliest external aid projects agreed upon after India became independent in August 1947.[3] This first Scandinavian effort in India reflected the enthusiasm and motivation of Norway's ruling Labour Party to extend concrete help to less developed countries, in an area where Norwegians could offer technical know-how on the basis of their own long experience, and also where the benefits were most likely to reach the lower income groups.

The Norwegians were quite understandably anxious that aid they provided should have a clear focus in terms of economic activity, beneficiaries, and location, and that it should be concentrated, so that its effects could be visible within a reasonable period of time. Kerala was chosen to begin the project because it was a major maritime state of India with a sizable part of its population depending on fishing for its livelihood. Also around that time, Kerala State itself was seriously considering the introduction of some degree of mechanization in fishing.

The three original fishing villages chosen for the modernization project lie within the Neendakara area and form a geographically compact block. Before the project's inception, the fish caught in this area were sardine, butter fish, and mackerel; due to the introduction of mechanized fishing and the discovery of extensive prawn grounds some ten to fifteen kilometres offshore during the latter part of the 1960s, the composition of the catch switched considerably in favor of the prawns, and today, fishing for prawns dominates the catch. In fact, it would not be an exaggeration to say that fishing in the Neendakara area has come to stand for prawn fishing, and that it is the most important prawn fishing center in India.

In theory, the trawling operations are carried out throughout the year, but in fact, the peak fishing activity is concentrated in a short period of about three months during the southwest monsoons, between June and September. By contrast, the unmechanized, or "traditional" fishing fluctuates seasonally, but not so drastically.

There was virtually no freezing activity connected with fishing before the mid-1950s in Kerala State. Prawns from inland waters were boiled in seawater or brine and dried or otherwise processed. The finished product was exported as prawn pulp, mostly to Burma. Prawn pulp was a low priced export article and prawn fishing was not a very profitable activity. Since not all species could be easily dried and processed, there was considerable waste through spoilage and delay in the transportation of fish to consumption centers. The use of ice had to be accepted and made popular. Today, ice is used extensively in handling prawns and other species, even by traditional fishermen and women.

The Study Villages

The fishing folk of these villages are drawn primarily from two quite distinct religious groups, Catholic and Araya Hindu. The impact of technological change was distinctly different between those groups, depending upon their closeness to the main boat landing center. Two of the villages— Sakthikulangara (pop. 3,144) and Neendakara (pop. 3,282)— are almost entirely Catholic; Puthenthura (pop. 2,607) is almost exclusively Hindu of the Araya caste. In all three villages, there is a very small number of Muslims (ranging from one-half to seven-tenths of one percent) (see Table 1). The Araya caste is designated as "backward" by Kerala State, but are not counted among the scheduled castes and tribes identified as particularly disadvantaged in the Indian Constitution. Statistically, the Araya-dominated village of Puthenthura differs from the other two study villages in the following ways: the men are much more likely to have remained in "traditional" fishing; a relatively small number of fishermen also own mechanized boats; women marry at slightly later ages (averaging from a few months to a year); and married women in Puthenthura have a smaller number of children (averaging 3.70 for married women of all ages, as compared to figures of 4.74 and 3.86 for Sakthikulangara and Neendakara, respectively) (see Tables 2, 3).

TABLE 1: Religious Composition of Fishing Households in Project Villages, 1978

Village	Total number of Households	Christians (Latin Catholics) %	Muslims %	Hindus (Arayas) %	Total %
Sakthikulangara	533	90.0	0.7	9.3	100
Neendakara	564	85.5	0.5	14.0	100
Puthenthura	464	5.1	0.5	94.4	100

Source: Unpublished statistics supplied by the Department of Fisheries, Government of Kerala.

TABLE 2: Percentage Distribution of Working Women by Civil Conditions, 1978

Civil Condition	Sakthikulangara	Neendakara	Puthenthura
Married	79.8	70.1	68.5
Widow/divorced/separated	13.1	12.4	9.0
Unmarried	7.1	17.5	22.5
Total	100.0	100.0	100.0

Source: Unpublished statistics supplied by the Department of Fisheries, Government of Kerala.

As of 1978, mechanized fishing occupied over 50 percent of the fishermen in Sakthikulangara and Neendakara, while traditional fishing occupied 23 percent of the fishermen in those villages. By contrast, Puthenthura, an Araya Hindu village, had 68 percent of

its fishermen engaged in activities labeled "traditional." Puthenthura is also, it should be noted, the furthest village of the three
from the main boat jetty. Among the working women of the these
villages, between 60 and 70 percent of the women in the Catholic
villages were engaged in prawn processing or prawn dealing; in the
Hindu village, nearly 70 percent of the women made nets, while 24
percent worked as prawn processors, and only one-half of one percent worked as prawn dealers.

TABLE 3: Average Number of Live Pregnancies Per Married Woman in Project Villages

Age Group	Sakthikulangara	Neendakara	Puthenthura
To married women of all ages	4.74	3.86	3.70
To married women of up to 60 years	4.19	3.69	2.28
To married women up to 40 years	2.95	2.60	2.07
Number of couples for which information was collected	262	250	251

Source: Data collected for this study, 1980.

With this background, the present analysis concerns itself with
the following major questions:

1. As a result of changes that have occurred in the technology of
   fishing, what change has occurred in the work status of women?
2. Is this change different for the two religious groups?
3. As a result of changes in women's work participation, has there
   been any change in the status and roles of women?
4. What change has occurred in the fertility behavior of women
   from these fishing households?
5. Are there any differences or disparities that exist with regard to
   fertility behavior between the two religious groups?

In order to answer the questions posed above, the present
analysis relies considerably on case studies. At the same time, use
has been made of information available on the basis of surveys and
censuses from these villages. In addition, new surveys were undertaken as part of the present study where it was found necessary to
have supplementary information or to check information available
from other surveys, since information on the status and roles of
women in fishing households was very scanty. However, a comprehensive survey of households to elicit all relevant information
was beyond the scope of this study. Moreover, it was our feeling that
while a sample survey would enable generalizations at the macro
level, it is only through case studies that one gains insight into the

real processes at work at the micro level. Second, but not less important, it was felt that the impact of change which this study was focusing on could better be studied through intensive autobiographical case studies.

WORK AND CHANGE FOR WOMEN IN KERALA FISHING VILLAGES

The Indo-Norwegian Project has resulted in a number of changes in women's lives. Many more women are occupied in income-generating activities than ever before. Moreover, the type of these activities is somewhat better. The new work opportunities are less demanding physically and offer a little more income, even when the women continue to be subject to no less exploitative relationships. If today one notices a greater use of medical facilities, both private and public, it is possibly due not only to the establishment of hospitals but also to the increased awareness of their usefulness as a result of the expansion of education, particularly among the women of fishing households. The trend towards higher female age at marriage and smaller family size in all three villages may be the combined result of the spread of education, women's increased involvement in work, and greater access to medical facilities.

The original analytical study of the Indo-Norwegian project, from which this paper is drawn, examined the lives of thirty women in considerable detail, gathering data from interviews, government statistics, macro survey data and church records. The investigation focused on questions regarding family planning, health care, age at marriage, infant mortality, literacy and dowry, as well as type of work and economic status. This chapter extracts sections from interviews with four of these women to illustrate the significance of change for individuals and for generations.

The ideal norm, both now and in the previous generation, among both the Araya Hindu and Catholic fishing households, has been for women to devote all their time to household activities, and not to seek work outside the home. Working outside the home is considered to be essentially a male job, whereas housekeeping and childcare are considered to be women's jobs. Women feel that, by going out to work, they would come into too much contact with men outside their families. However, from the autobiographies we find that quite a few women from the study village were doing something besides their day-to-day housekeeping (even in the previous generation), in spite of the cultural ideal. Women in the Catholic villages report remembering their mothers husking rice, dealing in broken rice, collecting shells, vending fish, making nets, and defibering coir. Among the Araya, coir defibering appears to have been the single most important occupation of the previous generation. Net making came next. The fact is that most grandmothers and mothers did have some remunerative occupation. Fish vending by headload was an occupation most frequently reported in the Catholic villages, whereas midwifery was more common in the Araya village.

Some Examples of Women in the Fishing Villages

Four women are briefly discussed here to illustrate women's perspectives on their own lives: Maggie and Mary, from the Latin Catholic village of Sakthikulangara; Kadalamma, from the Latin Catholic village of Neendakara; and Pankajakashi, from the Araya Hindu village of Puthenthura. Each woman's story portrays a different aspect of life in the Kerala fisheries and how it has changed. Maggie is a fish vendor, Mary is a prawn peeler, Kadalamma is a fish auctioneer and the owner of a mechanized boat, and Pankajakashi is a retired prawn peeler. Their accounts reveal a kind of dogged vitality, a determination to struggle against the vagaries of the market, the limitations of small-scale enterprise, the dominance of men, and the constant frustrations of life in a precarious and changing occupational community.

The first case is that of Maggie, a headload fish vendor. She is 36 years old, a Catholic who has had no formal education, and who married at the age of 15. She has borne eight children, and earns her living as a house-to-house vendor of fish. Her husband, Xavier, is a former coolie fisherman who now owns a small traditional boat. Her daily routine begins at 6:00 a.m., when she sets out with her basket for the beach to wait for incoming boats. Her husband and sons fish in separate boats to minimize the risk at sea. Maggie buys fish from any craft which comes in and does not wait for the family craft to return. Then, carrying her basket on her head, she vends fish to her regular customers in households and tea shops. Maggie explains her reasons for buying from other crafts:

> Apart from the fact that the time when Xavier comes back with his catch may not always suit me most, it makes little difference from whom I buy my fish. Even Xavier's fish catch must go through an auction, for often he has to share the proceeds with one or two persons from outside of our own family who work as crew members. [This is to prevent the accusation that one is underselling for one's own family.]

> I sell mostly on a cash basis but there will always be some who cannot immediately pay me either in part or in full. Usually they pay up the next day or the day after that. So I go back to them after disposing of the leftover fish in a wayside market. If the quantity I

have to dispose of is large, I go to the main market where there is a special place for women fish vendors. We all squat on the floor with our baskets placed in front.

In the afternoons, Maggie goes to the boat landing center to participate in the shrimp auction, where female buyers must compete with men.

The auction agents are all men and the bidders cluster around the basket. If the basket contains expensive prawns, mostly men bidders bid for it. If it contains a mixed assortment then women compete with each other for it. I sell to the representatives and agents of exporting firms who do not have the time and energy to watch out for every boat and participate. I often stay on at the jetty till about 6:30 or 7:00 in the evening. Late in the evening the bidding does not go very high since fewer people are there to participate. If and when I buy at the evening auctions, the prawns have to be taken home to be sorted, peeled, and cleaned. Then they have to be taken to one of the factories with which I have an arrangement to sell. Though there is much more money in bringing the prawns home, peeling and then selling them, I cannot do it on a large scale. For that I must put up a peeling shed of my own and have a number of women working for me. Also it is becoming very difficult to get someone to cart the prawns home at a reasonable price. I do plan to give up fish vending because it is both time consuming and low paying and concentrate on just buying of prawns and selling them away at profit without processing it.

For participation in the auction I need ready cash with me, though on resale the reimbursement is immediate. But when I sell directly to the factories as I do the cash I generally carry with me runs between Rs. 300 and Rs. 500. During the monsoon months, there are times when I make a profit of Rs. 50 in a single day. But then there are lean months and also months when there is no business at all to do. All the same, I am now a full-fledged worker in my own right. In fact, I sometimes wonder if I should not cut down on my work so as to devote a little more time to my family, particularly to my two sons still in school.

Maggie's account indicates pride in her accomplishments, along with doubts about what she perceives as a conflict between her work as fish vendor and mother.

Case two is that of Mary, a 37-year-old prawn peeler. She is married to a fisherman who owns a small traditional craft and ten different kinds of nets. She has borne five children. She entered the prawn peeling business because her older sister, Augustina, was already engaged in it. Her story illustrates both the social and the emotional difficulties women face when they compete against men in bidding for fish. Women must face hostility and ridicule from male

---

competitors in fish auctions, and must consciously renew their courage to persist.

At the boat yard there is not only much physical jostling and pushing about, but also a lot of aggressive male talk that relatively younger women find it rather hard to take, regardless of whom the talk may be aimed at. Most men at the jetty are, no doubt, from Sathikulangara and known to us. Still it is different when you meet them at the jetty than when you see them socially. Probably when you participate in an auction, every one is on his own and has to stand his ground firmly. To gain acceptance as an equal bidder with men takes time, probably for all women. It is particularly so if you are young and on your own with no male support. Further, one has to deal with agents, peeling shed owners, auctioneers, peelers, and coolies. All of them except peelers are men. We women have therefore to develop a thick skin in order to be successful in this type of work.

Initially, we women prefer to participate in small auctions. These consist of small baskets of low-quality shrimps. Strictly speaking, there is no rule against us participating in bigger bids. In actual practice, however, for large expensive lots of prawns, where the bidding opens with Rs. 1000, mostly men participate in auction. Women like me with modest cash on hand bid only in the smaller auctions where prawns both smaller in quantity and of inferior variety are auctioned. But I cannot say that there is any segregation in work based on sex. While participation of women in the bigger bids may be close to 10 per cent, the ratio of men to women participating in smaller auctions is very much in favour of women.

It is usually around 1:00 in the afternoon that Rita and I go to the jetty. Each of us carries three to four hundred rupees in cash. This is the minimum working capital one needs to operate in a modest way. Many other women as well as men are there already. It gets very crowded by 3:00 p.m., when the boats come in quick succession to land their catch. The land including the jetty on the western side of the highway belongs to twelve Christian families. All of these have become rich both because of the regular income from the use of the land by incoming boats and because of the enormous increase in the prices of the land.

As and when necessary, Augustina, Rita and I pool our capital. Then it is Augustina who participates in the bidding on our behalf. Often, however, we operate separately to be able to bid in more than one auction since several auctions are going on simultaneously. When a bid materialises in my favour, I transfer it to the nearby peeling shed of the firm with which we have been having our dealings. Three teenage Hindu girls from a neighbouring village who have been working for us for some years now peel the prawns. The girls get paid according to the number of prawn basins peeled. On an average, they each make five rupees a day. While we don't pay for the use of the shed, we have to buy our own ice. However, we have to leave behind the shelled peels so that the shed owner can sell it as manure. We sell our peeled prawns to the export firms at a price, as I have already mentioned, according to the size and weight, but the prices keep fluctuating from day to day, indeed hour to hour, depending on the incoming catch. When the catch is good, the price is low. Each firm displays the price it is willing to pay for various sizes. On a good day, Rita and I can net as much as 75 rupees together after deducting our expenses for sorting, transporting, ice and peeling. The peak months are June to August when the catch is maximum. On a lean day, our earning may be as low as ten rupees, even though on such days we try to do quite an amount of peeling ourselves. Then there are several days when there is little to buy, peel and sell. So one makes next to nothing.

The firm we deal with clears its bills only once every week and that is what creates headaches for us, particularly during days of peak business. For, to be able to buy shrimps worth Rs. 1000 in the course of one day, the weekly working capital we both require works out to be Rs. 5000, a sum that is not always quite easy for us to mobilize. Both Rita and I subscribe to chit funds to keep our savings in a form that we can tap readily.

Mary's story not only illustrates female solidarity in the face of male antagonism and domination of the fish auction, but a sophisticated understanding of women's need to be flexible in the face of local market forces.

Case three is that of Kadalamma. She is a fish auctioneer and a mechanized trawler owner who is married to a fish trader. She and her husband own two mechanized boats, a gill netter and a trawler. She has had 13 pregnancies. Her life history illustrates a long, but relatively successful entrepreneurial struggle.

Everyone at the boat yard in Sakthikulangara calls me Kadalamma. This is the way we refer to the sea. It means the sea mother goddess. After all, it is the sea that nourishes us and sustains us. She is like a mother to all of us fisherfolk. We are totally dependent on her bounties for our livelihood.

I did not belong to an affluent fishing household. My father was only a coolie fisherman and my mother a headload fish vendor...When I married John, he was considered a good fisherman, though still very poor...All these 40 years I have been married, I have been working for a living. To start with, it was a sheer necessity that I should make my contribution to the family's subsistence expenses. Later, however, as things started improving there was not such great pressure, but I felt restless just sitting at home. To begin with, I sold fish in Neendakara itself. Later, I started going to Sathikulangara. There I had many contacts of my own. Many young men whom I knew as a girl would oblige me and sell me fish at reasonable prices. Other fish vendor women soon became jealous and stories started circulating that my old boy friends were trying to entice me for sexual favors. Naturally, it made John angry. So I decided to give up fish vending altogether. I took to collecting shells...I tried to go back to fish vending, but it was hard.

It was around this time in 1957 when we were really struggling that our first break came. The Norwegians had been around for some time already. After an initial period of experimentation, it was announced by the government that mechanized boats would be distributed through the Cooperative Societies...Things really started brightening for us only when we purchased our second boat— a trawler— in 1962...I gave up headload fish vending and started going to the boat yard to wait for our boat to return from the sea. As soon as the catch was landed, it had to be auctioned and money recovered and shared. Though our sons also joined the crew along with John, sharing had to be done if even one of the crew was not from the family. Since the boat was in John's name, he got not only his share as crew-hand, but also as the boat owner. A boat owner gets sixty percent and the rest is shared by the crew. I participated fully in the supervision of all transactions involved after the fish was landed by our boat, so John and our sons did not have to worry about them.

John gave up fishing and switched to trading in fish. Soon he became very good in the buying and selling of fish and was able to make a reasonable profit. Ever since, I have been handling the affairs of the boats. With John completely off work for a few years now, the responsibility of overseeing the business of the family is completely on my shoulders.

I wake up early, much before sunrise. After a wash, my first job is to go to the boat jetty in Sakthikulangara...on my way I stop for tea. Being sixty years old now, I do not have to worry about where to have tea. Women younger than me have to be more careful and avoid tea shops popular with men. The gill netters go to sea only in the morning before sunrise and return to shore in the afternoon. I am always there before our gill net boat returns to supervise the auction proceeds of the fish at the jetty. By ten o'clock, most of the work is over and I go for my breakfast...then I go back home. The running of the house is now in the charge of my youngest daughter-in-law. Between my daughter and daughter-in-law they have divided the chores. We take our lunch around noon. The menfolk eat first and then it is the women's turn. Again I go to the boatyard in the afternoon also...I do not take any part in the household chores. My hands are full looking after the business operations of our two mechanized boats. In addition, I participate in buying and selling prawns. I find work at the jetty quite exhausting, particularly now that I suffer from high blood pressure.

No doubt we have come a long way, but it was by dint of hard work put in by both my husband and myself that we have been able to achieve our present level of well-being. It is reflected in our present assets and income. After we are both gone, the assets will belong to our eight sons. The daughters have already been given their share in the form of dowry, so they have no legal claim on anything more. But we cannot altogether wash our hands of our daughters, particularly when they are in difficulties. Brothers are supposed to protect the interests of their married sisters but knowing my sons as I do, I cannot leave my daughters quite to their brothers' mercy.

Kadalamma's case highlights one dimension of the impact of the Norwegian project upon women. Kadalamma started out as a head-load fish vendor, but at the age of sixty, she has become the manager of a family business. She tells us that while it has been necessary for her to work throughout most of her married life, she has also learned to enjoy it, and to feel bored within a purely domestic role.

Our last case study is that of Pankajakshi, a retired prawn peeler and homemaker from Puthenthura. Pankajakshi belongs to the Araya Hindu fisher caste. Interviewed at age 55, she was married at 15 and has had seven children. Her husband tutors schoolchildren, but has also worked as a coolie fisherman; she worked for many years as a prawn peeler. Now she makes nets at home and worries about the future for herself and her family, particularly about her daughters, two of whom have married into Catholic families.

Our first daughter, who got married in caste, has four sons and two daughters. Her husband owns a *kochuvallom*, the smaller of the two traditional boats found in the village, and her eldest son goes with him on it. My daughter supplements the family earnings by making nets at home with nylon cord supplied by the village dealer. She has now gone in for a sterilization operation, though late, as a result of great pressure from the hospital authorities. She had all her children at the Indo-Norwegian Medical Centre Hospital. They live in one of the 100 brick houses built by the government for fishermen in this village. Our second daughter was also married in caste, but some years after her marriage she developed a relationship with a Christian man who was working with her in the same peeling shed in Sakthikulangara.

There are no fixed hours of work for these women. When the catch is poor, not all sheds have work to offer. Also on some days one may get work for just a couple of hours. On the other hand, when the catch is very good, the peeling sheds ask you to work overnight because peeling cannot be put off for the next day. The families have no way of knowing why their girls have not returned home, on account of work or something else. The men, who have become newly rich over the past ten to twenty years because of the enormous increase in the availability of business in prawns in this area, will exploit any situation to acquire what money can bring them. Our second daughter fell prey to the lures of one such man. We have had no contact with her ever since she went away to him. Our third and fourth daughters are married to Christian boys and are staying in our own village. It came to us as a great shock when our third daughter, Suprabha, announced that she was getting married to the Christian boy in our neighborhood. When we tried to persuade her against it on the ground that it would go against her next sister, who too was marriageable, because no one in our caste would then accept her, immediately her fiance offered that his brother would marry the younger sister. Thus we were left with no option. Velu has, however, never reconciled himself to this. At the same time, we have not altogether cut ourselves off from these two daughters. After all, we did give our consent to their marriage even though it was, more or less, forced down our throats. Of these two girls, the first has two daughters and her husband has undergone vasectomy. The second has three sons and she herself has undergone sterilization. There children of these two girls were born in the Project hospital.

We decided to move to Puthenthura for various reasons. It was where our first daughter was living already with her husband and children. Also, quite a few of our other relatives, other than our daughters, also lived there. Then, there were opportunities for work for myself and my daughters in close proximity to Puthenthura thanks to the large increase in prawn catches in the area. Not the least important consideration was that living in a village of our own caste would help our children grow up better.

When we moved to Puthenthura, plenty of work was available for women in Neendakara, the neighboring village, only 3 to 4 kilometres away. My three girls and I started working for the peeling shed of a big exporting firm...Different people worked for different peeling sheds. There were nearly 200 to 300 sheds to choose from. It was a three kilometre distance which we would easily commute by walking. On the days when there was too much peeling to be done and it got late, we would be dropped back in the village in one of the company's vans...It is true that we have some success at work, but this has meant that several of our daughters have moved out of caste and away from us. We have had to pay a heavy price.

Pankajakshi's case represents the lives of those whose ability to participate in economic development has been marginal, dependent and erratic. She and her family have had to pursue a purely reactive path, and have not been able to turn themselves into fishery entrepreneurs.

When we look at these actual women's lives, we find that several of them had started doing work at an early age, helping their mothers even before they got married. Some worked independently of their mother, although in related activities. It would appear that Araya women worked less as children since they attended school. Catholic women respondents had practically no schooling and were totally illiterate. Some of the Catholic women gave up work after they got married, while others took work that would bring in slightly higher earnings. For example, Maggie became a headload fish vendor soon after her marriage. Now she is engaged in fish trade as an agent and does not hawk fish from door to door.

Other cases, which are not detailed here, also indicate substantial change in a woman's work over the course of her lifetime, as well as from the previous generation. One woman spent her childhood defibering and spinning coir with her mother and has now become a prawn agent. Another woman, who used to gather shells, now trades fish. A third woman has been able to leave headload fish vending and take over the management of her household's boats. A fourth woman runs a mutual savings club and a woman's tea shop; a fifth makes nylon trawl nets for the mechanized boats; a sixth now makes nets at home, after years of working as a prawn peeler.

Several of the informants were confined to their houses bearing and rearing children for the first few years after their marriage. It is noteworthy that the work they are now engaged in is quite different in nature and income generation from what their mothers were engaged in or what they themselves did as children.

Not only has the type of work changed in each case, but also the income such work yields has improved considerably. Since fishing, mechanized as well as traditional, is still highly seasonal, the associated activities have tended to be equally seasonal in terms of the employment and income they offer. For both groups in the present generation, particularly those born in the 1950s, work opportunities definitely seem to have increased, the main difference being that work opportunities within easy reach of women from Catholic villages were far more remunerative than those open to women from the Araya village.

What is the involvement in paid work of our respondents' daughters and daughters-in-law? Many women of childbearing age are primarily engaged in childrearing. There is no doubt about the economic pressure under which their mothers and mothers-in-law were forced into work. But it is not certain that once these younger

women are free from the responsibilities of bearing and rearing
children that they will be satisfied doing just the domestic chores,
particularly when economic opportunity knocks at their doors. Also,
they will not have to play the subservient role they now play as mere
housewives-cum-mothers.

Overall, young women have had better levels of education and
better access to medical facilities than their mothers. It is very likely that most, if not all, of these women will take steps not to undergo
excessive childbearing. To the extent that this comes about, many
of those not working now may decide to take up some work activity
or other once their children are sufficiently grown up. Thus, whether
or not one subscribes to the view that work participation by fisherwomen was rather low when fishing was pursued on traditional
lines, the fact remains that women's work participation under
changed technological conditions is vastly different and better paid,
judging from the inter-generational changes that our case studies
reveal.

Involvement in work has brought major changes in the life style
of several of our respondents. Work now means not only going out
of the house, but also meeting, dealing, and competing with men
other than those from their own households, making independent
financial decisions, and handling comparatively large sums of
money. Those of our respondents who, by dint of their hard work
and business acumen, have become reasonably successful in their
work, carry a lot of weight in their households. Many contribute significantly to the family income and enjoy within their respective
households a status all their own. In fact, no important decisions
are taken without consulting them.

Such cases have also meant a new kind of role for men. Normally, men in the fishing households are not in the habit of helping in
any of the so-called female tasks or taking care of the children, even
when they are not occupied full-time in their own work activity. Now
with women going out for long stretches of time, men have to take
on some responsibility for the care of children coming back from
school. Also, men in these households generally get more involved
than before in the running of the day-to-day affairs of the house.

The two non-working respondents (both Catholics) do not have
the kind of freedom and status enjoyed by our working respondents.
They continue to play the dependent, subservient role of the traditional home-bound wife. For these women, their contact with the
outside world is only through their husbands or the extended family. These women ask no questions and try not to differ in any way
with their husbands. It ought to be borne in mind, however, that at

least part of the reason why these women have not entered the labor force so far is because of their childbearing and relatively young age (mid-'30s). Of course, each of them has already six living children and has now been sterilized, but child-rearing might well keep them tied to the house for a few more years. Moreover, husbands' reluctance to allow their wives to mix freely with other men may inhibit their economic activity for a while.

There are limits to the kinds and extent of change, however. For example, there appears to be no change with regard to the ideas about universal marriage. Among both Catholics and Araya Hindus, marriage is universal. Moreover, both groups believe that sons are essential. Among the Arayas, a woman who gives birth only to daughters or one who has no children can be cast off. Both groups subscribe to the idea that life is incomplete without marriage.

However, one of the most dramatic changes that seems to have occurred in the study villages in recent years is with respect to family size. All of our respondents were born into large families of six to ten children. The respondents themselves have continued this practice. It is when we come to the married sons and daughters of our respondents that we notice a distinct tendency towards a decline in the number of children. This group has begun to limit families though sterilization, some after the birth of only two children. Family limitation is particularly noticeable among the Araya fisherwomen.

Evaluation of the experience of the three study villages of fisherfolk in Kerala indicates clearly that, although women from fishing households were altogether excluded from the core program aimed at modernizing fishing and fish preservation, women still availed themselves considerably of the various opportunities and facilities the new situation created. This was true of not only women from Catholic villages which had accepted the new technology of fishing, but also women from the Araya Hindu village.

The case of Araya women is remarkable in that their menfolk had not been totally forthcoming in the acceptance of the program of mechanization. These women came forward to take up whatever new opportunities of work were created as a result of the phenomenal growth in economic activity in the wake of mechanization and the discovery of prawn grounds in the area.

Because of problems of access, while women from Catholic villages were able to take up self-employment in trade and processing, women from the Araya village could only enter wage employment either in processing factories or as casual workers at or near the public jetties in the various peeling sheds. The fact that their men-

folk were engaged in the fishing trade or related activities was a matter of great support to Catholic women. The Araya women, on the
other hand, had to go it on their own with little support from their
menfolk. Several of these Araya women who, for some reason or
other, could not go out of their village for work for wage employment,
began making nylon nets, work that fetched some income, however
small, and could be combined with housework.

POLICY IMPLICATIONS

In terms of policy implications, the experience in the three villages
clearly demonstrates that there is hardly a development project
which does not have a women's dimension. Here was a program for
the modernization of activities which were generally considered as
male activities. In the design of the principal project, women were
assigned absolutely no role. Still, looking back over the past thirty
years or so, it is difficult not to notice the distinct increase in
women's involvement in economic activities very closely related to
the operations that the project sought to modernize. One is, therefore, strongly led to suggest that as a general rule, no development
project should overlook the possibilities which the realization of
development would throw open for women on the project's completion. It is not enough to provide for the building up of social
infrastructure as part of a development project, as, for instance, was
done in the design, as well as implementation of the study project.
     The women of these villages responded with energy and initia-
tive to the new opportunities they perceived: there can be no doubt
that if, in the design and implementation of the program, care had
been taken to assign fisherwomen of the study village a role in the
processing, freezing, and trading of fish, the participation of women
in these activities would not only have been larger than today, but
also at a different level. Today, their participation in these activities
is doubtless very much beyond any expectations they could have
entertained, but it is still at a level which is either marginal, as in
the case of the Catholic women who do small-scale trading and
processing of prawns, or very subservient, as is the case with Araya
women working for wages in processing factories or engaged in pre-
processing activities right at the jetties when the fish catches are
landed from mechanized boats. Wages are low and work is highly
seasonal, and the environment and the conditions in which these
women are made to work call for considerable improvement in terms
of both general hygiene and the health of the working women.
     In net making, where Araya fisherwomen predominate, the
relationship is even more exploitative, though women engaged in

net making have the advantage of working at home. The wage they earn per hour of work from net making is less that half of what a woman earns from work in a prawn processing factory. Net making in the study area shares this aspect of low wage with several other industries in the countries where production is organized on a putting out system, under which women from very poor households can be enlisted for work. The point of the analysis is that the study project could have been so designed as to provide adequately for such forms of organization for different types of activities, duly supported by facilities that would have allowed less exploitation.

The battle is, however, not altogether lost in that a number of steps could still be taken to improve matters:

1. provision of training for women in the basics of preservation and processing of marine products;
2. training in the elements of trading and commercial accounting;
3. encouragement to operate in cohesive groups, wherever it is a workable proposition, so that women can undertake to work jointly on a profit-sharing basis and middlemen can be eliminated;
4. construction and maintenance of peeling sheds on scientific lines to be rented out to groups of working women from day to day or even shift to shift in peak season;
5. orientation of deposit-cum-credit policies of various financial institutions to meet the financial needs of these women from the fishing households undertaking activities related to fishing;
6. organization of net making on a cooperative basis by encouraging and training housewives from fishing households to work together (any scheme or project which proposes to mechanize net making and undertake it on a large scale would be an absolutely disastrous way of tackling the present situation);
7. where women must still work for wage employment, in factories or at home; minimum wage legislation and enforcement machinery to see to it that the legislation is implemented.

While the importance of taking the women's dimension fully into account in all core programs cannot be overrated, it goes without saying that all development projects and programs, regardless of the attention they are able to pay to the women's participation in the core programs, must always have a strong social infrastructure component. All that it has been possible to achieve in the three study villages in terms of demographic improvements demonstrates that investment in social infrastructure can yield considerable dividends. We have seen that women from all three villages, regardless of religion and irrespective of the extent of response to the core programs, availed themselves fully of the new public health and medical facilities created as part of the study project for the benefit of their villages. As a result, once they gained a greater sense of security with respect to survival of children, and as the awareness of both the importance of limiting family size and the availability of sterilization facilities increased, women from our study villages showed a remarkable readiness to take to family planning.

Looking back at this brief intervention of the Indo-Norwegian Project, which lasted only ten years in these villages, we can see that village women made substantial changes in terms of health education and economic independence. These gains are significant only when we compare them with the lives of other fisherwomen on the Kerala coast where no such intervention has taken place. However, whatever it has been possible to achieve in the three project villages, particularly in terms of demographic improvements, demonstrates in good measure that investment in social infrastructure has yielded considerable and lasting dividends. A good lesson to be learned from the project is that all development projects, in India and elsewhere, should address social infrastructure problems if they are to take care of women's needs.

Notes

1. This chapter was compiled from a much longer and more detailed description published as *Fisherwomen of the Kerala Coast*. I thank the International Labour Office in Geneva for their generous permission to reissue this material.

2. The original, longer study relies considerably on case studies. A comprehensive survey of households to elicit all relevant information was beyond our scope. Fishing households were chosen on the basis of a random stratified sample; ten households were chosen from each of three villages. For each of the thirty chosen households, information was collected on family genealogy, relationships of all relatives, age, place of birth, education, dowry, occupation, number of children born alive or dead, and family planning status. On average it was possible to collect information for each family on 26 related couples covering three generations. Thus, information was collected on 784 married couples in all. Only ten households were chosen out of these 30 for biographical sketches, and four cases from these households were selected for the chapter presented here.

3. See A.M. Klausen (1968) for a discussion of the project's impact on the Kerala fishermen.

The Sexual Division of Labor and Social Change in a Portuguese Fishery

9

Sally Cole

INTRODUCTION

In recent years, anthropologists working within an historical materialist framework have analyzed the impact of economic change, with specific reference to the development of industrial capitalist relations of production, on the definition of women's work in tribal and peasant agricultural societies (Beneria 1981; Etienne and Leacock 1980; Young et al. 1981). In their work they have documented how these processes of social change have tended to privatize women's work and to erode women's economic autonomy. Harris has summarized the model and the general consensus of these anthropologists:

> As many studies have shown, shifts from household production for subsistence to household-based petty-commodity production, to an economy based on the sale of labor-power, affect radically the structure of households, power relations within them and the resulting changes in the power to command the fruits of one's own labor (1981:57).

The model has not incorporated cultural definitions of gender roles and relations, nor has it considered how such cultural definitions become in themselves factors in the processes of social change. Maritime societies have not, by and large, been examined in this literature.

In this chapter, I use an historical approach which incorporates local definitions of gender in an analysis of social and economic change in a small-boat fishery on the north coast of Portugal.[1] I describe the transformation in the definition of women's work in the fishery in Vila da Praia, a rural parish on the north coast of Portugal. Using historical and ethnographic evidence, I document how, over three generations, the role of women has been redefined from one of productive worker (*trabalhadeira*) in a household-based fishery to one of consumer and housewife (*dona de casa*) in the home. Flexibility in the sexual division of labor was essential to the survival of maritime households and required that women engage in a myriad of economic activities which had given them both economic autonomy and authority within the household. Since the late 1960s, increased dependence on wage employment and the consumption of manufactured goods, combined with the local systems of status and gender, has placed new burdens on women at the same time that it has curtailed their autonomy within the household.

THE VILA DA PRAIA FISHERY IN HISTORICAL CONTEXT

The development of the fishery in Vila da Praia is similar to the development of small fisheries in other European peasant societies. In many coastal communities, households dependent on fishing emerged from the lowest strata— those without sufficient land to farm— and depended on an intensive seasonal round of economic activities (Löfgren 1979:98). Andersen (1979:20) describes small fishermen as "part-time peasants" or "fishermen pluralists" in reference to the range of seasonal economic activities and multiple occupational skills which characterize non-industrialized fishing populations. Acheson (1981:291) describes this attribute of small fishing societies as "fishery switching," meaning that it is common for fishermen "either to hold multiple jobs, in which fishing is alternated with nonfishing jobs, or to switch between different fisheries in the course of the annual round." Löfgren, describing the nineteenth century development of a Swedish fishery found that "a viable household economy could only be upheld through a composite pattern of exploitation with land and sea activities fully integrated. This composite pattern gave both security and flexibility" (1979:97).

In Vila da Praia, by the mid-nineteenth century, the population had grown beyond that which could be supported by agriculture, and local inheritance practices were forcing some young households to look beyond the land for a livelihood.[2] These land-poor members of the parish sought to earn a living through the pursuit of a range of economic activities, including keeping their own small gardens and working seasonally as day laborers for the landowning farmers (Oliveira 1975). By the late nineteenth century, intensification of land cultivation had increased the need for fertilizers and created a reliable market for the local seaweeds and *pilado*.[3] At this time, a number of the land-poor households settled on the coast on a small stretch of beach sheltered by two rock outcrops and began to commit themselves fully to the exploitation of marine resources. In 1870, for the first time, the occupation of *pescador* (fisherman) appeared on the voter's list; six of 52 voters were described as fishermen. The number increased steadily, until by 1905 fishermen represented almost 30 percent of the voting population, a proportion they maintained until the 1960s.[4]

Households dependent upon marine resources developed a seasonal round of activities: in the summer months, from June to October, they harvested and dried a variety of seaweeds; from August to November they went to sea in small open boats to net the *pilado*; from October to February they concentrated on the sardine fishery; and year-round they used line-and-hook to catch a variety of fish, principally the *faneca* (whiting-put, *Gadus luteus*) and the *congro* (conger, *Leptocephalus conger*). They sold the dried seaweeds and *pilado* to the local *lavradores* (landowning peasant farmers) and they sold their fresh fish on the beach in Vila da Praia or by carrying it to neighbouring parishes. In addition, they worked as day laborers for the *lavradores* during peak times in the agricultural cycle and kept their own kitchen gardens.

The fishery provided a tenuous livelihood, and emigration offered fishermen an escape from the uncertainty of fishing and from the lack of other employment for them in Portugal. During the 1920s and 1930s, fishermen developed a pattern of emigrating to Brazil to work in the fishery there when fishing was poor in Vila da Praia. One woman, born in 1917, reported that her father went to Brazil seven times while she was growing up. Again in the 1950s and 1960s, fishermen emigrated to Brazil, Angola, and Mozambique or signed on Portuguese boats fishing off the Grand Banks of Newfoundland, and were absent from the parish for periods of four to six months each year.

Until the 1960s, the Vila da Praia fishery continued to be household-based and to operate on a small-scale: the fishermen and women fished from small, open boats they powered by sail and oars; they made daily trips to fishing grounds six to seven miles offshore; they concentrated on fishing for sardines and *faneca*; and they marketed their fish locally. Survival of the fishing household depended on a diversity of seasonal economic activities, and in years when the fishing was poor, the men emigrated temporarily from the parish. This "composite pattern" (Löfgren 1979) of economic activities required flexibility in the organization of the fishing

Between 1920 and 1940, 54 Vila da Praia women took out their licenses to fish from the Capitania do Porto in Vila do Conde. The majority of these women began fishing as young girls with their fathers. Fourteen was the legal age at which boys and girls could be licensed as members of a boat's crew. One *pescadeira* (fisherwoman) explained to me:

> There wasn't anything special about it. It was either work on the sea or go to work for the *lavradores*. I wasn't going to do that and leave my parents alone down here with the younger children and all the work to be done on the *praia*. Besides, the *lavradores* paid almost nothing—just a little something to eat. And they worked at all hours. A lot of their work was done at night. It wasn't like it is today—all done by machine. At that time all the work was done by hand. It was hard work and all day long. My father had no sons. We were five girls. There was only one boy but he died at 11 months old. My father had no sons so we went with him. This way he didn't have to pay someone from outside the family [to crew] and what we earned was our own [the household's]. But it wasn't anything special, my dear. In those days many women in Vila da Praia worked on the sea.

Lucilia took out her fishing license in 1923 when she was 17 years old. She went to sea as a *pescadeira* every year after that until 1959. She never married. When she stopping going to sea, she kept up her license with the Capitania for almost ten more years because she now owned a boat and had others fishing for her. Her sister started fishing in 1928 at age 13 and fished illegally for a year with her father and sister until she was 14 and old enough to be licensed as a fisherwoman. She continued to fish with them until after she was married, stopping only in her seventh month of pregnancy. When the child was seven months old she began to go to sea again with her father (her husband having emigrated temporarily to Brazil), stopping again when she became pregnant with her second child. This time she did not return to active fishing but continued to assist with the work on the shore.

Girls began fishing as crew for a father or a brother, but several women stressed that they had, at times, fished with men who were no relation to themselves. Once married, women often found their shore work too time consuming to enable them to continue fishing on a regular basis. It was rare for a husband and wife to fish together. One fisherman reported that it was considered unwise because in the event of tragedy, children would be orphaned. Some women did, however, continue to fish, whether regularly or irregularly, after marriage. Women deserted by emigrant husbands were often required to return to fishing in order to support their children. Other married women continued to fish when they could because they enjoyed the work and because it was always a way of earning extra money at times when the household required it.

One fisherwoman, Ines, described how her husband would crawl quietly out of bed in the early hours of the morning and go down to the beach hoping she wouldn't hear him. She would get up after him, get dressed and go to the beach where she would find someone else who would take her fishing. This was when the boats were going out line-fishing, and as she could jig *faneca* "as fast as any man" she was always a welcome crew member. She paid the boat owner a share for the boat and the rest of the fish she was free to sell for herself. She said that, although her husband would have preferred that she not fish, he accepted the fact that he could not stop her, and he never objected to the income she generated by fishing for the household. Ines began fishing with her father in 1931 when she was 14 years old and fished full-time "as a man," she says, until her marriage in 1946. After this she fished on an irregular basis and until a few years ago she would often go out line-fishing with other women. Ines was one of seven children and would not be inheriting her parents' house. Although they lived with her parents for the first two years of their marriage, Ines explained that, in order to move out of her parents' house and set up their own household, she and her husband needed the money that she could make only by fishing. "Besides, I enjoyed the work," she says. "I have such fond memories of those days."

Three women (now ages 59 to 67) took the exam for the *carta de arrals* (skipper's license) which authorized them to skipper boats along the coast between Povoa de Varzim and Matosinhos. The last of these women retired in 1979. The case of this skipper, Maria, is illustrative. The daughter of an unmarried woman, Maria began fishing at the age of ten and took out her license in 1941 when she reached the legal age of 14. She married a fisherman from a neighboring parish when she was 20. He moved in with Maria and her mother. Maria and her husband had three daughters in the next five years. In 1951, when she was pregnant with the third daughter, Maria's husband emigrated to Brazil. He was gone for almost four years when she decided to go after him, leaving the children with her mother. In Brazil, she found him living with another woman and she returned to Vial da Praia to full-time fishing and seaweed harvesting, and to raising her daughters alone. In 1961, she was able to buy a boat of her own and in 1965, she bought the small house on the beach which she had been renting from a *lavrador*. In 1979, she sold her boat and gave her fishing gear to her son-in-law. Today, a married daughter, son-in-law and grandchildren live with Maria in her home. In 1982, Maria bought a house-building lot for her other two married daughters, where they hare now building a modern duplex. Her estranged husband in Brazil has recently began writing to ask Maria to take him back: he needs someone to care for him now in his old age. At age 59, Maria, with the support of her daughters, is refusing to receive him. Maria's independence from men— she supported herself, her mother and her three children without the help of her husband or any other man— is due to the local perception of fishing as a possible occupation for women. Through her industriousness and thriftiness, Maria was able to solidify her economic security and independence by investing in property and in her daughters.

In Vila da Praia, women also inherited fishing property. Writing of rural northwestern Portugal, Pina-Cabral (1984:82) has noted that among the poorer households where there was little property involved, daughters tended to be favored over sons to inherit the entirety of whatever household property there was. It was felt that sons could always emigrate but daughters had to stay at home and marry. He also noted that uxorilocal residence tended to be practiced in these households. Practices were similar in the fishing households of Vila da Praia: daughters were frequently chosen over sons to inherit the property of the fishing household— the house, the boats, nets and lines, and the *casa do mar*, a small shelter on the beach for storing fishing gear and dried seaweed. In return, these daughters were expected to look after their parents in old age (and to tend their graves after death). In such cases, on marriage the daughter's husband moved in with her parents.

Women who did not go to sea were in other ways indispensable to the operation of the fishery and the management of the household economy. Women were responsible for unloading the boats, sorting the catch, selling the fish, and looking after the nets. The latter task was heavy work. The sardine nets (*pecas*) were made of cotton and when wet were extremely heavy. Women working in pairs rinsed the nets in fresh water after each use, then carried them on their heads from the river to the beach where the nets were spread to dry. Once dry, the women rolled up the nets and carried them to their boats ready for use once more. Both men and women were responsible for making and mending the nets. Boat maintenance was a male task but women assisted if necessary. Sails were made and mended by both men and women.

The women were responsible for the sale of the fish and for management of the household earnings for the fishery. The women

watched on the shore for the return of their husband's or father's
boat and they auctioned the fish on the beach or carried it to neighbouring inland parishes for sale door-to-door to *lavradores*. Women
received the cash from the sale of fish and kept accounts of the earnings and expenses associated with the operation of the household
boat. No household could survive on income from the fishery alone,
and because women managed all the income and spending for the
household, the job of "making ends meet" became their responsibility. Thus, in addition to their work in the fishery, women
engaged in a variety of income-generating activities.

All women of fishing households harvested seaweed. They spent
long hours on the beach during the summer months. They waded
in the shallows, often in water up to their necks, harvesting the loose
seaweed in their handnets (*ganha-pao*)[7] or they collected the seaweed as it washed on shore with the incoming tide. They carried the
heavy wet seaweed to the high water mark to be spread on the beach
to dry and, once dry, they rolled it up into bundles which they carried on their heads to a larger pile ready for sale to *lavradores*.
Women made the necessary contacts to sell their seaweed and they
controlled the earnings. Seaweed provided a source of income for
women which was independent of the household earnings in the
fishery, and therefore independent from the work they shared with
their husbands. The economic autonomy of Vila pa Praia women is
in large measure due to their access to a market for a product which
they alone controlled.

The women also kept small gardens where they grew potatoes,
several varieties of cabbage, turnip greens and onions. Men and
women would work together and exchange labor with other fishing
households during the peak times of soil preparation and planting
in the spring, but at other times the *quintal* was a woman's responsibility. Women would also keep hens for their eggs, and chickens
and rabbits for meat. And when times were hard, it was the women's
responsibility to beg from the *lavradores* a handful of flour to make
some bread for their children. The women were each careful to
develop and maintain a special relationship of *cunha* (Smith
1980:88) with one or two *casas de lavoura*. They would offer their
labor to these *lavradores* during peak times in the agricultural cycle
and it was from these households they would beg during the hungry
winter months when the sea was too stormy for the boats to go out
for fresh fish.

Domestic tasks of housecleaning, meal preparation and laundry
were simple and were performed as secondary activities to women's
work in the fishery. A woman could direct any member of the

household to prepare the basic meals: cabbage soup, grilled sardines and bread, or boiled fish and potatoes. Usually food was eaten in the hands or from a bowl, leaving few dishes to wash. Homes were scantily furnished: often there was no table to eat from and only a dirt floor to sweep. There were few clothes to wash; everyone owned only one change of clothing for Sundays and holidays. Children were raised on the beach. They followed their parents, grandparents, aunts and uncles around and, as the adults went about their work, all watched out for the children.

Prior to 1960, the sexual division of labor in Vila da Praia had required flexibility in the definition of gender roles: when there were no sons, daughters fished with their fathers; when husbands emigrated, wives fished or hired crew to fish in the household boat. The tenuousness of the fishery as a livelihood required the economic autonomy of women: women owned and inherited fishing property; they controlled the harvest and sale of seaweed; and they had decision-making power over the allocation of household resources.

Local gender ideologies reflected the social realities of gender roles in the sexual division of labor in the fishing household. Specifically, the cultural construction of women's identity reflected the central role women played in the organization of the fishing economies.

THE "GOOD WOMAN," THE "GOOD MAN": THE CULTURAL CONSTRUCTION OF GENDER

Complementing the economic role played by women, there developed an ideology of women's role, of women's work and of what makes a "good woman." Married women described themselves as *trabalhadeiras* (lit. hardworking women). In cultural terms, the definition of women as *trabalhadeiras* signifies local recognition that women performed a productive role in the household economy and that their work gave them autonomy from men in the household and freedom of movement within the community. After 1960 young married women begin to describe themselves as *donas de casa* (lit. housewives). This changing self-image signifies the redefinition of woman's role in the household and the loss of the economic autonomy and control which the *trabalhadeiras* had enjoyed. What were the central qualities of a *trabalhadeira*? And what were the socioeconomic changes which removed women from active roles in the fishery and identified them with domestic work in the home?

Girls in fishing families were raised to a life of hard physical work and instilled with a set of character attributes which firmly established the female self-image of *trabalhadeira*. Women remember a grandmother or aunt fashioning a small *ganha-pao* for them, and at age seven or eight they were following their mothers, aunts and grandmothers around in their work on the beach and collecting their own small piles of seaweed for drying and sale or exchange. By the time they were ten, they were accompanying mothers and grandmothers on their fish-selling trips, carrying a small load of fish in a wooden *giga* (tray) on their heads like the older women and walking long distances on foot to neighbouring parishes. Similarly, they learned agricultural work either in their mother's *quintal* or working alongside their mother for a *lavrador* in his fields. And by age eight or ten they were also effective workers at the domestic tasks associated with keeping the home: preparing the simple meals, cleaning the house or washing clothes at the river.

Girls learned that the job of the woman of the house was to be "*o governo de lar*" (the manager of the home). As one woman said: "*Sempre houve a ideia que a mulher tinha que aprender a ser poupadeira, a ser uma boa governadora de casa.*" (There was always the idea that a woman had to learn to be thrifty, to be a good manager of the household.)

The woman of the house was responsible for managing the household economy. In order to do this well in a life of accepted poverty and hardship, she must be "*muito trabalhadeira, poupada e lutar p'ra a vida*" (very hard working, thrifty and struggling constantly). A woman's job was "*fazer a vida*"— she was to make ends meet in order to ensure the economic well-being of the household. Girls learned that: "*A mulher e como uma formiga: arrasta, arrasta, faz a vida.*" (A woman is like an ant: she toils and toils, making a livelihood). And they learned that the possibility of their finding a good husband depended on their ability to "*fazer a vida.*" As one fisherwoman told me:

> We used to say, '*A mulher faz dinheiro, o dinheiro nao faz a mulher. Mais vale casar com uma mulher trabalhadeira do que com uma gastadeira com dote.*' (Women make money. Money does not make a woman. There's greater value in marrying a hard-working woman [implied lacking a dowry] than to marry a woman with a dowry but who likes to spend money.)

By contrast, they learned that men could not be expected to have the women's virtues of hard work and thriftiness. Men were possessed with *vicios* (vices). Husbands were an expense for the household. In order to be men, men had to engage in manly pursuits and pastimes which involved wasting (*gastar*) both time and money. They passed all hours when not fishing or working on their boats and nets in the *loja*,[8] where they were expected to engage in

games of dominos or cards. This involved gambling and paying gambling debts in hospitality in the form of a drink. Wives budgeted for
their husband's expenses in the *loja*. Because wives managed the
household budget, men were required to ask their wives for money
for beer, wine and tobacco. The most common catalyst of domestic
quarrels was a woman's decision that there was no money to give
her husband for his trip to the *loja*. He would accuse her of mis-
management for it was her job to ensure that there were funds to
meet his needs, but she would hold firm to her decision, reminding
him of the needs to their children. These confrontations would often
lead to violence: the husband beating his wife and his wife sometimes fighting back. I was told that husbands responded in different
ways to these inevitable times when there was not enough money
for them to fulfill their male responsibilities in the public life of the
loja. Common was the husband who resorted to violence to express
his frustration at his powerlessness—a sense of powerlessness
which was based on his recognition, first, that his wife was right
and that there *was* no money and, second, that the division of labor
in the household gave women power over the allocation of household
resources. Some husbands, however, were known to cry when confronted by their wives and by this sense of powerlessness. A "good
husband" was one who spent sparingly in the *loja* and who accepted
his wife's decisions about the management of the household income.

Girls also learned that they were members of the land-poor (*os
pobres*) in the parish and that they could only hope to find a husband from among those boys who were also poor. Girls from fishing
households married boys from fishing households or from other
landless households such as those of craftsmen or *jornaleiros*
(agricultural day workers). Marriages between households of *lavradores* and households of *pescadores* were rare. *Lavradores*
married their daughters to the sons of other *lavradores* with property. Among the *pescadores.*, however, parents exerted little control
in their daughter's choice of a husband and would only advise the
girls to choose a boy who came from "*una boa familia*," a good family, one which was "*muito trabalhadeira*" (very hard-working).
Parents directed their daughters to look at the way a boy had been
raised, the way that his parents had organized their household, and
the way that his mother had managed the household. In this way
they might determine whether or not he had properly learned the
roles and relations of men and women upon which the economic
viability of the fishing household depended. Men and women understood that: a "good woman" worked hard on the *praia* and was a
skillful manager of the household's resources; a "good man" was a

hard worker who trusted his wife (*tem confianca na mulher*) to manage the household. One fisherwoman described her good fortune in her marriage:

> We married because we were fond of each other. But it's after marriage that the trouble always started because in those days there was never enough to eat. Life was a misery (*uma miseria*). But marriage is a cross; you must pick up that cross and carry it (*carregar uma cruz*). It's only luck (*sorte*) if your marriage is a happy one. I was lucky. My husband was my friend (*muito meu amigo*): He didn't beat me and he didn't spend the money.

The meagre subsistence provided by fishing required that women in Vila da Praia fulfil productive roles in the household economy and make decisions about the management of the household. Women needed to be industrious and independent, and the cultural construction of a female self-image of *trabalhadeira* ensured that women would learn the necessary virtues of hard work and industry. The ideology of the hard-working women was necessary for the survival of the fishing household; at that same time it gave women a certain autonomy both in their marriages and in the community.

SOCIOECONOMIC CHANGE IN THE PARISH AND IN THE
FISHERY: 1960 TO THE PRESENT

In the 1960s, changes in the organization of the fishery and in the economy of the parish began to bring about changes in the structure of the household. For over forty years, economic policies opposing industrialization had offered the rural poor little alternative but emigration; those who stayed behind engaged in a continuous cycle of seasonal economic activities and a struggle to survive. Socioeconomic change in Portugal began in the 1960s with the replacement of Salazar by Marcel Caetano, the introduction of basic social services, and limited planning to open up of the country to industry. With the Revolution of 25 April 1974, the pace of change escalated. The succession of governments since 1974 has endeavored to modernize the economy and to "Europeanize" the Portuguese people in preparation for a role in the European Economic Community. The final Portuguese withdrawal from Angola and Mozambique (1974-76) returned a flood of refugees to Portugal, many of whom settled in rural areas bringing with them new social attitudes; these *retornados* were accustomed to a standard of living and a consumer lifestyle which they sought to reproduce in the rural communities in which they now found themselves. Finally, freedom from the censorship by which Salazar had controlled cultural and political development in Portugal has introduced the rural population to European and North American media, and images and aspirations of the West. These large-scale changes have had an important impact in rural parishes such as Vila da Praia. Changes in gender roles and relations are among the most notable: the role of hardworking, independent *trabalhadeira* is disappearing in favor of the *dona de casa*, a woman who identifies herself with her home instead of with her work. The transformation of women's work has increasingly created contradiction between gender roles and gender ideologies and few young women are able to realize their aspirations to be *donas de casa*.

Today Vila da Praia is a bustling, growing community. Its population of approximately 3000 residents represents an increase of 1000 from the parish population in 1966.[9] In 1966 the parish economy was based on subsistence fishing and agriculture; only 6.1 percent of voters worked for wages in industry. A household survey in 1985 revealed that today, 33 percent of the labor force in Vila da Praia is employed in industry; primarily women, they work in fish plants or in one of the numerous small garment factories which have opened in neighbouring parishes since 1966. Another 30 percent of the labor force (primarily men) is employed in skilled and unskilled trades related to construction. The proportion employed in fishing has decreased from more than 33 percent in 1966 to less than 9 percent in 1985.[10]

Since 1966, the Vila da Praia fishery has undergone extensive changes in technology and in the organization of labor. Outboard motors (15 hp) have replaced oars and sails making fishing possible on a year-round basis in all but the most stormy weather. Only two crew members are required to manage the motor-driven boats instead of the three or four who were needed when the boats were driven by sail and oar. The boats are still of the same open design but because they are power-driven they can be longer (5.5 m) and fortified to carry heavier loads (1400 kg). Fishermen who had emigrated to work in fisheries in Brazil, Angola, Mozambique, Germany and other parts of Europe returned to Vila da Praia in the late 1960s and early 1970s; they introduced new types of nets and traps and diversified the resource base of the local fishery. Today each boat is equipped with several varieties of nets and traps, and fish caught include not only the sardines, whiting-pout, and conger, but also varieties of sea bass and cod, sole, flounder, and mackerel and several types of crabs, shrimp, lobster and octopus. Nets are of nylon and do not require the daily maintenance the cotton nets had needed. These and other technological innovations have reduced the households and is central to understanding the nature of the sexual division of labor which developed. Pursuing a seasonal round of economic activities and experiencing prolonged periods of male absence, the fishing household in Vila da Praia depended on the economic participation of all its members, on flexibility in the sexual division of labor and on the economic autonomy of women.

THE SEXUAL DIVISION OF LABOR IN THE FISHERY: PRE-1960

Descriptions of the sexual division of labor in maritime societies have tended to view men's work as based on the sea and women's work as based on the land; the sea is male terrain and the land is female terrain (Andersen and Wadel 1972). This dichotomization of gender roles does not describe the division of labor in the fishery in Vila da Praia until after 1960. In the first half of this century, women were active in all areas of the fishery; the livelihood earned from the fishery was too tenuous to support a strict separation in gender roles. Although some tasks were performed primarily by men and others were performed primarily by women, the flexibility required in the economic organization of the fishing household required that women be able to replace men and men be able to replace women in the tasks associated with both the fishery and the running of the household. All men went to sea, but some women also went to sea; women controlled the seaweed harvest but, when called upon, men assisted their wives with this work; and, while domestic tasks were performed primarily by women, fishermen also assisted with cooking when necessary and were active in child rearing.

The role of women in Portuguese fisheries has not been analyzed although their contribution has been noted in general descriptions of fishing (Inquerito Industrial 1891; Lino Netto 1949) and descriptions of women's work have been central to at least two works of fiction (Brandao 1923; Costa 1980). Vila da Praia is known on the north coast of Portugal as the only fishery in which women went to sea.[5] An 1891 government report, the *Inquerito Industrial e Comercial: a Pesca*, provides a detailed description of the organization of labor in each of the more than 30 fisheries on the north coast from Porto to the Minho River. Vila da Praia was the only fishery in which women were sea-going. In a letter dated 1897 (BMVC), the marine authorities solicited the aid of the county administrator of Vila do Conde in an effort to prevent the women of Vila da Praia from going to sea. In this letter the official said that the women continue to insist on going to sea although it is against marine regulations, and that whenever officials have gone to Vila da Praia to enforce this regulation, they have been met with "hostile manifestations."[6]

extent to which women are engaged in fishing: today it is rare for women to go to sea; women's primary role is in unloading the boats and selling the fish.

A government-run fish auction (*lota*) was established in Vila da Praia in 1970 but the women continue to insist on selling the fish in the *lota* themselves and collecting the money from their buyers. They say they do not trust the *lota* and that by selling the fish themselves they know exactly the value of their boat's catch and the value of their equal share as partners. Today it is customary for two men to fish together as partners; their two wives work together unloading the boat and selling the fish and divide the proceeds of fish sales equally between them. In the fishing households, management of the finances is still the responsibility of the women: women keep the accounts and pay the bills for gas and maintenance of the boat; they give their husbands money for beer and cigarettes and control other household spending.

These changes in the technology and organization of the fishery have brought about changes in the work that women and men do and have developed a sexual division of labor which more closely resembles the dichotomization which Andersen and Wadel (1972) had described: today men's work is on the sea, women's work is on land. Furthermore, wider socioeconomic changes in the parish have introduced a new definition of women's work: the center of their work today is not the fishery but the home. Women describe their work in the fishery as *ajuda na prais* (lit. assisting on the beach), meaning they help their husbands in the work on the beach; but, when asked to describe their jobs, they say they are *donas de casa*. Maria, the retired skipper, speaks of how the women today don't know what it means to be a *pescadeira* (fisherwoman): "To be a *pescadeira* is to make decisions; to know where the fish are and to know how to get them. These women today don't know how to bring home a boatload of fish."

In 1966 there were 115 fishermen, in 1973 there were 105 fishermen, and in 1985 there were only 42 active fishermen. Only a handful of men and women active in the fishery today are under age 35 and all fishing households have at least one member working fulltime in wage employment. Sons and daughters go out to work as soon as they reach the legal age of 14 and complete the compulsory six years of formal education. When daughters approach the age of 14, their mothers canvas the nearby garment factories, speaking with the owners to arrange employment for their daughters. At about the same age, sons make the choice between taking up fishing or apprenticing in a trade. Unmarried sons and daughters deliver their wages to their mothers. Sons keep a small amount for cigarettes and for their expenses in the cafe; by working overtime on Saturdays they earn the extra money needed to buy and look after a small motorcycle. Daughters give all their wages to their mothers on the understanding that their mother is saving money for the furnishings of their kitchens when they marry.

Few fishermen's daughters today want to marry a fisherman; they want a husband who brings home a regular wage. They describe the life of a fisherman's wife as a life of poverty and hard work, and say that their mothers and grandmothers were *escravas* (slaves). A marriage based on wage earnings appears to them to offer the opportunity to escape their position as low-status women in the parish and to define themselves as *donas de casa*.

The construction of new homes in Vila da Praia symbolizes the importance of the *dona de casa* role for women in the community. From 1966 until recently, construction boomed in the parish: new homes were built and new shops opened— two butcher shops, a furniture store, three clothing stores, and numerous cafes. The homes are colorful and large. Emigrants with new wealth built the first new homes in Vila da Praia in the 1970s and today every young couple aspires to build a modern house. The most envied homes are those with the decorative outdoor mosaic tiles (*azulejos*), marble stairs and balconies and colorful, carefully tended flower gardens. The women of Vila da Praia today are house-proud and continually compare the appearance of their home to the homes of other women in the parish. They measure all houses in the parish on a scale from best to worst and thus are engaged in an endless struggle to improve their homes and to be considered the best or, at least, excellent housekeepers. They are fastidious about cleanliness, every day scrubbing their marble steps and washing the *azulejos*. They polish their beautiful carved mahogany bedroom suites and consume hours crocheting elaborate bedspreads and tablecloths. Their concern with cleanliness extends to their children, who are always meticulously turned out in a fresh full change of clothing. And, as modern housewives, they shop for new types of processed foods and learn to make a greater variety of more elaborate meals.

Although young women aspire to be *donas de casa*, few are able to realize this role. Dependence on wage-earnings has made the household more vulnerable to the high rate of inflation of the cost of living in Portugal since 1974. Furthermore, wages remain low and wage increases have not kept pace with inflation rates. The employment available for men is often only seasonal and irregular, and few households can survive solely on male earnings. Permanent and salaried, though low-paid, jobs are, however, available for women in the garment factories and fish plants. In order to "make ends meet," as Vila da Praia *trabalhadeiras* have always done, young women continue to work in factories after marriage. The difference for young women today is that their preferred identity is that of *dona de casa*, rather than that of *trabalhadeira*. They devote all leisure time to domestic work in the home, and take on the well-known "double day" of work for women.

The structure of the wage-earning household is in important ways different from the structure of the fishing household. Although women continue to be culturally defined as household managers, the former power and autonomy associated with the role has been eroded. Working for wages separates production from the activities of the household. Formerly a unit of production and consumption, the household is now the center of consumption only; productive activity takes place outside the household and is not controlled by household members. The role of women as managers of fishing households becomes, in the wage-earning household, the residual role of consumer. The ideology of women as managers persists, but what women are managing is consumption, not production. Furthermore, the consumer orientation of the wage-earning household has changed the nature of the domestic tasks associated with running the household, and the role of housewife in a consumer-based household is now more elaborate. In the fishing household, the tasks of meal preparation, house cleaning, child care, and so on, were simple and complemented women's productive work in the fishery. In the wage-based household, these tasks are all more elaborate and more time-intensive for the housewife. The process by which domestic tasks in wage-earning households become increasingly more time- and labor-intensive for women has been well-documented (Luxton 1980).

Women in wage-based households also find that they have less control over their husbands' earnings than women in fishing households. The separation of income-generating activities from the household has weakened women's control over the management of household resources and has limited their access to economic resources. Men who work for wages now receive their earnings themselves, and many wives today have to ask their husbands for money to go to the grocery shop. Even wives with full-time factory jobs find themselves in this position because they cannot meet all household expenses on their low salaries. By contrast, in the fishing household women received and controlled household earnings and husbands had to ask their wives for money for beer and cigarettes. While women in wage-earning households take on a double day of work, men are experiencing increased leisure time and greater economic independence from women.

The older women have noted this change in relations between husband and wife. One woman in strict confidence lamented: "Do you know, my daughter is not even *governadora* in her own house? It is he who rules. I can't understand it. She was raised always to be *muito trabalhadeira*." Another woman said: "I think it's a terrible thing when a husband doesn't trust (*nao tem confianca*) his wife with the money. When she always has to be asking (*a pedir*) him for money to go to the shop then she is *mais escrava* (more of a slave, servile)." Different generations of women now hold different images of a woman's role: the young married women value the status of *dona de casa* and say that their mothers and grandmothers were *escravas* because of their life of hard physical work; the older women, proud of their work as *trabalhadeiras*, worry about the dependent position their married daughters are in. They perceive some of the contradictions in the role of *dona de casa*.

When older generations of women criticize their young married daughters and young husbands enjoy increased independence from their wives, it is difficult to appreciate why the young women have accepted and aspired to fulfil the *dona de casa* role. In order to understand how the elaboration of the *dona de casa* role and ideology occurred, it is necessary to understand the historical experience of the fishermen and women as the land-poor in the parish. In the wealthier agricultural households of the parish in the first half of the twentieth century, wives stayed in the home. They were never seen in dirty, ragged clothes working in the fields. When wage employment opportunities opened up in the 1960s, members of fishing households moved into wage labor in much greater numbers than did members of the agricultural households. Industrial wage labor offered the land-poor men and women the possibility of defining new statuses for themselves within the changing parish social structure. In the parish, one symbol of achieving higher social status is the *dona de casa* role for women. For the young married daughters of fishing households, to work in the home and not in the fields or on the seaweed harvest, as their mothers and grandmothers had done, is a symbol of status and of the economic well-being of the household. Since 1974, commercial images of women as housewives abound in consumer advertising and have further developed this local image of women's work.

The socioeconomic reality of life in post-1966 Vila da Praia allows few women to achieve this ideal role and, as noted above, most women also work fulltime for wages. The increasing contradiction between the work that women actually do and the prevailing idea of the work that women do is extremely stressful for young married women. Emerging from the contradiction are signs that women themselves are beginning to struggle. Their struggle has begun in the household and centers around domestic work. Women factory workers are recruiting the labor of husbands and children in the tasks of shopping, meal preparation, and household maintenance.

CONCLUSION

An historical approach to the analysis of gender relations in a maritime society reveals important changes over time. Fishing in Vila da Praia developed as part of a household-based economy and was carried out in conjunction with other subsistence activities. In this context, the domestic work of running a household was an integral part of household production. The sexual division of labor in the fishing household was flexible in order to meet the demands of the relentless seasonal round of activities. Periods of male absence left women the dominant role in the management of the household. Women undertook additional production activities, notably seaweed harvesting, in order to "make ends meet" and these in conjunction with their role as manager of the household (*governadora da casa*) gave women economic autonomy and decision-making authority. A cultural definition of women as *trabalhadeiras* described and reinforced this role for women. Female socialization instilled young girls with this self-image and effectively reproduced the structure of gender relations within the fishing households, the gender relations around which the subsistence-based fishery was organized.

After 1960, as members of the fishing households increasingly engaged in wage labor, control of production was removed from the household. In this context, women's role of household manager was reduced to the residual role of consumer. In order to run the household, women now depend on wages earned outside the household, wages they themselves must earn in addition to the unpaid work they do in the home or wages they must depend on husbands or other household members to earn for them. Domestic work not only has been separated from productive work (now defined as paid work) but domestic tasks are now more time-consuming, more elaborate and more rigidly defined as women's work.

As social and historical constructs, gender roles and relations undergo change in a context of general socioeconomic change. In the circumstances of rapid change in a rural Portuguese fishery, women's roles and ideas about women's work have changed as the local economy has changed over three generations. Households of wage-earners and consumers in an industrial economy have replaced households of producers in a household-based fishing economy. Women, once considered *trabalhadeiras* and producers in a household economy, are now viewed primarily as *donas de casa* and providers of services for other members of the household—even when they are also full-time factory workers. The contemporary sexual division of labor which offers men increased leisure time and greater economic independence from their wives, places a double burden of work on women as both factory workers and *donas de casa*. There is evidence, however, that the *dona de casa* role is beginning to undergo further transformation. The roots of this transformation lie in the contradiction between gender ideology and the contemporary social reality of women's work. The locus of change is the household, where women are demanding changes in the sexual division of labor.

Notes

1. Research for this chapter is based on fieldwork conducted in Portugal from February 1984 to June 1985, and is part of a Ph.D. thesis currently in preparation for the Department of Anthropology, University of Toronto. Funding was provided by the Social Sciences and Humanities Research Council of Canada (SSHRC). Vila da Praia is a pseudonym.

2. In law, all children were entitled to an equal inheritance; however, the *de facto* inheritance system in Vila da Praia was based on a belief in the importance of keeping the *casa de lavoura* (the agricultural household, meaning all lands, livestock and buildings) unified. Thus, only one heir (a son or daughter) inherited the *casa*, but that heir was legally bound to pay the siblings (the non-heirs) their equal share of the value of the *casa*. In wealthier households, this payment took the form of a *dote*, a cash payment which ideally enabled marriage to the heir of another *casa*; in poorer households, it was more difficult for the heir to pay the siblings their legal share. Instead, they might receive a small plot of land on which to build a house. The non-heirs then became essentially landless in that they could not attempt to farm. Members of this land-poor group set up households dependent on fishing and emerged as a low status group in the parish hierarchy, a subordinate status of which the fishermen were always aware. Social relations in the Vila da Praia were characterized by antagonism between the *lavradores* (landowning peasant farmers) and the *pescadores* (land-poor fishermen). In order to rationalize their relative positions in the parish social structure, members of each group attributed unfavorable qualities to members of the other. The *lavradores*, for example, describe the *pescadores* as *maleducados* as lazy, uncouth

drunkards who do not know how to work the land. These images persist and continue to be an important factor in contemporary social relations in the parish.

3. The *pilado* (*Portunus puber*) is a species of small crab which travels in schools, making it easy to net in large quantities. Until the mid-1940s, it was common on the north coast of Portugal. The *pilado* was dried on the beach and then used as fertilizer. The *lavradores* were the first to develop the *pilado* fishery. Since at least the mid-eighteenth century, the *lavradores* had owned small boats and either gone to sea themselves for the *pilado* or sent their *criados do servir* (lit. servants) or employed agricultural day workers (*jornaleiros*) to fish for them. The harvest of seaweeds and *pilado* was at that time part of the work of the agricultural household and the fertilizer produced was for use on their own lands. In the mid-nineteenth century, the need for fertilizer began to exceed the amount that the *lavradores* themselves could produce, and it was at this time that the seaweed and *pilado* harvest began to offer a source of livelihood for the landless households.

4. Electoral censuses for Vila da Praia are available for the years 1862 to 1877 inclusive; and for 1905, 1911, 1918, 1928, 1966, and 1973. These list all adult males eligible to vote. Women did not appear in the censuses until 1966 and then only women who were heads of households or who had a secondary school education. The first fishermen were enumerated in 1870 when of 51 eligible voters, six were described as fishermen. By 1877 there were 84 voters, 25 of whom were fishermen. By 1905, 33 of 116 voters (28.5%) were fishermen. In 1928, 44 fishermen were enumerated, representing 28.9% of voters. By 1966 there were 115 fishermen representing 33.6% of the voting population. By 1973 the proportion had begun to decrease. In the 1973 census 22% (105 men) of voters were fishermen and in a household survey I conducted in 1984-85 only 8.7% of the households were engaged in fishing.

5. Brandao (1923) and Lamas (1948) both mention seeing women in other fishing communities punting small boats near the shore as they line-fished or harvested seaweed. The local view that Vila da Praia women were the only women in Portugal to go to sea would seem to refer to the greater extent of their involvement in fishing: they took out fishing licenses; they went greater distances out to sea and travelled up and down the coast between Povoa de Varzim and Matosinhos; and, they stayed out in boats overnight with male crew members during the sardine fishing which took place between sunset and sunrise. *Why* Vila da Praia women were more sea-going than were other women on the north coast, is a question for further examination. Vila da Praia women were sea-going at least as early as 1876 when eight women were shipwrecked returning with a load of *pilado*. Six were saved (BMVC).

6. When I checked with the Capitania do Porto in Vila do Conde they could find no record of there ever having been a regulation prohibiting women from going to sea. Officials there suggested that this 1897 reference to

a "regulation" probably reflected marine authorities' unofficial attitudes and not their legal authority.

7. A *ganha-pao* (lit. bread-earner) was simply constructed by attaching a piece of old netting to a small iron hoop. It was the basic tool used by men and women to net fish and harvest seaweed.

8. The *loja* is a small shop which sells basic groceries to women and beer and wine to men. The shopkeeper stands behind the counter serving all customers. Women come and go with their purchases; men sit at a small table in the corner or stand at the counter with their drinks.

9. In the 1966 census the parish population was 1,933. In the 1981 census the population was 2,781. In 1985 the Junta de Freguesia was in the process of conducting a census, and the Secretary of the Junta estimated that the population was now closer to 3,000.

10. These data are based on: the 1966 and 1973 censuses (Recenseamento Eleitoral do Concelho de Vila do Conde), the last official censuses of the parish; and on the results of a household survey I conducted in 1985. In 1966, 115 fishermen were enumerated (33.6% of voters); in the 1973 census there were 105 fishermen (22.0% of voters); in the 1985 household survey there were 74 men and women (8.7% of employed labor force) employed in the fishery. During these years (1966-1985) the proportion employed in agriculture declined on a similar scale. Meanwhile the proportion employed in waged labor increased from 6.1% in 1966 to 10.1% in 1973 to 33% in 1985. Those employed in skilled and unskilled trades increased from representing 19.4% of voters in 1966 to representing 27.6% of voters in 1973 and 29.6% of the employed labor force in 1985.

A Fisher Laddie Needs a Fisher Lassie: Endogamy and Work in a Scottish Fishing Village

10

Jane Nadel-Klein

INTRODUCTION

Two images represent women in the history of Scottish fishing: the fishwife and the "gutting quine." The fishwives worked as part of the domestic division of labor; the gutting quines worked for large curing companies in faraway places. Both now exist only in memory. In Scotland the fishwife is a creature of almost legendary status. Highland Character Dolls produced by Scottish artist Sheena MacLeod for sale in craft and "tartan" shops now include several models of fishwives, each complete with petticoat, shawl, and creel. The most famous of all is the Newhaven fishwife who was renowned in Edinburgh for her cries of "who'll buy my caller herrin'?" She can be found on postcards and paintings all along the east coast. The gutting quines have not been so romanticized. Photographs of them working at their stations in the Hebrides or the Shetlands show them standing, youthful and strong, in obviously industrial settings.

The fishwives gradually vanished along with the inshore small-boat fishing that had made their way of life possible. Essential participants in the fishing life, they also linked the fishing community to the external world of farmers and townspeople. In doing so, they came to publicly symbolize the radical differentiation of the fishing community from the surrounding, often antagonistic, landbased society. However, with the progressive domination of herring over inshore species, beginning all along the east coast in the middle of the nineteenth century and peaking shortly before the twentieth, women's domestic or village roles in white fishing began to give way to a more capital-intensive mode of production. The gutting quines, who were drawn from the same communities as the fishwives, cured and packed herring for marketing firms based in Scottish towns and cities. Their jobs lasted in some places until the late 1940s. The gutting quines came to symbolize the increasingly proletarianized condition of Scottish fishing.

It is important to pay attention to both fishwives and gutting quines, because they raise several interesting points about the status of women in Scottish society. They also evoke more general questions about the relationship between status and the division of labor, or the sources of gender ideology. The fishwives' status appears to have been relatively high, compared with that of women in other working-class and agricultural sectors of Scottish society. They were direct economic participants, vital actors in the production and exchange systems of their communities. Most of the time, male and female worlds were sharply separated, and the division of labor clearly marked, but there is no evidence that the fishwives' work was devalued, or that they were not acknowledged as "breadwinners" in their own right. At the same time, women were excluded from certain male domains and ritual activities. Also, as I explain below, women's "world" included contact with the "polluting" landward territory which men found threatening. While women's contribution to subsistence was large and visible, and while their status was *relatively* high, I believe that the ideology of gender in Scottish fishing communities still consigned them not only to a separate status, but to one which contained aspects of inferiority. This reminds us, as Quinn (1977:182) points out, that status cannot be treated or explained as a unitary construct. This underscores our need to look at the larger social context which affects the construction of status in general, cautioning us to remember that communities are seldom, if ever, social isolates, and that the primary features of gender ideology are not necessarily constructed within village walls.

The literature on North Atlantic fishing communities often places great emphasis upon male solidarity through work groups. For example, Breton's analysis of bilateral kinship in a Quebec fishing village focuses upon bilateral kinship in the structure and recruitment of male work groups in cod-fishing, trapping, and caribou hunting (Breton 1973). Likewise, Nemec (1972) looks at "brotherhood" as both the actual basis for crew recruitment and as the metaphor for male solidarity and egalitarianism in the Newfoundland outport of St. Shotts. These and other studies tend to assume that male work groups are the primary lynchpins of the social order of fishing communities. A Scottish student, for example, reports on her attempt to do research about the women in Scottish fishing as follows:

> ...a Reader at the University said to me that he thought that no one had ever considered talking to a humble fisherwife. Most academics were more interested in the men and the fishing methods which they used and the contribution which they made to the National Economy (Buchan 1977).

However, to focus exclusively on male activities and male social organization in Scottish fishing would greatly obscure the structure and dynamics of fishing communities. Throughout the history of Scottish fishing villages, women were a vital part of the fishing system, not merely as mates and childbearers, but as workers. In this paper, I stress the importance of women's work and work groups as major factors in village social organization. Women's work enabled men to go out to sea: women baited lines and processed and marketed fish. They even carried their men to and from the boats to keep them dry.

The fishermen themselves were well aware of women's contribution to the fishing economy and consciously sought wives who would be effective helpmates. Scottish fishing villages were widely known to resist intermarriage with outsiders. Outsiders tended to regard this endogamous pattern as insularity and generally ascribed it to shyness or to some inbred "racial" peculiarity. It is certainly easy to view it purely as a defensive reaction against the social stigma attached to fishing villages by Scottish society in general. However, I believe that kinship in Scottish fishing society was not harmoniously bilateral, but manifested a tension between agnatic and uterine solidarity which village endogamy alone could mediate. The extent of the kindred tended to be defined by village boundaries. In other words, endogamy not only protected fisherfolk from the hostility of outsiders, it also provided a way to reduce conflict between men's and women's interests and to enhance women's contribution to the fishing economy. It was an adaptation to a mode of subsistence which required both male and female work groups and companionship.

CONTEXT: STIGMATIZED OCCUPATIONAL COMMUNITIES

In order to understand the social life of Scottish east coast fishing communities from the mid-eighteenth through the early twentieth centuries, we must look at the political and economic context of their emergence and survival. Many of these communities were created between the seventeenth and eighteenth centuries as occupational villages spawned by the extension of capitalist interests and institutions during the eighteenth century.[1] Until the 1740s, fishing along the east coast, in particular, had been relatively underdeveloped, and specialized fishing villages were mostly very small.[2]

Many lowland lairds in the northeastern counties of Forfar (now Angus), Kincardine and Aberdeenshire already owned farming hamlets (*fermtouns*) on their estates. During the late seventeenth and eighteenth centuries, as land in Scotland increasingly came to be regarded as a source of capital, some entrepreneurial lairds decided to try to exploit the sea as well by adding fishing villages (*fishtouns* or *fishertouns*). The fisherfolk were bound by debt and tenancy to fish part of the year for the laird's profit.

Fishing had long been regarded on the east coast as an undesirable and low-prestige occupation, and the social isolation of the fisherfolk was intensified with specialization during the eighteenth century. (For a fuller discussion of this occupational stigma, see Nadel 1984.) The only relationships which regularly cut across these boundaries were economic, based either upon a limited and direct exchange of goods, that is, fish for farm produce, or upon the exploitation of their fishing and fish-processing labor as dependent producers for rising capitalist entrepreneurs. In no case for which recorded evidence is available were Scottish fisher communities perceived either by themselves or by outsiders as standing on an equal footing with either agricultural or market-based communities. It is only in very recent years that a few of the remaining fishing communities have achieved any degree of real economic prosperity (Knipe 1984).[3]

The Origins of Ferryden

An ethnohistory of the North Sea village of Ferryden provides the focus for this paper.[4] Ferryden is surrounded by the agricultural district of North Angus and the Mearns, and sits across from the harbor and market town of Montrose. In its heyday in the 1880s, Ferryden was one of the busiest fishing villages along the east coast of Scotland, with over 160 boats, but its fishing days are long gone. The way of life and division of labor described here began to collapse with the onset of the First World War.[5]

Ferryden was one of those villages born in the 1740s as a laird's herring colony. The early settlers of Ferryden participated in a dual, seasonally determined fishing system which characterized the whole east coast, pursuing herring in the summer and inshore

"white fish" species during the rest of the year.[6] The herring fishing
belonged to the laird: fishermen exchanged their catch for the use
of boats, gear, and houses. In the 1840s, the estate was broken up
and herring fishing declined precipitously until new capital interests revived it in the 1860s and '70s. However, ties to the laird and
to herring were quickly replaced by dependence upon the market
for white fish.

THE SEXUAL DIVISION OF LABOR IN WHITE FISHING:
FISHERMEN AND FISHWIVES

Each of the two fisheries, herring and white fish, generated a distinct division of labor within the family and the community. Each
involved both men and women, but in the case of herring, both sexes
came to work for the fish-curers in an explicitly capitalist setting.
White fishing, however, can be regarded as having supported a
household-oriented mode of subsistence in which men's and
women's work was complementary and mutually supportive. Each
woman worked to support a particular boat and one or more crew
members. Ferryden women's involvement in fish marketing was largely ended after the First World War, but in other communities where
inshore fishing persisted, some women sold fish until the 1940s, or
even later.

The white fishing boats themselves were purely male domains
and women were not allowed to set foot on board. Like cats, pigs,
salmon, and ministers, women were bad luck for boats. (See discussion below.) The three- or four-man inshore crews were recruited
agnatically. Groups of brothers or brothers and their sons were
preferred, and the catch was divided into shares. Men went out to
sea on trips which could last from twelve to fourteen hours. They
sailed in small, undecked wooden sailboats to the fishing grounds
which lay from five to twenty-five miles offshore. Each man took a
woven basket packed with coiled fishing lines. There were several
thousand feet long of line strung with hooks at short intervals.
Anson claims that around 1840, "in the summer months it was not
an uncommon event for fifteen or sixteen boats at Ferryden to come
in...with a thousand haddocks each," and that these would sell for
roughly a farthing per pound (Anson 1930:117).

Women were responsible for preparing these lines. This was very
time-consuming, arduous, and dirty labor. The first step was to
gather the mussels which were used as bait. Ferryden was well-
situated, for it lay right next to an abundant source: the mussel
beds of the tidal estuary which opens up just behind the harbor
mouth. For the first century of the village's existence, the mussel

bait was a free, common property resource. Mussels grew in the section of the tidal basin called the Back Sands. They were exposed during low tide, when the Back Sands became a sticky, oozing mud flat. Groups of fishwives left the village every few days armed with mussel rakes. Working in hymn-singing groups of two or three, their skirts hiked up to their thighs to protect them from the mud, they piled thousands of mussels into the pack-baskets and hauled them back up the bank to the village, where they were dumped into shallow pools dug out on the foreshore to keep the shellfish fresh.

Then began the long and monotonous work of baiting the lines, work which often began at first light. Each line required several hundred to several thousand mussels, shelled and fixed expertly on a hook. Sometimes older children helped their mothers in this job, and often older daughters were required to take over such household tasks as cooking and childminding in order to free the fishwives for the crucial line-baiting work. A woman from a more northerly village recalls:

> I hated the small lines for this meant so much more work for the adults, shelling the mussels, baiting the lines...My parents' day began at three in the morning and often ended at midnight...I have seen both of my parents fall down with exhaustion at the end of a day, after my father had come in from the sea (Fraser 1983).

In both line-baiting and in bait-gathering, women worked in small groups of uterine kin. This was true all over the east coast, as well as in Ferryden. Margaret Buchan quotes an old lady from the area of Peterhead:

> She said if the weather was fine we all sat outside and baited lines on the pavement, my mother, my sisters and myself. If the weather was bad, we then had to work in the kitchen, and then the place was in a right 'steer.' However, she said if anyone needed help it was given gladly (Buchan 1977).

It seems unlikely that men, women, and their families could have spent much time together. People in Ferryden remember that children would often be turned out of their beds to make room for their fathers and older brothers upon their return late at night from the fishing. Their houses were called "but-and-ben": one room front, and one back, and in these, fisherwomen raised families of ten or twelve.

Women had additional responsibilities during the inshore fishing season. They had to knit the fishermen's stockings and jerseys, and clean and mend lines and nets. When the tide was low, they helped to launch the boats. When the boat was launched, women had to hand the lines and ballast to the men on board. Upon the

boats' return, women helped to haul them back in again. And finally, women in Ferryden and other fishing villages carried their men
to the boats on their backs, wading through waist-high water to
protect them from the cold North Sea, and when the fishing was
done, carried them back to shore. Line drawings from the late
eighteenth century depict brawny fishwives, skirts tucked im-
modestly up to their waists, with relatively small but heavily clothed
and leather-booted fishermen slung on their backs like creels.
Bertram describes this scene for the neighboring village of Auchmithie, a few miles south of Ferryden:

> I have seen the women of Auchmithie 'kilt their coats' and rush
> into the water in order to aid in shoving off the boats, and on the
> return of the fleet carry the men ashore on their brawny shoulders
> with the greatest ease and all the nonchalance imaginable, no mat-
> ter who might be looking at them (Anson 1930:113).

It is doubtful that the fishermen in these early years saw much
of the cash their fish realized. When the catch had been divided into
shares, the women took over. They reserved part of it for their
family's consumption and loaded the rest of the fish into their creels
for sale, either to inland households or to local markets and cadgers.
The following describes the winter haddock fishery in Auchmithie:

> The boats would set off from the open beach at 2 a.m., the men
> being carried to the boats on the backs of the women; by 10 a.m.
> the crews would be back with the daily haul...There followed in-
> tense activity by the whole family around each fisherman's cottage.
> One woman would decapitate and gut the haddocks, another would
> slit and clean them, another put them in salt in a tub and yet
> another tied them by the tails in pairs on a pole. The fish were then
> hung on a scaffolding to dry before being sent for sale...the baiting
> of the hooks, of which there were 6500 to each set of lines, was
> done by the children (Gray 1978).

Often, the fish were carried directly to inland households. Each
fishwife had a regular clientele among the farm workers of her territory. She was usually paid in kind, particularly butter, eggs,
cheese, and grain. However, "towards the end of the six-monthly
period after payment of their wages, rural laborers' incomes were
unable to buy fish regularly and the fishwife would have a walk to
the nearest town in an attempt to sell off surplus stocks" (Hay and
Walker 1985:37). In the early years before the development of a rail-
way system, all marketing expeditions were made on foot. A woman
might cover fifteen to twenty miles in a day. Even more prodigious
exploits were recorded for the fishwives some villages farther south
near Edinburgh, where four fishwives from Dunbar were reported

to have "trotted" with a full creel, twenty-six miles in five hours (Bertram 1883). Women often preferred to travel in groups, for these expeditions could be dangerous, as well as fatiguing. "Fishwives were often attacked both for money and carnal knowledge. All carried sharp gutting knives" (Fraser 1983). Children of both sexes occasionally went along, and "by fourteen a daughter was able to cover the round on her own" (Hay and Walker 1985:37).

Sometimes the Ferryden fishwives carried the fish straight to Montrose, where the catch could be sold to itinerant cadgers or middlemen for cash. The return was poor—a hundredweight of fish fetched only a few shillings. This money was used to pay debts and to purchase some household necessities in the town. The fishwives' marketing labors earned them a reputation for aggressive verbal ability, and the stereotype of the fishwife is, of course, that of a shrill, loud-voiced, or shrieking woman. In any case, their labors were essential for household survival, for unlike the fisherfolk of the west coast or those of Scandinavia, or, for that matter, their east coast predecessors, the Ferrydeners and other specialized east coast fishers were not crofters. That is, they held little or no ground to supplement their fishing income. There is no record in Ferryden of potato patches or of the keeping of pigs or chickens.[7] They were, for all intents and purposes, exclusively fisherfolk—people of the sea.

Changes in marketing made the first serious impact on women's roles in the Ferryden white fishery. Beginning in the 1830s, women faced increasing marketing competition from Montrose-based fish cadgers. At first these were merely itinerant entrepreneurs with a cart and a few barrels, who entered the village to purchase fish for resale. Some bought fish directly from the men on the shore, frequently concluding these transactions in one of the many ale-shops which flourished in the village. The fisherfolk were believed to be hard drinkers, and the cadgers paid for a significant amount of the catch in whiskey, a compensation that the fishwives could not provide. An additional advantage, from the fisherman's point of view, was that cash paid directly to the fishermen meant that liquor could be purchased before the housekeeping expenses could be extracted.

Fishcurers became serious rivals for the marketing of both white fish and herring: the fishwives had to compete with middlemen for their husbands' catches. The fishermen quickly went into debt, for curers were glad to extend credit in exchange for the fisherman's guarantee of exclusive rights over the catch, sometimes for an entire fishing season. The curers soon acquired a reputation among the fisherfolk for rapacity, an image that was expressed and reinforced by the saying, "The fishcurer is the enemy of the fisherman." To be more accurate, the saying should really have been, "the enemy of the fisher man and woman," for women began to lose their control over the household livelihood.

In Ferryden, this situation was soon exacerbated by the establishment of a powerful fishcuring firm, the Montrose Curing Company (a pseudonym) which moved in from the Border town of Berwick. By the 1870s-'80s, this company had acquired a near-monopoly on commercial fishcuring and fishmarketing within the greater Montrose region. Taking advantage of a boom market for herring, the firm introduced bigger, more efficient boats and hired the fishermen directly to work as employees. They gained control over the mussel beds of the Back Sands, changing them from a common resource into a private, profit-making one. Extending credit to the generally impoverished fishermen, they secured mortgages on virtually all of the fishermen's boats and houses within a few years and effectively compelled the fishermen to sell all of their herring catch and much of the white fish catch exclusively to them. Some of the women managed to continue selling fish, but their control over the inshore catch declined. This trend was not confined to Ferryden, but in ports near Edinburgh, some of the fishwives kept control over the transaction by selling the fish to the middlemen themselves.

> The labor of the females in the olden time was heavy, but it is less so now that so much of the fish caught by their husbands and sons is disposed of at the side of the boat in wholesale fashion, to buyers from those large seats of population, which are always demanding supplies of fish, and are never able to obtain all they want. Some of the fishwives make excellent auctioneers; they possess a rude eloquence which is difficult to resist...(Bertram 1883:6).

The Company also began to change the seasonal rhythm of work and increased the distance between the fisherman and his family by encouraging the fishermen to spend a greater portion of their year in following the herring shoals around the north and west coasts of Scotland, as well as down to Yarmouth in England. Inshore white fishing continued, but its significance was greatly reduced.

Change: From Fishwives to Gutting Quines

Over the course of the nineteenth century, the balance in Scotland between the white and herring fisheries shifted, with herring taking on a greater and greater importance. In 1812, roughly 100,000 barrels of cured herring were exported; in 1850 the figure rose to nearly 600,000 barrels; by the early 1880s, Scotland was exporting approximately a million and a half barrels of herring (Gray 1978). Ferryden's participation grew accordingly. By the 1880s it was said that one could walk across the river between Ferryden and Montrose over the fishing boats, most of which were owned by or mortgaged to the Montrose Curing Company.

With the expansion of the herring industry, there was a greatly increased demand for female labor in the curing process and this produced a significant alteration in the relationship of male to female labor.[8] Now the curers' demands dictated the rhythm of work as well as the division of labor.

> Herring fishing's demand for ancillary labour was not contained within the framework of the family group as had been the older forms...during the fishing itself the crew would operate without the direct aid of their women-folk. Nets had to be spread for drying but it was done either by the crew or by laborers hired for the purpose. The transport of fish from boat to yard was the responsibility of the curer and he would engage specialized carters for the purpose. The women, on the other hand, finding employment within the yards as gutters and packers, did not directly support the crews in which their men-folk were organized. Rather they were hired as wage-earners by the curers to share impersonally in the work of a yard into which the catches of many boats might be discharged (Gray 1978).

The Montrose Curing Company sent several women to Sweden to learn Scandinavian herring curing methods. They began to hire Ferryden village women directly as wage-earners. These women were expected to follow the herring fleets. Women from Ferryden were put in small open boats, lashed in to protect them from being washed overboard in heavy seas, and sent to Shetland, Yarmouth, and the Hebrides to gut, cure, and pack what the people of Aberdeen call the "silver darlings"—the herring.

Girls could start in the gutting as early as the age of ten, although they usually waited until leaving school at the age of fourteen. Both unmarried and married women went, though photographs indicate a preponderance of younger women. They were housed communally, under conditions that were often less than ideal. "The huts were overcrowded and the women were overworked so if disease struck it took a terrible toll" (Buchan 1977). The hours were long, sometimes up to fifteen hours a day. They were generally paid at piece rates.

> In the early years of this century the women received 8d. between the crew [in other words, to be divided three ways] for each barrel of herring packed and gutted. Later it rose to 10d., then to 1/-. The most anyone ever remembers receiving was 2/6d. per barrel. My

mother says when she received £40 for working at the summer fishing she thought that she had made a fortune (Buchan 1977).

Later they also received a weekly wage. They were hired and worked in groups of threes: two gutters and a packer to a barrel. The packer was also responsible for keeping track of all financial transactions (Buchan 1977).

> With their razor sharp knives flashing at lightning speed they could deal with as many as 50 herring a minute. The fish were first sprinkled with salt otherwise they would have been too slippery to handle at such speed (Elliott 1979).

Scots fisher girls became known for their strength and hard working habits:

> In their leisure time they were equally industrious. They could usually be seen strolling round the town engaged in animated con- versation with each other, but knitting quickly as they walked (Elliott 1978).

Some of the older women in Ferryden today remember those days with a mixture of pride and pain. They speak of the long hours of standing over barrels of brine. They wrapped their fingers in cot- ton rags, for gutting made sores and the brine inflamed them. The salt alone cut holes between their fingers, and they remember hands cracked, raw, and bleeding. "Even in the late autumn they were ex- pected to continue working in the open 'exposed to rain, sleet and wind,' standing into the night ankledeep in 'quagmires of mud, sand and fish refuse'" (Thompson et al. 1983).[9]

Not all curing operations were done in faraway places. There were a number of smaller, local curing stations. In the summer, the Curing Company hired women to gut herring in Montrose. They sent coopers round Ferryden village to gather the women by crying out "A'body! A'body!" The work was hard and long. One old Ferryden lady recalls that her mother would often return home at two or three in the morning. "A woman was finished at fifty in those days."

The relationship between the fish-curing firm and the people of Ferryden was tense, and it grew increasingly antagonistic as the herring boom began to decline and as fishermen competed for scarce work. When the company tried to introduce trawlers briefly after the turn of the century, many Ferrydeners refused to work on them, loathing the conditions of work, and fearing (presciently) that the trawlers would ruin the fishing. After World War I, the curing firm withdrew its investment from herring and white fish altogether, preferring to concentrate on salmon exports, and mussel sales (both lucrative, low-labor activities compared to sea-fishing.) Many fishermen emigrated. Some tried to get work netting salmon, but were refused because, according to informants today, they had been insufficiently deferential to company officials. Some women, however, were paid to make nets for the salmon fishers. According to a Ferryden informant, two women working together could make about one net a week, for which they were paid a few pennies. With the men gone or unemployed, however, more and more women also were forced to leave the fishing industry, and many of them found work as low-paid laborers in the flax and jute mills or the jam factory in Montrose.

ENDOGAMY, GENDER, AND SOCIAL ORGANIZATION

Throughout Ferryden's fishing days, village endogamy was practiced intensively. Occasionally men brought in fisher lassies from other villages along the coast, but for years even this was relatively rare. As one author says, "none of the communities would easily absorb outsiders, whether male or female" (Gray 1978). There were several reasons for this. For one, as we noted in the beginning, Ferryden, like other fishing villages, suffered from a stigmatized identity. Montrosians regarded Ferrydeners, as one Ferryden man put it, as "savages." Thus no Montrosian was likely to consider marrying a Ferryden woman. Montrose boys were not apparently above trying to set up sexual liaisons, however. At least the Ferrydeners believed this, for villagers today rather fondly recall hearing of episodes in which outside males venturing across the bridge would be met by a gang of village males hurling sticks, stones and refuse from the mussel middens which lined village streets.

I believe that another reason underlay the strong preference for village endogamy. This emerged from the nature of male and female work groups. Both male and female work groups were organized around core groups of male and female kin. Boat crews were organized agnatically. Men said that they felt more comfortable working with their own kin. Women felt the same way, however, and women's groups often consisted of mothers, sisters and daughters, and the evidence suggests that women were extremely reluctant to break these ties. "When the men were away, as they often were, for eight to ten weeks at a time then the women and children had each other for company and protection" (Buchan 1977:4). Parish birth records from Ferryden reveal a strong pattern of women having given birth at least to their first and second children in their mothers' houses. Some women even returned from North America to do so.

Naming practices also indicate the strength and persistence of uterine ties. Despite a formal change in surname after marriage, married women in the village continued to use and to be addressed by their maiden names. Thus Mary West might be Mrs. James Watt for official documents, but she remained Mary West within the village. Even the official parish birth and death records from the mid-nineteenth through the mid-twentieth century recognized this equivalence of maiden and married names. They gave women's names according to the formula: (1) "given," (2) "married," (3) "or maiden." Thus, "Mary Watt West" is listed as "Mary West or Watt." In the village, women also were often identified simply through their uterine genealogy: Mary's Catherine's Betty, for example. My observations of older village women, daughters of the fisherfolk, show a great deal of closeness between mothers and daughters, between sisters, and between aunts and nieces. Some sisters in the village today are said to be so close that "they even go to the bathroom together." Village endogamy allowed both women and men to maintain consanguineal ties and thus, even marriages to fisherfolk from other fishing villages were discouraged. They were not unknown, however, and "if a fisherman married from outside the community, then usually his mother took over and instructed the outsider in her duties. Sometimes this situation worked very well, at other times it led to bitterness and rancour" (Buchan 1977:5).

In the densely woven social fabric of Scots fishing villages, men's and women's lives were largely separate, but complementary. There was a strong embracing ethic of bilaterality which united all villagers as kin and as equals within the stigmatized community. Ferrydeners said (and still say today), "we're all 42nd cousins." In addition, there was a tendency for women and men to emphasize and interact with different sections of the kindred. Women stressed female links to female kin; males stressed male links with male kin.[10] Perhaps this can be (if only frivolously) expressed by a ditty which a group of female old age pensioners sang on a bus trip during my field work:

Oh, ye cannae shove your granny aff a bus,
Oh, ye cannae shove your granny aff a bus,
Oh, ye cannae shove your granny,
'cause she's your mammy's mammy,
Oh, ye cannae shove your granny aff a bus.
Oh, ye can shove your other granny aff a bus,
Oh, ye can shove your other granny aff a bus,
Oh, ye can shove your other granny,
'Cause she's your *daddy's* mammy,
Oh, ye can shove your other granny aff a bus!

Village endogamy, therefore, provided men and women with mates whose skills and values were complementary to their own, and it also enabled male and female solidarity to persist unchallenged.

The fisher women were widely perceived as strong and domineering. Outsiders have depicted them as tough and strong, and the observers' surprise at women's roles indicates the fishwives' difference from the women in landward communities.

> It may not, perhaps, be generally known to those who are not in possession of special sources of information, that in all fishing communities, the woman is head of the house...She is ruler over her household and chancellor of her husband's exchequer (Bertram 1883:4).

Despite Bertram's conviction of female dominance, I believe that women's "rule" over men was limited, and, in fact, countered in other spheres of activity. Male superiority was institutionally promoted within the realm of public organization and ritual activity. For example, since the mid-nineteenth century, the churches have been the main political arena for the Ferryden fisherfolk, but the elders of the church have nearly always been male, and community or parish associations were until very recently solely male domains. The white-fishing boat itself constituted a kind of semi-sacred realm, hedged about with ritual restrictions, of which the prohibition of women on board was central. When a fisherman died, his coffin was carried across to the Burying Ground at low tide, followed by an exclusively male procession.

Unfortunately, little has been recorded of the fishwives' own perceptions of their status or of their relationships to men. Some revealing information comes from the period of Protestant revivals and the Temperance movement (roughly from the 1860s through the 1920s), when fishing villages all over Scotland were transformed from (reportedly) "pagan" communities to devout, God-fearing ones. Accounts from this period indicate that women were often the first to respond, and they were certainly very prominent in promoting Temperance. (Given the strain which male drinking habits must have placed on households, and the fishcurers' exploitation of this through the fish-for-alcohol payment system, this hardly seems surprising.) Fishwives began to hold prayer meetings, and some were subject to hysterical conversions, "stricken down" by God, sometimes in prayer meetings, sometimes out on the Back Sands (Mitchell 1860; see also Nadel 1986).

Life for both men and women was unpredictable and dangerous. Women were forced to bear continuous anxiety and stress. Childbearing was done at home in all but very exceptional cases, and people today indicate that women had little time for rest. Since a fisherman's activity depended upon his wife's cooperation, he could ill afford her incapacity. One informant claims that women could be seen raking mussels in tidal water before they had healed, "and the water around them was red." In a novel written about the northeast fisherfolk of the nineteenth century, we see a fishwife refusing to see a doctor, despite the agonizing pain of a mysterious, and ultimately fatal disease, because "in the Fishertown you had the doctor only when you died" (Patterson 1950: 37). They worked long hours in the cold and wet, and they had to face the ever-present threat of losing their husbands, brothers and sons to drowning. The lifeboat was often busy and some boats went down in sight of land. Even after a rescue, they might still succumb to pneumonia. The Ferryden lifeboat records make stark reading: "Alexander Paton died of exposure and shock after being thrown overboard. Left widow and two children" (Duncan n.d.:25).

The words of Christian Watt, a fishwife from a northern village who lived from 1833 to 1923, bear eloquent witness to the toll this could take. She spent the last forty years of her life in Aberdeen's Cornhill Asylum, a victim of depression:

> The Congregational Minister came to the door. I asked him which one of my folk was lost, he said, 'It is the husband'...It was the 21st August, exactly three years and two weeks to the day since my son Peter was drowned and in that time I had lost five of my nearest...My son James was 17, so Maritime laws would not allow him to skipper the boat, which meant I would have to pay somebody to do so. Shortly afterwards I was to lose another son and daughter...I had my trust in Christ the Man of sorrow, and knew what he felt as he stood before Pontius Pilate the Procurator of Judea (Fraser 1983).

THE SYMBOLIC REALM: FEMALE STATUS AND MALE AMBIVALENCE

Despite, or perhaps because of the pattern of what Bott (1957) calls "segregated conjugal roles," women's status in Ferryden and other fishing villages seems to have been relatively high. Domestic social organization and inheritance patterns indicate a fairly evenhanded attitude towards women. For example, house inheritance patterns reveal no clear-cut bias towards one sex or the other, unlike the neighboring farmers, who display a marked preference for male primogeniture. Women often inherited their parents' houses. In a 1792 will from the northern village of Broadsea, the fisherman James Lascelles left all my worldly goods and chattels whatsoever and wherever situate to my great grand daughter Helen Noble or Lascelles widow of Andrew Noble a White fisher and to her eldest child...to be left in fee in her Mother's lifetime in time to be her own absolute property (Fraser 1983).

This property included not only household goods, but "my great lines and my small lines," as well. And a number of elderly women in Ferryden today, both married and never-married are living in houses inherited from their kin.

Despite this relatively high status, the Scottish fisherwomen's world was largely separate from that of men, and there is evidence that men feared it. I believe that men's anxiety can be partly explained by examining women's relationship to the landward world beyond the fishing village. Thus, while the ocean was perilous, so was solid ground. One could say, in effect, that the fishermen of Ferryden saw themselves as caught between the devil and the deep blue sea.

Women in Scottish fishing villages were essential to the survival of the fishing economy, and men recognized this. At the same time, however, women's work—in marketing and in curing— associated them with the land and with land-bound people who were seen as hostile and threatening. Buchan points out that "the fisher wife...acted as a link between land and sea—few of these existed" (1977:12). A fisherman had neither any access to land as a productive resource, nor a chance of getting any. For Ferrydeners, to acquire land or a land-based occupation usually meant leaving the village and the fisher-identity behind. The village itself constituted a narrow edge of tiny cottages all clustered at the water's edge. Behind it lay fields and farms; across from it was the town. From the fisherman's perspective, all land belonged either to the laird, the farmer or the fishcurer. The very tenancy of his house depended upon his ability to capture sea resources for others' profit. With the advent of the fish-curing firm's monopoly, the fisherman was caught in a cycle of credit and debt which both supported and threatened his livelihood. His only allies were other fishermen. Land people looked down on him and classified him as a member of an alien and inferior race. The inland world was hostile territory, where the fisherman had no place. The fisherwoman, on the other hand, whether as fishwife or gutting quine, did have a place there, albeit a lowly one. First, the land was where the fisherman's lines and gear must be prepared. But second, and more importantly in this context, the fishwives could go where the men could not. As white fish marketers, they transformed their husbands' labor into income by negotiating barter and sale. They could penetrate the world behind the coast. In that role, or as gutting quine employed by the curing firm, women regularly left the village for landward destinations. In contrast to the women of many Mediterranean societies, where women's activities are largely confined to private places and domestic spheres, Scottish fishwives performed publicly interstitial roles, standing, as men are so often said to do, between the domestic and the outside world.

While women transformed men's marine labors into earthly rewards, the fishermen had to risk their lives in one of the world's most perilous occupations. The North Sea took a steady toll, its rocks and storms snuffing out fishermen's lives with frightening regularity. The fisherman did not even bother to learn to swim, for he believed that once the sea had gotten a hold on him, it would not let go again. (Given North Sea conditions, and the fishermen's heavy leather boots, this was not an entirely irrational belief.) As Malinowski long ago pointed out, danger and magic go together (Malinowski 1860). Accounts of Ferryden and of other fishing villages are replete with rituals, charms and prohibitions designed to ward off danger and bring luck and safety to the fishermen. Many of these refer to women. Anson records the belief that "if a woman steps over a fishing-line, no fish will be caught in it" (Anson 1975). Several Ferryden village women were reported to be unlucky, and a few old women were even said to be witches. A fishermen who encountered any one of these on his way to the boat might well decide to turn back and forego the day's fishing, for it would be fruitless. A woman had magical power when her husband was out to sea, and could, wittingly or unwittingly, sever his "lifeline" with the shore. A fishwife must never comb her hair while her husband's boat was out to sea, for if she did, he would surely drown.

Women's associations with land and the extreme segregation of men and women for most of their working lives generated a degree of tension which was mirrored in the symbolic and supernatural realm. The women of Ferryden were seen as both powerful and dangerous, necessary and polluting. Without them and their labor, the fishing economy could not operate; without them and their reproductive capacities, the fishing community could not continue. However, from the men's point of view, women were not only helpmeets, they were sources and representatives of danger. As we noted above, women were not allowed to set foot in a fishing boat. Some women could not even go near them. Thompson says that "in the past fishermen might take it as a bad omen, and perhaps even turn back home, if they met with particular women on their way to the harbour. Sea work was men's work; and for women to have any place in it would be a pollution" (Thompson et al. 1983:173).

However, it is interesting in this context to consider the symbolic implications of women's role in carrying the men to the boats and back again. By carrying them from the dry land of the village to the boats, the women, whose domain was on land, transported the men to their domain, the sea. They raised them above the liminal tidal zone, the beach (sometimes land and sometimes water), which separated the two domains, so necessary and yet so antithetical to each other. The women kept the men out of the water which the men feared to enter, lest they never leave it. In a sense which is reminiscent of their reproductive roles, women delivered men to safety while they delivered them to danger.

The fishwives thus served a critical mediating function, practically and symbolically. They carried men across the water, keeping their feet dry and their status secure. They raised the next generation and managed the domestic world of the village. They marketed fish and worked as fish-curing laborers, transforming the catch into cash. Thus "a fisher laddie needed a fisher lassie" for more than her ability to bait the lines: a fisher lassie both literally and figuratively negotiated his passage between land and sea.

CONCLUSIONS

Women in Scottish fishing played a number of essential roles, both in the household-subsistence and in the capitalist modes of production which co-existed in the rural economy. Communities in the early, pre-herring years of household-oriented inshore fishing exhibited some of the characteristics of a peasant economy, with partial participation in the market and a reliance upon kin-based labor (Wolf 1969). Most fishermen and fisherwomen lived within stigmatized, encapsulated and internally unstratified communities which defended their social boundaries through a strong insistence on endogamy. I have suggested here that endogamy in Scottish fishing villages was also connected with the need to satisfy both male and female desires for same-sex kinship-based solidarity in work groups.

As we have seen, the sexual division of labor in such communities was quite clear-cut. In examining patterns of conjugal relationships within an urban setting, Bott (1957:60) says that:

> The degree of segregation in the role-relationship of husband and wife varies directly with the connectedness of the family's social network. The more connected the network, the greater the degree of segregation between the roles of husband and wife.

Bott attributes this relationship to the magnetic pull which pre-existing networks impose upon spouses, and the corresponding degree of conformity within the network which develops. An occupational community such as a fishing village, which offered no alternative forms of work, presents another dimension from which to look at the relationship. The requirements of inshore fishing were such that men could not make a living without the support of skilled females. For the white fishing, this was organized within the nuclear family, so that a wife's labor supported her husband's directly. As Friedl points out, subsistence technology is critical for determining both the division of labor and the quality of relationships between the sexes (1975:7). Inshore fishing was labor-intensive and un-mechanized. It required the men to be away from home for long hours, so that for many times in the year, husband and wife spent relatively little time together. Women relied upon their children and upon other women for companionship and assistance. The bonds set up between mother and daughter or between sisters grew very strong, so that it would be equally logical to say that "a fisher lassie needed a fisher lassie."

As long as inshore fishing provided a significant proportion of the fishing economy, herring fishing does not appear to have seriously changed gender relationships within the home villages. However, the division of labor generated by the herring fishery ultimately worked to increase the already considerable social distance between men and women. Men went out for voyages lasting several weeks or months and women also left home for long periods of time. Women still worked in female kin groups, but their labor now supported herring boats crewed by unrelated males.

The total impact of herring fishing on women's status is not clear, but there is I think, some reason to consider a possible analogy with agriculture. As Ester Boserup (1970) pointed out and as others have continued to document, women's status may decline dramatically with the transition from subsistence to commercial agriculture (Linares 1985). The new division of labor in cash cropping tends to reduce women's control over the domestic economy, along with her direct contribution to subsistence. As herring fishing gradually came to predominate in the east coast communities, the power of middlemen and fishcurers grew, and the domestic role of women in the fishery lessened. Women's enthusiastic participation in the Temperance movement may well have been an early response to these changes. Later, as gutting quines, women's wages contributed to household subsistence, but their work no longer directly supported male family members. Away from home, they may also have been the targets of increased male aggression, particularly within a proletarianized situation where both men and women were subject to exploitation by their employers.

Fisher women's economic activities and group solidarity gave them a status which women in most other sectors of Scottish social life did not enjoy. As many authors have noted, social and cultural segregation of the sexes and the social devaluation of women in much of Britain tends to be quite strong (Whitehead 1976; Bell and Newby 1976; Jackson 1968). However, gender status asymmetry did exist in fishing villages and its content reflected the dependent condition of these communities. If the fishermen's perception of gender was that women were to land as men were to ocean, that does not necessarily indicate a maritime version of the nature/culture divide. Rather it suggests a response to the very material marginality of fishing communities within the larger social setting. A fisher laddie needed a fisher lassie— he even respected her— but he also feared her.

Notes

1. This period is known as the age of the agricultural "improving movement" (Smout 1970). It was also the time of the notorious Highland Clearances, when landlords replaced "inefficient" humans with wool-producing sheep.
2. The exception is the region known as the East Neuk of Fife, where fishing settlements had been active since the sixteenth century (Gray 1978).
3. It is often stated that the fishermen owned their own boats, and legally, or formally speaking, this was true for many (Buchan 1977; Knipe 1984). However, by the middle of the nineteenth century in Ferryden at least, boats, like houses, were either owned outright by the fishcuring company, or the company held their mortgages.
4. Fieldwork was conducted in 1975-76 and in 1984. The data are drawn from the memories of old people, from local archives, and from a variety of published sources.
5. The combination of a drop in the market for cured fish, the depletion of the herring stocks, and increased competition from mechanized, capital-intensive trawling from Aberdeen proved lethal for the Ferryden fishing industry, along with that of a number of other small communities. Village population peaked during the herring boom of the 1880s at roughly 1600; today it has half that number and serves largely as a dormitory suburb and site for an offshore oil support base (Nadel 1979, 1983).
6. White fish is a term used generally to refer to such species as cod, ling, turbot, and haddock.

7. Fisherwomen and children in Ferryden did perform some casual harvest labor for the nearby potato farmers, and they kept their gleanings underneath the box bed inside their "but-and-ben" (two-room) cottages. Fisherfolk in some other villages also grew their own "tatties" in tiny patches of ground. A famous folk song tells of the endless round of "tatties and herrin'" which provided the Buchan fisherfolk's diet.

8. Earlier, women from some of the more northerly villages had also been hired to cook and clean for the herring crews and in some places, for men employed as gutters. "In 1844, most Broadsea fishers went to the west coast and the Hebrides. We as lassies went to cook for the men...the coastline was dotted with the bothies of girls; it was hard work to bake wash and cook to 27 men...at this time the fishermen did most of the gutting, it had not yet become wholly a female job" (Fraser 1983).

9. These exploitative conditions sometimes led to strikes, which deserve much more discussion than there is room for in this paper. Thompson (1983) and Buchan (1977) both discuss fisher girls' strikes:

> So far as I can ascertain the women were not unionised but if there was a strike then they all went on strike to a woman. Two strikes which I have been told of several times was one which occurred in 1911, and another which occurred in 1935. The 1911 one was started by someone putting a red rag on the end of a broom and going around all the yards thereby managing to encourage everyone to come out on strike...The women were the hub. If they did not work then the curers did not buy the fish so then there was no money for anyone (Buchan 1977).

A note on Margaret Buchan: she herself is descended from a fisher community in Peterhead, and many of her informants are friends and relatives.

10. The older men and women of Ferryden today express this separation in their social groupings and activities. A casual glance around the village reveals small clusters of older people sitting together and chatting. These are almost invariably sex-segregated. Even the church has largely become (the Elders aside) largely a woman's domain.

"Shore Skippers" and "Grass Widows": Active and Passive Women's Roles in a Newfoundland Fishery

11

Dona Lee Davis

INTRODUCTION

Fish plant laborer, shore skipper, and grass widow are three contemporary, community level, fishery-related roles which may be filled by women in the southwest coast Newfoundland fishing village of Grey Rock Harbour.[1] The fish plant worker takes an active, instrumental role in the village fishery. She cleans, processes and packages fish caught by the Harbour fishermen. The shore skipper's fishery-related role is also active and instrumental. She keeps the books and accounts for her seabound husband's vessel and acts as his onshore agent. By contrast, the grass widow appears to be a more passive and expressive role. While more esoteric and thereby difficult for the outsider to readily comprehend, proper performance of the grass widow role is integral to the success of the fishery as a family and community enterprise. The grass widow provides female, landbound, emotional support to those fishery activities that are male and seabound.

Many studies of women in fishing economies focus on the material aspects of the division of labor in the fishery, e.g., the exceptional women who actually fish or work at sea, women who process and market fish, or women whose domestic activities indirectly support the fishing enterprise. Male/female and husband/wife realms of activity in the fishing enterprise are usually portrayed as separate albeit complementary domains. Although it is important to differentiate between the material aspects of male and female work roles, the more expressive, impalpable domain where male and female concerns merge or overlap should not be neglected. This is particularly true for any analysis of a fishing society. In this chapter, the analysis goes beyond the actual economics of fishing to demonstrate the ramifications of women's share in the occupational identity of their fishing menfolk on the day-to-day operations of the structural and ideological facets of community life. Fishing in Grey Rock Harbour is part of local, village, collective life. Fishing is not merely men's work, but is part of the outport tradition and heritage— a way of life for a people. A fishery ethos pervades the entire community. In the analysis that follows the Grey Rock Harbour village fishery will be presented as a sociocultural system characterized by complex, multi-dimensional, overlapping instrumental and expressive male/female roles.

In the first section of this chapter, local notions of the shore skipper and the grass widow are presented. Each of these roles is described in terms of (a) instrumental and expressive functions, and (b) acceptable and unacceptable roles for women. The second demonstrates how fisherwomen give meaning, purpose, and legitimacy to their activities in the community. Culture change is the topic of the third and final section. Since the indigenous ideals of outport women cannot be understood apart from the impingement of urban Newfoundland and mass Canadian society on the local identity, the collective ethos of the fishery is examined in light of the peripheral nature of outport communities, in general, and of Grey Rock Harbour, in particular.

THE SETTING

Grey Rock Harbour (a pseudonym) is a small fishing village of 800 inhabitants located on the southwest coast of Newfoundland. The physical community is clearly bounded by high, rocky cliffs which surround the "gut" or passageway to the sea. Brightly colored houses are perched on the cliff-sides, looking like houses lining the inside of a bowl. By Newfoundland standards, Grey Rock Harbour is a comparatively new settlement. Earliest census reports show 100 inhabitants present in 1845. Unlike some other outports, Grey Rock Harbour is a very homogeneous setting. Fishing is and has always been the economic mainstay of the community. The villagers are Anglican and share a common southwestern English heritage. There are no village factions based on occupation, religious affiliation, ethnicity or social class.

Grey Rock Harbour is a stable fishing community. Seventy-four percent of the men are involved in fishing— 40 percent as fishermen and 34 percent as fish plant laborers. Unlike some outport villages on the north and east coasts of Newfoundland, Grey Rock Harbour has had a bountiful year-round fishery. Historically the villagers were poor by Canadian standards, although economic conditions in Grey Rock Harbour were never as severe as in other outports, where fishing was seasonal and more sporadic, and where fishermen did not have the option of selling fish to local merchants or those in Nova Scotia. Living conditions improved dramatically beginning with confederation with Canada. In 1960, Grey Rock Harbour was designated a resettlement community. People from small, isolated communities along the southwest coast were resettled (see Iverson and Matthews 1968) into Grey Rock Harbour and the construction of a road was begun. The underlying reason was that it would be cheaper to bring outporters to modern services than it would be to bring modern facilities to isolated areas. In 1960, a preliminary dirt road was completed and connected to the village proper by a bridge, which continually washed out. In the early 1970s isolation ceased when a solid bridge was built and the road was straightened and paved. A new school, public electricity, telephones, and indoor plumbing followed soon after. During the most of the year villagers can readily travel to the local town to purchase goods and receive medical services. However, during winter the road can become quite impassable and local stores sell out of goods. Each household must have supplies to last several weeks. Villagers who are prone to severe episodes of sickness or who are in advanced stages of pregnancy are packed off to live with relatives in towns with local hospitals.

Despite the fact that villagers have most of the conveniences and services of modern Canadian society, their distinction from mainstream Canadian life styles stems, in part, from their long history of isolation. Two themes dominate the essence of village life for both men and women: (1) the fishery and (2) the "hard times past." Village activities center on fishing. Aside from work as store clerks, postal officers, and one or two multipurpose fix-it men, the people who work in the community are involved in fishing. The fishery permeates the landscape in Grey Rock Harbour. Each house has a picture window overlooking the Harbour. Men (even those who do not fish) wear distinctive fishermen's dress, consisting of high rubber boots, plaid flannel shirts, slickers, and fishermen's toques. Villagers' seasonal and daily work schedules and income fluctuate with the fishery. Catches are a major topic of everyday conversation for men and women alike. The second theme of "hard times past" describes the abiding recognition of how easy life today is compared to the poverty and hardship of the past. Grey Rock Harbour villagers have forestalled a headlong rush into mass, middle class society

(Davis 1983b) by consciously attempting to blend the best of the old traditions with the advantages of present-day life in order to offer a meaningful choice of life styles for their children— children who will have to decide whether to stay in the village and perpetuate valued outport traditions or leave and become uprooted figures in mass society. It is against these two themes, fishery and hardship, that women's roles in the local community are discussed.

WOMEN AND THE FISHERY

Studies of women and the fishery tend to regard women's contributions in two different ways. The first mode is tangible and functional and entails women's fishery-related work roles. The second contributory mode is less tangible and involves the emotional, ideological, more rarefied contributions women make to the fishing enterprises— in terms of their roles of wife, mother, and sister of fishermen and as carriers of the family tradition. While the instrumental roles of women remain as prominent (although changed in kind) today as in the past, the cultural forces of localism and traditionalism have actually enhanced the expressive role of women in the Grey Rock Harbour fishing enterprise.

At this point it becomes necessary to further elaborate on what is meant by instrumental and expressive roles. Parsons (1951:49) makes a functional distinction between the two types of roles. Instrumental roles are related mainly to task performance, making big decisions and taking responsibility for economic security. Expressive roles are concerned with nurturance plus the emotional aspects of nurturant tasks. How can each of these roles be related to women's conduct in fishing economies?

Instrumental Roles

An instrumental focus on women's fishery-related roles dominates most of the literature on women in fishing economies. These studies (reviewed in the second chapter of this book) focus on active roles of women in the fishery, such as catching, processing and marketing fish; financing gear and boats; and keeping family business records; or actively lobbying for legislative change. Other, less obvious, instrumental functions of women in a fishing economy include the "subsidiary" (Smith 1977a:8) functions of women, who take over the responsibility of running the household and raising the children, so that the men are free to fish.

The role of women in the Newfoundland outport fishery has not been ignored by observers of Newfoundland society and culture. However, it is the traditional, pre-confederation fishery-related roles of Newfoundland women that have been the primary focus of ethnographic description. Murray (1979) stresses the role of women as "work horse" in the traditional fishery. Historically, women's direct contribution to the fishery included drying and salting of cod, making sails, and giving birth to future fishermen. Indirect or subsidiary functions included tending gardens, keeping cows and chickens, shearing sheep, picking berries, preserving food and overall household care and maintenance. The old saying was that women gave "more than 50 percent." The theme of complementary but separate male and female spheres of activity characterizes much of the literature on the instrumental roles of women in the outport family fishery. Antler (1977, 1980, 1982) and Antler and Faris (1979) negatively contrast present female roles of fish plant laborer and housekeeper to what they view as the more rewarding traditional roles in primary, family-based, saltfish production. Porter (1983) also describes how modernization has undercut the traditional, instrumental roles of Newfoundland fisherwives, reducing their fishery contribution to the level of subsidiary functions. According to Porter, in the contemporary Newfoundland, post-saltfish fishery, the lists of men's tasks and women's tasks hardly overlap.

Studies such as those of Porter, Faris and Antler have focused on fisheries on the northeast coast. Although at various junctions of their individual life histories, women in Grey Rock Harbour had to adapt to prolonged periods of husband absence (Davis 1983a), they were never actively involved, to any large extent, in saltfish production. Villagers have not commercially prepared saltfish for over 65 years. Even the historical saltfish production was slight, conducted by the local merchants rather than families, and only employing two or three women who were widowed or were from needy families. Thus Grey Rock Harbour women have not "lost" a traditional productive role in the fishery—nor have they historically performed subsidiary household productive functions such as raising garden produce, cows for milk, or shearing sheep, since the local ecology is incompatible with agriculture or foraging. On the contrary, through modernization they have gained an instrumental role in the fishery—fish plant laborer. Over 56 women now work at the fish plant, which came with the road in the 1970s. Presently, the occasional Harbour woman fishes or hunts with her husband, and women keep all household accounts, yet the predominant instrumental fishery-related roles of Grey Rock Harbour are limited to those of fish plant worker and household/family caretaker.

Expressive Roles

The economic analysis of women's work roles is central to understanding the nature of male and female contributions to fishing economies. However, it should not preclude analysis of the more ideational, emotional, or expressive aspects of the fisher husband-/wife relationship, nor should it obscure the relationship of the fishing enterprise to the overall community ethos. These non-material, less palpable aspects of the fishery have been relatively ignored, and almost totally ignored when it comes to women. The exceptions can be illustrated by the passing attention given to the emotional realm on the one hand, and the phenomenal realm on the other. Studies of the emotional realm tend to focus on the strain that separation puts on a fisherman's marriage (Acheson 1981; Acheson and Lello 1980; Orbach 1977; and Tunstall 1969), or on the task of coping with the anxiety generated in a high risk and dangerous occupation (Danowski 1980; Poggie and Gersuny 1974). Studies of the phenomenal realm focus on women as polluters or contaminators of gear and boats (Gladwin 1970; Tunstall 1969; and Wadel 1966). However, there is minimal theoretical or ethnographic elaboration of these themes. The most explicit and comprehensive account of the expressive and ideological realms of life in a fishing community, although not specifically concerned with women, comes from Cohen's (1982a, 1982b) analysis of the Whalsay fishermen of Britain on the ideology of localism. According to Cohen (1982a:2, 3, 4, 19, 36, 199) communities should be studied in terms which are meaningful to their own members. He is an advocate of the "ethnology of locality"— going beyond "objective manifestations" to capture the collective, "experiential sense of belonging"— that immensely complex ideology which informs every aspect of a community's social life. Cohen's thesis on localism and belonging recognizes two aspects of community ideology that become relevant to the subsequent analysis. First, he recognizes that men who fish have moral support from those who are ashore (1982b:36). Second, he notes how localism can function to enhance the survival of community identity when a historically traditional community is threatened by culture change and assimilation into mass, nonlocal culture (1982a:4).

The few studies of female expressive roles in the Newfoundland outport setting focus on the affective aspects of the male/female relationship. Stiles (1972) demonstrates how the emotionally satisfying, highly interdependent relationship that characterizes outport marriages may be temporarily undermined by the wife's inappropriate use of radio information. Andersen and Wadel (1972) comment on how a husband's presence at home can disrupt a woman's schedule to the extent that she is glad to see him leave. Antler (1982:133-134) notes how village exogamy can result in a woman's low, constant stranger status in her husband's community. As outsiders, women lack easy means of friendship and cooperation. On a more phenomenal level, Faris (1972) points to village exogamy and its consequent production of negative hostile views of women as polluters and jinxers. Brake (n.d.) and Szala (1977) are among the few observers of outport life, who have gone beyond a simple observation of the affective, relational aspects of the female expressive role to address the greater complexity inherent in the more esoteric aspects of outport women as symbols of occupation and community. Brake provides a precise account of one woman's role as community intermediary to the supernatural. Aunt Lydia, an outport woman, was so good and kind that her prayers for fish were answered. When fish were scarce, Aunt Lydia was chosen to lead a prayer at prayer meetings. The following day the fish always came. In a less dramatic vein, Szala's interpretation of female expressive function is couched in an analysis of the family and community as strong metaphors for outport life—a life synonymous with fishing.

It was women's response to the tragic sinking of a local dragger that attuned me to the ideology of femininity in terms of women's affective, rarefied roles in Grey Rock Harbour. Elsewhere (Davis 1983c), I have discussed the female expressive role of "worrier." A Grey Rock Harbour woman's worry or concern over her absent husband is a kind of deeply felt spiritual empathy. It is the Harbour women who actually deal with the risk and uncertainty of fishing. Worrying is one of the jobs a fisherman leaves to his wife. Worry is a status enhancing moral duty of women. Symbolically it is the woman's worry that keeps her husband's boat afloat. Worry is all pervasive among Harbour women.[2]

While it may be true that only men fish, the danger and drama of fishing and a wife's concern for her husband's safety and well-being generate a sense that "we're all in it together." In Grey Rock Harbour, male and female roles symbolically overlap and it is necessary to understand the quasi-spiritual supportive roles (as well as instrumental roles) that women play in the fishery in order to understand what differentiates Grey Rock Harbour from urban and town Newfoundland, in particular, and from Canadian mass society, in general.

General, passive worry as well as actual, direct participation, reinforces a woman's sense of belonging to the community fishery.

Worry is a highly elaborated and complex female expressive function. It is the moral duty of women to worry, but worrying must be
done properly according to highly restrictive community standards.
Similarly, although active, direct instrumental participation by
women in the fishery is acceptable there are informal rules which
govern female comportment in the material, everyday, mundane
operation of the fishery. Strictures on behavior are particularly important in the area where male and female concerns merge because
they are inextricable from the overall community ethos. An analysis
of the roles of shore skipper and grass widow— the former to be envied but never honored, the latter to be honored but never
envied— provides a background against which to elaborate on local
roles which govern proper and improper behavioral norms for
women in this particular fishing community.

THE SHORE SKIPPER

"Shore skipper" is an epithet that may refer to different kinds of persons. If the referent is a retired skipper or fisherman it is a term of
respect. Skipper may be used affectionately to refer to children. It
may be used to refer to any temporary leader or even the driver of a
car. Husbands and wives may use it as an expression of endear-
ment. However, when preceded by "shore," the term skipper, as
applied to women, implies a negative tease or outright insult. A
woman shore skipper is bossy and interferes excessively in her
husband's affairs. Not all communities would share the meaning of
this particular idiom. Locally specific situations and individuals
provide the referents and context for the use of the term "shore skipper" as a form of ingroup argot. To my knowledge there were two
shore skippers in Grey Rock Harbour: (1) Flossie, a skipper's wife,
who in the view of the locals took too active a part in her husband's
fishing affairs and who sought to get ahead at the expense of others;
and (2) Mabel, who publicly criticized the fishing abilities of harbour
men in a misguided attempt to enhance her own husband's reputation as a good fisherman, and who was thought to get ahead at the
expense of others and whose boisterous and aggressive behavior
was unacceptable to her neighbors. Both women were bright, independent, assertive and self-determined women, who had difficulty
living up to the community ideal of the quiet, clean woman.

My curiosity about shore skippers arose one afternoon as I was
having tea with two sisters. One of them made a comment about
that "ole shore skipper." The second followed up with "Oh yeah! The
woman with three stomachs." Asking what "shore skipper" meant
and who it referred to, I was told that shore skipper was a local

description of a woman who was bossy, had little respect for the feelings of others and took too much interest in her husband's fishing affairs. I was told that while there were a couple of shore skippers around the harbour this one was the worst. The same woman was subsequently identified as a shore skipper again and again by many different villagers during my stay. A brief account of the sins of the shore skipper follows.

> Flossie rides on that poor Jack [the husband/captain] some awful. All she cares about is more money. She can't get enough of it. That Jack goes out [fishing] when no one else will. My poor man, Ted, trip fished with him for years. That skipper drives them some hard. Ted's getting older now and can't take it no more. Everytime he comes home Ted looks like death warmed over. Poor dear Ted, everytime he went out I thought it'd be his last. Ted's proud— all he knows is hard work. He's loyal to the skipper too, just like any good man. But Jack abuses it. He works his crew harder than any other skipper, but they don't get no more pay for it. He wouldn't be so bad, you see, if it weren't for all her push, push, push. Ted's got a brother with a good wife. He's a good skipper, best kind. But this Flossie's some hard ticket, I tell you.

> When the men are at sea, skipper's wife is supposed to check up on the crew wives, see how they're doing, pass on information— that sort of thing. But that Flossie, you can't turn 'round but she doesn't have her nose in your business. She don't take no mind to respect your personal [privacy]...wants to know all your comings and goings. Just so's she can yap it on to someone else.

> That fat old witch [Flossie], sees that Jack gets fair shares. More than fair shares if you ask me. The last straw was when she made him take a share of the fishes' peas.[3] After that my Ted quit. Good riddance I say. Skipper Jack couldn't find no one else who'd work like slaves, so he had to fish short handed. That burned her. It did. She yapped on the phone for hours, to anybody who'd listen— about how Jack should have put Ted ashore last year. She said he wasn't pulling his weight. She got some nerve. Now she complains that Jack has to do all the dirty work cause he can't trust no crew. She'll get him some other sucker (crew member) sooner or later. You can count on that.

Flossie also took charge of all her husband's accounts. She made out checks, purchased equipment, etc. Her husband was the first man to own his own boat after the modern fish plant opened. He lost his first boat by (what was rumored to be) ill-considered seamanship, yet, was able to purchase a second. Many locals felt that it was not fair for one man to get two chances. All other trip boats including the one skippered by Jack's brother, were owned by the local plant.

A second shore skipper, Mabel, like Flossie, was called a shore skipper behind her back and her interfering manner hurt rather than helped her husband's fishing career. Mabel and her family were outsiders, who had been resettled into Grey Rock Harbour about five years ago. Mabel not only took an active role in her husband's fishing affairs, but she committed the additional sin of maligning the skills and commitments of local fishermen. According to Mabel, the harbour fishermen were nowhere near as hardworking, courageous or skilled as the fishermen of her former outport home. Mabel would publicly state that her husband was so much better as a fisherman that none of the local men would fish with him. Her husband fished alone in a motor boat and was constantly on the look out for a fishing partner. He was regarded as a "good sort" by most folk. ("Tis none of his doing, mind you....It's her bad mouthing us that sets them against him.") However no man would fish with Mabel's husband, because of the comments that his wife so constantly made. While defending her own man's reputation, Mabel was insensitive to the harm that she caused him. Yet this alone was probably not the sole reason that Mabel was labelled a shore skipper. Like Flossie, Mabel compounded her sins as an interfering fisherman's wife by being boisterous and "acting superior." Unlike Flossie, Mabel was also viewed as a bad mother. She yells at her children and curses and cuffs them. The children are so used to her behavior that they simply shrug it off. Moreover, while Flossie's actions affected the lives of her husband's crew members, the affect of Mabel's actions was limited to her own family.

As we shall see in the section on impression management it is not simply interference in the husband's fishing affairs which generates the epithet of shore skipper. If that were true surely Ted's wife would have been so labelled. Rather it is the notion, held by others, that you think you are better or above them. The proper role of women in Grey Rock Harbour— and this is synonymous with fisherwomen who are part of parcel of fishing collectivity (ethos)— is that of the grass widow. Ted's wife was able to maintain her image as grass widow and hence is esteemed and accepted as "in the right" by her peers. We will return to this theme after a more detailed look at the grass widow.

GRASS WIDOW

The term "grass widow" is synonymous with female dignity. Grass widow refers to a woman whose husband is not dead but gone away. Grass widow formally describes a very passive female expressive role— the woman who sits on the grassy hills (actually mossy rocks) overlooking the shore, staring out to sea, wondering when and if her husband will come home from fishing.[4] The image of grass widow connotes the ideal woman, the long suffering, ever dependable fortress of community and domestic life. Her appropriate behavior and quiet concern for the safety of loved ones insures that all is right with the world.

Actually, grass widow conjures up a physical image that has little relevance to everyday, mundane values. No self-respecting Harbour woman would waste time lollygagging and daydreaming on the grass. Rather, grass widow is a symbol of the endless energy for organizing and keeping the family together that is so admired in Harbour life. She is not a specific individual but an idealized representation of the quiet dignity and competent, controlling, self-effacing female expressive role. She is an embodiment of the collective ethos. She is a part of the village fishery.

The term grass widow expresses women's emotional involvement in the fishery. This section discusses several dimensions of the concept of grass widow— going from the surface meaning to the deeper significance of the term as it represents the role of the female in Grey Rock Harbour life.

In many ways grass widow is a personification of values of the past. Grass widow symbolizes the adaptation to cyclical patterns of male absence. Grass widow symbolizes the excitement of homecoming, intense companionship and the mutual admiration that traditionally characterized the husband/wife relationship. Grass widow denotes the shared emotions of husband and wife. For the older woman it brings back past memories of excitement for the returning hero after a long trip; an excitement intensified by the promise of sexual activity after long periods of abstinence. Women would bake homemade pies and gather on the cliffs to spot the boats coming in, to await proof that they had escaped widowhood this time. When husbands were home, wives felt they should spend every minute together. Women admired men for fishing and voiced pride in their ability to do hard work, fish successfully and build boats, etc.

Although today most men day fish rather than trip or seasonally fish, the grass widow still symbolizes the woman who is both mother and father to her children. She represents the good woman, who keeps the family together and functioning through good times and bad. She depicts strong landbound networks that exist among women. Since Grey Rock Harbour women tend to marry within the community they never leave their own matrikin (Davis 1983b).

Women draw on each other for emotional support, companionship and labor or monetary assistance when it is needed.

The idealization of the traditional role of women has been modified to fit current post-confederation circumstances. A close look at female impression management will show how women exploit the fishery ethos for status enhancement. The fine line between the acceptable behavior of grass widow and the unacceptable behavior of shore skipper will be discussed in terms of the local value system.

IMPRESSION MANAGEMENT

Parson's (1951) distinction between active, instrumental roles and more passive, emotional roles is a prerequisite to understanding the nature of shore skipper and grass widow roles. However, a more cogent analysis requires that the performance of these roles be related to the overall community value system, such as the all-pervasive egalitarian ethos of Grey Rock Harbour.

The key to understanding the acceptability and admirability of the grass widow role and the unacceptability of the role of shore skipper rests not so much in the instrumental, material or performance aspects of these roles as in a woman's management of the impression of herself that she conveys to others. In this section the problems of impression management are discussed. Successful impression management generates high self-esteem and the admiration of other community members, men and women alike. The trick is to do it without the appearance of conceit, self-centeredness, or of being unnecessarily critical of others.

In his discussion of British local culture, Cohen (1982a:10-11, 1982b:24) notes that people on the village level interact with each other as "whole" persons, rather than in terms of the more clearly analyzable sociological concepts of status or roles. In the local community, the member's personal characteristics and their life and family histories are public knowledge— the "currency" for public action. Social control does not need a formal or authoritative office. Individuality is subordinated to the community, which is pervaded by an egalitarian ethic. Assertiveness of any sort is not allowed, unless it is conducted within highly conventionalized and limiting idiomatic forms. Individuality is recognized and legitimized only within rigidly enforced limits. Cohen's statements are equally applicable to Grey Rock Harbour life.

Danowski (1980:1) states that, "there is no one way to be a fisherman's wife." This is true in Grey Rock Harbour. However, there is not much latitude for individuality in outport life— particularly in as isolated and homogeneous a setting as Grey Rock Harbour. As described by Szala (1978:4) the ideal wife is a "clean woman." She is a good housekeeper, modest, reticent, loving, nurturant and supportive. Women's contribution to their society involves their commitment to maintaining what they perceive to be the high quality of family, home, and village life.

Part of Flossie's problem of being labelled a shore skipper rested in her inability or unwillingness to abide by the egalitarian ethos of her community. Flossie was different and proud of it. She had married into the village and was more educated than most. All of her grown children had left the community except her teenage daughter, who was known as the "junior shore skipper." Flossie was direct, assertive and determined to improve her lot of life, in a community that values indirectness, unassertiveness, and self-sacrifice, e.g., "We all go up together or we don't go up at all." Until recently, Flossie's husband was the only skipper who owned his own boat. Therefore, he was the only man in the Harbour to receive both skipper's and owner's shares for his boat. Despite the fact that most of his owner's profit returns to the boat, in the form of equipment, insurance, etc., the locals saw him and his family as having an unfair advantage. Flossie's crime was not that she was active in her family's business but that she felt herself to be above others and "lorded it over them."

The extent to which Flossie "intended" to do this is questionable. Whenever I talked to her she was the very image of the grass widow. Worrying, busy, supportive and self-sacrificing. Obviously, however, her attempts at impression management failed in the community at large. Whether she was right or wrong in her actions she was an outsider and "better off than most."

Mabel's case was similar. She also was an outsider, but not better off than others. Her entire family had been resettled to Grey Rock Harbour. She, too, interfered with her husband's fishing. Mabel's unflattering comments about local fishermen were cited as the major reason that he could not find a fishing partner. To a limited extent, Mabel's loud mouth was tolerated ("After all, she's a stranger and for all we know, they all screech like that where she comes from"). Like Flossie, however, Mabel broke from the egalitarian ethic. In addition to repeatedly asserting that her man was better than anyone else's man, Mabel is reputed to have told another woman how "beautiful she [Mabel] was" and how local women did not dress very tastefully. Unlike Flossie Mabel did not even try to pull-off the grass widow role. She was hostile, bellicose and crude in most of her encounters with local folk and refused to participate in any community social activities. Although Flossie took an active responsible role in community affairs, Mabel's position was closer to that of pariah. Mabel became the laughing stock of village women and was referred to as "that other shore skipper."

This is not to suggest that grass widows are not allowed to protest nor does it imply that females actually are passive or saint-like in their relationships with other community members— either women or men— as the following cases illustrate:

> Once when Steffie was a young married woman she was up at a friend's house talking. This friend had a woman living with her who was pregnant by a married man. She was noticeably pregnant at this incident. In her house she always kept a long narrow bottle full of knitting needles by the window. Steffie saw two boats come in. She started to jump up and down and to shout "The men are coming, the men are coming." The pregnant woman looked at her and said, "If you're in such a state you'd probably be better off using that bottle." This really burned Steffie but she couldn't think of a come-back. It shamed her too. The next year the very same thing happened. Steffie was up there and the woman was holding her illegitimate baby in her arms. The boats came in, four this time. Steffie jumped up and down and shouted "The men are coming." The girl with the baby said "If you are so bad off you should use that bottle." This time Steffie was ready. She looked at the woman and then at her baby and said "I think there are some others who should have used the bottle." Steffie had waited a whole year to say this.

Women pride themselves in being "yary." Men and women alike enjoy feisty women. Women who let someone "walk all over you," a wife who lets her husband do "just as he wants" and is afraid "to put her foot down" is called "low lifed." Women will stand up to and stick up for their husbands. As Ted's wife repeatedly told me:

> I sure hope someday when we're out together (husband and wife) we'll meet up with Skipper Jack and his fat so and so. I'll tell him a thing or two. My old man don't dare talk back to a skipper. We women can and do. I can come up with all kinds of sass. Men can't. We wives can get away with it. Next time I see him I'll ask about the "fishes' peas" and how's he's cheaten my man to feed his fat wife.

She did. Ted's wife will never be called a shore skipper. She may be bossy at times but she is considered a good wife and shore skippers make "safe victims." Ted's wife functions within the parameters of the local ethos. Successful maintenance of the long suffering grass widow expressive role enhances one's image in the eyes of others.

Women do play various roles in Harbour life, as wife, mother and worker, yet they are evaluated as total persons. Adequate performance in one area does not guarantee freedom from criticism in another. This is why impression management in its abstract, highly generalized, expressive grass widow form is so important. It's the glue that holds the multiple images of the good woman together and affixes them into the everyday operations and drama of the fishery. In the concluding section, I would like to argue that these roles, particularly that of grass widow, are more salient and pervasive in the Harbour today than they were in the more traditional past. The idealization of grass widow, the disparagement of shore skippers and the complex patterns of impression maintenance cannot be understood apart from the changes that currently permeate every level of village life.

SOCIAL CHANGE

The role of grass widow is not so much a relic as it is a current adaptation. The contemporary roles of grass widow, and to a less important degree, shore skipper, are best understood as idioms for creating a rhetoric of historical and cultural continuity. They serve to mask culture change in everyday life and to present young people with real and viable life style options from which to choose.

The image of the good woman or grass widow is easy to maintain. Bad women or shore skippers are few and far between. They are the women who want to be different, who want to get ahead. Shore skippers are the villains, who can be pointed to as examples of what can happen when one breaks with the highly valued traditional egalitarian ethic. Shore skippers are shunned and ridiculed. "Being good" in Grey Rock Harbour means "being the same as everyone else."

Smith (1977a:15) warns against overemphasis on the closed nature of local communities. My emphasis on traditionalism in Grey Rock Harbour directly confronts and incorporates culture change. If social change and amalgamation into mass society were not so pervasive in the outport, then Grey Rock Harbour would not have to be so traditional. According to Cohen (1982a:6-7) the strength of local culture does not necessarily diminish as the locality becomes increasingly precarious. As local people come to recognize their own culture as distinct from others, they may come to value such distinctions as a condition of survival. The grass widow role and the fishery ethos, romanticize the past. They are idioms used by locals to express their difference from others and to justify their existence in a remote, expensively serviced community. The stoic supportive role of ideal women and the successful presentation of self as living up to that traditional ideal pervades everyday village life and links generations to a collective village, coast and island identity. Change offers the opportunity to combine the best of today with the resurrection of the ideals of the past.

The value of the grass widow role is enhanced rather than undermined by change; and change is pervasive in Grey Rock Harbour (Davis 1983a, Chapter 5). The fact that many fishermen dream of a 9 to 5 job cannot be overlooked. Some women encourage their daughters to leave the outport so they do not have to marry a fisherman. With the predominance of day fishing and fish plant work, fishermen are not even as "absent" as they used to be. Fishing is no longer as dangerous as it was traditionally. Houses are full of modern conveniences. Everyone dresses in the latest styles from the Simpson-Sears catalogue. Women have fewer children. Afternoon television is avidly watched and teens play all the latest tunes on their stereos. Yet, the comfort of the modern day conveniences and the fact of changing times provides a background against which locals can evaluate and idealize the past. No one wants to turn back the clock but they do want to preserve "what's best."

Wright (1981:62) also deals with this theme and shows how the seal hunt has become important as a symbol of the desire to keep Newfoundland rural and protected from outside interference. Lest one jump to the conclusion that such "mystification of the superficial" results in a "false consciousness" which conceals the reality of class and state and delays constructive confrontation of problems (a warning voiced by Cohen 1982a:2-3), let me point to a positive role of reinterpretation and intensification of the traditional. The caveat here is that one must accept the value of localism and survival of local tradition. Although localism may seem superficial to the outsider, the villagers have combined modernization with the continued maintenance of self-esteem. This is especially true for women. The self-esteem the maintenance of traditional values generates on the inside is real.[5]

The relative primacy of the expressive over instrumental roles in the traditional Grey Rock Harbour culture and the consequent ascendency of the expressive role in modern life can best be illustrated by comparing Grey Rock Harbour to other outports where female fishery-related, instrumental roles were traditionally more salient.

Men in Grey Rock Harbour have always fished. Grey Rock Harbour women have never been involved in the fishery as were women in other outports who were active in primary saltfish production. Nor were their subsidiary functions as complex or instrumental as in those areas more conducive to gardening and livestock. Grey Rock Harbour women have not lost productive roles. However, they have always considered themselves important in the emotional life of the community.

CONCLUSION

Because of its isolation and/or because of its preservation of tradition, Grey Rock Harbour has been successful with the maintenance of localism and commitment to local lifeways among contemporary generations of women. Here women have parlayed an apparently passive role into the construction of a gender ideology which has been used to establish a coherent and powerful position for women in this tightly bound community. This is not true for other parts of Newfoundland. Antler and Faris (1979) point to alienation and apathy among women. Porter (1983, 1985), while her overall assessment of outport women's status in the village of Aquaforte on Avalon Peninsula is positive, points to a lack of shared values among contemporary adult mothers and daughters. According to Porter, middle-aged women and all ages of men in the outport are committed to the preservation of the best of its fishery and its traditional values and life styles. However, the loyalty of young women to the outport system is at best a reluctant loyalty. In Aquaforte a generation gap has fractured the "women's culture." As Porter sees it, options of employment for women and their temporary absorption into sophisticated materialistic life style of the nearby city, St. John's, has undermined the structural base of traditional society. Drawing their new outport husbands into the big city, young women are forced by financial exigencies to return to their husbands' outport after the first child is born. The young women of Aquaforte are bored, lonely and frustrated.

Aquaforte women can no longer live the traditional life style the way Aquaforte men can. According to Porter (1983) the fisherman's wife role— based on the primary instrumental function of participation in saltfish production, and subsidiary instrumental functions of gardening, livestock rearing and household maintenance in times of crushing poverty— exists no more. Additionally Porter sees the tensions among Aquaforte women as enhanced by village exogamy. Women in Aquaforte are strangers to the community. Here the pre-confederation past ranks as idle tales of old women. Younger women show no inclination for keeping traditions alive.

The situation in Grey Rock Harbour is different: saltfish production and household production such as gardening were never salient features of women's life. Women here have not lost primary productive or subsidiary work roles in their community. If anything they have gained a primary productive role in the fishery— that of fish plant laborer. Another very important distinction between the two communities lies in a comparison of marriage patterns. Unlike Aquaforte, Grey Rock Harbour has been and continues to be characterized by female endogamy (Davis 1983b). The mother-daughter relationship in the Harbour continues to be strong, reciprocal and reinforced by mutually held values. The middle-aged woman, the woman who functioned and survived through the "hard times past" continues to be the model of the ideal woman for all generations and both sexes.

Maybe the case of Aquaforte foreshadows the future of Grey Rock Harbour. Certainly the comparative isolation from urban life contributes to survival of the traditional. However, at present, those women who continue to choose the options of outport life, and marry within the community (as they always have) delayed or avoided the onset of a generation gap between women and a sex role gap between women and men. Men and women alike in Grey Rock Harbour continue to identify themselves with the community fishery and all the cultural baggage it entails. Maybe this is due to the fact that in Grey Rock Harbour women's contribution to the fishing has always been more symbolic than substantive as compared to other coasts, and women had long ago become the masters of the "emotional and expressive" contribution to the fishery, a role they have not relinquished in the face of culture change and modernization but actually intensified.

Notes

1. Fieldwork was conducted from October 1977-December 1978, with a return visit in Fall of 1979. Research was supported by the National Institutes of Child Health and Development for a two year traineeship, which was administered by the Carolina Population Center at the University of North Carolina at Chapel Hill. For additional publications on this study, see Davis 1982, 1983a, 1983b, 1983c, 1984a, and 1984b.

2. Worry can be equated with the complaint of "nerves." Over 80 percent of women between ages 35 and 60 complain of nerves (Davis 1986c). Although four village men were recognized as suffering from nerves, nerves stemming from a lifetime of worry is viewed as a female complaint.

3. Fishes' peas are roe. Liver and peas money is considered the property of the fisherwife.

4. Grass widow, in local use, refers to a woman whose husband is temporarily away from her. Although in common English usage the

term can also be used to refer to a discarded mistress or woman with an illegitimate child, local women had never heard the term used in this way. Women were quite surprised when I told them that the term could refer to 'bad' as well as 'good' women.

5. This is corroborated by the self-esteem indices I administered as part of my menopause study (see Davis 1983 a: Chapters 6, 7, and Appendix I).

Women Fishermen in the Pacific Northwest   **12**

Charlene J. Allison

INTRODUCTION

In the United States, commercial fishing, as an occupation dominated by men, is considered to be a "nontraditional" occupation for
women. Although the social sciences have begun to study the lives
of women in nontraditional professional occupations, the lives of
women in laboring occupations lack documentation and remain un-
examined (see U.S. 1976; Kanter 1977). This paper is concerned
with two important questions: what working conditions, roles, and
tasks characterize an occupation as nontraditional for women, and
how do these conditions relate to contemporary theories or perspectives on the relationships between women, work, and marital
status? Four primary perspectives which continue to dominate U.S.
sex role research in the 1980s include: (1) assessment of sex differences; (2) the study of sex roles and the "norms which govern
them"; (3) a look at women as a minority group; and (4) a consideration of the "politics of caste" (Hochschild 1973:1012-1013; see also
Richardson and Wirtenberg 1983). Of these four perspectives, the
study of sex roles and norms is most applicable to the analysis of
women fishermen in the Pacific Northwest. Hochschild (1973:1016)
points out that "role studies usually deal with women in the family
and in the economy and the 'cultural contradictions' of being in
both." However, I agree in this chapter with Kanter (1977) and Finch
(1983) who assert that, since women have always been involved in
productive contributions to the economy in one form or another,
there are no contradictions involved. The minority perspective,

which deals with discrimination, and the politics of caste perspective, which deals with the distribution of power, also inform the analysis that follows.

In developing a new theoretical framework for studying women's roles in nontraditional occupations, we need to avoid presenting cultural assumptions as theory. Therefore, we must turn to the body of data itself to see what it can tell us. This is the direction taken in this chapter. The first half describes the roles and activities of women on board Pacific Northwest boats. The second half discusses issues needing further research. These issues fall into two broad categories: aspects of women's participation which need to be studied to provide further documentation; and factors affecting women's entry and participation in Northwest Coast fishing, especially those related to the working environment and sociocultural factors.

ROLES AND ACTIVITIES ON BOARD

Women who fish in the Pacific Northwest identify themselves simply as "fishermen," not as "women fishermen" or by any other name.[1] That is, they identify with the occupation, and, although they readily discuss gender issues, do not differentiate themselves within the occupation on the basis of gender. They are found on board fishing boats in a variety of capacities and roles: as captain, cook/deckhand, and occasional or substitute cook/deckhand.

The data on which this paper is based were collected as part of a project on "Sociocultural Roles of Women in Commercial Fishing in the Puget Sound Area," undertaken at the University of Washington in Seattle during 1979 and 1980.[2] The information was collected through open-ended interviewing, recording life histories, and participant-observation. We talked with numerous women and men involved in the commercial fishing industry in a variety of activities, not just in the harvest. Of the 18 women for whom we collected life histories, 11 go (or have gone) fishing. Of these 11, three skipper their own boat (or have done so in the past, having retired by 1980); four crew (or have crewed) regularly; and four crew (or have crewed) on an irregular basis. The lives of these 11 women provide illustrations of women's roles on board Pacific Northwest boats.

Captain

The captain of a fishing vessel often owns the boat, though not necessarily, and has the primary responsibility for running the vessel, managing crew members, finding the fish and determining a fishing strategy, and organizing and directing the fishing effort. One of our informants, Laura, whose home port is Port Angeles, Washington on the Strait of Juan de Fuca, trolled for salmon and albacore (longfin tuna— *Thunnus alalunga*) for 20 years,[3] primarily in southeast Alaska (usually simply referred to as "Southeast") and off the coasts of Washington and Oregon, although she did range as far as California. Laura fished for salmon in the spring and albacore in the summer during the regular trolling season. She said:

> [I would] leave here around the last week in March and go to Alaska. Then [I would] fish up there until about the second week in July, [and] then either come down the inside [passage] or the outside— not fishing down....Down the inside...[in] Canadian waters, you don't fish there....[I would] just come right down with the fish. Then [I would be] either delivering [in] Port Angeles,...or go on down...and deliver in Astoria, or go down to Charleston— we call it Charlietown, and deliver down there....Then [for a few years] I [would] go down to California and usually go into Frisco and ice up down in Frisco [in October]....It seemed like I did that [go to California] three, four years in a row.

While trolling, Laura generally stayed out on the ocean, fishing for eight to ten days at a time, coming in to deliver fish and obtain more ice.[4] Trolling is hard, intense work. Trollers, including Laura, fish 12 to 14 hours a day, as long as weather, seas and regulations permit. When a troller is "in fish," it keeps working until the fish no longer bite. Once the fish are on board they must be gutted and iced. Laura commented:

> [The work] is hard. It's not difficult. There's no difficulty in working if you keep organized. Like...I had leaching tanks [aft]. If I got into a school of fish, I pulled by myself the most number of fish....[There] was 315 silvers [coho salmon— *Oncorhynchus kisutch*] in one day. That means icing down clear 'til three o'clock in the morning. But I had leaching tanks, so when I was catching a whole bunch, I put 'em in the tanks. There was fresh seawater running through 'em all the time, and two sides to them— one for cleaned and one for not cleaned fish. When you get a little, little tiny bit of slack, you just— always keep your knife sharp, keep 'em handy, and start cleanin' fish really fast. That's something else I enjoyed. I love to clean fish. Oh boy, you betcha'. I can clean fish real fast.

Laura primarily fished alone, although some years she had a teenage deckhand— sometimes male, sometimes female, and occasionally had a husband along. Even when a husband was along, she was the captain of her boat. Laura has been married several times; her refusal to limit or give up fishing was the direct cause of

a few marital breakups. Trollers remain in constant radio contact
with each other, and Laura was no exception. In fact she used this
to her advantage when she first started fishing. She said:

> Because being a woman when I first started fishing, I was never
> gonna tell anybody I was lost. That's something that I always im-
> pregnate[d] in my mind—I was not going to get lost. Well, all
> fishermen listen to their radios. If you mention something about
> catching a fish, they can take a direction finder and zoom—they
> got you and they run right out to you. So I figure[d] if I ever got
> lost, I'd just call a friend of mine and tell 'em I've just got into a
> whole bunch of fish. And then I'd never be lost no more. 'Cept I
> never had to use that. But I always figured that was my ace in the
> hole.

Some trollers also form what are sometimes called "code
groups." These code groups are often referred to as "fleets," an extremely general term fishermen apply to any number of different
groupings of boats. A code group consists of a number of friends
who will share information with each other on the type and location
of fish when they find them. This information is transmitted to other
members of the group in code so that non-group fishermen will be
unable to take advantage of it.[5] Laura was not a member of such a
group. She said: "A fleet [that is, a code group] is a tightly knitted
group of friends—that try to eat each other's throat[s]. That's about
the way it goes. No...[I fished with] no particular group because,
when I first started fishing, you had to kinda prove yourself."

Laura took care of all her own boat and engine maintenance and
repair, and other fishermen used to come to her to get advice on
various mechanical problems. She had learned engine repair when
she joined the army at age 17. She related the following story to illustrate some people's reaction to her mechanical abilities:

> I overhauled my engine one time....I needed a torque wrench, cause
> I was gonna tighten the head back down. This young kid— he was
> about 19 years old—was watching me all the time. He was sitting
> there. I got everything taken apart and doin' what I was doin'—
> cleanin' all the garbage off the valves, 'cause they were pretty badly
> burned. He says, 'Wait a minute, I'll go ask my dad' [for some
> wrenches].... [It turned out] I didn't need 'em....Pretty soon, this
> kid's father come down [to] tell 'em it was time for him to go to bed.
> He says, 'I want to see if it'll run after she [has] got through ruin-
> ing it.' Of course, when I got it goin' 'bout ten o'clock, the kid was
> so happy. [He said,] 'Wait till I go home and tell my mother! Wait
> till I go home and tell my mother!'

Laura retired from fishing in 1974, as she became paralyzed for almost eight months due to fishing related injuries. She explained what happened:

> See, there's a trolling cockpit...right in the back here....You stand down in there, so your waist is pretty much down....And behind me, I have put these Gresen valves for hydraulics....[In] the rough weather I would hit back against that Gresen valve here so much...[the] lower part of my spine started disintegrating. Then it got so I couldn't hardly move. I have to take spinal fluid injection shots.

But Laura loved fishing and still does. She said:

> You've heard of the expression...'being called to the sea'? That's exactly what I had....When I get away from the water, any place, I feel like I'm landlocked. I've gotta be near the water. Even after I've sold my boat and everything, I go down [and] look the boats over. Like one fella said to me, he says, 'L..., you look at boats like most men look at women.' And I think that's my biggest calling right there. I've always had confidence. I've never had a fear of drowning. I've been in some pretty bad storms, too.

Trolling is only one of many gear types available to northwest fishermen. Our second captain, Wilma, gillnets for salmon "inside," that is, in Puget Sound.[6] Puget Sound gillnetters fish at night and deliver their catch daily. Salmon gillnet season is roughly June through October, although the actual number of days gillnetters can fish is becoming more and more limited by state regulations. Wilma was 42 years old when she began fishing in 1969. She said that if she had been younger when she started fishing, fishing would have been her life. She said, "I done everything that a fisherman's required to do— get your net back in, pick the fish out of the net." When she was not fishing she also spent a lot of time mending her nets. One of her teenage sons went along as "crew." She has never gone out alone, as she believes it is too dangerous to be out alone in a small boat at night— mainly because it is all too possible to get caught in the net. When her son was unavailable— sometimes "my son wanted a night off to go to the junior prom or to the senior prom or something"— friends went fishing with her. Her son also helped her maintain her boat. Her husband, who was at one time a gillnetter but did not care for night fishing, did not go fishing with her. She said, "Well, he'd sooner have me stay at home. But, when I go fishing, why, he doesn't say anything." But they do keep in contact by radio. Wilma, who lives in Friday Harbor, Washington, is now semi-retired. Sometimes she goes fishing with her son. But now the roles are reversed and her son is captain. She says, "My son is one of the top ones [fishermen] now, due to the experience of every mistake that I ever made....I mean, I'm real, real proud of him, and I'm proud to feel I had something to do with it."

Our third captain, Marilyn, has skippered her own charter boat for 21 years. Marilyn lives with her husband in Port Angeles, Washington, and operates out of that port in the winter. In the summer, she lives on board her boat at Neah Bay, a Makah Indian town just inside the Strait of Juan de Fuca and very close to the Pacific Ocean. She basically trolls for salmon (for her passengers) using sport gear. She said:

> [In Ilwaco and Westport— two ports further south on the Washington coast, there are] three or four hundred charter boats in each place. [This is in 1979 - 1980.] We only have maybe eight or nine charter boats at Neah Bay and only two or three here [at Port Angeles]....We fish differently [here] too. They drift down there in the ocean, and I can't imagine...how many people must get sick, drifting. But we keep our boats moving....We only get maybe two or three in a whole week they might get sick.

Her charter boat license allows her to fish within 20 miles of a safe harbor. She says, "That's far enough to go. If you have to go...any further than that, it's too far when you've got all those people on board." She also has a commercial bottomfish license she uses when the charter business is slow. In 1980 she was booked "right to the ears," but when she was just starting out she had to rely more on her commercial licenses:

> When I started back in '55...I had four guys one time. They looked at me and they looked at the fog and they said, 'I'm not goin' out with a woman in the fog.' I said, 'Suits me fine 'cause if you aren't going, I'm goin' fishin'.' I cast off the dock and left 'em standing there. I made way more money going out and commercial fish[ing]— I had a commercial license— than I would've if I took them out. But I knew I was building a job for the future....I guessed that some-day commercial fishing would peter out, and that's what's happening....I'd go out when I didn't have a charter. Many years I'd go out and I had always had a commercial license. The only thing I have now on commercial license is a bottomfish license.

Marilyn's husband is a troller who owns and operates his own boat out of Neah Bay during trolling season, and does chartering out of Port Angeles in the winter. They remain in constant radio contact. Marilyn stopped chartering one year and went trolling with her husband. However, she says she missed the people. Her boat can carry 22 passengers, although in 1980 state regulations limited her to 16. She enjoys her passengers, except in August:

August. Now speaking of getting fish for the thrill of it! August becomes a meat month. People are after meat and they are not after
the sport. That's one month of the whole year I would like to cancel out and take my vacation. People are just fish hogs. They want
the biggest and the most and they won't give up their poles. Talk
about...sportsmen!...They come aboard and they come in droves.
You have to turn down people every day that...don't have a reservation. And the ones that do get aboard, they get grabby. They'll
swipe other people's fish. They'll swipe your gear. They'll take off
your lures. They'll get in your drawers and take stuff out of your
drawers. That's why I would like to cancel August out.

Marilyn does the routine maintenance on her boat's engine and
on the boat itself (bottom painting and so forth) while her husband
takes care of any engine repairs. During the summer when she has
a large number of passengers, MJ takes along a deckhand— sometimes a female, sometimes a male— to help out.

These three women are or were all skippers of their own boats.
All of them are responsible for navigating their boats, finding the
fish, and catching enough fish to make a living. While she was fishing, Laura did all of her own engine, boat, and gear maintenance
and repair. Marilyn has some help on engine repairs but does the
rest herself. Wilma has help on both boat and engine maintenance,
but repairs all the nets. Only one of the three, Laura, stays out for
days at a time on the open sea. The other two fish on a daily basis—
one in the relatively calmer Puget Sound, and the other at the mouth
of the Strait of Juan de Fuca and up to twenty miles out into the
ocean. Informants mentioned several other women who skipper
their own boats. Had the project been able to continue, we would
have doubtless been able to interview additional women captains.

Cook/Deckhand

Though there are women captains in the Pacific Northwest, northwest women are more likely to be found on fishing boats in the role
of cook and/or deckhand than skipper. As with the role of captain,
women in the role of cook/deckhand perform the same tasks as do
men in these positions. For most of the women we interviewed who
are cook/deckhands, however, the registered owner and captain of
the boat was usually a husband or sometimes a boy friend. Four of
the women who fish or have fished regularly filled the role of
cook/deckhand on boats skippered by their husbands. Two of these
boats were referred to as "family boats," as the couple's children
went along.

Elena and her husband Ken established a family boat because they did not want to be separated. Neither liked the idea of the husband, Ken, going off alone to fish for days or months at a time. During their first year in commercial fishing (1957), they trolled on a daily basis out of Neah Bay, taking their children along. Elena and the children did not go every day during that first season. That fall they met a commercial fishing couple from Alaska. Elena reported: "They said if you're gonna fish with your family, why don't you consider Alaska? There's quite a few people up there doing it. It's just a whole lot easier on families, because there're harbors....If you don't want to trip fish, you can sell your fish every day to a buying boat." The next year they took their boat to southeast Alaska and have been trolling for salmon in Southeast ever since. While their children were small, they day fished, always putting into a safe harbor at night. They also made sure the children had enough time to play on shore. When the children got older, and after they had purchased a bigger boat, they began to trip fish, staying out for ten days at a time. During the first years, Elena steered the boat while her husband did the fishing and gutting. She cooked, and her six and ten-year-old daughters helped look after the baby. Then her youngest daughter, and later her son, began to clean the fish. Later on, when the children were grown and had gone their own ways, Elena began cleaning the fish. She says she can handle anything that comes up in running the boat, except for mechanical work. She and her husband do not run the gear at the same time. She said: "He doesn't ever really want me back there pulling gear when he's back there. It's fine when he goes down for his nap. He knows that if I see fish, I'm going to bring 'em in and land 'em. But we never work in the [cock]pit together." Their home is Port Angeles, Washington. When their children were in school, Elena's husband would go to Alaska around May 1 by himself and begin fishing. Elena and the children would join him when school was out and stay until school started again in the fall. Her husband continued fishing by himself until October 15, after which he would return to Port Angeles.

Glenna is also part of a family boat. Like Elena and Ken, she, her husband, and two children troll for salmon in southeast Alaska. The children were four months and three years old when they began fishing in Alaska in 1977. They chose Alaska for the same reason as did Elena and Ken— they did not have to fish on the open ocean and safe harbors are plentiful. She said:

> I mean there was no way I wanted to take two kids on a boat off the California-Washington-Oregon coast. No way. Because it's

just— it's constant offshore. There aren't very many places to
anchor up. If you're in a blow, there are very few [places]. [And] because [on the coast] you're hassling with bar situations [bars which
need to be crossed to enter harbor] which are very dangerous at
times. And it's a whole other perspective when you have two other
helpless bodies dependent on you.

Glenna says that their motivation in establishing a family boat was
not economic, but rather to keep the family together. She said,
"When we left San Francisco, we left with the idea that we wanted
to get a larger boat so that we could all go out as a family. My husband didn't want to make ten day trips on his own, leaving us at
home. And we felt that the only place we could feasibly do that was
Alaska." Glenna and her husband reached Alaska by way of Provincetown, Massachusetts and San Francisco, California. Glenna, who
had previously lived on the west coast, met and married her husband while living in Provincetown. He did longlining and trawling
out of Provincetown.[7] When they moved to San Francisco, he
gillnetted for herring. He did not have a hydraulic wheel to pull in
the net, but rather pulled it in by hand. He then bought a troller to
fish off the coast of California and finally another troller to fish in
Alaska. Glenna commented:

> I was involved in our getting the boat [the first troller] and outfit-
> ting it to fish, and maintenance and the bookkeeping and all of that
> aspect of it, but I did not fish at that time. Then we sold that troller
> and bought a bigger troller which we now use mostly in Alaska. I'm
> still involved in all those other aspects of it, but I also run the boat
> and fish the boat.

Glenna and the children did not go along until they began fishing
in Alaska. Glenna and her husband live in the Puget Sound area
and go to Alaska during the month of April. In 1980, they intended
to diversify into gillnetting herring in Bristol Bay, Alaska during
April and then go trolling in Southeast during the summer. They
were also thinking of going after halibut when the trolling season is
over. Glenna did not indicate whether she and the children would
go fishing with her husband for herring or halibut.

The other two women who fish or have fished regularly with their
husbands, Monica and Katherine, worked as "boatpuller"— deckhand on a troller— with their husbands. Monica described the work
as follows:

> The first thing that they [boatpullers] do is they clean fish....That's
> the initial reason that they're hired is to help clean the fish. And,
> you pull the gear up and down— run the gear up and down through
> the gurdies, and check the lines, and you ice the fish and you cook
> the meals. With trolling, you learn how to do everything else. You

end up—you know how to navigate the boat and if you do it long enough you get an idea of where to look for fish. You end up learning everything, but what you don't have is the responsibility of worrying about whether you are on the best fishing or not. The captain gets that.

When Monica and Katherine and their husbands started trolling for salmon in 1971, both couples were part of the same code group. The code group originally consisted of nine boats, each of which was operated by a couple. Two of the boats were family boats. During the first few years, all of the members of the code group lived on board their boats at Fishermen's Terminal, Seattle. Older fishermen named their code group "The Hippie Fleet." The name has stuck with the code group even though its members are now older, more experienced, and have moved off their boats. When they first started out, their aim was just to get by. Now they are professional fishermen, and identify themselves as such.

The membership of the code group has fluctuated over the years, with some people leaving fishing altogether, or just leaving the group. New people have joined. Monica said that, in 1979, there were 20 boats in the group—too many as far as she was concerned. The code group fishes primarily off the coasts of Washington and Oregon.

Katherine was one of the code group members who left fishing, but she did not leave "the fish business." Katherine trolled with her husband for five years. After her marriage broke up, she and another "retired" woman fisherman started a roadside business selling smoked salmon. After doing that for a few years, she linked up with yet another retired woman fisherman and began a fish buying operation in the San Juan Islands, in Puget Sound, buying salmon from gillnetters for a fish store in Seattle. They also marketed their fish to restaurants and to private residences in the islands. In addition, Katherine did independent brokering—arranging for the sale of fish to restaurants and domestic markets between Washington and California.

Monica has remained in fishing, and is still part of the same code group. When her first marriage broke up, she stayed on shore for a year. She says her year on shore made her feel "claustrophobic," and she decided to return to fishing. During her first summer back in fishing, she worked as a boatpuller on two separate trollers. The next summer she hired onto one of these trollers again (she was the third woman to work as boatpuller on the vessel, over the years), and later married its captain. She was then back in fishing as part of a husband/wife team, rather than as hired deckhand. In 1980,

Monica was uncertain both about the future of trolling (because of decreasing salmon stocks and increasing regulations) and about her future in fishing. She identifies herself as a fisherman and enjoys fishing, but is uncertain about how to combine fishing with having children. She feels it would be possible to take infants fishing, but not toddlers. Their boat is quite small, she says, and there's too much gear in which a curious young child could get caught.

Occasional or Substitute Cook/Deckhand

An additional four of the women we interviewed go or have gone fishing on an irregular basis. The first of these is Nora. Nora fished with her husband off and on for approximately six years. Her husband had extensive fishing experience working as a deckhand on other boats before they were married. In the early years of their marriage they tried various gear types while trying to become established in commercial fishing on their own. Nora said: "I didn't like trolling at all. It was 14 or 18 hours a day, and we were out on the open ocean. You didn't see land for hours at a time. I hated it." Her husband ended up trolling without her while she taught in a Native American school in LaPush, Washington. They then changed gear types, and began gillnetting for salmon in the San Juan Islands in Puget Sound. She said, "I think the reason [we chose gillnetting] was for him. Since he did the majority of the work, why should I give my two cents about it? He preferred net fishing...." She worked with her husband, picking fish out of the net. By her own decision, she did not go when the water was very rough. She said of her work on the boat:

> [I do] just about anything that has to be done. I do a lot of navigating. I do a lot of picking fish, when there's lots of fish. Usually one person can pick the fish most of the time. But when you're in real heavy fishing, it's nice to have people with whom you can get the fish picked and bring it [the net] out again. It's a lot faster.

After the Boldt Decision (United States vs. Washington 1974) allocating treaty Native Americans 50 percent of the harvestable salmon in Washington waters, the number of fishing days gillnetters were allowed was substantially reduced. Nora and her husband felt there was no future for them in the Puget Sound fishery. They again changed gear type and fishing area. Nora and her husband now own a salmon purse seiner operated out of Kodiak, Alaska.[8] In 1980, they were considering moving to Kodiak. Nora said of their first season in Kodiak (summer 1979): "I didn't fish [on the seiner] because you need a crew of four people and the boat is so small that there is no foc's'le. The bunks are just all exposed. And to have a woman on board, and then three guys, is just too close quarters.

So, I went up to Kodiak and worked in a cannery." Nora did not know whether she herself would fish commercially again in the future.

Another two of the women we interviewed were asked by their husbands to work for short periods of time as cook/deckhand, to temporarily replace regular crewmen. Both husbands operate salmon purse seine vessels. Susan worked as cook for two months one fall, seining in Puget Sound. She said:

> My husband is a little bit more harsh on his cooks than most....He wants homemade bread and that kind of thing....They make a set right about the time you have to punch it down and knead or something. So, if you're cook, you have the hardest job on the whole boat. Because for one thing, you have to keep everybody happy....I did bake bread and in between sets went out and did my share on the nets and operated the buttons and got jelly fish in my eyes and the whole business.

She had brought her baby along. He sat on the galley table in an infant seat while she helped with the net. Susan now has three children. She says, "I would do that again if I had one child, but probably not if I had the three."

Joan has gone fishing with her husband only for two weeks, again simply to replace a regular crewman. She worked as a cook, seining for salmon in southeast Alaska. Joan loved it, and would like to do it again. However, she says her husband does not believe in family boats. Their son has worked as a deckhand on board in Alaska, and their daughter has gone fishing with her father on Puget Sound. But, she said, her husband does not feel it would be fair to the rest of the crew to have the whole family on board at the same time. Her husband did have a woman cook on board in Southeast one season. Joan said: "She was one of the better crew members he's ever had....There wasn't anything that she couldn't do....In fact, she bought herself a gillnetter and she went up to Bristol Bay [Alaska] herself." Joan commented that she was jealous of the woman crew member, not because she was on the same boat as her husband, but because she was fishing and Joan could not.

The situation of the fourth woman who fishes on an irregular basis is entirely different from that of any of the other women we interviewed. Christina started and continues in the fish business as a fish processor— cleaning and packing first shrimp, then crab and more recently salmon. In the past, her primary base of operation had been Dutch Harbor, Alaska, in the Aleutian Islands. Depending on the fishing season, she migrated between Dutch Harbor, Adak (further out in the Aleutian chain), Akutan (also in the Aleutians),

Seldovia (on the Kenai Peninsula) and other places. In between, she hired on a boat as cook/deckhand for two weeks. She says:

> It was in the middle of the springtime and we were going tanner [crab] fishing. So [I] went out in this 85 foot boat. The boat had two guys on deck plus the skipper and me. I had to work on deck. I went out and had a really good time for two weeks. I cooked, did my job.

Later on that same year, she went crab fishing again as cook/deckhand with the same skipper. That time they spent six to eight weeks in the Pribilof Islands, in the Bering Sea:

> We only got 12,000 crab for six weeks of work. We spent Christmas out there; we spent New Year's out there; went to Kodiak twice. Just rotten weather. It blew 70 every single day. There were days when I was seasick and there were days when I wasn't seasick....But, I did my job, and that's all that counts to them....The crew is the greatest bunch of guys I've ever been with. They were really supportive.

Then, one summer she worked as a cook/deckhand on a 42 foot salmon seiner out of Kodiak. The crew consisted of the skipper, two other men and herself. She said of the skipper: "He was crazy, just crazy. [He said,] 'You're going to work hard. You're not going to be lazy, are you?' And then he gave me all the jobs on the boat to do."

In 1979 she moved her base of operation from Alaska to Seattle, primarily because the company she had been working for had passed over her for a higher level position for which she felt she was very qualified. She had just finished managing an entire tanner crab operation for the company— from hiring the crew to cleaning up after the season was over. She said: "I thought, 'Whoa! This is where I want to be!' But then, they brought in this guy— it's always they bring in the guy— and he's spent 20 days in the king crab business, and I'm not kidding you. Twenty days!" He got the job. (She has since been offered better positions with the company.) In Seattle, she began working for a fishing/processing operation run by fishermen. During the summer of 1979, she worked on the company's processor-freighter boat off the Alaska Peninsula, and also worked as cook on board when the boat was brought back to Seattle at the end of the season. She had several options for 1980, one of which was to work as a cook on board one of the company's boats while tanner crabbing off Seward during January and February. A second option was to run the processing operation on board the processor-freighter for the same tanner season.

ISSUES FOR FURTHER RESEARCH

Documentation Issues

These, then, are some of the roles women fill on board Pacific Northwest fishing boats: captain, cook/deckhand and occasional or substitute cook/deckhand. The results of the project establish that women do indeed go fishing in a variety of capacities in the Pacific Northwest, and the oral histories provide illustrations of their activities and roles on board and the tone of their lives as fishermen. Because commercial fishing is perceived as a nontraditional occupation for women, the fact that women go fishing at all calls for comment on whether the Pacific Northwest is unique, the numbers of women involved, and the history of women's involvement in Pacific Northwest fishing. We can move on at that point to examining some of the salient issues concerning women's entry into fishing and participation in the harvest. As the project was largely aimed at documenting rather than explaining— at providing a basis for current and future theory building, this study identifies and informs areas of possible future inquiry rather than providing definitive answers.

Uniqueness of the Pacific Northwest

The Pacific Northwest appears to be unique in having women who regularly fish commercially. Yet it is true that in other areas of the United States, some go fishing with their husbands. An informant reported that in Maine, some women fish with their husbands and at least one has seined herring as a crew member; and a few skipper their own lobster boats (P. Kunhikannan, personal communication 1984). Another informant, Glenna, mentioned a woman who worked on a dragger in Massachusetts. Glenna said of this woman: "She did the best she could do with what she had, and she was respected for that. She got jobs. Not I wouldn't say on the highline fishing boats.[9] In smaller operations [like] scalloping [and] that kind of thing." Danowski mentions that a few women in the southern Rhode Island community she studied "fish as crew or co-owners" (1980:44). Carolyn Ellis found that in one of the two Chesapeake Bay communities she studied women participate in crabbing from small skiffs (personal communication 1984). However, it seems quite probable that far fewer women go fishing in the northeast U.S. than do in the northwest. Glenna, who has been involved in fishing in both areas, said: "Fishing in Provincetown [Massachusetts] was very much at that time a man's world....I think that the west coast fishery lends itself to a family operation....Even though there aren't a whole lot of women fishing on the west coast,

I think there are a whole lot less on the east coast." Another informant had come west because she heard that it was much easier to
hire onto a boat in the northwest than it was in Maine. She added
that in Maine some men felt women were "bad luck" on boats and
others felt that, if a woman was on board at all, she should be there
only as the wife of the man running the boat. Further research needs
to be done in all areas of the United States on the extent to which
women actually do go fishing, where and how they fish, and on the
roles they fill on board.[10]

Numbers of Women Fishing in the Northwest

If the number of women who fish in the Pacific Northwest is probably greater than elsewhere in the United States, just how many
women in the Pacific Northwest *do* fish? Considerable further research is needed to answer this question. It is difficult to estimate
the number of northwest fishermen, let alone the number of women
fishermen. The following will illustrate some of the problems.

   One can begin by estimating the number of fishermen generally by multiplying the number of vessels landing salmon in the state
by the estimated crew size for the various gear types. The figures
presented here are for Washington state non-Native American salmon fishermen only. Granger notes: "Very few fishermen use more
than one commercial salmon gear type during the year, so the numbers of fishermen in these categories can be added. The numbers of
fishermen in other fisheries and gear groups should not be added
since they are frequently salmon fishermen who are using their vessels in alternative fisheries during winter month" (Granger 1979:10).
Table 1 presents information by selected gear types on the number
of vessels for 1975 and 1981 landing salmon in the state of
Washington.

   A troller can be operated by one person, but is more usually
operated by two people. A Puget Sound gillnetter is more likely to
be a one person operation, but often carries two people. Charter
boats, too, often operate with a skipper and a deckhand. Purse
seiners on the other hand, operate with a crew of four or five. Thus,
the total possible number of salmon fishermen fishing in the state
of Washington using these gear types during 1981 could be as high
as 12,352.

   The percentage of these who are women is not known. Licensing information for the state of Washington does not include the
applicant's gender.[11]

TABLE 1: Number of Vessels Landing Salmon in Washington, State-Wide

	1975	1981
Trollers*	3,030	2,601
Gillnetters (Total in State)	2,361	2,107
Puget Sound Gillnetters	1,659	1,448
Purse seiners	385	396
Charter boat operators	404	478
Total	6,180	5,582

Note: This table lists only the major gear types and is based on information provided by the Pacific Fisheries Management Council (1983:Table V-9).

* These numbers include trollers with vessel delivery permits which allow trollers to fish beyond three miles from the state's coast, and land their catch in Washington. Regulations in other northwest states vary.

In any case, if a married couple operates a vessel, ownership and other papers and licenses are usually issued in the husband's name. Elena said: "As far as owning a share in it [the boat] and what not, I own the half that's mine by law [referring to Washington State community property laws] and knowing that's it." Marilyn said:

> When I had this one [boat] built [in 1958]...the bank didn't want to finance it in my name. We had a little trouble over that. I told them I would go where I could find a bank that would finance it in my name. I said, 'Even though my husband backs me up, I want it in my name.' So we got it in my name, but the Coast Guard fellow, when he filled it out, put my husband's name on my Certificate of Inspection. We intend to correct that in a couple of weeks.

The State of Alaska handles the situation a bit differently. Sex of applicant is requested on applications for crew licenses which are valid anywhere in Alaska in any fishery. Anyone who sets foot on a commercial fishing vessel, even for just a very short period of time, or picks a single fish out a net, needs a personal license.[12] In 1971, approximately 9 percent of all personal licenses were held by women of all ages (see Table 2). In addition, children under the age of 15 held 8 percent of the licenses, with approximately 15 percent of these licenses being held by girls (Alaska Governor's Study Group 1973:80, Table 19). In 1973, the Alaska Governor's Study Group on Limited Entry noted among the reasons for the practice of obtaining licenses for children that "many children also accompany parents on harvesting vessels" (1973:79). This licensing information, however, is for the entire state of Alaska, and is not available by area of the state or by gear type. The women we interviewed who fish primarily in Alaska power troll for salmon in Southeast. We can try to estimate the number of women involved by using figures for gear licenses. In 1971, there were 857 power troll licenses issued for Yakutat (which is just north of "Southeast") and for southeast Alaska (Alaska Governor's Study Group 1973:157). The total number of possible power troll fishermen in Southeast and Yakutat during 1971 is therefore 1,714 (allowing two persons per vessel). Using the all-Alaska percentage of women who held personal licenses in 1971 (9%), 154 of the 1,714 possible power trollers could be women fishermen. The figures would probably be higher for 1980, as there was an increase in the number of power troll vessels from 1971, and the number of women fishing has probably increased (see below).

TABLE 2: Number of Women Holding Personal Licenses, Alaska, 1971

		Female		Male	
	Total	Number	%	Number	%
Resident	13,918	1,546	11	12,372	89
Non-resident	6,315	225	4	6,090	96
Total	20,233	1,771	9	18,462	91

Note: This table is based on information presented by the Alaska Governor's Study Group on Limited Entry (1973:80, Table 18). More recent information is available on computer tape from the Alaska Department of Revenue, Fish and Game License office. Skippers are not included in these statistics, however, as under the limited entry permit system introduced in 1974, a skipper's entry permit includes his/her personal license.

The above estimates of the total numbers of male and female fishermen harvesting salmon in Washington and Alaska provides a ceiling for the number of women who could possibly participate in the harvest, although clearly their actual participation is a small percentage of this number. In addition, salmon fishermen often fish for other species and clearly there are some fishermen who do not fish for salmon at all. This is one of the reasons it is so difficult to count northwest fishermen. Another is their extreme mobility. They may fish in Alaska with the entry permit for their area, species, and gear type being provided by a processing plant and also hold a license in their own name in Washington and/or Oregon and/or California for a variety of species.

Women and Fishing: Historical Background

However long at least some women have been fishing, there has no doubt been an increase in their numbers in recent years. This may be the result of particular historical events such as the Depression and World War II. Elena thought, for instance, "Just around World War II was when women first started getting into the [fleet]....When the war came along,...it wasn't so easy to get fellas to work. So some of the wives just started going alone. [It] worked out fine, so why not?" It could also be the result of changes within the industry and/or historical trends in American society.

The history of large scale commercial fishing by whites in the Pacific Northwest, and of women's participation in the industry, began with the rise of canneries. Canning allowed large amounts of fish to be processed for sale in distant markets. The first salmon cannery on the Pacific coast was built in 1864 on the Sacramento River in California. The later 1860s through 1880s saw the rise of canneries elsewhere in the Pacific Northwest. The first cannery in Washington was built on the Columbia River in 1866 and the first in the Puget Sound area was built in 1877 (Cobb 1911:12-22).

The fishing industry seems at first to have been dominated by members of various ethnic groups who began immigrating to the Pacific Northwest in the late 1800s and early 1900s.[13] They settled down in Puget Sound area towns and neighborhoods with members of their own ethnic groups, to carry on their traditional fishing occupations. The three most important ethnic groups as far as fishing itself is concerned are: Scandinavians (particularly Norwegians), Greeks, and Yugoslavs. The Yugoslavs came to dominate the purse seine industry on Puget Sound and in Alaska. Many Yugoslavs are still purse seiners today. The Greeks took up gillnetting for salmon on Puget Sound, but most of them have since moved on to other occupations. The Norwegians dominated the halibut fishery, making up 90 percent of the fleet (Droker 1980:7). According to Hage, in 1969 all but one of the halibut fishermen who were based in Seattle and fished in a particular regulatory area in Alaskan waters were Norwegians (or of Norwegian descent) and had previously fished in the U.S. or Norway (Hage 1971:8-9). Norwegians and other Nordic peoples are still active in all types of fishing.

The ethnic fishermen are still present in the fleet, and many of them still appear to reside in neighborhoods consisting of other fishermen of their same ethnic group. At the same time, they no longer dominate the industry. Many participants in commercial fishing in the northwest are members of an occupational community rather than of ethnic communities.[14] This change in the industry appears to provide women with easier access to fishing. (See below in this paper for further discussion of this issue.)

At the same time, other changes in U.S. social and cultural values may also be affecting women's participation. During the 1970s, for instance, there was an apparent influx of women into the fleet. Monica, Katherine and Nora all first started fishing in the early '70s, and Glenna and Christina in the mid or later '70s. Zoe Landale, who writes of fishing off the British Columbia coast, began in 1970: "On the whole, the fishermen didn't know what to make of me, as in those days there were few women, especially young ones, in the fleet" (Landale 1977:34). Elena commented on this influx:

> I think this is evolved recently, since there've been so many of the young women pulling into the fleet with their boy friends, husbands, and what not. I don't remember seeing women doing this 20 years ago. It's just been in the last 10 years there's been such a change in the whole world as far as young women and young men being together...I never recall seeing it years ago.

The next question to ask is whether women's involvement in Pacific Northwest fishing is entirely a recent phenomenon. This does not appear to be the case. There is some indication that women have participated in the industry as fishermen for some time. Documented historical instances of women who have fished in Washington waters in the past are sparse. The earliest we found during the course of the project was in the late 1940s. Marilyn began as a kelper—hand trolling on a daily basis for fish found in and around the kelp on rocks near the shore—in 1947. She says there were other women fishing when she began. Laura began in 1955 and Elena in 1957. In 1980, a fishing newspaper printed a notice of the death of a woman who had fished with her husband since 1950 (*Fishermen's News* 1980a). The presence of women fishermen in Alaska is better documented. Ballard Hadman began trolling with a brother in Southeast in 1937 (Hadman 1955). There were other women fishing when she first came to Alaska. She married a fisherman and continued fishing with him. She also took her young son along. She says:

> Because other boats had children aboard, living the same life, absorbing the same independence, I had not considered how deeply just how unusual Jamie's childhood was—usual to his place, his environment, but unusual to his time, to other environments. Jamie will have to know eventually what the world to southward is like, what other lives are like (Hadman 1955:225-226).

Other women trolled or seined in Southeast during the 1940s and 1950s as captains as well as deckhands (Alaska Department of Education 1979).

FACTORS AFFECTING ENTRY AND PARTICIPATION— ISSUES RELATING TO THE WORKING ENVIRONMENT

Although the percentage of women fishing in the Pacific Northwest is perhaps only nine to ten percent of all fishermen, it appears to be a greater number than fish elsewhere in the United States. Historically, the number of women fishing seems to have been increasing over time. At least some women were fishing as early as the late 1930s, with an influx occurring in the 1970s. Further research is required to confirm this apparent trend.

Given that women are fishing commercially in the Pacific Northwest, we now turn to factors affecting their entry and participation in the harvest— issues which seem inevitably to arise in connection with women's participation in nontraditional occupations. These include a description of the physical demands of the occupation and women's access to resources. Social and cultural factors, which are perhaps more at the heart of the matter, will be discussed in a following section.

Gear Types

Pacific Northwest fishermen rank commercial gear types in terms of a hierarchy of difficulty. The rank of a specific gear type depends on a combination of factors: estimates of the physical strength needed to operate the gear, characteristics of the species sought, and the area and seasons fished. The more "difficult" gear types are accorded greater prestige. In his study of southeast Alaska salmon gillnetters, Houshower mentions this differential prestige: "But as a former seiner and a crabber, Bob occupied a special niche within a kind of unspoken ranking system among gillnetters which accorded more respect and prestige to individuals who had experience in the purse seine fleet and even more to those who had worked on a crab boat" (Houshower 1982:155). We found trolling and gillnetting to be considered of approximately equal difficulty, with seining, then dragging, and finally Bering Sea crabbing at the top. Most of the women we interviewed are concentrated in gear types at the bottom of the hierarchy: most of the women who fish regularly are trollers; two are gillnetters. The remaining three women have worked as cook/deckhand on seining boats, and one has worked as cook /deckhand on a Bering Sea crabber.

Trolling and gillnetting require the least amounts of physical strength. Trolling is a hook and line fishery, with the lines being reeled in by power gurdies. Once the fish reach the surface of the water, they must be brought on board using a gaff hook, bludgeoned, and then cleaned and iced. Hand trollers do exist—where the lines must be reeled in by muscle power alone. Gillnetting is a net fishery. Most boats have an hydraulic reel to bring the net in, but on older boats it was done by muscle power. Everyone we talked to, both men and women, thought women were quite physically capable of doing the work on a troller or gillnetter.

Seining is considered the next most difficult gear type after trolling and gillnetting. A power block is used to haul the net along with its tons of fish out of the water. Most of the women we have talked to or been told about who work on seiners work as cook/deckhands. Dragging, mainly for bottomfish, involves yet another gear type. Draggers, or trawlers, drag a net along the bottom of the ocean, or at mid-level. This is considered a more difficult gear type. None of the women we interviewed worked on draggers, although we were told of a few who do. Finally, at the top of the scale of danger and difficulty is king crabbing, particularly in the Bering Sea. Christina, who worked as cook/deckhand on a crabber said:

> Handling a six to eight hundred pound pot is not the easiest thing in the world, you know. Take my word for it....One night we were out off of Dutch Harbor...and I helped stack 32 pots. I got to work on deck and I did my part. I helped stack and put the hook on and all that. Boy, that's not easy....Even with winches and stuff....What they usually do is let the woman run the winches...But she can't now because you have to spell off the guys. They can't stand it either. But they're of course physically stronger in a lot a ways, but then again they're not....Endurance, women have more endurance. It's just such hard work, so physically demanding. And, you have to realize your limitations....As far as net fishing is concerned, like gillnetting or purse seining or that, or longlining, there's no reason why a woman couldn't do that. But, as far as crab fishing is concerned, in particular, I don't think I would ever see the day a woman could hold her own on deck.

Besides the gear itself, Bering Sea crabbers have to deal with strong winds, high seas and the icing problems which can result from the combination of these two with Bering Sea temperatures. Excessive icing can cause a boat to capsize.

We discovered that fishermen's perceptions of what a woman is physically capable or not capable of doing seems to depend largely on the gear type with which that person is most familiar. Nevertheless, women do seem to be more concentrated in the less demanding gear types. There are, however, at least a few women fishing in even the most demanding ones. Several articles in fishing newspapers mention women who work as cook/deckhand on Alaskan crabber or combination dragger/crabber boats (*Fishermen's News*, 1980b, 1980c; Goforth 1980). We were also told of a crab boat out of Kodiak, Alaska entirely run by women. We can thus lay aside the physical strength issue as the sole reason women do not participate in fishing in many areas of the world.[15]

The other considerations in ranking and also in choosing a gear type involve the species, seasons, length of trip, and areas fished. With one exception, the fishing activities of all the women we interviewed are targeted primarily on salmon. A few of the trollers also fish albacore tuna and pick up incidental halibut. Halibut are considered very dangerous fish. Monica said, "Halibuts are all muscle, and even the small ones are dangerous." A few of the women have also fished for bottomfish (such as ling cod or sablefish). Their fishing choices are also influenced to some degree by preferences for daily versus trip fishing, day versus night fishing, open ocean versus "inside" fishing, the availability and closeness of safe harbors, and weather conditions. Nora, for example, did not like trolling for salmon off the Washington coast because it is done on the open ocean out of sight of land. Monica, on the other hand, did not like trolling for albacore off the coast, but loves trolling for salmon. She said:

> Fishing salmon, you're close to shore. It's far more work, fishing salmon, in some ways. You're close to shore, though, and you can go and anchor up, if it's really bad weather....Tuna fishing, you're out there 250 miles or 200 miles—you can't do anything.

Elena and Glenna and their husbands decided to troll in southeast Alaska rather than off the Washington coast because, although the weather might be somewhat worse, if they fish the inside passage, they are protected from ocean swells. In addition, compared to the Washington coast, safe harbors in Southeast are plentiful. Whatever species they are pursuing, almost all of the women fish only from approximately May through October each year. Marilyn does chartering in the winter further inland on the Strait of Juan de Fuca rather than near the ocean. Christina is the only one who has gone fishing commercially in the winter (and in the Bering Sea for tanner crab).

Resources and Earnings

There are other reasons, however, why women may be found in some gear types more frequently than in others. As it happens, the hierarchy of gear type difficulty roughly corresponds with both the hierarchy of expense to enter and operate a particular gear type and the amount of money to be made from that gear type. Trolling and gillnetting are low budget operations when compared to seining and crabbing. Nora commented that she and her husband went gillnetting because "there was no way we could afford purse seining, so we chose gillnetting, which is the lesser money out of the net fishing." Bering Sea crabbing is even more expensive than seining. Crab boats can cost in the millions and are often owned by nonfishing corporations.

All of the women we interviewed started out with very small operations. Laura hand trolled for ling cod in the winter in the Strait of Juan de Fuca. Marilyn began as a kelper, hand trolling near shore. Through the years, all of our informants gradually upgraded their boats and equipment, although some upgraded further than others, depending on their resources. Nora and her husband had help from her husband's fishing family. She said:

> His Dad builds Kodiak seiners, and his Dad could build us a boat a lot cheaper than us having to buy one off the street. And we have fished for a cannery down here...that could finance us for a license. A license [in Alaska] is as much as buying a boat....They could finance us, 'cause we just didn't have the money.

Some of the expenses involved in operating a boat and gear include the cost of the boat and gear, insurance, moorage, operation and maintenance of boat and gear, crew shares of the take, and licenses. All of this comes out of the total gross income of the fishermen. Monica estimated that a fisherman trolling off the coast of Washington could make $20,000 to $30,000 in an average season, before expenses. After expenses, Washington trollers take home much less than this and their incomes could not be considered extravagant. In 1980, Alaska Sea Grant and United Fishermen of Alaska co-sponsored a study of Alaska fishermen's incomes. They received only a 14 percent response rate to their questionnaire. Of those who responded, the net 1979 income of southeast Alaska salmon purse seiners (after the deduction of expenses) was $19,871; of salmon drift gillnetters $14,151; of power trollers $17,925; and of hand trollers $585. The "returns to labor and management (how much a skipper of a vessel earns for his labor in fishing and skills as an operator)" for each of the above in 1979 was $2,519 for purse seiners, $3,103 for salmon drift gillnetters, $7,642 for power trollers, and $427 for hand trollers (*Alaska Fisherman's Journal* 1981).

At the present time the cost of licenses constitutes a major expense for a person trying to enter fishing or upgrade their operation, and the cost of the licenses and permits can be taken as a rough index of the monetary returns to be expected from a gear type. The states of Washington and Alaska have limited the number of entry permits and licenses available to fishermen, particularly for salmon fishing. This has resulted in competition for licenses and permits, and the price of a permit or license is determined by what other fishermen are willing to pay. During 1984, the Washington State buy-back program—a program aimed at reducing the fishing effort—was paying $1,600 for troll vessel licenses. The resale value of these licenses to other fishermen is not documented, but was rumored to be $700 to $2,000.[16] Puget Sound gillnet licenses were worth more than trolling licenses, primarily because gillnetting is considered more lucrative than trolling. In southeast Alaska, where fishermen can earn more money than in Washington, the resale value of permits in 1984 was even higher. When one compares the potential income with the initial cost of a permit alone for any gear type, one can see that the cost of entering fishing for the first time is very high.

Factors Affecting Entry and Participation: Social and Cultural Issues

Although women are concentrated in the less demanding gear types, and lack of resources may hinder women's participation in any of them, we must look to social and cultural factors as the most important ones affecting women's participation in fishing. For instance, one reason women may be more prevalent in trolling and gillnetting is that these are one or two person operations. Other gear types require larger crews living together on board for at least a week at a time. Nora went fishing with her husband when he was a gillnetter. She does not go seining. She said: "If it was another husband and wife sort of set-up, where there would be two of us, that would be okay, but to have...three guys and a gal, it just doesn't work out well." Another (male) fisherman said that women are not hired because the boats lack "facilities." There are usually no showers on board, and the ocean itself constitutes the toilet facilities. Sleeping arrangements are similarly makeshift on smaller boats, and on seiners usually consist of a small open area foc's'le with bunks. The quarters are considered too tight for the mixing of unrelated male and female crew members while maintaining a degree of decorum.

While a different arrangement of space on newer boats may alleviate this problem to some degree, the core of the issue seems to be that introducing women into a crew introduces sexuality into the work place. Kanter points out that "sexuality has for a long time been considered the enemy of work discipline" (1977:9). The work place attempts to exclude the element of sexuality and all lines of authority and allegiance which might compete with the organization. To many male fishermen, having one woman on board among many men introduces the element of sexuality into their work place and thereby, in their view, causes disruption. If that woman is allied with the captain, the usual vertical line of authority remains intact. If she is allied with a crew member, then the allegiance becomes horizontal and interferes with the vertical line of authority from captain to each individual crew member. This, perhaps, explains the feelings of the Maine fisherman who said that a woman should be on board only as the wife of the man running the boat.

When a male captain and his wife (or "significant other") are the primary operators of a boat, it becomes in effect a family business. It has the same characteristics in terms of interpersonal relationships as a land based business. Many of the women we interviewed are involved in this type of relationship. They were either married to men who were already fishermen, or went along with them when they decided to become fishermen. The remaining women also entered fishing through a personal relationship with a man. Laura bought her first working boat with her husband, although she had an interest in fishing and had done ocean sport fishing by herself before that time. Marilyn's husband was an avid sport fisherman before becoming a commercial fisherman, and she used to go fishing with him. Wilma's husband had a gillnet boat, but lost it. Then a son had a boat he couldn't insure and Wilma and her husband took it over for him. Christina took advantage of job offers made to her by male skippers, although she entered the fish business on her own accord. She says her job as cook on the crab boat was simply a job. Of her Kodiak salmon seining job, however, she says: "But, yeah, I was still his girl friend. I wasn't just hired because I knew what I was doing." Some of the daughters of women we interviewed are now gaining access to fishing through their fathers. Christina summed up the situation in her description of what she saw in Chignik, Alaska.

> Chignik [Alaska] is a lagoon and there's a very...superclosed fishery. In fact, it has its own permit...and the people who live there live there most of their lives. Very small, very few boats....One reason I really enjoyed Chignik this summer...[is that] I saw women

working with their husbands, or daughters working with their fathers, on deck, paid....But yet it was still, like I say, related women. They were related. Never just a woman. In fact, the only woman in Chignik that I know of who fished strictly as a woman was put down by her whole crew. And not very nice things were said about it.

It thus seems that although these women are working in an occupation considered nontraditional for women, most of them are on board in customary male-female relationships. The women who are captains usually fish alone or with unrelated crew members. Laura attempted to have a husband as crew member but this reversal of the customary lines of family authority did not work out. Marilyn and her husband operate separate vessels. Wilma had a son, not a husband, as a crew member. Here the mother-son line of authority coincided with the captain-crew line of authority.

Women who attempt to enter fishing as wage earners or for shares of the catch are being nontraditional in every respect and have a much harder time entering and remaining in fishing. One woman we met went to the docks in Ketchikan, Alaska and hired on a seine boat. Although she enjoyed fishing and would do it again, she fished for only one season. The second season, the skipper's wife complained—this is apparently common—and the skipper could not hire her back even though he wished to. The third season, her boy friend told her that if she went fishing, he would not be waiting for her when she returned to Seattle. His objection was that she would be the only woman on board with a number of men and she was forced to make a choice between her boy friend and fishing.

All of these women have the problem of how to combine fishing and child rearing. Most of the women had no children (Laura, Katherine, Nora and Christina), or at least no small children (Wilma and Joan) during their fishing days. Elena and Glenna regularly take their children fishing and when she first started fishing, Marilyn did so occasionally. Elena and Glenna are the two women with "family boats." Elena's children were on board only during summer vacation from school. She and her husband day fished when the children were small and began trip fishing only after they had bought a larger boat when the children were older. Glenna's youngest child was four months old when she began fishing and her eldest was three years old. She said:

> My six year old [in 1980] has been on the boat since he was three. And he can do just about anything: he can clean fish; he can run the gear; and he can bait up; he can throw his own gear over the side and fool around with that; he can cook; he can—whatever. He

loves the boat and he really is very capable. The little one is something else. He started on the boat when he was four months....He's not as careful with himself, and I'll have to watch him a lot more. I can't, for instance, have him on deck if we're running the gear. It's just too dangerous. One false step and fingers are in the gurdies and— disaster. So he has to do more wheel house activity than the other. They play together a lot, and they swing off the boom and catch their own kind of fish.

Glenna and her husband regularly do trip fishing. She did not say how they would handle schooling when the children reach that age. The situation of Monica, who was the youngest woman fisherman we interviewed— she entered fishing at age 20— provides an illustration of the dilemma to be worked out. Monica was expecting a child in 1980. She was undecided about which path to take. She did not want to give up fishing, but, on the other hand, did not want to take the baby out on the boat.

One possible factor in taking children fishing appears to be the size of the boat. Glenna and her children began fishing only after the family had bought a larger troller; Elena and Ken began trip fishing with their children after they bought a larger boat; and Monica mentioned the small size of the family boat as an obstacle to taking a baby along. In addition, Ballard Hadman notes in her book that one of the contributing factors in her and her husband's decision to buy a larger boat was to have better accommodations for their child (Hadman 1955). It should be noted, however, that only those women who fish alone or with a relative, particularly a husband, have the option of taking their children fishing. Those women who fish with unrelated skippers do not have this choice.

Other sociocultural factors affecting women's entry and participation in commercial fishing command attention when we look at the women's natal family background. Of particular interest is the role of ethnicity. None of the women fishermen we interviewed identify with any of the three major ethnic groups (described earlier in this paper) which have traditionally been strongly involved with commercial fishing in the Pacific Northwest. Only one of our informants, Joan, was both born and married into one of these ethnic families. She has fished for only two weeks as a substitute cook/deckhand and her husband does not believe in having a "family boat." She did not go fishing on her father's boat when young, as women were considered bad luck. She recalled that when she was about twelve years old, she was on her father's boat when he was taking it through the locks in Seattle.[17] There was an accident; it was blamed on her because she was the only woman on board. Their daughter, however, has gone fishing with her father, and in 1980 hoped to work as a regular crew member (rather than as a cook) on a boat that summer in order to earn money for college. Another informant, Nora, married into one of these families and went gillnetting with her husband. Now that he is seining, she no longer goes along.

In examining the role of ethnic values, we must be careful to look at women's attitudes as well as the men's. Many of the women from these ethnic families declared they wanted nothing to do with the "old, smelly boat." This may have been their way of avoiding entanglement with what Kanter would call an absorptive occupation (1977:25). We were told also of one older Yugoslav woman who had regularly worked as a cook on her family's seiner. When we contacted her for an interview, she replied, "You'd have to talk to the menfolk about fishing."

As pointed out previously, participants in Pacific Northwest commercial fishing are now primarily members of an occupational community rather than ethnic communities. If our women fishermen's natal families were members of the ethnic communities, were their families from the occupational community? This does not appear to be the case. With one exception, none of the women we interviewed who fish or have fished regularly come from natal families which engaged in commercial fishing. They come from a variety of urban and farm environments. Marilyn was born on a farm in eastern Washington, and her family moved to Seattle when she was five or six years old. Elena is also from an eastern Washington farm family. The younger women, such as Monica, Christina and Katherine are from urban or suburban families who did not engage in fishing. None of these women knew women fishermen who might have acted as role models, and only a few of the women knew male fishermen. Laura grew up in Everett, Washington, on Puget Sound. There were several fishing families in the neighborhood, but the women in these families did not go fishing. Laura says: "[They] just didn't do things like that. The women prepared the meals, and usually a man went out and then came back in the evening, or [would be gone] just maybe overnight." Laura's father, however, was a seaman, and her mother used to go out on a tug with him. She says she was within four days of being born on a tug. Wilma's family moved from Kansas to Friday Harbor, Washington, an island community, when she was nine years old. While none of her family were fishermen, she grew up around fishing. She worked in Friday Harbor canneries and occasionally did net mending for fishermen. Nora is the only one of the women who

comes from a family which was involved in fishing. She never went
fishing with her father (although her brothers did) and grew up as
a farmer rather than a fisherman. Two other women we interviewed
who neither go fishing nor are from fishing families, married men
who are second generation fishermen. These men, however, do not
identify with one of the three major ethnic groups associated with
commercial fishing in the Pacific Northwest. All the women we interviewed who fish therefore lacked role models, and most had little
or no experience on board when they first entered the industry as
fishermen.

From all of the foregoing we can identify four major ways women
may enter commercial fishing: through their natal family; through
hiring on; through marriage (or alliance with a "significant other");
or through having the resources to buy their own gear. The last is
usually done by both men and women only after they have gained
experience through one of the other avenues. The avenue most used
by the women we interviewed is marriage. Even if their natal family was involved in fishing, this did not provide access (although this
may now be changing). Once in fishing, their continued participation seems to depend on how they manage to combine fishing with
child rearing. In addition, some women hire onto vessels operated
by unrelated skippers. Their entry and participation in the industry
is hampered by social and cultural values and attitudes, as is illustrated by the "decorum" issue; and participation is likely to be
sporadic for just such reasons as is illustrated by the situation of
the woman who hired on a seiner out of Ketchikan. These values
and attitudes need to be identified and defined.

CONCLUDING REMARKS

The study of women in nontraditional occupations, especially voca-
tional ones, is a relatively new area of research. In the past, cultural
assumptions about women's roles and activities have either dis-
torted or replaced social science theory. Recent work by Kanter and
Finch provides a breakthrough in the study of women and work.
There is still much to be done. Although theory necessarily informs
description, scholarly documentation of social phenomena is prior
to and necessary for theory building.

When we began our study on women's roles in Pacific Northwest
fishing, we had little to guide us in our inquiries. No documentation
of women in northwest fishing existed except for a few popular accounts and newspaper articles. Theoretical insights provided by
scholarly literature were limited. We could not, therefore, take the
usual social science approach of defining a single (usually narrow)

theoretical problem or issue, researching the question, and presenting the findings. Rather, we set out to document that women in the northwest do fish commercially and to define the issues concerning women's entry and participation in the industry which need further research. The more salient issues are discussed in the second half of this chapter. It is hoped that this discussion will aid other scholars in their research and advance the study of women in society.

Notes

1. This paper addresses only the participation of non-Native American women in commercial fishing. The topic of Native American commercial fishing in the Pacific Northwest and the roles of Native American women in the industry calls for a separate study. Further, the paper primarily reflects conditions prevailing within the industry during the years 1979 and 1980. All of the names used in this chapter are pseudonyms.
2. The project was conducted jointly by the Women Studies Program and the Institute for Marine Studies at the University of Washington, Seattle. Funding was provided by Washington Sea Grant. Sue-Ellen Jacobs, Director of the Women Studies Program, and Marc Miller, Institute for Marine Studies, served as Principal Investigators. The research staff included myself, Karen Blair, Leona Pollock and Judy Hodgeson. At this point I wish to thank all of those in the fishing industry who helped us in our research. I also wish to thank in particular Victoria Foedisch, Sue-Ellen Jacobs, and Mary Porter for commenting on a draft of this paper, and Margie Ramsdell for typing it.
3. Trolling is a hook and line fishery usually done on the open ocean. Typically, a troller will have six lines, with anywhere from one to ten hooks on a line. The boat pulls the lines through the water.
4. Some trollers are called "ice boats," as the fish are stored on ice. Ice boats usually stay out at sea 10 to 14 days, depending on how long their ice will last. Thus, there are 10 day ice boats, 14 day ice boats and so on.
5. For more information on code groups and "running partnerships," see Stuster (1978).
6. In gillnetting, fish are caught by their gills when they try to swim through the net. There are two types of gillnetting— drift gillnetting and set netting. Set nets are legal only in Alaska. In addition, a few set nets are in (legal) use by Washington state Native Americans (Higgins 1978:15).
7. A longline is a long length of line, or many lengths of line, with a series of hooks on leaders of various lengths fastened to the mainline. The line is anchored to the ocean bottom and marked with a buoy. In trawling ("otter trawling"), also called dragging, a net is towed through the water behind the boat.

8. In purse seining, a net is used to encircle the fish. The bottom of the net is then drawn together, or pursed, and the fish entrapped. Michael Orbach's book on tuna seining in San Diego gives a complete description of how the gear operates (Orbach 1977). The San Diego tuna vessels described by Orbach are floating palaces compared to most Pacific Northwest seiners.
9. A highliner is a fisherman who consistently lands a large amount of fish due to both luck and skill as a fisherman.
10. Thompson, Wailey and Lummis report very few instances of women fishermen who skipper their own boats in Northern Ireland (1983:378). They also report instances of women who fish close to shore in Sweden, Norway, northwest France (Brittany) and Spain (1983:174); of women fishing further off shore in Sweden in small boats (1983:175); and of women in Sardinia who serve as temporary crew members when no men are available (1983:378). They also report that in the Newfoundland cod fishery from the late eighteenth to the mid-twentieth century male fishermen took women along as fishworkers and cooks to work on board the boats as well as in huts on shore (1983:173-174).
11. Washington State Department of Fisheries, Licensing, Olympia, WA (personal communication, June 1984).
12. Alaska Department of Revenue: Fish and Game License Office, Juneau (personal communication, June 1984).
13. See Cobb (1911:68) for the number of members of each ethnic group involved on shore. Filipinos began working in the canneries shortly after the Chinese and Japanese, and remain one of the dominant ethnic groups working in fish processing plants today. (V. Foedisch, personal communication, 1984.)
14. See William Pilcher's book on Portland longshoremen for a general description of a dispersed occupational community (Pilcher 1972). Van Maanan, Miller and Johnson use this concept in discussing commercial fishing in Bristol Bay, Alaska (1980).
15. Andersen and Wadel come to a similar conclusion. They say, "When we consider available information about the division of labor, however, this viewpoint [that women's lack of physical strength prevents them from fishing] seems facile, and somewhat ethnocentric....Fishermen in the Northern Atlantic exclude women from direct participation in many fishing activities. That the explanation for this must be sought in cultural terms (...) is reinforced by the fact that many fishing 'cultures' resort to prohibitions restricting female access to the fishery" (1972:141-142).
16. Washington State Department of Fisheries, Licensing, Olympia, WA (personal communication, June 1984).
17. The Hiram M. Chittenden Locks in Seattle connect Puget Sound with two fresh water lakes. Fishermen's Terminal, which provides moorage for commercial fishermen, is located to the east of the locks in fresh water.

Managing Uncertainty: Family, Religion, and Collective Action Among Fishermen's Wives in Gloucester, Massachusetts

Margaret Elwyn Clark

Spurred by the women's movement in the 1960s, scholars have begun to examine women's social roles and power. One early hypothesis was that women are universally subordinate to men (Rosaldo and Lamphere 1974). However, ethnographic data demonstrate the cross-cultural variation in women's social roles and power. Many studies have documented that in different societies, women may control valued resources, make socially important decisions, and have personal autonomy (Friedl 1967; Rogers 1978). This diversity points out the complexity of the issue and the need to expand our definition of women's power and influence. Stamm and Ryff (1984) suggest that to define the mechanisms of women's power, it is necessary to specify the social roles and arenas within which women interact—that is, to study women on their own terms. This chapter focuses on the Gloucester Fishermen's Wives Association (GWFA), with the aims of elucidating the ways and contexts in which women in Gloucester, Massachusetts, exert control and influence and of identifying some of the social norms and constraints which affect their power.

The fishing life style is filled with uncertainty. The occupation is physically dangerous. A fisherman's life is at risk when he is out at sea. Every trip, the size of the catch varies depending on the season, the weather conditions, the skill of the skipper, the quality of the boat's equipment, and chance. In addition, there is economic uncertainty. When the fisherman leaves the shore, he does not know how much money he will receive per pound of fish. The price of fish is based on the Boston fish auction and prices fluctuate daily. Further, government policies which regulate fisheries are continually changing. An additional risk factor is that most of the men do not have the training to do other types of work.

Some of the fishermen's wives in Gloucester manage this high-level of uncertainty in their lives through the combined reliance on family, religion, and collective action. Using profiles of two women, this chapter explores the manner in which the women keep the round of everyday activities going and at the same time address the chronic problems and crises which beset the fishing industry. The central hypothesis is that women are acting to ensure the well-being and continuation of the family in four spheres: the biological (by having children), the social (by maintaining strong family networks), the cultural (by preserving religious values, Sicilian traditions and the fishing heritage), and the productive (by participating in the GWFA).

This chapter is divided into three sections. The first describes the city of Gloucester and provides the historical background of the GFWA. The next contains biographical sketches of the two women. In the last section, their negotiation of family network, religion, and collective action will be discussed, using the events of one day, 28 July 1983.[1]

GLOUCESTER AND THE GLOUCESTER FISHERMEN'S WIVES ASSOCIATION

Gloucester, population 28,000 (United States Census 1980), has a long tradition of seafaring. The town was originally settled in 1623. Gloucester's active marine business began in the 1700s, making it the oldest fishing port in the United States. Although Anglo-Saxons dominated the fishing industry for two hundred years, they were gradually displaced by immigrants from Scandinavia, Nova Scotia, Ireland, Portugal, and Sicily who moved into the area beginning in the early 1900s.

While tourism and light manufacturing are growing, today, Gloucester's economy is still dominated by all facets of the fishing industry: catching, landing, and processing fish. It is consistently the top port in New England in terms of landings. In 1983, 150.9 million pounds of fish were landed (*Commercial Fisheries News* 1984a). The dollar value was 38 million dollars, making Gloucester the eighth richest port in the nation (*Commercial Fisheries News* 1984a). Seventeen international companies import/export 17 tons of fish annually through the Gloucester harbor (Cape Ann Chamber of Commerce 1980b). Some marine repair and small craft businesses can also be found. Despite its high ratings, the success of the Gloucester fishing industry is undermined by chronic problems: lack of public dockage; low prices received by the fishermen; foreign fish imports; rising costs of fuel, equipment maintenance, and insurance; as well as numerous, constantly changing government restrictions.

While the processing and marketing aspects of the fishing industry have become increasingly modernized, the commercial fishing business has remained small-scale and family-oriented. There are about 275 boats over 30 feet fishing out of Gloucester, the majority of which are wooden and were built before 1950.

The fishing community consists of approximately 1100 fishermen, most of whom are of Sicilian descent with Portuguese and Yankee families making up the rest. Since fishing families share a unique life style and set of problems, the people involved directly in fishing can be said to form an occupational community that is distinct from its non-fishing counterparts (Miller and Maanen 1979). This seems to be true in Gloucester. However, as Miller and Maanen (1979) point out, there are five distinctions made within the Gloucester fishing community which affect its solidarity. Two are work-related and represent visible and different work patterns: off-shore versus inshore day fishing and captain versus crew. Three additional factors— kinship, ethnicity, and length of time in the United States— influence the work strategies, networks, and life styles of the fisherfolk.

In the past, these internal differences have weakened the ability of the fishermen to work together to improve economic conditions and their ability to influence government policy decisions in their favor. None of the existing men's organizations— the Seaman's Union, the Saint Peter's Club, or the Boatowner's Association— are politically active.

The Gloucester Fishermen's Wives Association (GFWA) was formed in 1969 in large part due to the realization that a cohesive, informed voice was needed to represent the interests of the fishing fleet. Originally named the United Fishermen's Wives Association (UFW), the organization was conceived by Carmine Gorga and Grace Parsons, two community organizers with Action, a community-based social service agency. The association was part of an anti-poverty campaign in Gloucester, one branch of which was directed at addressing economic problems within the fishing industry. Although the association's creation was not initiated by the women themselves, the organizational setup developed through meetings with the Action staff, representatives of the fishermen's wives organization in New Bedford, Massachusetts, and about 50 women from Gloucester. The officers of the association were fishermen's wives, with the Action staff acting more as facilitators.

The major focus of the organization was political action at local, state, regional, and federal levels to make officials aware of the economic difficulties confronting the fishermen. In particular, the UFW pressed the United States Senate to pass Senator Edward Kennedy's bill (S2825) to aid the industry by limiting imports of fish and giving grants to fishermen's co-operative associations. Among the other issues the group addressed were the curtailment of the foreign fleet off the United States shore and pollution control.

Plans were also made for a fishermen's co-operative, a fresh fish restaurant, and a fish cookbook. In 1972, the group faltered. Their efforts to complete these projects were not successful and Action's funding was not renewed. One of the women explained, "Some of the members lost interest, some got jobs or were involved with other activities and the leaders got discouraged because the same group did everything all the time."

However, in 1976, the organization was revitalized by the fishermen's wives and was renamed the Gloucester Fishermen's Wives Association. The first project was to join in the fight to pass the 200-mile limit thereby extending the territorial waters of the United States to 200 miles. This would keep the large foreign factory ships from further depleting areas where the Gloucester fleet has traditionally fished. The GFWA also wanted some federal assistance for the Gloucester fleet since it was competing against foreign boats being subsidized by their governments. Once the 200-mile limit was passed, the association was very active in negotiations with state and federal officials regarding the management of the fisheries.

At the same time, the women worked on promoting the consumer's understanding of underutilized species of fish by holding fish fries. Since these efforts were successful locally, the women decided in 1976 to broaden their audience by compiling their recipes in a cookbook. *The Taste of Gloucester: A Fisherman's Wife Cooks*, published jointly by the GFWA and the Cape Ann League of Women Voters, is currently in its seventh edition.

The GFWA has continued to grow. It is listed in the Cape Ann Directory of Organizations as "advocates for the fishing industry" (Cape Ann Chamber of Commerce 1980a). Incorporated in 1979, the organization has 170 members and is headed by a 12-woman Board of Directors. The majority of the members are of Sicilian descent. Of these women, 34 percent are Sicilian-born and the remainder are first-generation Americans. However, three of the more active women are Americans of Anglo-Saxon origin.

The women continue to work to protect the fishing businesses of their families through lobbying and creative marketing techniques. Both aspects of their campaign have expanded. Current political issues in which the association is involved include: working with environmental groups to fight offshore drilling on Georges Bank, pressuring government agencies to regulate the imports of Canadian fish, and monitoring local issues such as the use of the waterfront property. The marketing campaign of the association focuses on promoting the consumption of domestic fresh fish and broadening the public's awareness of underutilized, cheaper species such as pollack. The women give cooking demonstrations in supermarkets throughout Massachusetts and cater dinners for local organizations. To publicize their cause further, the association would like to raise a statue in honor of fishermen's wives around the world.

To summarize, the GFWA was formed in response to threats to the fishing industry from new United States government interference, changing economic conditions, and the fragmented nature of the Gloucester fishing community. The organization has existed for 15 years and has become a force to contend with at local, state, and federal levels both as a political lobby and an economic marketing agent for the industry. Yet the members are all women—wives, mothers, grandmothers, and daughters. Most of them grew up in traditional Sicilian households either in Gloucester or in Sicily.

The GFWA, then, appears to present a paradox for several reasons. The literature indicates that men's integration in the public domain precedes women's and that men, not women, are usually articulate in the public sphere (Nelson 1979; Tinker and Bramsen 1976; Rosaldo and Lamphere 1974). Further, the gender role norms in the Sicilian cultural tradition clearly confine women to running the household and raising the children. It is the men of the family who manage the external affairs. The honor of the family is linked to female chastity, fidelity and motherhood, all of which are better safeguarded in the domestic domain (Dolci 1981; Cornelison 1976; Giovannini 1981). Of course, the actual behavior of men and women is tempered by the demands of daily life. However, options for women to participate directly in economic and political affairs in the public domain are quite restricted (Giovannini 1981).

In order to explain the existence and effectiveness of the GFWA, it is important to include the women themselves in the discussion.

At this point, then, the reader must be introduced to Rose and Maria, two women who are active in the organization.

PROFILES OF ROSE AND MARIA

Rose

Born in Gloucester in 1917, Rose is the oldest daughter of nine children: six boys and three girls. On both her father's and mother's sides, the men have been fishermen for generations. Rose's parents were born in Sicily and emigrated to the United States as young adults. As they did not speak English, and the family lived in the Italian section near the waterfront, Rose grew up speaking Sicilian. She did learn English in school, which she attended through the seventh grade. At the age of thirteen, she was taken out of school in order to help her mother take care of the other children, do housework, and prepare for the fishing trips of her father and brothers.

By this time, Rose's father had become a fishing captain and boat owner, which meant additional responsibilities for his wife and daughters. Since Rose could speak English, she translated for her father in many of his dealings concerning the boat and the business side of fishing. For example, Rose would accompany her father when he went to buy parts and equipment for the boat or to negotiate with the banks for loans. Rose would also handle the money for the crew members— many of whom were single men who would come over from Sicily to fish on her father's boat during the mackerel season. She speaks of the time when the currency was revalued: "My father was fishing off Cape May and he called me to tell me to take all the money to the bank and exchange it. I walked to the bank with a paper bag full of bills. I was only 8 or 9 years old at the time."

One consequence of these experiences was that Rose met businessmen who were outside the fishing community in Gloucester and learned about financial affairs. At that time, the Italians were not treated very well. Rose explains the work she does now for the industry in terms of the fact that she saw how hard it was for her father and her uncles. She does not want the fishing heritage to be lost, nor does she want the current generation of fishermen to be faced with such difficulties. She says: "I do all this now because I know how hard it was back then but those fishermen gave us a beginning— not only the Italians but the Yankees, the people from Nova Scotia and Portugal too. Without them, there would be no industry for us today, so it's up to us to keep it going now."

Despite her responsibilities for the boat and money, Rose was brought up very strictly. In speaking of her childhood Rose says that she was not allowed down on the wharves at all, and that she could attend only one movie a year.

At the age of 21, Rose married Sal. Sal was also born in this country into a fishing family. He became a fishing captain, boat owner, and renowned net designer and net maker. In addition to raising her six children and maintaining the household, Rose was the land agent for her husband's boat, work she continues to do for her son who now skippers the family boat. Her tasks include informing the fish dealers of when her son is coming in from fishing and of how much fish he has landed. If any repairs to the equipment or the boat are needed, Rose will make these arrangements. In addition, Rose is an active participant in the boat corporation and is the major decision-maker in such matters as the disbursement of money to pay the bills, and the negotiation of the boat insurance policy and the mortgage. She also makes sure that the boat has the required licenses and meets the safety regulations.

All of Rose's children are married except for the youngest daughter who is in her early 20s and still lives at home. Rose also takes care of her mother, aged 94, who lives next door.

Rose is a staunch advocate for the fishing industry as an individual, as well as through her work in the GFWA. As part of her personal campaign, she has written letters to Avon and Arm & Hammer protesting their use of fried fish in advertisements for room deodorizers; and she has fought to have the employment status of the fishermen changed from unskilled to skilled labor. An active promoter of fresh fish, Rose would get her female relatives to help her put on fish dinners for community groups before the GFWA was even formed. She is recognized in the town as an excellent cook and was Yankee magazine Cook of the Month in March 1978. Currently, she is experimenting with ways to make her home recipe of fish soup for babies a marketable item. All her work is an attempt to increase the consumption of domestic fresh fish.

A founding member of both the United Fishermen's Wives Association and the GFWA, today Rose is the Treasurer. She attends public meetings regularly to speak out for the industry. She says: "I don't have no degrees like the lawyers or marine biologists, but I got four generations of fishing in me. That's my degree, so I guess I got something to say."

Maria

Although Maria is much younger than Rose, there are many similarities in the childhood experiences and responsibilities of the two women. Born in 1950 in a fishing village in Sicily, Maria is descended from a long line of fishermen. Both her grandfathers and her father were licensed fishermen and boatowners. Her mother was a seamstress who worked at home. Like Rose, Maria is the oldest daughter.

Maria says: "As I was growing up, I did not learn anything but about fishing boats and equipment. Between the ages of six and ten, I went to school but being the oldest I had to perform many duties for my father such as buying twine for the nets and assisting in the sharing up of the money." When Maria turned ten, it was no longer considered ladylike for her to be down on the wharf so she had to stay away. However, like Rose, she continued to help with the financial affairs of the boat.

As fishing became more difficult in the early 1960s, Maria's father decided to come to the United States. The family moved to Gloucester in 1965. Her father's skill in making and mending nets secured him a site on an offshore dragger.[2] This meant he was out fishing six to ten days and in port for two. Since he was a member of the crew and did not have the added responsibilities of being an owner, Maria was not as involved in fishing although she maintained an interest in the industry. Maria's mother did not continue her dress-making business. She now had four children to raise in a country far away from her own mother and the relatives who used to help her in Sicily.

By taking extra courses in English, Maria graduated with honors from high school in 1969. That same year she became a United States citizen. Since she spoke English, she was the intermediary between her family and American life. She did her parents' banking, helped to negotiate the deals when they bought their house and car and translated for them when they would go to the doctor, the store or the school. Today, Maria continues to interpret for her parents and other relatives who do not speak English.

After working one year as a bookkeeper, Maria married Tony, a fisherman from the same town in Sicily, who was then fishing on a boat in Gloucester. In 1975, they bought their own fishing boat and Maria became the president of the fishing vessel corporation and the onshore agent, positions which she still holds today. She does many of the same tasks as Rose but Maria also works with the bookkeeper to settle the boat accounts. While many boat owners' wives act as the land agent, Maria is one of four who actually go to the settlement house. Maria and Tony have three children: a 13-year-old boy and two girls aged nine and five.

Maria did not get involved with the Fishermen's Wives Association until August 1977 when Rose called her to come to a meeting with the National Marine Fisheries Service. As a conservation measure after the 200-mile limit was passed, the United States government implemented a fishery management plan which included creating regional fisheries councils and establishing quotas for the amount of groundfish which could be landed by American fishermen. To involve industry people in the development of the fishery management plan, the National Marine Fishery Service held a series of meetings in the major ports in each region of the country. Gloucester was the site of one of the meetings for the New England region.

Fishermen's attendance at public meetings was often poor for a combination of reasons: they were out fishing, they were not familiar with meeting procedures, and frequently, the men were not comfortable speaking English. On this occasion, Rose had telephoned several skippers she knew were in port, as well as fishermen's wives, to urge them to come to the meeting and stand up for the fishing industry. Rose thought of Maria because she had seen Tony recently and he had mentioned that his wife should get involved. Rose knew Maria slightly because Maria's brother-in-law fished on Rose's husband's boat. Maria knew who Rose was since Rose was already a public figure but the two women had not spoken much prior to this meeting.

Although this was Maria's first meeting, she spoke out against the quotas on the catch, which the fishermen were afraid would close the fisheries and force them to tie up their boats. As she says, "Suddenly, I found my hand raised and I gave my speech. When I sat down, they were clapping. It was my first time speaking out in public. That was the start of the whole thing. I just kept going to more meetings and in January 1978, I was elected president of the Association." Six years later, Maria is still president of the GFWA.

As president, she is the spokesperson for the organization. Reporters from the *Gloucester Daily Times* and local TV stations call her for the reaction of the fishing community to a fishery-related event; public officials and people from environmental groups and other fishery associations contact her when they want the support of the GFWA and the fleet. In turn, Maria feeds information to the other members through phone calls if the matter is urgent, at a Board of Directors meeting (held approximately every other month) or at the semi-yearly membership meetings.

While Rose initiates much of the GFWA cooking projects and political action at the local level, Maria's major focus is political work at state, regional, and federal levels. She, along with Rose and two other Wives, has attended meetings with the Governor and the Secretary of Environmental Affairs of the State of Massachusetts. She also serves on the Advisory Board of the New England Regional Fisheries Commission, a unique advisory board mandated by the City Charter of Gloucester whose members represent all aspects of the fishing industry. The purpose of the group is to advise the Mayor on issues relating to the industry. Maria is known for her broad knowledge of the issues and her simple eloquence.

As a consequence of the contacts she has made in working with the GFWA and the management skills she has honed, Maria was asked to be on the Board of Directors of the Gloucester Fishermen's Museum. She also serves on the Board of Directors of a new local branch of a Boston bank.

The particulars of the biographies of Rose and Maria, as well as their degree of involvement in the GFWA, are unique. However, their stories conform to the outline of the lives of most of the Sicilian women in the GFWA. Mothers and wives typically have the primary responsibility for the biological and social reproduction of the family. For fishermen's wives, the manifestation of this caretaker role includes raising the children and maintaining the house, but also managing the family finances and handling a host of other responsibilities such as emergencies, illnesses, car repairs, and yard work which might normally fall to their husbands if they worked on shore (Danowski 1980). The women are the decision-makers and managers in these arenas. In addition, these women do the work of keeping the kin network strong and cohesive. Thus the women not only maintain their own families, but also keep the family intact as a social institution.

Family

Rose's and Maria's political activism derives in part from their family roles and kin ties. Both women are oldest daughters. In the Sicilian family system, the parents look to the oldest daughter to take responsibility for the welfare of the extended family. In this context, where the parents were immigrants and did not speak English, being an oldest daughter meant that Rose and Maria acted as interpreters in family dealings with the American world. Consequently, the two women have become involved in the family fishing businesses, in addition to assuming active roles in running the household. Further, as oldest daughters, the women are integral in maintaining the strong ties within the extended family, ties which can be activated when there is a crisis in the fishing industry.

As wives of skipper/boatowners, Rose and Maria have more invested in the fishing industry than do the wives of crew members. In working as land agents for the family boats, the two women have learned about all aspects of the industry and have sharpened their managerial skills. Also, since the skipper receives a higher percentage of the boat's income, neither Rose nor Maria have had to take paying jobs.

Rose and Maria have acquired skills in business, management and negotiation as a consequence of being oldest daughters and wives of boat owners. The development of these empowering skills, however, has been accompanied by additional family responsibilities. Thus, for Rose and Maria, the family both constrains and facilitates their autonomy. This interplay can be seen by looking at the number and variety of the women's daily activities and the ways in which they manage to fit everything in.

The experiences of Rose and Maria on one day exemplify the strength of the women's commitment to their cause in the face of the demands and obstacles of daily life. On 28 July 1983 the two women were going to Boston to testify at a public hearing concerning the ecological effects of the proposed oil drilling on Georges Bank. (This issue will be discussed in the section entitled Collective Action.) However, this was not all Rose and Maria had to do that day.

Rose's day began at 5:30 a.m. Since last winter, Rose had been sleeping at her mother's house because her mother is afraid of falling during the night. However, on this day, Sal was going fishing so Rose had to go home to wake him up because he is going deaf and would not hear the alarm.

Once up, Rose started doing laundry. Around 8:00 a.m. she bought fresh bread and made coffee to be ready for her daughter, her two sisters and the various nieces who usually stop in. By 10:30 a.m. she had done five loads of laundry, checked in on her mother, talked with two sisters-in-law on the phone and visited with her sisters. Sal had come in because there was too much wind to fish. Since he wanted to eat, Rose was quickly frying some cod for him. Recently her mother decided she did not like fish anymore, so Rose had to cook spaghetti with broccoli especially for her. As her mother loves this dish, Rose was hoping that she wouldn't say too much about Rose leaving to go into Boston. Even though Rose's sisters were there and they knew she was rushing to go to Boston, neither offered to cook for their mother, though Rose did get one of them to agree to sit with her mother in case she fell. To a certain extent, cooking for their mother was seen as Rose's responsibility, yet Rose's sisters' behavior also indicates a degree of dissent from her involvement and commitment.

Maria was also up early to take her son to work at 6:30 a.m. Normally, when she returns home, she has a cup of espresso before getting the girls up and ready for summer school. If Tony is in, it is often their time to talk. But on this day, her husband was out fishing and as Maria explained: "I didn't have the luxury of being quiet. Last night my cousins came from Milwaukee but all the motels were full so I had five people sleeping on my sofas and floor. My mother and father came over at 7:00 a.m. and with all the commotion the girls missed their bus and I had to drive them to school."

After making several calls, Maria had finally found a motel for her cousins. She said: "I think everything is under control here. My father will get the girls from school. My cousins' kids are staying with my mother and the parents want to come with us to Boston. I just hope I have some time to make a few notes for this afternoon. Sometimes when you're up there, you forget things."

During the drive into Boston, Rose and Maria described the arrangements they each had made to ensure that the other members of the families would be taken care of in their absence. Both commented that going into Boston with the wives to speak out for the fishermen made it easier for them to get away than if they were going out of town to shop or to eat lunch or to spend the day with friends.

On the trip back to Gloucester in the late afternoon, the two women's thoughts turned back to their families. Before taking Rose home, Maria stopped to check on things at home. Everything had gone smoothly: Maria's aunt had spent the day doing Maria's laundry and cleaning; the children had played in the yard. Maria's parents were on their way over with food for dinner.

When Maria took Rose home, she went in to call her husband on Rose's ship-to-shore radio. He said he was having trouble with the boat and told her to call the dealer to let him know the boat would be unloading fish the next morning. Maria told him about testifying in Boston. He said he hoped that she and Rose had set the people straight about what's going on out on the Bank.

It was 8:30 in the evening before Maria headed home to get ready for dinner and Rose went over to sit with her mother. As the two women said good-bye, they agreed that, "you never know what the day will bring."

Relating these events demonstrates how the roles of oldest daughter, boat owner's wife and mother are translated into daily life in Gloucester. Concern for the immediate and extended family pervades the thoughts and actions of the women. They have become involved in the GWFA and lobbying activities by circumstances which they perceive as endangering their families.

Religion

Religion is very important to Rose and Maria, as it is for other Sicilian fishermen's wives in Gloucester. To analyze religion as an external factor would be to mask the integral role Catholicism has in the women's cultural and personal interpretations of life. The family is the place where religion is most explicitly and intimately played out. Daily life is experienced in terms of "what the Lord meant to be." In talking about some future plan, Maria will frequently end the conversation with "God willing" or "if the Lord wants." After a recent tragedy, Maria explained, "God sometimes makes us go through these things to make us strong." Rose finds evidence of the hand of the Lord in the lobster. There are two bones in the head which she feels resemble the Madonna and Child in profile. This supports her view that the fishing industry of today is linked to that of the disciples who were casting their nets when Jesus called them. Events such as a woman becoming pregnant after many months of trying are defined as "miracles of the Lord." Rescues after close calls at sea are seen to be answers to prayers to the saints.

The ways in which Rose and Maria practice their faith differ. When Rose's children were growing up, her mother-in-law was living and her own mother was more mobile, so Rose could go to early mass every Sunday. Now she only goes on special holy days and in honor of a family member or loved one. At one time Rose was very ill. She explains her recovery and subsequent good health as a sign that the Lord was giving her extra energy to live in order to help people. Part of her mission is the work she does with the GFWA and in the community. Raising money to erect and maintain a statue of St. Ann, the saint of the parish, and arranging a special ceremony on St. Ann's day every year are other aspects.

In contrast, Maria goes to mass regularly on Sundays as well as on holy days. She tries to say the rosary every day. Every June, she holds a novena to Saint Anthony, the patron saint of the town from which her family emigrated in Sicily. She builds an altar in her home and leads the rosary and songs to Saint Anthony every afternoon for 13 days. On the last day a priest comes to celebrate mass and bless loaves of bread which are eaten at the following feast. Anyone who wants to attend the novena in the hope that Saint Anthony will hear her or his prayers is welcome.

Catholicism enables Rose, Maria, and other Sicilian women in the GFWA to deal with the insecurity inherent in the fishing life style. Several women remarked that religion is what makes them strong enough to live with the knowledge that every time their fathers, husbands or sons go out fishing, they may not come back. Faith helps the women to persevere in their efforts to protect the fishing businesses of their families.

Religion, fishing, and Sicilian customs are intertwined parts of the cultural identity of the fishing community in Gloucester. It is the women who maintain this communal sense of self. By integrating religion into daily life, maintaining the Sicilian customs, and keeping the lore of the fishing heritage alive, the women preserve all of these values for their children to absorb.

Collective Action

Over the past ten years, a major focus of the GFWA has been the fight to prevent the leasing of tracts for oil drilling on Georges Bank. The primary fishing grounds accessible from Gloucester are off the northern end of Georges Bank, one of the richest fishing areas in the world. The shallow waters of Georges Bank mark a confluence of the warm Gulf stream coming north from Florida and the cold plankton-filled Labrador current coming south from Canada. The constant turbulence and tidal mixing result in high phytoplankton levels. These levels are responsible for creating one of the world's most important spawning grounds (Bates 1981).

At present, the major use of Georges Bank is as a commercial fishery. The area supplies approximately 16 percent of the United States' food fish and about 8 percent of the world's total catch (Bates 1981). However, according to a 1974 United States geological survey, Georges Bank is also a potential area for new oil finds. The estimated yields of oil vary. The government's own figure is around 123 million barrels to be extracted over 20 years. Measured in terms of daily national use, this is equivalent to seven to eight days (Bates 1981). As a means of alleviating the energy problems in the United States, the government has been encouraging oil companies to drill along the entire Outer Continental Shelf. Tracts in three areas of Georges Bank have been nominated for sale: Lease Sale No. 42 in November 1979; No. 52 in 1982; and No. 82, which is currently being discussed.

People in favor of leasing claim that drilling for oil will not affect the fisheries. They argue that there is only a one-in-a-billion chance of a major oil spill. Although at present there is no provision of adequate safeguards for fishing activities in the plans submitted to the government, the oil companies guarantee that something will be worked out when the drilling actually starts.

The GFWA and the fishing industry, as well as environmental groups, the Boston Law Conservation Foundation and some government officials from the Coastal Zone Management agency, all disagree. They cite the effects of previous oil spills in other coastal waters in their defense: the oil fouls the fishing gear, preventing the boats from going out (Marsden 1980) and contaminates the water, destroying the fish. The oil companies admit that they cannot do anything to prevent a spill if the waves are over six feet. At the Bank the waves average five feet and are much higher in the winter (Marsden 1980). Further, the seabed is constantly shifting making it difficult to build an oil rig safely. Also the drilling itself stirs up mud which damages the fish (MacLeod and Prescott 1981).

Ever since 1974, when the plans to open Georges Bank for oil exploration were first announced, the GFWA has participated actively in the struggle to save Georges Bank. The women have spoken at rallies in Gloucester and meetings in Boston and Washington. The association was able to convince the Gloucester city council to donate money to the Conservation Law Foundation to aid them in their efforts to halt the leasing on legal grounds. Both Rose and Maria have testified at Senate hearings in Washington, met personally with state and federal officials, and made themselves heard in the local and national press. In addition, the GFWA sponsored a rock concert and a panel discussion in order to heighten public awareness of the issue. Rose, two other Wives, and other community representatives travelled to Washington to present a dory full of fish and a petition to stop drilling signed by over 4,000 people, to the White House in an appeal to President Carter.

Despite the growing evidence of the harmful effects of oil drilling, increasing opposition to the drilling, and the waning interest of the oil companies in oil exploration on Georges Bank, the Department of the Interior is continuing its program of leasing. In May 1983, the Department of the Interior published its proposed Notice of Sale for Lease No. 82. On 28 July 1983, the Office of Environmental Affairs sponsored a hearing in Boston on Lease Sale No. 82. The public was invited to comment on the Draft Environmental Impact Statement prepared by the Department of the Interior, which dealt with the ecological effects of drilling in these tracts. Maria and Rose represented the GFWA and were scheduled to speak at 4:00 p.m.

When Rose and Maria are going to make a speech they never write out extensive notes beforehand or read prepared statements. Instead, they like to arrive early in order to hear what the other speakers are saying. Based on their remarks, the women decide what to stress when it is their turn. Since issues such as Georges Bank are matters of real everyday concern, the women are very familiar with the points that need to be made. In addition, family conversations provide ample opportunities for them to test ideas and hone their positions. On this occasion, to avoid repetition, Rose and Maria reviewed briefly what they wanted to say over lunch in Boston.

Each adopted a different strategy. As Maria explained: "I give them the facts of what is happening out there now with the fishing. I let Rose do the part about what Georges Bank means to us. She's good at that."

Maria began by introducing herself as the president of the Association: "I am here to represent the women in my organization, their husbands and their children who have made their living by going out to sea in ships and to protect the heritage of our beloved Gloucester, who has for the last 356 years sent children out to Georges Bank and sometimes they never come back." She stressed that "the fishermen who go to Georges are producing food—food for the people of this country and that food is first before oil." After giving some statistics on the percentage of the United States' food fish which comes from Georges Bank, she closed by stating that the Wives are fighting not only to protect their own family businesses and livelihood but also to benefit all the American people.

Rose began by saying she wanted to approach the issue of drilling on Georges Bank "with the way of the feelings." "As a child, I seen a lot of disaster. I seen a lot of accidents happen; people being lost at sea. It was always to go out there to make a living at fishing. Fishing a food to bring in to feed the people. Now this Georges Bank was not manmade. It was created by Almighty God. It is up to us to protect it." While Rose also mentions that Georges Bank supplies food, throughout her remarks the main emphasis was that Georges Bank, the fishing industry, and fish are not of man but all were begun by the Lord. To Rose, Georges Bank is a symbol that the Lord will provide for His flock. This illustrates the manner in which the women's religious beliefs pervade the way they experience life.

At the end of the hearing, Maria and Rose went up to talk to the convener, to say hello in person and to reenforce their position opposing the lease sale. Rose and Maria often employ this tactic of "having a word" with the officials after a meeting. The two-pronged approach—factual followed by rhetorical—made the two women an effective team. The convener told them he found their testimony particularly valuable: "What you say comes out of your husband's and son's experiences fishing on Georges. It is more effective because it comes from the heart: your voices and thoughts show feelings. We want to copy the tape and use it at special meetings if you don't mind." Both women told him to do anything to change Watt (then Secretary of the Interior James Watt) and the oil companies. Several other speakers told the two women that their comments had been more interesting and clearer than anyone else's.

When asked how she thought it had gone, Rose replied, "Good, very interesting to hear the other people. It's good when you stand around and talk after." Maria added, "We got to explain how it really is out there."

The GFWA is not solely a means for the women to fight for the fishing industry. It also provides opportunities for the women to meet new people, to go out of town, and to do different things. Participation in the organization's activities then, enables the women to put aside daily family responsibilities for a period of time. Several times after taking part in an association event, women remarked that a particular activity had come at a good time because they needed a break that day. On July 28, Maria and Rose went to the North End to buy Italian pastries, cheese, and fruit and to have espresso before returning home. As Maria explained, "The GFWA is not for work only; we deserve to have some fun with it too."

As stated earlier, fishing is a high-risk occupation and now fishermen in the United States are part of a competitive, international market. If the women did not organize to fight for the fishing industry, their families' livelihood would be affected. In turn, the women's ability to ensure the reproduction of the family would be jeopardized. Thus, the GWFA is a creative response to the economic problems facing a traditional fishing industry that is situated in the highly-developed capitalist economy of the United States. In addition, the organization offers women a socially legitimate outlet for their concerns.

CONCLUSION

Family, religion, and the Gloucester Fishermen's Wives Association are three resources which fishermen's wives in Gloucester use to manage the uncertainty which is built into their daily lives. The women turn to their families and religion for comfort, stability, and strength in all aspects of their personal and social lives. Involvement in the GFWA is a new means for dealing with this uncertainty.

Rose and Maria stand out in the GWFA for their initiative and activism. A combination of factors in their family background seems to enhance their autonomy and to account for their leadership roles in the organization. These factors include their position as eldest daughter, decision-making and managerial responsibility for the household and family finances, strong family networks, their role as onshore agents in the family fishing business, their command of the English langauge, and their ability to exploit a flexible schedule.

As members and leaders of an organization, the two women are able to maximize their effectiveness in dealing with the officials who decide the policies affecting the fishing businesses of their families and the industry as a whole. Although the styles of the women differ, through their involvement in the Gloucester Fishermen's Wives Association, both Rose and Maria are able to maintain their traditional wife/mother role and at the same time to exercise power in shaping their participation in conflicts within the fishing industry.

All of the women who are members of the GFWA are in the public arena to varying degrees, depending on their level of participation. However, first the women are wives, mothers, and daughters. Their political activism and fish marketing efforts are motivated largely by a concern for their families' fishing businesses. They define their work in the GWFA as a necessary element in fulfilling the nurturing and sustaining mandate of the mother/wife/daughter role. The women are acting in new ways to achieve the same end— the well-being of their families and the preservation of their way of life for future generations.

However, the GWFA does create opportunities for changes in women's roles. Participating in the organization enables them to begin to develop a new sense of self which is separate from that of their families. Thus, while participation in the GFWA cannot be seen as a transformation of the social roles of fishermen's wives in Gloucester, it does represent an expansion of the traditional mother/wife/daughter role.

Notes

1. Acknowledgements: A version of this chapter was presented at the 82nd Annual Meeting of the American Anthropological Association in Chicago in November 1983. It was part of a panel entitled Women in Fishing Economics organized by Dr. Jane Nadel. The paper is based on fieldwork conducted in Gloucester, Massachusetts in 1983 and 1984. I would like to thank the Department of Anthropology and Syracuse University for funding this research project. I also want to thank the women in the Gloucester Fishermen's Wives Association for their time, patience, and friendship.
2. A site is a job on a fishing boat.

The Right to Choice: Power and Decision-Making   **14**

M. Estellie Smith

INTRODUCTION

The chapters in this volume address a number of issues ranging from the particular—e.g., the ethnography of fishing and family dynamics—to such general concerns as development in marginal areas, political economy, and feminist issues.[1] However, the theoretical thread of interest that seems to me to bind these papers is one that runs through much of recent scholarship, drawing increasing attention from those in many disciplines and of a variety of persuasions. That thread is the multidimensional issue of power. There is, in point of fact, a growing conviction that this "theoretical issue" is of growing common concern to those in all walks of life. Thus, whether the goal be pure science or the arenas of practical concerns, we are trying to understand power: its interrelations with its concomitants, authority and decision-making; its composition, distribution, and intended functioning, as well as actual functions; and the explicit goals and unintended consequences of all these aspects.

The material in this volume examines various aspects of the distribution of the power to make choices, whether about gender or occupational roles, economic goals or life styles, incorporation or autonomy. Explicitly or implicitly, the studies focus on one aspect of the question discussed above, how *power*— rather crudely defined here as *the ability to set and achieve one's own goals*— is distributed among the participants of a group or groups with which an individual or a set of individuals identifies.

Allison's chapter indicates that an engagement with capitalism has been an important factor in the increase of women's presence in the formerly male domain of fishing. As she emphasizes, "the growth of large scale commercial fishing in the Pacific Northwest, and of women's direct participation in the industry can be said to have begun with the rise of canneries." Thus, as in other industries (e.g., the early employment of women in the coal mines of Victorian England and in textile manufacturing at large), women and men are being occupationally "degendered" by capitalism. This is not always the case, nor is it unique to capitalism. The ethnographic literature offers ample evidence for similar situational flexibility of occupational gendering or degendering in pre-capitalist societies. There are, for example, similarities of degendered prestige and privileges in polities with ranked lineages where women and men have equal access to high or low positions (e.g., the Ivory Coast Baule and the Polynesian Tonga). There is also, however, equally ample evidence for marked gender differences in certain of the most "primitive" societies (e.g., Radcliffe-Brown's (1922) study of the Andaman Islanders, passim).

The majority of recent studies has focused more on (industrial) capitalism's power to generate inequalities and the ways in which it has reduced the standing of women, than on capitalism's potential for workplace degendering and the possible implications this has relative to the rise of the feminist movement and other human rights groups. As a case in point, however, the suffragist movement, with its call for political, legal, and economic sexual equality was (along with the rise of trade unions, demands for general education, and public assistance programs) the product of industrial capitalism. Some might even note evidence for such stirrings with the advent of mercantilism. In sum, production needs and the necessity to rationalize labor costs decrease the utility of age and/or sex marking relative to the identity of the "worker" (or, for that matter, the holder of capital) while increasing differentiation among economic classes and occupational categories.

Broch's description of the simultaneous (and thus paradoxical) existence of egalitarianism and hierarchy indicates how complex one's analysis must be. Miang Tuu males and females exchange duties and share equally in decision-making (though males between the approximate age of 18 and 40 apparently are discriminated against by being forced to regularly absent themselves during the annual four to five month period when foods are scarce.) Alongside this, though, there is also a sharp consciousness of ethnicity and of social inequality: rich and poor kin distance themselves socially from each other, the poor fearing they might be viewed as disrespectful, the more affluent to avoid embarrassment; further, "no fate is worse for a man than to marry a woman too far above his own status." Broch's data compel us to recognize how intricate the ordering of even the smallest and technologically limited societies can be—and therefore how much more difficult our task will be when addressing these same questions in macro-systems.

Clark's study of the Gloucester women complements Allison's study of women in the Northwest fishery. In Gloucester's Sicilian fishery-based households, the female members have taken on the additional task of coping with the impact of the federal involvement in fisheries following the passage of the Magnuson Act (the so-called "200 mile act"). Though still maintaining the deferential role of women relative to men that marks Mediterranean culture, Gloucester women have assumed public positions and thus garnered greater decision-making rights and duties. It is the women who consistently track data from the economic and political spheres (at both the formal and informal levels), as well as decide what critical information should be circulated to such audiences as the media, the public, fishery managers, and, most of all, to their menfolk. Without this involvement, the fishermen would be at a real disadvantage in many spheres. Away at sea much of the time, men would have little voice in the public process of management. They would also be in jeopardy, legally and economically, for they have little search time to assign to the work of information-getting, so necessary if they are to keep abreast of changing laws and regulations as well as market conditions. Finally, the fishermen would have small opportunity to sway public opinion on such issues as whether or not oil leases should be granted on the rich fishing grounds of Georges Bank, and to what extent waterfront development can conflict with commercial fishing usage.

What is striking here, I think, is that despite this increased involvement in the political and economic decision-making of the larger society, both the women and men in the fisheries community see a decline in individual decision-making rights. In Gloucester, for example, many maintain that the new bureaucratic regime of fishery management has created higher costs and introduced new and/or greater risks, but offered, at best, negligible benefits. That a fisherman has lost much of his former freedom to make decisions as to where, when, and how to fish, or that a woman has more demands on her time and less freedom to schedule her day as she wishes, are counted as weighting the scales negatively relative to any amount of increased participation in the public arena (which, in any case, they claim was unnecessary prior to management).

Cole makes the argument that in the four generations of its existence, the settlement of Vila da Praia on the coast of northern Portugal has undergone a rather dramatic change, that both generated and reflected a shift in the role of women in the economy. Unusually, the women of the hamlet, almost from the beginning, took to going to sea to fish along with the men. In more typical fashion, the women also took charge of marketing the fish; the income from the fish (plus monies earned from the sale of the seaweed they gathered for fertilizer, seasonal work in the fields and even remittances from some males who "temporarily" emigrated) constituted the family fund, which was largely controlled by the senior female of the household. It must be noted that men as well as women demonstrated a willingness to put a loose construction on gender marked roles; the exigencies of survival required this sort of adaptability. Cole maintains that the shift out of fishing and into wage labor in the post World War Two period has led to a decline in the independence of women, a greater reliance on the income earned by male household members and, above all, despite the persistence of the role of women as household managers, a transformation in that managerial role from control of production to consumption. Given that both men and women are shifting from petty commodity maritime production to an infant factory system and wage labor, it is clear that males have also lost control of production. On the other hand, men now have a greater say about personally earned discretionary income, and I see their use of their wages to pursue male leisure activities as the counterpart of the female shift from production to consumption decision-making.

Beyond Cole's concern with the changing relationship between the men and women of Vila da Praia is, of course, the question of the degree of control which these local inhabitants— men and women, together or separately— ever had over their economy. Dependent from the beginning on a fluctuating demand for fish, seaweed, and their labor as seasonal field hands and domestics, the most that was controlled in any real sense of the word was the produce from the small gardens attached to their houses. Even the fish (if these people are similar to the Portuguese with whom I've worked) were eaten only if they were unsold at day's end. More in point, I think, is that both in earlier times and now, the hegemonic ideology supported the persistence of an underpaid, reliable, and available but irregularly utilized labor force that made a virtue of the necessity of hard work at whatever came along. *Trabalhadeiras* (and, interestingly, there is no masculine synonym for this term) are not just "hard workers"; they are women who can always find something to do, some way to earn (or save) a few pennies, opportunistically seizing whatever chance to work presents itself. Males accommodated the system by entering a pattern of what I have called "retromigration"— temporary migration when work and food were locally scarce, and returning home when there was a demand for their labor. Women, on the other hand, stayed to produce and reproduce the conditions of production. Today, the women of Vila da Praia continue to underwrite the economic needs of the larger region; where once they filled the productive slots to sustain peasant agriculture, they are now being used to support a burgeoning manufacturing sector, both as producers *and* consumers. They are being encouraged to ensure the profitability of that sector by using their wages to buy what most would label non-productive symbols of affluence (cf. Douglas and Isherwood [1979], who argue for the extreme productivity of such symbols).

From this perspective, then, the women and men of Vila da Praia, throughout their brief history, have been captive to the dominant ideology. Thus, Maria (whose "industriousness and thriftiness" allowed her to buy property, houses for her daughters and herself, a boat and gear which later served as capital for her son-in-law) is different only in form from her grandchildren, whose differentially phrased but ideologically comparable "industriousness and thriftiness" as waged producers allow them to acquire the commodities *they* see as necessary for "the good life." But the people of Vila da Praia continue to seem powerless to resist the hegemony exercised over them by those to whose productive aims they must accede.

Those who write about "power" (as differentiated from authority) often equate it with "influence." Davis's chapter on Newfoundland outports details the significant role played by women in their "non-authoritative" position as caretakers and nurturers. She notes that Grey Rock Harbour had been designated a relocation center— one of the amalgam ports targeted as favored loci by the provincial and federal governments in a former program responding to the perceived need (of the government) to eliminate certain isolated and economically marginal (thus costly) fishing communities. But what is it that, despite growing economic hardship, rising costs, lower catches, shorter fishing seasons and all of the attendant problems, supports the continuance of such outports?

Davis makes a strong case for some significant measure of outport durability stemming from family members' mutual reinforcement, especially the support flowing from wife to husband. Despite the marked "passivity" of Grey Rock Harbour women in economic or political decision-making, despite the jeers directed towards "aggressive, interfering" women so lacking in propriety they are labeled "shore skippers," women appear to exercise great influence on the qualitative factors that are cognitively weighed in decision-making. One suspects that here, as elsewhere, the rate of emigration depends largely on the extent to which women validate a male's choice to stay where he is. Thus, despite the lack of public power (and prohibitions against many of its expressions lest one seem a "shore skipper"), Grey Rock Harbour women, and women like them throughout the some 600 Newfoundland outports, are probably a significant force negating government attempts to alter the face of the fishery. In large measure, these communities persist not only because the men decide to keep fishing but because the women decide to support that choice and the way of life it can be said, literally, to engender.

The paper on the consequences of the pioneering Indo-Norwegian Fisheries Project, begun in the Indian state of Kerala in 1953, addresses the unanticipated consequences of that project on women in three villages, two Roman Catholic and one almost exclusively Hindu. Assuming (among many other things) that, "if men of the fishing households could be helped to improve their economic position, their womenfolk would automatically stand to gain," little attention was given to the particulars of the impact that such a shift in fishing stylistics would impose on women. Indeed, it is not certain that much attention was given to the local inhabitants of either sex, save in their anticipated role as producers. Such assumptions, unfortunately, are not unusual in the design of what have come to be tagged as "top-down" development projects.

The Kerala project, building on a viable, in-place fishing base, was designed primarily to increase India's GNP, especially in the export sector where the country's leaders were in desperate need of dollars to correct the badly skewed balance of payments. In terms of the goals built into the design, the project was very successful, and, as Gulati emphasizes, all in all, the project attained the specific goals intended.

There was, on the other hand, no special concern with the overall impact of the project, with the positive or negative "ripple effect" on the quality of life of the inhabitants in the Kerala coastal area. Regional goals were defined in terms of national problems. Were the changes that were intentionally wrought wanted by the local villagers? That is difficult to answer because such a question dangerously assumes a homogeneity of goals and effects among the pre- and post-project population, plus the *informed* consensus of the population— neither of which obtained in Kerala. In fact, the local population (women in particular) were very little involved in the initial planning and later modifications of the project. This does not necessarily mean that the population was totally bereft of strategies to restructure the program or at least segments of it to their own individual, familial, or village ends. It does mean—and I think this significantly accounts for so many program "failures" as well as unexpected results—that whatever control was exercised by those discounted individuals and communities was, perforce, opportunistic.

Prior to the introduction of what is locally labelled the Ghana boat fishery, the Sherbro coastal communities of Sierra Leone allocated adults to separate but equal gender-marked work roles. Men fished and consigned their catch to women (usually of their own household) for processing and distribution; women were in charge of shoreside, fishery-related activities and, as well, the majority of day-to-day decisions of the household economy. As was probably true of garden produce as well, whenever there was a small surplus beyond home consumption needs, women bartered or peddled it in order to augment the store of family necessaries (rice, salt, cloth, etc.).

As has been shown in several of the chapters, but is too often overlooked in research on household economies, such "surpluses" are often as much a result of a woman's diligence, cleverness, and frugality, as of the basic availability of resources and the production patterns themselves. Whether in Amerindian villages in New Mexico, Azorean fishing villages, the inner city of the United States urban poor, or the affluent suburb, there are households whose quality of life differs significantly from others in their economic group solely because of the capabilities and managerial skills of the female household heads.

The Sherbro women are, at least for now, in a fortunate circumstance. Many, especially the older ones, are still mindful of certain of the domestic roles and practices of the recent past, before the shift to the "Ghana boats." In this particular historical moment, not a few of these women still have the habit of practicing thrift and industry, and through such patterns a significant number have acquired sufficient surplus cash that they can—still with little *necessary* capital—build up a risk fund. This risk fund allows them to invest in ventures of fishermen (kin or non-kin) as well as underwrite the "penny capitalism" of entrepreneurial younger co-wives, children, and others. Such women have become "quite well off" and "frequently wield an economic influence over local affairs comparable to that of the wealthiest males." Krabacher shows that, given certain conditions of change and development, women need not suffer qualitative or quantitative losses and can even, on the whole, benefit more than the majority of their male counterparts.

This is a special case, I think, requiring ideal market conditions of (1) low entry costs, (2) low risk of unevenly available resources and/or a volatile market price for products, and (3) a reliable consumer sector. Such a situation is not an uncommon one in areas where artisanal fisheries are undergoing the transformation from labor- to capital-intensiveness, where fishery stocks are still relatively plentiful and "free," and where incorporation into the world economy is barely underway. It is especially the last factor that allows women to retain more power than most of their menfolk in making their own decisions about risks, consumption, investment, and the like.

Expanding the traditional niche of processing/marketing, the Sherbro women often accumulate enough capital to enlarge their own operations as well as to finance others. They retain a significant selectivity in strategizing— taking a high capital risk on one occasion (and potentially expanding their capital through repayment of the loan with interest); a low capital risk on another occasion (but, say, solidifying the household unit by financing the venture of a co-member); and, not to be overlooked, simply through their own labor. Her male counterpart has more constricted opportunities— if indeed, he really has any! He can continue to use traditional gear in a low-production fishery and, relative to the new, market-geared, prestige standards, run the social risk of seeing his spouse out-perform him; or he can take investment risks and face such dangers as equipment breakdowns, repairs, and rising fuel costs, a spate of poor landings, etc., all of which can result in his inability to meet the debt he incurred in shifting fishery modes. Thus, the current entrepreneurial climate favors women and, to a large extent, disfavors men. The result is that the relatively egalitarian, cooperative, subsistence-based system has altered and unbalanced the distribution of power between Sherbro spouses.

If, however, Quinn's (1978) analysis of Mfantse women has general applicability, one should expect to see capitalization continue to expand. This should lead to the replacement of most Sherbro women (whose potential for expansion is constrained) by urban buyers capable of operating on a much larger scale spatially and monetarily. After all, while competent and wealthy by local standards, the Sherbro women are in no position to compete with national and even internationally-based companies.

The current prosperity of the Sherbro women depends on small-scale market arrangements— e.g., social pressures primarily within local networks that ensure that no one undercuts the price of another ("a uniform price is offered along the beach on any given day"). Perhaps more significantly, we are told that "business arrangements between buyers and sellers tend to be long term" and thus, the linchpin of the capitalist market— impersonal, competitive shopping for lowest price/highest profit— does not yet dominate exchanges. A more manipulative context, however, should make it increasingly difficult for Sherbro women to maintain their current advantages.

What is also noteworthy about the present situation is that women (young or old) are no less likely than males to seize the advantage of the moment, if they can, discarding "traditional" household-based gender relations with their menfolk, despite the fact that they selectively (and somewhat paradoxically) seek to maintain established forms of relations at another level. Women desire to work within the more historically familiar framework of long-term arrangements between buyer and seller— implying a reciprocity basis that modifies purely commercial transactions; however, these same women are willing to forego such "traditional patterns" relative to economic relations in the more immediate and intimate domestic sphere (Smith 1982). Formerly when market surpluses were limited, a fisherman would hand his catch over to his wife or kinswoman without prior payment on the basis of a communal accounting system, but now domestically-based exchanges between spouses are treated largely as depersonalized trades, for each keeps a distinct account.

These data contradict yet another widely-held and almost axiomatic argument, still assumed in the design of some of the most otherwise sophisticated development projects: males are the focus of change, the risk-takers and innovators; females are innately more cautious, conservative, and timid about entering the public sphere (and complementary to this, more attached to the preservation of the traditional values of home and hearth). In addition to being tautological (and similar to the belief that peasants are, "by nature," more attached to their traditional ways), this assumption should be given short shrift by a growing body of data that offers more substantive and empirical reasons why men and women, young and old, rich and poor, may differ in time and place as to their categorical acceptance of or resistance to change. More work should be done in this area.

Nadel raises an intriguing issue in her chapter on Ferryden for, she tells us, the community was internally "fundamentally egalitarian"— despite the fact that it was established as an occupational "colony" by an entrepreneurial laird. Further, once the laird abrogated his interests, first the Montrose fish curers and, then, the vertically integrated Montrose Curing Company, controlled Ferrydeners' lives. Thus, at no time were the villagers engaged in truly independent household production; their origin and continuity rested firmly in the context of venture capitalism, and again, one cannot assume that capitalism per se generates a decline in the power of women relative to their menfolk. Nadel addresses the day-to-day world of household and village as well as external, market-dominated linkages— especially the significant decision-making roles women played in the domestic sphere. She argues that however unequal and exploitive were the relations between micro- and macro-system, Ferrydeners sustained a degree of egalitarian complementarity between the sexes.

This analysis suggests that we can err if we assume a consistently or unambiguously inferior female status when, as in Ferryden, (a) women's sexual characteristics are pejoratively labelled, (b) men hold all public positions, and (c) male activities control household economics (for example, Nadel stated that males received payment for a "significant amount of the catch in whiskey"). The thrust of Nadel's argument would seem to be that if women control that sector within which their daily affairs are primarily conducted, they are— relative to those with whom they interact in that sphere— in an egalitarian context. More importantly (and as with several of the other chapters), her analysis argues that existence within a macro-system of capitalism or even colonialism, and any inequalities resulting from this domination, need not *ipso facto* alter the fundamental internal egalitarianism of a society. This is an important statement since, for many scholars, evidence for female inequality relative to males is treated as an inevitable consequence of such conditions (cf. Leacock 1978). Nadel suggests, if I read her correctly, that this "explanation" is far too facile. Among other things, it does not address the question of whether the concern with equality of participation is: (a) a consequence of increasing equality in today's world, (b) a reaction to the corrosion of internal village or neighborhood sociocultural bonding, or (c) due to the diffusion of and/or sensitivity to a hitherto inconceivably foolish or (at best) quaintly idealistic concept of fundamental human rights (as a result, say, of broader accessibility to education and the intellectual awareness this brings).

In Nowak's paper on the Btsisi' we are told that at the same time the British began installing rubber and coffee plantations (c. 1890), Skeat reports the village elders instructing a young bride and groom in their "traditional" roles of, respectively, caretaker and familial breadwinner. Now, it is possible that these "traditional" instructions were, in point of fact, an early response to colonial "modernization." Indeed, they may have the same roots as the factors that led to women losing their positions on the village council and that influenced the value system to the point that today women maintain that they do not want to be leaders. If so, why were both male and female villagers so responsive to early external influences that deprived women of authoritive leadership positions? On the other hand, if it was a "traditional" pattern, one is left with the intriguing question of why, at the time Skeat wrote, such rules existed and instruction by the elders was accepted without question, whereas recent attempts by Malaysian government agents of change simply (apparently) to reinforce those roles has resulted in what Nowak labels "quiet resistance." Why did the Btsisi' accept the statement of the gender-marked ideal (and possibly *de facto*) roles when presented by the elders? And how can we account for the change?

Further, Nowak maintains that a gender-marked division of labor (but coupled with a pragmatically-grounded willingness for occupational cross over) actually serves as the basis for an "ideology of cooperation" that has allowed Btsisi' men and women alike to resist concepts of sexual inequality and "buffer the negative effects on women...commonly associated with 'modernization' and development." If this is indeed the case, it argues that no significant loss of power and decision-making resulted when women forfeited authority positions on the village council. This implies that evidence for gender-based exclusivity of decision-making in a particular sphere need not mandate a hierarchical ordering of those spheres relative to each other (say, males in the public and women in the domestic) and is not necessarily indicative of inequality within such a sphere as public decision-making. That is, despite the fact that the Btsisi' women lost positions on the council, an ideology of cooperation and *de facto* egalitarianism still prevails. Thus, according to Nowak, it must be that diminished or non-existent input into the choices made in one or more spheres by one set of actors relative to another cannot automatically be equated with a diminution of power and the subordination of the disfavored set. Finally, Nowak's chapter indicates that neither "modernization" nor colonialism generate so powerful a dynamic for inequality that the target population is docile in the face of their demands, unable to resist, reject, or exercise choice relative to demands for changes that challenge indigenous patterns.

Robben's study of conjugal relations in a Brazilian port town illustrates the significance of setting priorities in decision-making. The probable consequences of a man's choice to enter one or another fishery— and a woman's choice to become the wife of either a boat or canoe fisherman— must be very clear to the inhabitants of Camurim. Further, it must seem equally clear to all that, once a choice is made, there is little turning back. Canoe fishermen and their families can expect, so it would appear, to be more independent of market forces. Thus, within the microcosm of the household in this fishery mode, all members are able to live up to familial expectations and maintain a reasonably well integrated domestic life. The cost, however, is that they cannot expect to gain the heights of prestige and familial social standing nor match the display of material symbols that are the measure of success as it is defined in the larger world of Camurim. Alternatively, however, those who choose to enter the boat fishery, whether crew men or owners, elect and may even succeed in attempts to maximize potential economic gain— but face infinitely greater risks of failure and, in addition (whether winner or loser), pay higher social costs. In the case of those few successful enough to become boat owners, there is the constant economic pressure, the never-ending social striving, the limitations on rewardingly close family/cohort relations, and the need to maintain a facade behind which lies an existence of minimally affective social relationships. But it is those who must spend their lives in the world of the boat crew men who receive the fewest rewards. Those in this last category rarely succeed in escaping a devolutionary and circular path of poverty, indebtedness, marital stress, and loss of self-dignity. There seem to be no compensatory mechanisms and little opportunity for altering their condition of life.

The Camurim study emphasizes that if the word "strategy" is to be used only when there are genuine options available, one must acknowledge that "the boat people" (crew men, boat owners, and family alike) have few if any alternatives once the initial step is taken. While crew men "suffer under the power of capital owners," boat owners themselves are enthralled by the power of a market system of prices, as well as trapped within a rigid, ultimately unrewarding sociocultural cobweb.

Finally, one must ask "To what extent are women the powerless victims of the choice males make as to what fishery they will enter?" Though Robben does not say, it would appear that women have little choice as to whether males choose one or another path— and may not have much choice as to whom they will marry. Can women, through their own life style, demands, and expectations, influence or even program their sons and husbands into one or another mode? If males are susceptible to such programming, again, what determines female expectations? How free are women (including those of canoe families) to design the future for themselves and their menfolk?

De Grys tells us that in the Peruvian fishing port of San Jose, women control the purse strings (not only within the family but, apparently, in a significant number of public expenditures); that "men and women both acknowledge women's ability to run the household and the village....Women are not timid in the *municipalidad* or with public officials or with outsiders..." and that "women seem to make decisions with as much boldness and deliberation as men"—with men accepting this state of affairs with little difficulty since women's decisions "seem to stand the test of time." These circumstances in San Jose result from, "the pragmatics of the situation arising from men's absence which makes women structurally important." Despite all this, the *machismo/marianismo* complex is said to trap both men and women into a situation that Schweitzer de Grys summarizes as one where "women...are in structural positions which are disadvantageous" and "men's power is evident in *all* of the patterned social relationships, and the economic, political and religious organization" (my emphasis). In the juxtaposition of these seemingly contradictory findings, we see more of the problematic potential in these chapters and, as well, the risks we run when we choose to use instances of decision-making power to construct the analytical grid through which we filter our data (see Smith, M.E. 1982, 1983, 1984 for ethnographic examples of the approach and a more extended commentary on such an issue). In locales where much the same situation prevails (e.g., Ferryden, Grey Rock Harbour, Gloucester) the respective authors argue that there exists a complementary distribution of power, for a degree of gender egalitarianism. Schweitzer de Grys is more bold (or less consistent?) than the others and the full extent of the sociocultural contradictions emerges.

This essay began by calling attention to the common thread in all of the chapters in this volume— a concern with power/authority, their distribution, and the broad sociocultural consequences of that distribution. Nadel and Davis note in their introduction that fishing people in general seem to be constrained in their exercise of power. Numerous studies have also emphasized that once fishing communities lose an autonomy born of isolation or simply disinterest on the part of a larger polity to which they may be linked, the members of such communities become increasingly disenfranchised. It is also clear that one must beware of imposing upon females a male model for achievement. Though women may have considerable *de facto* decision-making powers, they are allowed to manifest it within fewer and/or more limited spheres and are often forced to exercise that power (or even authority) with a tact, subtlety or deviancy not always required of males in similar contexts. As a rule, then, fisher people, women in particular, have, relative to other comparable categories, less of an ability to set and achieve their own goals. The intellectual provocativeness of this issue and others raised in this volume should lure us into further exploration. Thus, though Fedigan has recently pointed out that "many authors now emphasize the importance of *sharing* between gathering women and hunting or scavenging men as the key human invention, i.e., the sexual division of labor" (1986:35), it would seem more critical to research that other human invention, the division and allocation of decision-making capabilities relative to issues of the general good. That, it seems increasingly obvious, is the crucial problem for the future.

Note

1. Support for the research in this paper was received from sabbatical funding from the State University of New York, College at Oswego and research supported by the J.N. Pew, Jr. Trust and the Woods Hole Oceanographic Institution's Marine Policy and Ocean Management Center.

References

Acheson, James. 1981. "Anthropology of Fishing." *Annual Review of Anthropology*, 10:275-316.

Acheson, James M. and J. Lello. 1980. "The Fishermen's Wives Association." In *Social and Cultural Aspects of New England Fisheries: Implications for Management*. Final report to National Science Foundation, University of Rhode Island, University of Maine, Study of Social and Cultural Aspects of Fishery Management. New England under extended jurisdiction. Vol. II.

Akerele, Olubanke. 1979. "Women and the Fishing Industry in Liberia: Measures of Women's Participation." United Nations Economic Commission for Africa.

Alaska Department of Education. 1979. "The Southeast Alaska Salmon Fishery: A Guide to Interviews with Men and Women Engaged in Commercial Fishing 1913-1978." Juneau: Alaska Department of Education, Division of State Libraries and Museums.

Alaska Fisherman's Journal. 1981. "Money Talk: A Study of Fisherman's Income." *Alaska Fisherman's Journal*, 4(2).

Alaska Governor's Study Group on Limited Entry. 1973. *A Limited Entry program for Alaska's Fisheries*. State of Alaska, William A. Egan, Governor.

Andersen, Raoul. 1978. "Extended Jurisdiction and Fisherman Access to Resources: New Directions, New Imperatives." Paper prepared for *Conference on Modernization in Fishing Industries and Communities*. Greenville, N.C. East Carolina University.

_____ 1979. *North Atlantic Maritime Cultures*. The Hague: Mouton.

Andersen, Raoul and Cato Wadel (eds.). 1972. *North Atlantic Fishermen: Anthropological Essays on Modern Fishing*. St. John's: Institute of Social and Economic Research, Memorial University of Newfoundland.

Andersen, Robert and Barbara G. Andersen. 1964. *The Vanishing Village.* Seattle: University of Washington Press.

Andrews, Raymond A. n.d. "Female Participation in the Port De Grave Fishery." Unpublished manuscript, Memorial University of Newfoundland, Queen Elizabeth Library, Newfoundland Collection, St. John's.

Anson, Peter. 1930. *Fishing Boats and Fisher Folk on the East Coast of Scotland.* London: J.M. Dent Sons.

_____ 1932. *Fishermen and Fishing Ways.* East Ardsley: Reprinted in 1975 by EP Publishing Limited.

_____ 1969. *Life on Low Shore.* Banff: The Banffshire Journal.

Antler, Ellen. 1977. "Women's Work in Newfoundland Fishing Families." *Atlantis,* 2(2):106-113.

_____ 1980 "The Economics of Home Economics." *Anthropology Resource Center Newsletter,* 4(2):4.

_____ 1982 "Fishermen, Fisherwomen, Rural Proletariate: Capitalist Commodity Production in the Newfoundland Fishery." Dissertation, University of Connecticut.

Antler, Ellen and James Faris. 1979. "Adaptation to Changes in Technology and Government Policy: A Newfoundland Example (Cat Harbour)." In Raoul Andersen (ed.), *North Atlantic Maritime Cultures.* The Hague: Mouton.

Atkinson, Jane M. 1982. "Anthropology." *Signs,* 8(22):236-257.

Ayampillay, Saktuna Devi. 1976. *Kampung Tanjung Sepat: A Besese (Mah Meri) Community of Coastal Selangor.* Social Anthropology Section, Report No. 6. Palau Pinang, Malaysia: Universiti Sains Malaysia.

Bacdayan, Albert S. 1977. "Mechanistic Cooperation and Sexual Equality among the Western Bantoc." In Alice Schlegel (ed.), *Sexual Stratification: A Cross-Cultural View.* New York: Columbia University Press.

Bailey, Fred G. 1957. *Caste and the Economic Frontier.* Manchester: Manchester University Press.

Bandarage, Asoka. 1984. "Women in Development: Liberalism, Marxism and Marxist Feminism." *Development and Change,* 15:495-515.

Bascom, William R. 1965. *Ponape: A Pacific Economy in Transition.* Anthropological Records. University of California Press.

Bates, Sarah. 1981. "The Struggle for Georges Bank." In Guy C. MacLeod and John H. Prescott (eds.), *Georges Bank: Past, Present, and Future of a Marine Environment.* Boulder, CO: Westview Press.

Bauman, Zygmunt. 1978. *Hermeneutics and Social Science.* New York: Columbia University Press.

Bay, E.G. 1982. "Introduction." In E.G. Bay (ed.), *Women and Work in Africa.* Boulder, CO: Westview Press.

Bell, Colin and Howard Newby. 1976. "Husbands and Wives: The Dynamics of the Deferential Dialectic." In D.L. Barker and S. Allen (eds.), *Dependence and Exploitation in Work and Marriage.*

Bellamy, G.C. 1895. "The Sakais of Selangor, Kuala Lantat." *Selangor Journal,* 3(14):224-238.

Beneira, Lourdes. 1982. *Women and Development: The Sexual Division of Labour in Rural Societies.* New York: Praeger.

Beneira, Lourdes and Gita Sen. 1981. "Accumulation, Reproduction, and Women's Role in Economic Development: Boserup Revisited." *Signs,* 7(2):279-298.

Benjamin, Geoffrey. 1968. "Headmanship and Leadership in Temiar Society." *Federation Museums Journal,* 13:1-43.

_____ 1973. "Introduction." In P. Schebesta (ed.), *Among the Forest Dwarfs of Malaya.* Kuala Lumpur: Oxford University Press.

_____ 1976. "Austroasiatic Subgroupings and Prehistory in the Malay Peninsula." In Philip Jennere (ed.), *Austroasiatic Studies,* Part I. Oceanic Linguistics Special Publications, no. 13, Hawaii: University of Hawaii Press.

Bertram, J.G. 1883. *The Unappreciated Fisher-Folk.* London: William Clowes and Sons, Limited.

Blauner, R. 1960. "Work Satisfaction and Industrial Trends in Modern Society." In W. Galenson and S.M. Lipset (eds.), *Labour and Trade Unionism.* London: Routledge and Kegan Paul.

BMVC. Letters and Files of the Administration of the County of Vila do Conde held in the Bibliteca Municipal de Vila do Conde.

Boserup, Ester. 1970. *Women's Role in Economic Development.* London: Allen and Unwin.

Bott, Elizabeth. 1957. *Family and Social Network.* London: Tavistock.

Bourdieu. 1977. "Outline of a Theory of Practice." *Cambridge Studies in Social Anthropology,* 16.

Brake, S. n.d. "The Role of Women in Hunt's Harbour." Unpublished manuscript, Memorial University of Newfoundland, Newfoundland Society and Culture Student Collection, St. John's.

Brandao, R. 1923. *Os Pescadores.* Lisboa: Bibliteca Ulisseia de Autores Portugueses.

Brandes, Stanley H. 1981. "Like Wounded Stags: Male Sexual Ideology in an Andalusian Town." In Sherry B. Ortner and Harriet Whitehead (eds.), *Sexual Meanings: The Cultural Construction of Gender and Sexuality.* Cambridge: Cambridge University Press.

Brandt, Vincent. 1971. *A Korean Village: Between Farm and Sea*. East Asian Series No. 65. Cambridge, MA: Harvard University Press.

Breton, Yvan D. 1973. "A Comparative Study of Work Groups in an Eastern Canadian Peasant Fishing Community." *Ethnology*, 12(4):393-418.

_____ 1977. "The Influence of Modernization on Modes of Production in Coastal Fishing: An Example from Venezuela." In M.E. Smith (ed.), *Those Who Live From the Sea*. New York: West Publishing Company.

Britan, Gerald. 1979. "'Modernization' on the North Atlantic Coast: The Transformation of a Traditional Newfoundland Fishing Village." In R. Andersen (ed.), *North Atlantic Maritime Cultures*. The Hague: Mouton.

Broch, Harald Beyer. 1981a. "Cultural Variation on the Islands in the Sea of Flores, Indonesia." *Archipel*, (2):43-53.

_____ 1981b. "Ethnic Differentiation and Integration: Aspects of Inter-Ethnic Relations at the Village Level on Bonerate." Paper read at the Social Research Council sponsored conference at Monash University, Melbourne.

_____ 1983. "The Matrilocal Warp of Bonerate Culture." In Bo Utas (ed.), *Women in Islamic Societies: Social Attitudes and Historical Perspectives*. Studies on Asian Topics No. 6. London: Curzon Press.

_____ (in press). "Resource Utilization in Miang Tuu, Bonerate." *Contributions to South-East Asian Ethnography*.

_____ (in press). "Crazy Women are Performing in Sombali: A Possession-Trance Ritual on Bonerate, Indonesia." *Ethos*.

Brown, Cheryl. 1980. "The Newfoundland Pilgrimage to St. Anne de Beaupre: The Search of Home and Meaning." Paper presented at Canadian Ethnology Society Meeting, Montreal, Quebec.

Brown, Judith K. 1963. "A Cross-Cultural Study of Female Initiation Rites." *American Anthropologist*, 65(4):837-853.

_____ 1975. "Adolescent Initiation Rites: Recent Interpretations." In Robert E. Grinder (ed.), *Studies in Adolescence*, 3rd edition. New York: Macmillan Publishing. Brox, Ottar. 1972. *Newfoundland Fishermen in the Age of Industry: A Sociology of Economic Dualism*. St. John's: Institute of Social and Economic Research, Memorial University of Newfoundland.

Buchan, Margaret. 1977. "The Social Organization of Fisher-Girls." Conference Paper, Aberdeen, Scotland.

Buenaventura-Posso, Elisa and Susan E. Brown. 1980. "Forced Transition from Egalitarianism to Male Dominance: The Bari of Columbia." In Mona Etienne and Eleanor Leacock (eds.), *Women and Colonization: Anthropological Perspectives*. New York: Praeger.

Burdon, T.W. 1954. "Malayan Fishing Methods." In *Journal of the Malayan Branch Royal Asiatic Society*. Monographs on Malay Subjects, 2:5-76.

Burkett, Elinor C. 1978. "Indian Women and White Society: The Case of Sixteenth Century Peru." In Asuncion Lavrin (ed.), *Latin American Women.* Westport: Greenwood Press.

Burrows, Edwin and Melford Spiro. 1984. *An Atoll Culture: Ethnography of Ifaluk in the Central Carolines.* Westport, CT: Greenwood Press.

Burton, Michael L. and Douglas R. White. 1984. "Sexual Division of Labor in Agriculture." *American Anthropologist,* 86(3):568-583.

Byron, R.F. 1975. "Economic Functions of Kinship Values in Family Businesses: Fishing Crews in North Atlantic Communities." *Sociology and Social Research,* 60(2):147-160.

Cape Ann Chamber of Commerce. 1977. "Economic Impact Report: The Fishing Industry in Gloucester, Massachusetts." Unpublished paper.

_____ 1980a *Cape Ann Industrial Directory— 1980.* Gloucester, Massachusetts: Cape Ann Chamber of Commerce and the Essex County Economic Development Corporation.

_____ 1980b *Making It On Cape Ann: Cape Ann Industrial and Career Exhibit.* Gloucester, Massachusetts: Cape Ann Chamber of Commerce and the Essex County Economic Development Corporation.

Carey, Iskandar. 1976. *Orang Asli: The Aboriginal Tribes of Peninsular Malaysia.* Kuala Lumpur: Oxford University Press.

Caulfield, Mina. 1978. "Multinational Corporations and Political Change." In Ahamed Idris-Soven, Elizabeth Idris-Soven and Mary K. Vaughan (eds.), *The World as a Company Town.* The Hague: Mouton.

Chaney, Elsa M. 1979. *Supermadre: Women in Politics in Latin America.* Austin: University of Texas Press.

Chang, Kenne. 1971. "Institutional Changes and Development of the Fishing Industry in a Japanese Island Community." *Human Organization,* 30(2):158-169.

Chiaramonte, Louis. 1970 *Craftsmen Client Contracts: Interpersonal Relations in a Newfoundland Fishing Community.* St. John's: Institute of Social and Economic Research, Memorial University of Newfoundland.

Chodorow, Nancy. 1974. "Family Structure and Feminine Personality." In Michelle Z. Rosaldo and Louis Lamphere (eds.), *Women, Culture and Society.* Stanford: Stanford University Press.

Christensen, James B. 1977. "Motor Power and Women Power: Technological and Economic Change Among Fanti Fishermen in Ghana." In M. Estellie Smith (ed.), *Those Who Live From the Sea: A Study in Maritime Anthropology.* St. Paul: West Publishing Company.

Christiansen-Ruffman, Linda. 1982. "Women's Political Culture and Feminism in Canada." Unpublished manuscript.

Ciprianni, Lidio. 1966. *The Andaman Islanders.* London: Weidenfeld and Nicolson.

Cobb, John. 1911. *The Salmon Fisheries of the Pacific Coast*. Bureau of Fisheries Document No. 751. Washington, D.C.: Department of Commerce and Labor, Department of Fisheries.

Cohen, Anthony P. 1980. "The Anthropology of Proximate Cultures: The Newfoundland School and Scotland." *Scottish Journal of Sociology*, 4(2):213-226.

_____ 1982a. "A Sense of Time, A Sense of Place: The Meaning of Close Social Association in Whalsay, Shetland." In Anthony Cohen (ed.), *Belonging: Identity and Social Organisation in British Rural Cultures*. Manchester: Manchester University Press.

_____ 1982b. "Belonging: The Experience of Culture." In Anthony Cohen (ed.), *Belonging: Identity and Social Organisation in British Rural Cultures*. Manchester: Manchester University Press.

Collier, Jane F. and Michelle Z. Rosaldo. 1981. "Politics and Gender in Simple Societies." In Sherry Ortner and Harriet Whitehead (eds.), *Sexual Meanings: The Cultural Construction of Gender and Sexuality*. New York: Cambridge University Press.

Commercial Fisheries News. 1983. "Fight is Far from Over: Lease Sales on Hold." *Commercial Fisheries News*, November: 15.

_____ 1984a. "It's Official: New Bedford is Country's Richest Port." *Commercial Fisheries News*, May: 15.

_____ 1984b. "States Want Georges Bank Lease Sale Cut." *Commercial Fisheries News*, July: 36.

Connelly, Patricia and Martha MacDonald. 1983. "Women's Work: Domestic and Wage Labour in a Nova Scotia Community." *Studies in Political Economy*, 10:45-72.

Cook, Judith. 1984. *Close to the Earth: Living Social History of the British Isles*. London: Routledge and Kegan Paul.

Cornelison, Ann. 1976. *Women of the Shadows*. New York: Vintage Books.

Costa, Louis. 1980. *A-Ver-O-Mar Cronicas*. Figueirinhas.

Coull, James R. 1969. "Fisheries in the North-East of Scotland Before 1800." *Scottish Studies*, 13.

Couturier, Edith. 1978. "Women in a Noble Family: The Mexican Counts of Regla, 1950-1830." *Latin American Women*. Westport: Greenwood Press.

Dahlberg, Frances. 1981. "Introduction." In Frances Dahlberg (ed.), *Woman the Gatherer*. New Haven: Yale University Press.

Danowski, Fran. 1980 "Fishermen's Wives: Coping with an Extraordinary Occupation." Kingston, RI: *University of Rhode Island Marine Bulletin*, No. 37.

Davis, Dona L. 1979. "Social Structure, Sex Roles and Female Associations in a Newfoundland Fishing Village." Paper presented at the Canadian Ethnology Society annual meeting, Banff, Alberta.

_____ 1982. "Women's Experience of Menopause in a Newfoundland Fishing Village." *Maturitis*, 3(4):207-216.

_____ 1983a *Blood and Nerves: An Ethnographic Focus on Menopause*. St. John's: Institute of Social and Economic Research, Memorial University of Newfoundland.

_____ 1983b. "The Family and Social Change in the Newfoundland Outport." *Culture*, III(1):19-32.

_____ 1983c. "Woman the Worrier: Confronting Archtypes of Stress." *Women's Studies*, 20(2):135-146.

_____ 1984. "Medical Misinformation: Communication Difficulties Between Newfoundland Women and their Physicians." *Social Science and Medicine*, 18(3):273-278.

_____ 1986a. "Changing Self-Image: Studying Menopausal Women in a Newfoundland Fishing Village." In Tony Whitehead and Mary Ellen Conaway (eds.), *Sex and Gender Role Boundaries in Cross-Cultural Encounters: Exploring Problems and Prospects for Research and Communication*. Urbana, IL: University of Illinois Press.

_____ 1986b. "Occupational Community and Fishermen's Wives in a Newfoundland Fishing Village." *Anthropological Quarterly*, 59(3):129-142.

_____ 1986c. "The Meaning of Menopause in a Newfoundland Fishing Village." *Culture, Medicine and Psychiatry*, 10:73-94.

d'Azevedo, W.L. 1962. "Some Historical Problems in the Delineation of a Coastal West Atlantic Region." *Annals of the New York Academy of Sciences*, 96:512-538.

de Grys, Mary Schweitzer. 1983. "Would God Command Me to be Poor?" *Anthropology and Humanism Quarterly*, 8(3).

Dentan, Robert Knox. 1964. "Senoi-Semang." In Frank M. Lober, Gerald C. Hickey and John K. Musgrave (eds.), *Ethnic Groups of Mainland Southeast Asia*. New Haven: Human Relations Area Files Press.

_____ 1965. "Some Senoi-Semai Dietary Restrictions: A Study of Food Behavior in a Malayan Hill Tribe." Unpublished Ph.D. dissertation, Yale University.

_____ 1978. "Notes on Childhood in a Nonviolent Context: The Semai Case (Malaysia)." In Ashley Montagu (ed.), *Learning Non-Aggression: The Experience of Non-Literate Societies*.

_____ 1979. *The Semai: A Nonviolent People of Malaya*. Fieldwork edition. New York: Holt, Rinehart and Winston.

_____ n.d. "The Nature of Ethnographic Data." Unpublished manuscript.

DePauw, Linda Grant. 1982. *Seafaring Women*. Boston, Houghton, Mifflin Co.

Diamond, Norma. 1969. *K'un shen, A Taiwan Village*. New York: Holt, Rinehart and Winston.

Dixon, Richard et al. 1984. "Fishermen's Wives: A Case Study of a Middle Atlantic Fishing Community." *Sex Roles*, 10(1, 2):33-52.

Dolci, Danilo. 1981. *Sicilian Lives*. Justin Vitiello, Translation. New York: Pantheon Books.

Donnelly, Patricia. 1974. "Newfoundland Women in the Novels of Margaret Duley." Unpublished manuscript, Memorial University of Newfoundland, Queen Elizabeth Library, Newfoundland Collection, St. John's.

Doran, Claire. 1974. "Adaptation et Economie Familale dans une Petite Communauté Rurale Francophone, de Terre-Neuve". Masters thesis, McGill University.

Douglas, Mary and Baron Isherwood. 1979. *The World of Goods*. New York: Basic Books.

Droker, Howard. 1980. "Fishermen of Four Cultures." *The Seattle Times Magazine*, 6(22):6-7.

DuBois, Hazel. 1964. "Matrifocality and Courtship in Four Puerto Rican Communities." Paper read at the annual meeting of the National Council on Family Relations, Miami, Florida.

Dumont, Louis. 1957. "Hierarchy and Marriage Alliance in South Indian Kinship." Occasional Papers of the Royal Anthropological Institute, No. 12.

Duncan, D.C. n.d. *Lifeboat Work at Montrose*. Montrose: Review Press.

Ebert, James M. et al. 1987. "Botswana: Fishermen of the Two-Way River." *Cultural Survival Quarterly*: special Edition on Fishing Communities, 11(2):35-38.

Elliott, Colin. 1978. *Sailing Fishermen in Old Photographs*. Reading: Tops'l Books.

———— 1979 *Steam Fishermen in Old Photographs*. Reading: Tops'l Books.

Ellis, Carolyn. 1983. "Economic Organization and Family Structure in Two Fishing Communities." Unpublished paper.

Ember, Carol. 1973. "Feminine Task Assignment and the Social Behavior of Boys." *Ethos*, (4):424-439.

Endicott, Karen Lampell. 1979c. "Batek Negrito Sex Roles." Unpublished Master's Thesis. Australian National University, Canberra.

———— 1984. "The Batek De' of Malaysia." *Cultural Survival Quarterly*, 8(2):6-8.

Endicott, Kirk. 1979a. *Batek Negrito Religion. The World-View and Rituals of a People of Peninsular Malaysia.* Oxford: Clarendon Press.

———— 1979b. "The Hunting Methods of the Batek Negritos of Malaysia." *Canberra Anthropology,* 2(2):7-22.

———— 1979c. "The Impact of Economic Modernization on the Orang Asli (Aborigines) of Northern Peninsular Malaysia." In James C. Jackson and Martin Rudner (eds.), *ASAA Southeast Asia Publications Series,* No. 3. Singapore: Heinemann Educational Books (Asia) Limited.

———— 1983. "The Effects of Slave Raiding on the Aborigines of the Malay Peninsula." In Anthony Reid (ed.), *Slavery, Bondage and Dependency in Southeast Asia.* New York: St. Martin's Press.

———— 1984. "The Economy of the Batek Negrito of Malaysia: Annual and Historical Perspective." In B.L. Isaac (ed.), *Research in Economic Anthropology.* Greenwich, CT: JAI Press.

Erikson, Erik. 1978. *Childhood and Society.* Reprint. St. Albans: Triad Paladin.

Estioko-Griffin, Agnes and P. Bion Griffin. 1981. "Women the Hunter: The AGTA" In Frances Dahlberg (ed.), *Women the Gatherer.* New Haven: Yale University Press.

Etienne, Mona and Eleanor Leacock. 1980. *Women and Colonization: Anthropological Perspectives.* Cambridge: Cambridge University Press.

Evans, I.H.N. 1913. "Notes on the Besisi of Tamboh, Kuala Langat Selango." *Journal of the Federated Malay States Museum,* 5(1):1-14.

Faris, James C. 1972. *Cat Harbour: A Newfoundland Fishing Settlement.* St. John's: Institute of Social and Economic Research, Memorial University of Newfoundland.

———— 1977. "Primitive Accumulation in Small-Scale Fishing Communities." In M.E. Smith (ed.), *Those Who Live From the Sea: A Study in Maritime Anthropology.* St. Paul, MN: Westview Press.

———— 1978 "Modernization in Traditional Fishing Communities: The Example of Cat Harbour." East Carolina Conference.

Fedigan, Linda Maine. 1986. "The Changing Role of Women in Models of Human Evolution." In *Annual Review of Anthropology,* Vol. 15. Palo Alto: Annual Reviews.

Figueiredo, Mariza. 1983. "The Socioeconomic Role of Women Heads of Family in a Brazilian Fishing Village." *Feminist Issues,* 3:83-103.

Finch, Janet. 1983. *Married to the Job: Wives' Incorporation in Men's Work.* London: Allen and Unwin.

Firestone, Melvin M. 1967. *Brothers and Rivals: Patrilocality in Savage Cove.* St. John's: Institute of Social and Economic Research, Memorial University of Newfoundland.

Firth, Raymond. 1946. *Malay Fishermen: Their Peasant Economy*. New York: W.W. Norton and Company. Revised version published in 1966.

_____ 1967. *Tikopia Ritual and Belief*. London: Allen and Unwin.

_____ 1984. "Roles of Women and Men in a Sea Fishing Economy: Tikopia Compared with Kelantan." In B. Gunda (ed.), *The Fishing Culture of the World*, Vol. 2. Budapest: Akademiai Kiado.

Firth, Rosemary. 1966. *Housekeeping Among Malay Peasants*. London: Athlone Press.

Fisherman's News. 1980a. "Viola Knudsen Dies at 56." *Fishermen's News*, 36(8), April.

_____ 1980b. "'Vanguard' Takes the Lead." *Fishermen's News*, 36(11), May.

_____ 1980c. "F/V Raven Sets Course." *Fishermen's News*, 36(11), May.

Fishing News International. 1986. "Minister Defends Whale Research."

Forman, Shepard. 1970. *The Raft Fisherman: Tradition and Change in the Brazilian Peasant Economy*. Bloomington, IN: Indiana University Press.

Foster, George M. 1979. *Tzintzuntzan*. Boston: Little, Brown and Company.

Fox, Robin. 1978. *The Tory Islanders: A People of the Celtic Fringe*. New York: Cambridge University Press.

Fraser, Sir David. 1983. *The Christian Watt Papers*. Edinburgh: Paul Harris.

Fraser, Thomas M. Jr. 1960. *Rusembilan: A Malay Fishing Village in Southern Thailand*. Ithaca: Cornell University Press.

_____ 1966. *Fishermen of South Thailand: The Malay Villages*. New York: Holt, Rinehart and Winston.

Freyre, Gilberto. 1961. *Sobrados e Mucambos*. Rio de Janeiro: Livaria Jose Olypio Editora, Vol. 1, 3rd Edition.

Friedl, Ernestine. 1967. "The Position of Women: Appearance and Reality." *Anthropological Quarterly*, 40(3):97-108.

_____ 1975. *Women and Men: An Anthropologist's View*. New York: Holt, Rinehart and Winston.

Fyfe, C. 1979. *A Short History of Sierra Leone*. London: Longman.

Gadamer, Hans-Georg. 1979. "The Problem of Historical Consciousness." In Paul Rabinow and William M. Sullivan (eds.), *Interpretive Social Science: A Reader*. Berkeley: University of California Press.

Gaffney, M. 1972. "Cross-Handed Work Organization and the Development Cycle of South Coast Newfoundland Domestic Group." In R. J. Preston (ed.), *Papers from the 4th Annual Congress, Canadian Ethnology Service*. Ottawa: National Museum of Man, Mercury Series.

Gerrard, Siri. 1987. "Women in the Fishing Districts: The 'Ground Crew' of the Fishing Industry." In D. Grobech and S. Gerrard (eds.), *Women in*

The Norwegian Fisheries. Alta, Norway: Finnmark Distriktshogskole (FDH Report).

Gerrard, Siri and Bi Haavind. 1987. "Unionized Women in the Fishing Industry— On the Margin of a Male Organization." In D. Grobech and S. Gerrard (eds.), *Women in the Norwegian Fisheries.* Alta, Norway: Finnmark Distriktshogskole (FDH Report).

Geertz, Clifford. 1973. *The Interpretation of Cultures.* New York: Basic Books, Inc.

_____ 1983. *Local Knowledge.* New York: Basic Books, Inc.

Giovannini, Maureen. 1981. "Women: A Dominant Symbol with the Cultural System of a Sicilian Town." *Man,* 16(3):408-526.

Gissi Bustos, Jorge. 1980. "Mythology About Women, With Special Reference to Chile." In June Nash and Helen Icken Safa (eds)., *Sex and Class in Latin America.* Brooklyn: J.G. Bergin Publishers.

Gladwin, Christina. 1975. "A Model of the Supply of Smoked Fish from Cape Coast to Kumasi." In Stuart Plattner (ed.), *Formal Methods in Economic Anthropology.* Special Publication of the American Anthropological Association, Number 4.

Gladwin, H. and C. Gladwin. 1971. "Estimating Market Conditions and Profit Expectations of Fish Sellers at Cape Coast, Ghana." In G. Dalton (ed.), *Studies in Economic Anthropology.* Washington, DC: American Anthropological Association.

Gladwin, Thomas. 1970. *East is a Big Bird: Navigation and Logic on Pulowat Atoll.* Cambridge, MA: Harvard University Press.

Gloucester Fishermen's Wives Association. 1979. *Newsletter,* May.

_____ 1980. "Georges Bank Update." *Newsletter,* April and May.

Goforth, Penelope. 1980. "Out on the Crab Grounds on 'Hazel Lorraine I.'" *Alaska Fisherman's Journal,* 3(7):26-28.

Goldschmidt. 1966. *Man's Way.* New York: Holt, Rinehart and Winston.

Gonzalez, Nacie L. Solien. 1969. *Black Carib Household Structure.* Seattle and London: University of Washington Press.

Goodale, Jane. 1971. *Tiwi Wives.* Seattle: University of Washington Press.

Granger, Pete. 1979. *The Commercial Fishing Industry of Whatcom County: Some Economic Aspects 1977.* Seattle: Washington Sea Grant Advisory Program.

Gray, Malcolm. 1978. *The Fishing Industries of Scotland, 1790-1914.* Oxford: Oxford University Press.

Green, Gordon. 1976. *Don't Have Your Baby in the Dory.* Montreal: Harvest House.

Greenwood, David J. and William A. Stini. 1977. *Nature, Culture, and Human History: a Bio-Cultural Introduction to Anthropology.* New York: Harper and Row Publishers.

Grobech, Dagrunn and Siri Gerrard. 1987. *Women in the Norwegian Fisheries.* Alta, Norway: Finnmark Distriktshogskole (FDH Report).

Grumet, Robert S. 1980. *Native Americans of the Northwest Coast.* Newbery Library D'Arcy McNickle Center for the History of the American Indian Bibliographical Series. Bloomington, IN: Indiana University Press.

Gulati, Leela. 1981. *Profiles in Female Poverty.* Delhi: Hindustan Publishing Corporation.

_____ 1984. *Fisherwomen on the Kerala Coast: Demographic and Socio-Economic Impact of a Fisheries Development Project.* Women, Work and Development Series No. 8. Geneva: International Labour Organization.

Gunda, Bela. 1984. *The Fishing Culture of the World: Studies in Ethology, Cultural Ecology and Folklore,* vols. 1 and 2. Budapest: Akademiai Kiado.

Hadman, Ballard. 1955. *As the Sailor Loves the Sea.* New York: Harper and Brothers.

Hage, Karl Per. 1971. "On some Formal and Substantive Properties of a Maritime Communication System." Unpublished Ph.D. dissertation, University of Washington.

Hammel, E. A. and Ynez D. Hasse. 1962. "A Survey of Peruvian Fishing Communities." *Anthropological Records,* 21:211-230.

Harris, O. 1981. "Households as Natual Units." In K. Young et al. (eds.), *Of Marriage and the Market.* London: CES Books.

Hart, Kathy and Nancy Davis. 1982a. "Margaret: An Equal Partner in Family Style Fishing." *Coast Watch,* 9(10):3-4.

_____ 1982b. "Carol: Spell it 'Fisherman.'" *Coast Watch,* 9(10):1-2.

_____ 1982c. "Fisherman's Life Troubles—Wives Who Wait at Home." *Coast Watch,* 9(10):4-5.

_____ 1982d. "Social Barriers Don't Stop Women Who Fish." *Coast Watch,* 9(10):5-6.

Hay, Edna R. and Bruce Walker. 1985. *Focus on Fishing: Arbroath and Gourdon.* Dundee: Abertay Historical Society Publication 23.

Hendrix, M.K. 1983. "Technology and Tradition in West African Maritime Fisheries: Tombo, Sierra Leone." ICMRD Working Paper No. 8. Kingston, RI: International Center for Marine Resource Development.

Higgins, John. 1978. *The North Pacific Deckhand's and Alaska Cannery Worker's Handbook.* Eastsound, WA: Albacore Press.

Hochschild, Arlie R. 1973. "A Review of Sex Role Research." *American Journal of Sociology,* 73(4):1011-1029.

Hornell, James. 1950. "Fishing in Many Waters." *The Women Divers of Japan.* Cambridge: Cambridge University.

Horobin, G.W. 1972. "Community and Occupation in the Hull Fishing Industry." *British Journal of Sociology,* 43:1-14.

Houshower, Hans. 1982. "Fishing Tree Point: Gillnetting as Work and Self-Reflection. Unpublished Ph.D. dissertation, University of Washington.

Inquerito Industrial E Commercial. 1891. *A Pesca: Lisboa.* Inprensa National.

Iverson, Noel and D. Ralph Matthews. 1968. *Communities in Decline: An Examination of Household Resettlement in Newfoundland.* St. John's: Institute of Social and Economic Research, Memorial University of Newfoundland.

Jackson, Brian. 1968. *Working Class Community.* New York: Praeger.

Jaquette, Jane S. 1973. "Literary Archetypes and Female Role Alternatives: The Woman and Novel in Latin America." In Ann Pescatello (ed.), *Female and Male in Latin America.* Pittsburgh: University of Pittsburgh.

Jorion, Paul. 1976. "To Be a Good Fisherman You Do Not Need Any Fish." *Cambridge Anthropology,* III(I):1-12.

_____ 1982. "All Brother Crews in the North Atlantic." *Canadian Review of Sociology and Anthropology,* 19(4):513-526.

Kalland, Arne. 1983. "In Search of the Abalone: The History of the Ama in Northern Kyirsha, Japan." Paper presented to the XIth CAES.

Kanter, Rosabeth. 1977. *Work and Family in the United States: A Critical Review and Agenda for Research and Policy.* New York: Russel Sage Foundation.

Karim, Wazir Jahan. 1977. "The Belief Systems of the Ma' Betisek of Palau Carey, Malaysia." Unpublished Ph.D. dissertation, London School of Economics and Political Science.

_____ 1980. "Children of the Garden: Concepts of Size, Space, and Time in Child Socialization Among the Ma' Betisek and the Malays." *Federation Museums Journal,* 25:151-158.

_____ 1981. *Ma' Betisek Concepts of Living Things.* London School of Economics, Monograph on Social Anthropology, No. 54. London: Athlone Press.

Klausen, Arne Martin. 1968. *Kerala Fishermen and the Indo-Norwegian Pilot Project.* London: Allen and Unwin.

Knipe, Edward. 1979. "Boat and Fleet: An Analysis of Kinship Linkages in a Scottish Fishing Fleet." American Anthropological Association.

_____ 1984. *Gamrie.* Lanham, Maryland: University Press of America.

Kottak, Conrad Phillip. 1966. "The Structure of Equality in a Brazilian Fishing Community." Unpublished Ph.D. dissertation, Columbia University.

_____ 1983. *Assault on Paradise: Social Change in a Brazilian Village.* New York: Random House.

Kuchikura, Y. 1977. "An Ecological Approach to the Fishing Activity System of a Coral Island Community in Okinawa." In Hitoshi Watanabe (ed.), *Human Activity System: Its Spatiotemporal Structure.* Tokyo: University of Tokyo Press.

Kuhikannen, Ralangadan. 1980. *Sex Roles and Fishing.* Maine: North-East Anthropological Association.

Lamas, M. 1948. *As Mulheres do Meu Pais.* Lisboa: Actualis Lda.

Lamson, Cynthia. 1983. "Female Employment in the Seafood Industry: The Socio-economics of Fish Plant Work."A report prepared for the Canadian Research Institute for Advancement of Women.

Landale, Zoe. 1977. *Harvest of Salmon: Adventures in Fishing the B.C. Coast.* Saanichton, B.C.: Hancock Publishers.

Landes, R. 1938. "The Ojibwa Woman." *Columbia University Contributions to Anthropology,* 31:1-144.

Leacock, E. 1978. "Women's Status in Egalitarian Society: Implications for Social Evolution." *Current Anthropology,* 19:247-55.

Leacock, E. (ed.). 1979. *Women in Latin America: An Anthology from Latin American Perspectives.* Riverside: Latin American Perspectives.

Leap, William L. 1977. "Maritime Subsistence in Anthropological Perspective: A Statement of Priorities." In M. Estellie Smith (ed.), *Those Who Live From the Sea: A Study in Maritime Anthropology.* St. Paul: West Publishing Company.

Lee, Richard B. 1968. "What Hunters Do for a Living, or, How to Make Out on Scarce Resources." In Richard B. Lee and Irven DeVore (eds.), *Man the Hunter.* Chicago: Aldine Publishing.

Lenski, Gerhard. 1966. *Human Societies.* New York: McGraw Hill.

Lessa, William. 1966. *Ulithi: A Micronesian Design for Living.4* New York: Holt, Rinehart and Winston.

Linares, Olga. 1985. "Cash Crops and Gender Constructs: The Jola of Senegal." *Ethnology,* 24(2):83-94.

Lindsay, Beverly. 1980. "Women and Social Reality: A Conclusion." In Beverly Lindsay (ed.), *Comparative Perspectives of Third World Women: The Impact of Race, Sex and Class.* New York: Praeger.

Lino, Netto. M. 1949. *A Linguagem dos Pescadores e Lavradores do Concelho de Vila do Conde.* Coimbra: Revista Portuguese de Filologia.

Lipset, S.M. et al. 1956. *Union Democracy.* Chicago, Ill.: Free Press.

Löfgren, Orvar. 1972. "Resource Management and Family Firms: Swedish West Coast Fishermen." In R. Andersen and C. Wadel (eds.) *North Atlantic Fishermen: Anthropological Essays on Modern Fishing.* St. John's: Institute of Social and Economic Research, Memorial University of Newfoundland.

———— 1974. "The Making of a Fisherman." Paper presented at British Sociological Conference on Becoming a Seafarer, Socialization into Seafaring Occupations. Cardiff.

———— 1979. "Marine Ecotypes in Preindustrial Sweden: A Comparative Discussion of Swedish Peasant Fishermen." In Raoul Andersen (ed.), *North Atlantic Maritime Cultures.* The Hague: Mouton Publishers.

Lummis, Trevor. 1977. "The Occupational Community of East Anglian Fishermen: On Historical Dimension Through Oral Evidence." British Journal of Sociology, 28(1):51-74.

1985. *Occupation and Society: The East Anglian Fisherman, 1880-1914.* Cambridge: Cambridge University Press.

Lundström-Burghoorn, Wil. 1981. *Minahasa Civilization: A Tradition of Change.* Gothenburg Studies in Social Anthropology, No. 2.

Luxton, Meg. 1980. *More than a Labour of Love: Three Generations of Women's Work in the Home.* Toronto: Women's Education Press.

MacCormack, C.P. 1978. "The Cultural Ecology of Production: Sherbro Coast and Hinterland, Sierra Leone." In D. Green, C. Haselgrove, and M. Spriggs (eds.), *Social Organization and Settlement.* British Archaeological Reports, International Series, No. 47.

———— 1982. "Control of Land, Labor, and Capital in Rural Southern Sierra Leone." In E.G. Bay (ed.), *Women and Work in Africa.* Boulder, CO: Westview Press.

MacLeod, Guy C. and John H. Prescott. 1981. *Georges Bank: Past, Present and Future of a Marine Environment.* Boulder, CO: Westview Press.

Malaysia. 1981. *Fourth Malaysia Plan, 1981-1985.* Kuala Lumpur: Government Printer.

Malinowski, B. 1860. *Magic, Science and Religion.* Glencoe, Ill.: Reprinted in 1954.

Maraini, Fosco. 1962. *The Island of Fisherwomen.* New York: Harcourt, Brace and world Ltd.

Maranda, Elli K. 1974. "A Woman is an Alien Spirit." In Carolyn Matthiasson, *Many Sisters.* New York: Free Press (Macmillan).

Marsden, George. 1980. "The Rigging of Georges Bank." *Attenzione,* 2(6):56-63.

Martin, Kay M. and Barbara Voorhies. 1975. *Female of the Species.* New York: Columbia University Press.

Mattulada. 1982. "South Sulawesi, Its Ethnicity and Way of Life." *Southeast Asian Studies*, 20(1):4-22.

McCay, Bonnie J. 1981. "Development Issues in Fisheries as Agrarian Systems." *Culture and Agriculture: Bulletin of the Anthropological Study Group on Agrarian Systems*, 11:1-8.

_____ 1983. "Fish Guts, Hairnets, and Unemployment Stamps: a Female Proletariat in Newfoundland." Paper presented at the 82nd Annual Meeting of the American Anthropological Association, Chicago, Illinois.

Mead, Margaret. 1962. *Male and Female: A Study of the Sexes in a Changing World*. Reprinted in 1975, New York: Penguin Books.

Meehan, Betty. 1977. "Hunters by the Seashore." *Journal of Human Evolution*, 6:363-370.

Melo, D. Francisco Manuel De. 1650 *Carta de Guia de Casados*. Lisboa: Editorial Verbo.

Messenger, John. 1969. *Inis Beag: Isle of Ireland*. New York: Holt, Rinehart and Winston.

Miller, Mark. 1977. "Commitment and Mobility: the Diversity of the Pacific Fishing World." ECU Conference.

Miller, Mark and J. Van Maanen. 1979. "Boats Don't Fish, People Do: Some Ethnographic Notes on Federal Management of Fisheries in Gloucester." *Anthropological Quarterly*, 53(1):29-38.

Mitchell, William. 1860. *A Memoir of William Gutheri*. Montrose: George Walker.

Muir, Margaret. 1975. "The Paid Housekeeper: Socialization and Sex Roles in Two Fishing villages." In R. J. Preston (ed.), *Papers from the 4th Annual Congress Canadian Ethnology Service*. Ottawa: National Museum of Man, Mercury Series, 85-98.

1976. "Professional Women and Network Maintenance in a French and English Fishing Village." *Atlantis*, 2(2):42-55.

Mullen, Patrick B. 1969. "The Function of Magic Folk Belief Among Texas Coastal Fishermen." *Journal of American Folklore*, (82):214-225.

Murdock, George P. 1959. *Africa: Its People and Their Culture History*. New York: McGraw-Hill.

_____ 1967. *Ethnographic Atlas*. Pittsburgh: University of Pittsburgh.

_____ 1968. "The Current Status of the World's Hunting and Gathering Peoples." In Richard B. Lee and Irven Devore (eds.), *Man The Hunter*. Chicago: Aldine Publishing Company.

Murdock, George P. and Caterina Provost. 1973. "Factors in the Division of Labor by Sex: A Cross-Cultural Analysis." *Ethnology*, 8:329-369.

Murray, Hilda C. 1979. *More Than Fifty Percent: Women's Life in a Newfoundland Outport 1900-1950*. St. John's: Breakwater Books.

Nadel, Jane Hurwitz. 1979. "Till the Sea Runs Dry: The Social Impact of a North Sea Oil Support Base on an East Coast Scottish Village and Town." Unpublished Ph.D. dissertation, CUNY.

_____ 1983. "Houston's Little sisters: A Cross-Cultural Perspective on Offshore Oil." *Human Organization*, 42:142-167.

_____ 1984. "Stigma and Separation: Pariah Status and Community Persistence in a Scottish Fishing Village." *Ethnology*, 23(2):101-115.

_____ 1985. "Changing Waters: A Cross-Cultural Survey of Petroleum Development Impacts on Artisanal Fishing Communities." Paper presented at the 45 Congresso Internacional de Americanistas. Bogata, Colombia.

_____ 1986. "Burning with the Fire of God: Calvinism and Community in a Scottish Fishing Village." *Ethnology*, 25(1):49-60.

Nelson, Nici. 1979. *Why Has Development Neglected Rural Women: A Review of South Asian Literature*. New York: Pergamon Press.

Nemec, T.F. 1972. "I Fish with My Brother: The Structure and Behaviour of Agnatic-Based Fishing Crews in a Newfoundland and Irish Outport." In Raoul Andersen and Cato Wadel (eds.), *North Atlantic Fishermen: Anthropological Essays on Modern Fishing*. St. John's: Institute of Social and Economic Research, Memorial University of Newfoundland.

Nietschmann, Bernard. 1973. *Between Land and Water*. New York: Seminar Press.

Nimmo, Harry Arlo. 1972. *The Sea People of Sulu: A Study of Social Change in the Philippines*. San Francisco: Chandler.

Norbeck, Edward. 1954. *Takashima, A Japanese Fishing Community*. Salt Lake City: University of Utah Press.

Norr, James L. and Kathleen L. Norr. 1974. "Environmental and Technical Factors Influencing Power in Work Organizations: Ocean Fishing in Peasant Societies." *Sociology of work and Occupations*, 1:219-51.

_____ 1977. "Societal Complexity or Production Techniques: Another Look at Udy's Data on the Structure of Work Organizations." *American Journal of Sociology*, 82:845-53.

_____ 1978. "Work Organization in Modern Fishing." *Human Organization*, 37(2):163-170.

_____ 1982. "Impact on Urban Growth: Change in a South India Fishing Community from 1965 to 1980." *Ethnology*, 21:111-123.

Nowak, Barbara S. 1983. "Cooperation and Partnership: A Look at Gender Relations Among Hma' Btsisi' of West Malaysia." Paper presented at the 82nd Annual American Anthropological Association Meeting, Chicago, Illinois.

_____ 1984a. "Ideal Versus Real: Btsisi' Practicality in the Sexual Division of Labor." Paper presented at the Canadian Ethnology Society Meetings, Montreal.

_____ 1984b. "Can the Partnership Last? Btsisi' Marital Partners and Development." *Cultural Survival Quarterly*, 8(2):9-11.

_____ 1985. "You Give Us Saplings, But what About the Land?" Paper presented at the Symposium, "The Anthropology of Reservations," at the 83rd American Anthropological Association Annual Meetings, Denver, Colorado.

Nunez del Prado Bejar, Daisy Irene. 1975a. "El Rol de la Mujer Campesina Quechua Audina." *American Indigena*, 35:391-401.

_____ 1975b. *The Effects of Rural-Urban Migration on Women's Role and Status in Latin America.* UNESCO: Reports and Papers on the Social Sciences.

Nyseth, Toril. 1987. "The Young Girl's Migration from Finnmark." In D. Grobech and S. Gerrard (eds.), *Women in the Norwegian Fisheries.* Alta, Norway: Finnmark Distriktshogskole (FDH Report).

Okraku, Ismael. 1975. "Fishing and Fertility: A Study of a Nova Scotia Fishing Village." *Social Biology*, 22:326-337.

Oliveira, E. Veiga et al. 1975. *Actividades Agro-Maritimas em Portugal.* Lisboa: Instituto de Alta Cultura.

Olveira, Lygia Estevao De. 1966. *Cajui: Socializacao em uma Comunidade Prainana.* Recife: Imprensa Universitaria.

Oppeng, C., C. Okali and B. Houghton. 1975. "Woman Power: Retrograde Steps in Ghana." *African Studies Review*, 18-71-84.

Orbach, Michael K. 1977. *Hunters, Seamen and Entrepreneurs: The Tuna Seinermen of San Diego.* Berkeley, CA: University of California Press.

Ortner, Sherry B. 1974. "Is Female to Male as Nature is to Culture?" In Michelle Zimbalist Rosaldo and Louise Lamphere (eds.), *Women, Culture and Society.* Stanford: Stanford University Press.

_____ 1984. "Theory in Anthropology Since the Sixties." *Comparative Studies in Society and History*, 26(1):126-166.

Ortner, Sherry B. and Harriet Whitehead. 1981. "Introduction: Accounting for Sexual Meanings." In Sherry B. Ortner and Harriet Whitehead (eds.), *Sexual Meanings: The Cultural Construction of Gender and Sexuality.* New York: Cambridge University Press.

Pacific Fisheries Management Council. 1983. *Proposed Plan for Managing the 1983 Salmon Fisheries Off the Coasts of California, Oregon and Washington.* Portland: Pacific Fisheries Management Council.

Parkin, David. 1979. "The Categorization of work: Cases from Coastal Kenya." In Sandra Wallman (ed.), *Social Anthropology of Work.* ASA Geograph 19, London: Academic Press.

Parsons, Talcott. 1951: *The Social System.* Glencoe, IL.: The Free Press.

Patterson, Neil. 1950. *Behold Thy Daughter.* London: Hodder and Stroughton.

Philbrook, Thomas. 1966. *Fisherman, Logger, Merchant, Miner: Social Change and Industrialism in Three Newfoundland Communities.* St. John's: Institute of Social and Economic Research, Memorial University of Newfoundland.

Pilcher, William M. 1972. *The Portland Longshoremen.* New York: Holt, Rinehart and Winston.

Pina Cabral, J. 1984. "Female Power and the Inequality of Wealth and Motherhood in Northwestern Portugal." In R. Hirschon (ed.), *Women and Property, Women as Property.* London: Croom Helm.

Plath, David. 1986. "What Even Your Mother won't Show You—Though Your Mother-in-Law Might: How to Become a Shellfish Diver on the Shima Peninsula." Unpublished manuscript.

Poggie, J., Jr. and C. Gersuny. 1974. "Fishermen of Galilee: The Human Ecology of New England Coastal Community." Kingston, RI: University of Rhode Island Marine Bulletin, No. 17.

Pollnac, Richard B. 1974. "The Sociocultural Correlates of Fishing as a Subsistence Activity." Anthropology Working Paper, Number 4. International Center for Marine Resource Development, University of Rhode Island.

_____ 1976. "Continuity and Change in Marine Fishing Communities." Anthropology Working Paper Number 10. A State of Art Paper Proposal for the U.S. Agency for International Development.

_____ 1984a. "Sociocultural Aspects of Small Scale Fisheries Development in West Africa." Anthropology Working Paper Number 43. International Center for Marine Resource Development, University of Rhode Island.

_____ 1984b. "The Division of Labor by Sex in Fishing Societies." Anthropology Working Paper Number 44. International Center for Marine Resource Development, University of Rhode Island.

_____ 1986 "Peoples of the Sea and Coastal Zone: An Anthropological Perspective." In R. Grundy, R. Ford and M. Beardsley (eds.), *Marine Science Information: An International Commodity.* Gloucester Point, Virgina: International Association of Marine Science Libraries and Information Centers' Conference Series.

Pomponio, Alice. 1983. "Women as Middlemen in a Maritime Society." Unpublished manuscript.

Porter, Marilyn. 1982. "Women and Old Boats: The Sexual Division of Labour in a Newfoundland Outport." In E. Garminkow et al. (eds.), *Public and Private: Gender and Society.* London: Heinemann.

_____ 1983. "'She Was Skipper of the Shore Crew': Notes on the Development of Sexual Division of Labour in Newfoundland." University of Manchester.

_____ 1984. "'A Tangly Bunch': The Political Culture of Outport women in Newfoundland." *Newfoundland Studies*, 1.

_____ 1985. "Marginal Regions, Marginal Women? Sexual Divisions on the Periphery." Paper presented to the International Seminar on Marginal Regions, Galway, Ireland.

Price, Richard. 1966. "Fishing Rites and Recipes in a Martinequan Village." *Caribbean Studies*, 6(1):2-24.

Queen, S. and Robert Haberstein. 1974. "The Newfoundland Outport Family." In S. Queen and R. Haberstein (eds.), *The Family in Various Cultures*. Philadelphia, PA: J. B. Lippencott.

Quinn, Naomi. 1977. "Anthropological Studies on Women's Status." *Annual Review of Anthropology*, 6. Palo Alto: Annual Reviews.

_____ 1978. "Do Mfantse Fish Sellers Estimate Probabilities in their Heads.?" *American Ethnologist*, 5:206-226.

Radcliffe-Brown, A.R. 1922. *The Adaman Islanders*. Cambridge: Cambridge University Press.

Randall, Robert Alden. 1977. "Change Variation in Samal Fishing: Making Plans to 'Make a Living' in the Southern Philippines." Unpublished Ph.D. Thesis, University of California, Berkeley.

Ricoeur, Paul. 1981. *Hermeneutics and the Human Sciences*. Cambridge: Cambridge University Press.

Robben, Antonius. 1982. "Stratification, Scale, and Ranking: Social Change in Two Brazilian Fishing Communities." *Ethnology*, 21:125-135.

Rodgers, Silvia. 1984. "Feminine Power at Sea." *Rain*, (67):1-4.

Rogers, Barbara. 1980. *The Domestication of Women: Discrimination in Developing Societies*. London: Tavistock Publications.

Rogers, Susan Carol. 1978. "Women's Place: A Critical Review of Anthropology Theory." *Comparative Studies in Society and History*, 20(1):133-162.

Rosaldo, Michelle Zimbalist. 1974. "Woman, Culture, and Society: A Theoretical Overview." In Michelle Zimbalist Rosaldo and Louise Lamphere (eds.), *Woman, Culture, and Society*. Stanford, CA: Stanford University Press.

_____ 1980. "The Use and Abuse of Anthropology: Reflections on Feminism and Cross-Cultural Understanding." *Signs*, 5(3):389-417.

Rosaldo, Michelle Zimbalist and Louise Lamphere (eds.). 1974. *Woman, Culture, and Society*. Stanford, CA: Stanford University Press.

Roseman, Marina. 1984. "The Social Structuring of Sound: An Example from the Temiar of Peninsular Malaysia." *Ethnomusicology*, XXVIII(3):411-445.

Rubin, G. 1975. "The Traffic of women: Notes on the Political Economy of Sex." In R. Reiter (ed.), *Toward an Anthropology of Women*. New York: Monthly Review Press.

Russel-Wood, A.J.R. 1978. "Female and Family in the Economy and Society of Colonial Brazil." In Asuncion Lavrin (ed.), *Latin American Women*. Westport: Greenwood Press.

Sacks, Karen. 1975. "Engels Revisited: Women, the Organization of Production and Private Property." In M.E. Rosaldo and L. Lamphere (eds.), *Women, Culture and Society*. Stanford, CA: Stanford University Press.

_____ 1979. *Sisters and Wives: the Past and Future of Sexual Equality*. Westport, CN: Greenwood Press.

_____ 1972. *Stone Age Economics*. Chicago: Aldine, Atherton Incorporated.

Sahlins, Marshall and Elman Service. 1970. *Evolution and Culture*. Ann Arbor: University of Michigan Press.

Sanday, Peggy Reeves. 1974. "Female Status in the Public Domain." In Michelle Rosaldo and Louise Lamphere (eds.), *Woman, Culture and Society*. Stanford, CA: Stanford University Press.

_____ 1981. *Female Power and Male Dominance: On the Origins of Sexual Inequality*. Cambridge: Cambridge University Press.

Sather, Clifford A. 1975. "Bajau Laut." In Frank M. LeBar (ed.), *Ethnic Groups in Insular Southeast Asia, Volume 2: Philippines and Formosa*. New Haven: HRAF Press.

_____ 1976. "Kinship and Contiguity: Variation in Social Alignments Among the Semporna Bajau Laut." In G. N. Appell (ed.), *The Societies of Borneo: Explorations in the Theory of Cognatic Social Structure*. Special Publication of the American Anthropological Association, (6):40-65.

Saugestad, Sidsel. 1986. *Partners in Enterprise: The Social Organization of Paid and Unpaid Labour: Case Studies of Household Viability in Northern Norway*. Tromso, Norway: University of Tromso, Institute for Social Sciences.

_____ 1980. "The Caring Farmer—A Time Utilization Perspective on Job Combination, Work Sharing and Social Change." *Tidsskrift for Samfunnsforskning*. (Periodical for Sociological Research) (b.d.) 21:283-296.

Schlegel, Alice. 1972. *Male Dominance and Female Autonomy*. New Haven, CN: HRAF Press.

_____ 1977. *Sexual Stratification: A Cross-Cultural View*. New York: Columbia University Press.

Sealy, Nanciellen. 1975. "Consequences of Development Strategies in an Acadian Maritime Village." In R. J. Preston (ed.), *Papers from the 4th*

Annual Congress, Canadian Ethnology Service. Ottawa: National Museum of Man, Mercury Series.

Sider, Gerald. 1976. "Christmas Mumming and the New Year in Outport Newfoundland." *Past and Present*, 71:102-125.

Skeat, W.W. 1896. "Sakei Tribes in Selangor: Kuala Langat District." *Selangor Journal*, 5:325-338, 361-366, 392-396.

Skeat, W. W. and C. O. Blagden. 1906. *Pagan Races of the Malay Peninsula.* Two Volumes. London: Frank Cass and Company Limited. Reprinted in 1966.

Smith, M. Estellie. 1977a. *Those Who Live From the Sea: A Study in Maritime Anthropology.* St. Paul: West Publishing Co.

_____ 1977b. "Comments on the Heuristic Utility of Maritime Anthropology." *The Maritime Anthropologist*, 1(1):2-8.

_____ 1978. "What You Wants is Results: What You Gets is Consequences." Paper presented for the Symposium of Modernization in Fishing Industries and Communities. East Carolina University.

_____ 1980. "Women and Migration: On the Fringe or the Cutting Edge?" *International Migration Review*, 14(1):77-92.

_____ 1982a. "Fisheries Management: Intended Results and Unintended Consequences." In J. Mailo and M. Orbach (eds.), *Modernization and Marine Fisheries Policy.* Ann Arbor: Ann Arbor Science Publishers.

_____ 1982b. "The Process of Sociocultural Continuity." *Current Anthropology*, 23:127-142.

_____ 1983. "Pueblo Councils: An Example of Stratified Egalitarianism." In E. Tooker (ed.), and M. H. Fried (symposium organizer), *The Development of Political Organization in Native North America.* Proceedings of the American Ethnological Society. Washington, DC: AES.

_____ 1984. "The Impetus for Affluence: The 'Good Life' or Material Wealth?" In R. Salisbury (ed.), *Affluence and Cultural Survival. 1981 Proceedings.* American Ethnological Society, Washington, DC: AES.

_____ 1985. "The Elite: A Necessary Evil." *Reviews in Anthropology*, 11(3):21-33.

Smout, T.C. 1970. "The Landowner and the Planned Village." In N. T. Phillipson and Rosalind Mitchison (eds.), *Scotland in the Age of Improvement.* Edinburgh: Edinburgh University Press.

Stamm, Liesa and Carol D. Ryff. 1984. *Social Power and Influence of Women.* Boulder, CO: Westview Press.

Stevens, Evelyn P. 1973a. "Machismo and Marianismo." *Society*, 10:57-63.

_____ 1973b. "Marianismo: The Other Face of Machismo in Latin America." In Ann Pescatello (ed.), *Female and Male in Latin America: Essays.* Pittsburgh: University of Pittsburgh Press.

Stiles, Geoffrey. 1972. "Fishermen, Wives and Radios: Aspects of Communication in a Newfoundland Fishing Community." In Raoul Andersen and Cato Wadel (eds.), North Atlantic Fishermen: Anthropological Essays on Modern Fishing. St. John's: Institute of Social and Economic Research, Memorial University of Newfoundland.

_____ 1979. "Labor Recruitment and Family Crew in Newfoundland." In Raoul Andersen (ed.), North Atlantic Maritime Cultures. The Hague: Mouton.

Strange, Heather. 1980. "Some Changing Socioeconomic Roles of Village Women in Malaysia." In Sylvia A. Chipp and Justin J. Green (eds.), *Asian Women in Transition.* University Park: Pennsylvania State University Press.

Stuster, Jack. 1978. "Where 'Mabel' May Mean 'Sea Bass.'" *Natural History,* 87(99):64-71.

Suttles, Wayne. 1968. "Coping with Abundance: Subsistence on the Northwest Coast." In Richard B. Lee and Irven DeVore (eds.), *Man the Hunter.* Chicago: Aldine Publishing.

Szala, Karen. 1977. "Family as a Source for Metaphor: A Newfoundland Account." In R. J. Preston (ed.), *Papers from the 4th Annual Congress, Canadian Ethnology Service.* Ottawa: National Museum of Man, Mercury Series, 45-58.

_____ 1978. "Clean Women and Quiet Men: Courtship and Marriage in a Newfoundland Fishing Village." M.A. Thesis, Department of Anthropology, St. John's: Memorial University of Newfoundland.

Tanner, Nancy. 1974. "Matrifocality in Indonesia and Africa and Among Black Americans." In Michelle Rosaldo and Louise Lamphere (eds.), *Woman, Culture and Society.* Stanford: Stanford University Press.

Taylor, Lawrence J. 1980. "Colonialism and Community Structure in Western Ireland." *Ethnohistory,* 27(2):169-181.

_____ 1981. "'Man the Fisher': Salmon Fishing and the Expression of Community in a Rural Irish Settlement." *American Ethnologist,* 8:774-788.

_____ 1983. *Dutchmen on the Bay.* Philadelphia: University of Pennsylvania Press.

Thompson, Paul. 1985. "Women in the Fishing: The Roots of Power Between the Sexes." *Comparative Study of Society and History,* 27(1):3-32.

Thompson, Paul, Tony Wailey and Trevor Lummis. 1983. *Living the Fishing.* History Workshop Series. London: Routledge and Kegan Paul.

Tiller, Pier Olvav. 1958. *Father Absence and Personality Development of Children in Sailor Families.* Oslo, Norway: Institute for Social Research, Nordisk Psykologiis Monograph Series, No. 9.

Tinker, Irene and Michele Bo Bramsen. 1976. *Women and World Development.* Washington, D.C.: Overseas Development Council.

Tunstall, Jeremy. 1962. *The Fishermen: The Sociology of an Extreme Occupation.* London: MacGibbon and Kee.

UNECA/FAO. 1975. *Women, Population and Rural Development—Africa.* New York: UNECA/FAO.

Unites States Bureau of the Census. 1980. *Massachusetts Profile of Gloucester.*

United States Department of Health, Education and Welfare. 1976. *Women in Non-Traditional Occupations: A Bibliography.* Prepared by Koba Association for H.E.W. Office of Education, Bureau of Occupational and Adult Education. Washington, D.C.

Van Maanan, John, Marc Miller and Jeffrey C. Johnson. 1980. "An Occupation in Transition: Traditional and Modern Forms of Commercial Fishing." Working Paper 11 24-80, Alfred P. Sloan School of Management, Massachusetts Institute of Technology.

Wadel, Cato. 1966. "Capital Management Under Extreme Uncertainty". Unpublished M.A. Thesis, University of Bergen.

_____ 1969. *Marginal Adaptations and Modernization in Newfoundland.* St. John's: Institute of Social and Economic Research, Memorial University of Newfoundland.

_____ 1973. *Now, Whose Fault is That? The Struggle for Self-Esteem in the Face of Chronic Unemployment.* St. John's: Institute of Social and Economic Research, Memorial University of Newfoundland.

_____ 1979. "Folk Work Concept." In Sandra Wallman, *Epistemologies of Sex.* Chicago: Beresford Book Service.

Wallerstein, Immanuel. 1974. *The Modern World System: Capitalist Agriculture and the Origins of the European World-Economy in the Sixteenth Century.* NY: Academic Press.

Wallman, Sandra. 1978. "Epistemologies of Sex." In Lionel Tiger and Heather Fowler (eds.), *Female Hierarchies.* Chicago: Beresford Book Service.

_____ 1979. *The Social Anthropology of Work.*

Ward, Barbara E. 1965. "Varieties of the Conscious Model: The Fishermen of South China." In Michael Banton (ed.), *The Relevance of Models for Social Anthropology,* ASA Monographs. New York: Praeger.

Weatherburn, M. 1977. "Changing Ecological Adaptation in a Newfoundland Fishing Community." Masters Thesis, Memorial University of Newfoundland.

Weiner, Annette. 1980. "Stability in Banana Leaves: Colonization and Women in Kiriwina, Trobriand Islands." In M. Etienne and E. Leacock (eds.), *Women and Colonization: Anthropological Perspectives.* New York: Praeger.

Werner, Roland. 1973. *Mah Meri: Art and Culture*. Kuala Lumpur: Museums Department.

_____ 1974. *Mah Meri of Malaysia: Art and Culture*. Kuala Lumpur: Penerbit Universiti Malaya.

White, Walter Grainge. 1922. *The Sea Gypsies of Malaya*. Philadelphia: J.B. Lippincott Company.

Whitehead, Ann. 1976. "Sexual Antagonism in Herefordshire." In D. L. Barker and S. Allen (eds.), *Dependence and Exploitation in Work and Marriage*. London: Longman.

Willems, Emilio. 1953. "The Structure of the Brazilian Family." *Social Forces*, 31:339-345.

Wilson, Peter. 1973. *Crab Antics: The Social Anthropology of English-speaking Negro Societies of the Caribbean*. New Haven: Yale University Press.

Wipper, A. 1972. "The Roles of African Women: Past, Present, and Future." *Canadian Journal of African Studies*, 6:143-146.

Wolf, Eric. 1969. *Peasant Wars of the Twentieth Century*. New York: Harper Row.

Woortmann, Klaas. 1982. "Casa e Familia Operaria." *Anuario Antropologico*, 80:119-150.

Wright, Guy. 1981. "Why Do Sealers Seal? Cultural Versus Economic Reasons for Participating in the Newfoundland Seal Hunt. *Culture*, 1(1):61-64.

Young, K. et al. 1981. *Of Marriage and the Market: Women's Subordination in International Perspective*. London: CSE Books.

Zulaika, Joseba. 1981. *Terranova: The Ethos and Luck of Deep-Sea Fishermen*. St. John's: Institute of Social and Economic Research, Memorial University of Newfoundland.

ISER BOOKS